Oh!great

TRANSLATED AND ADAPTED BY
Makoto Yukon

LETTERED BY
Janice Chiang

D0282327

BALLANTINE BOOKS · NEW YORK

2006 Del Rey Trade Paperback Original

Emblem design by Kei Machida

Published in the United States by Del Rey Books, an imprint of The Random House Publishing Group, a division of Random House, Inc., New York.

Del Rey is a registered trademark and the Del Rey colophon is a trademark of Random House, Inc.

Publication rights arranged through Kodansha Ltd.

First published in Japan in 2003 by Kodansha Ltd., Tokyo

ISBN 0-345-49278-1

Printed in the United States of America

www.delreymanga.com

9 8 7 6 5

Translator and Adaptor—Makoto Yukon
Lettering—Janice Chiang

Honorifics

Throughout the Del Rey Manga books, you will find Japanese honorifics left intact in the translations. For those not familiar with how the Japanese use honorifics and, more important, how they differ from American honorifics, we present this brief overview.

Politeness has always been a critical facet of Japanese culture. Ever since the feudal era, when Japan was a highly stratified society, use of honorifics—which can be defined as polite speech that indicates relationship or status—has played an essential role in the Japanese language. When addressing someone in Japanese, an honorific usually takes the form of a suffix attached to one's name (example: "Asuna-san"), or as a title at the end of one's name or in place of the name itself (example: "Negi-sensei," or simply "Sensei!").

Honorifics can be expressions of respect or endearment. In the context of manga and anime, honorifics give insight into the nature of the relationship between characters. Many translations into English leave out these important honorifics, and therefore distort the "feel" of the original Japanese. Because Japanese honorifics contain nuances that English honorifics lack, it is our policy at Del Rey not to translate them. Here, instead, is a guide to some of the honorifics you may encounter in Del Rey Manga.

-san: This is the most common honorific and is equivalent to Mr., Miss, Ms., or Mrs. It is the all-purpose honorific and can be used in any situation where politeness is required.

-sama: This is one level higher than "-san" and is used to confer great respect.

-dono: This comes from the word "tono," which means "lord." It is an even higher level than "-sama" and confers utmost respect.

-kun: This suffix is used at the end of boys' names to express familiarity or endearment. It is also sometimes used by men among friends, or when addressing someone younger or of a lower station.

-chan: This is used to express endearment, mostly toward girls. It is also used for little boys, pets, and even among lovers. It gives a sense of childish cuteness.

Bozu: This is an informal way to refer to a boy, similar to the English term "kid" or "squirt."

Sempai/Senpai: This title suggests that the addressee is one's senior in a group or organization. It is most often used in a school setting, where underclassmen refer to their upperclassmen as "sempai." It can also be used in the workplace, such as when a newer employee addresses an employee who has seniority in the company.

Kohai: This is the opposite of "sempai" and is used toward underclassmen in school or newcomers in the workplace. It connotes that the addressee is of a lower station.

Sensei: Literally meaning "one who has come before," this title is used for teachers, doctors, or masters of any profession or art.

[blank]: Usually forgotten in these lists, but perhaps the most significant difference between Japanese and English. The lack of honorific means that the speaker has permission to address the person in a very intimate way. Usually, only family, spouses, or very close friends have this kind of permission. Known as *yobisute,* it can be gratifying when someone who has earned the intimacy starts to call one by one's name without an honorific. But when that intimacy hasn't been earned, it can also be very insulting.

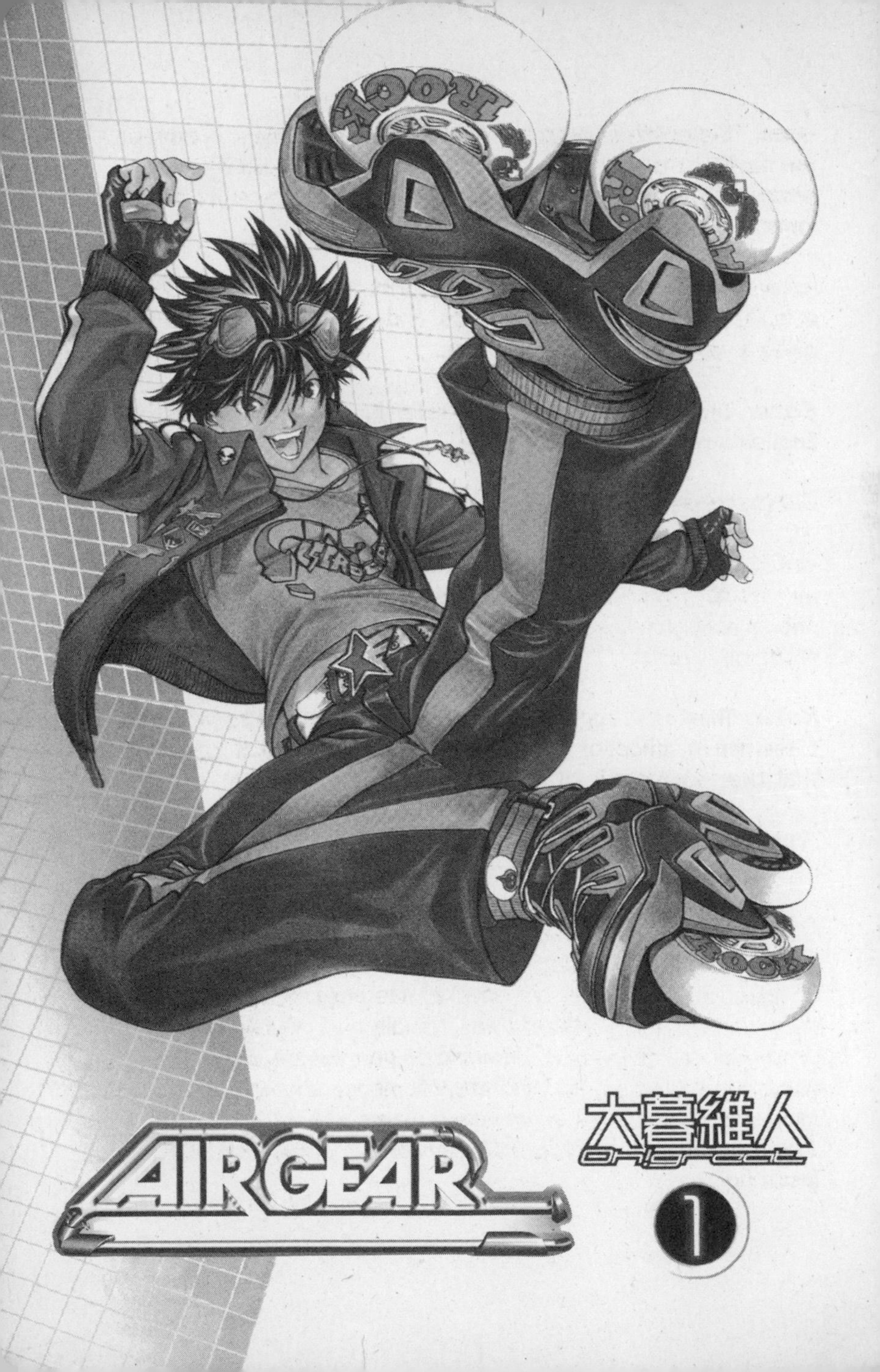

AIR GEAR
大暮維人
oh!great
1

CONTENTS

Honorifics	iii
Trick:1	3
Trick:2	75
Trick:3	133
Trick:4	163
Trick:5	183
Character Sketches	203
Translation Notes	208
Preview of Volume 2	212

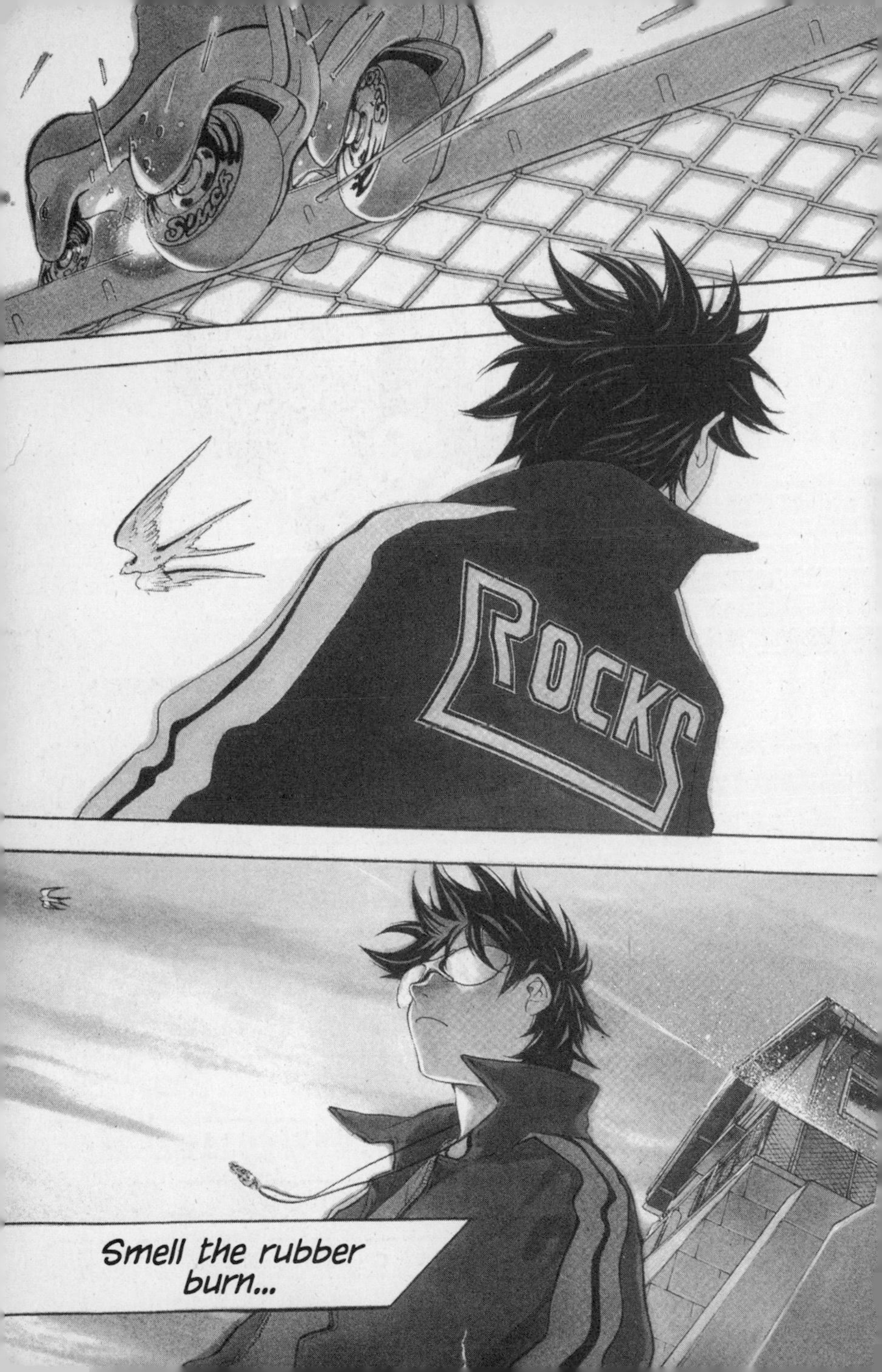
ROCKS
Smell the rubber burn...

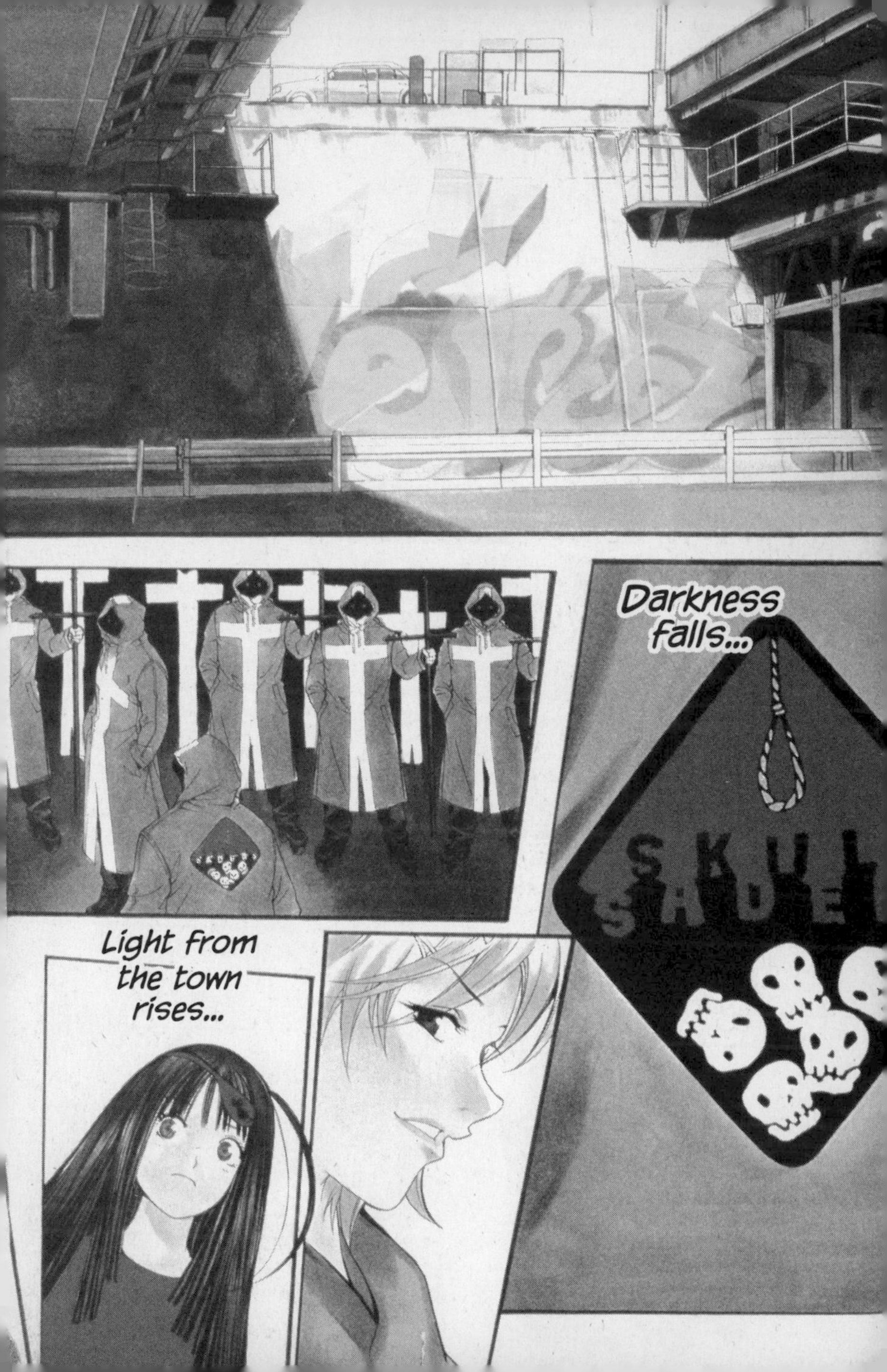
Darkness falls...
Light from the town rises...

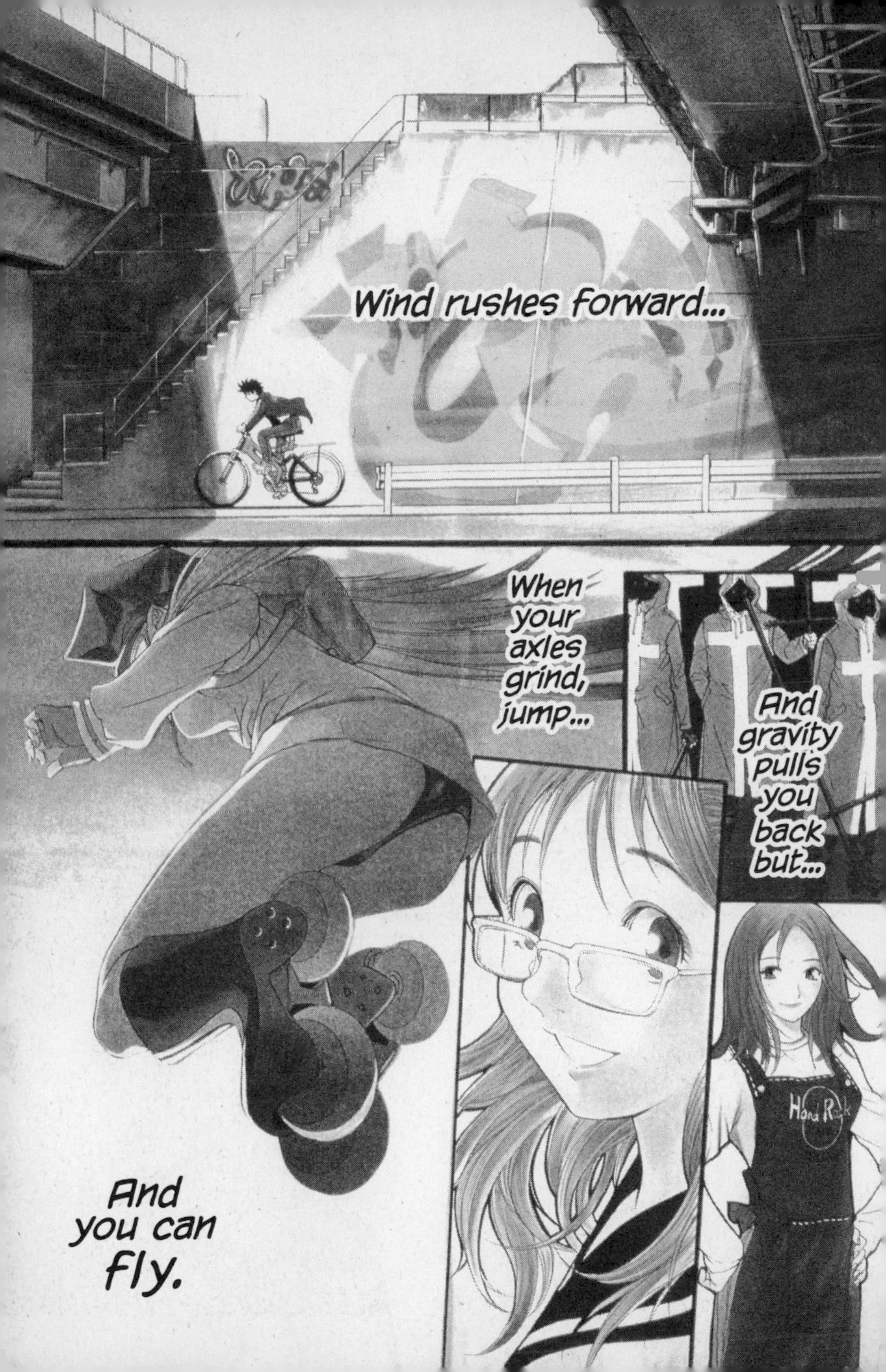
Wind rushes forward...
And gravity pulls you back but...
When your axles grind, jump...
And you can fly.

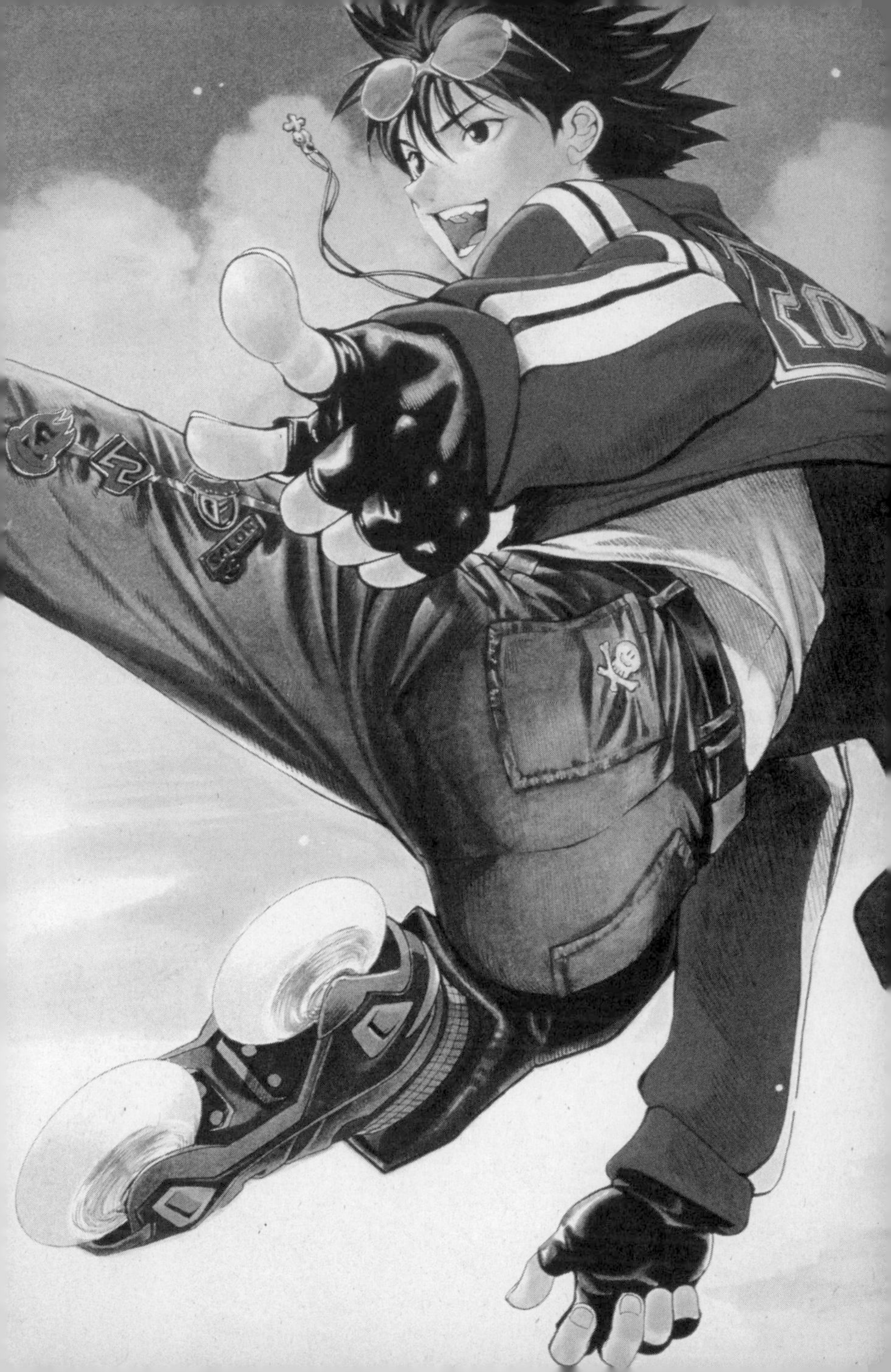

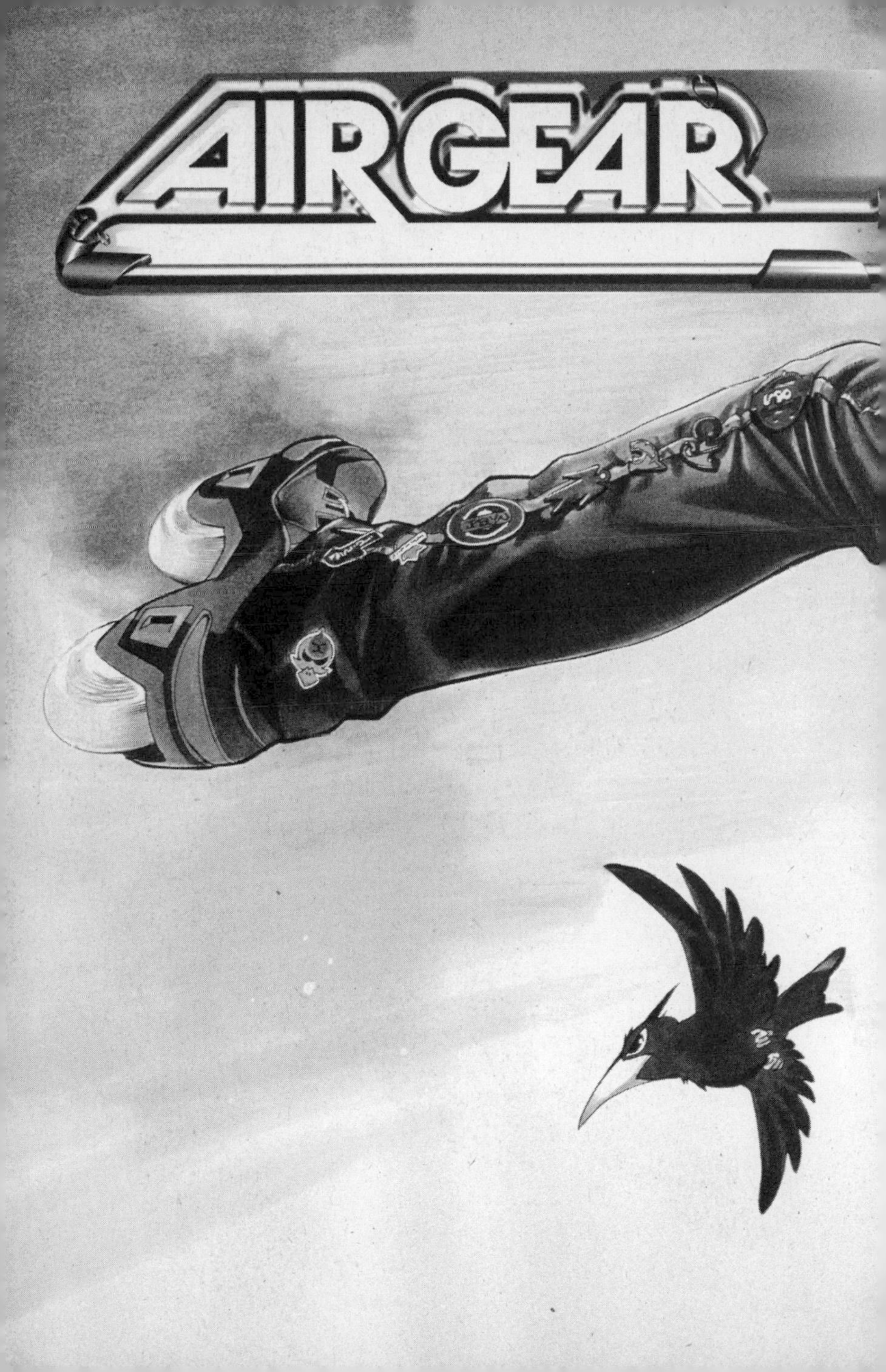
AIRGEAR

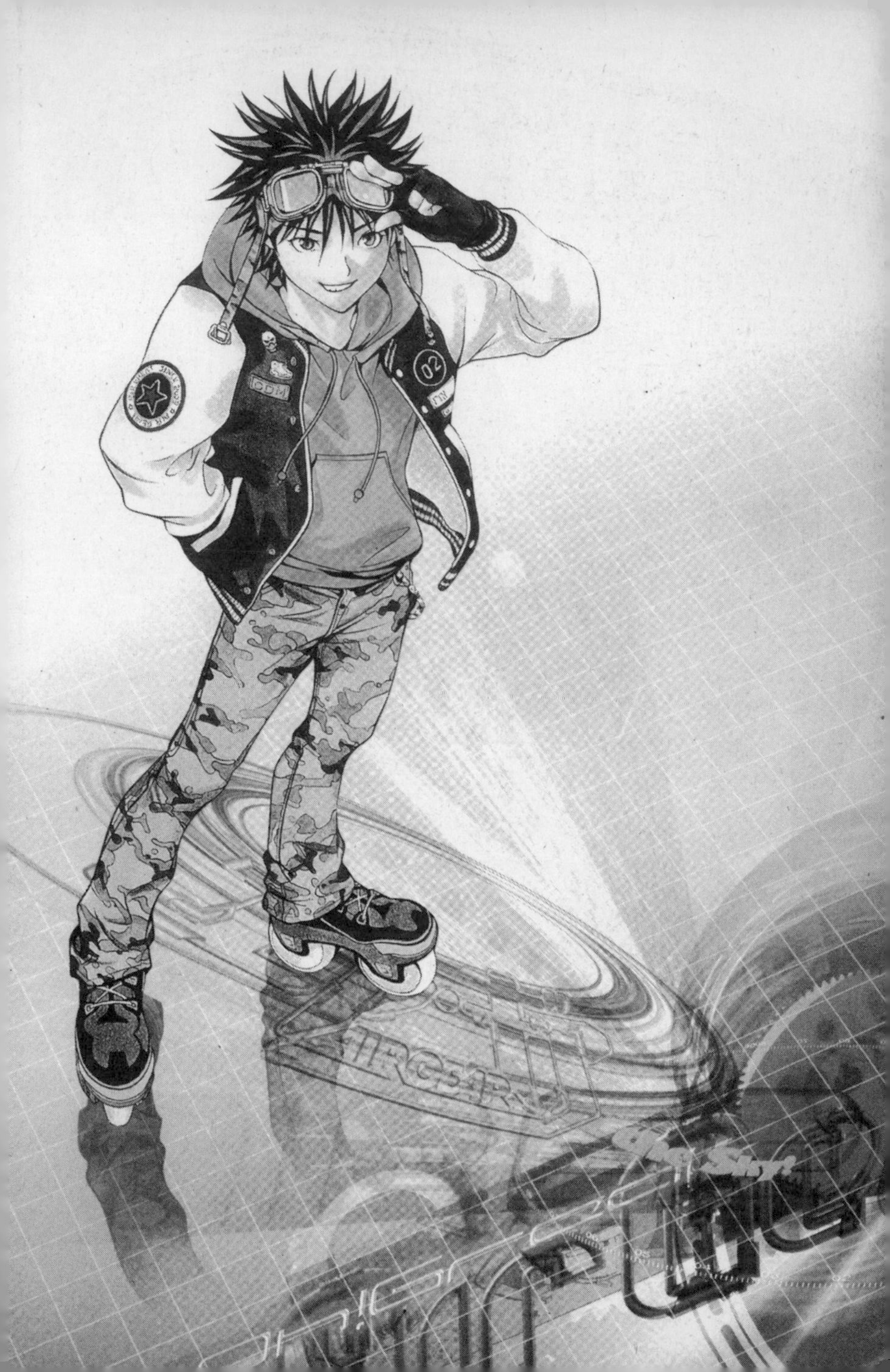

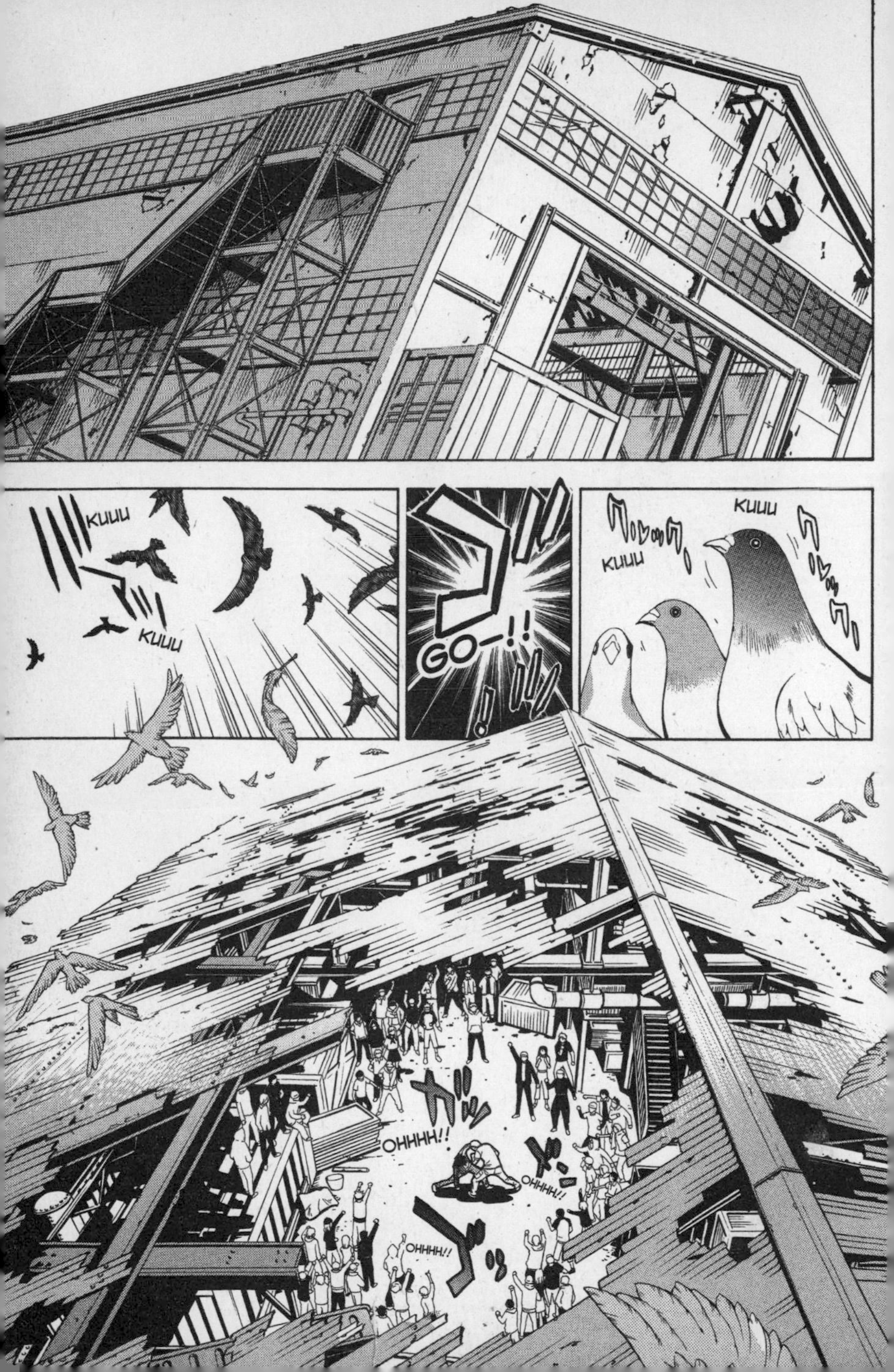
KUUU
KUUU
GO—!!
KUUU
KUUU
OHHHH!!
OHHHH!!
OHHHH!!

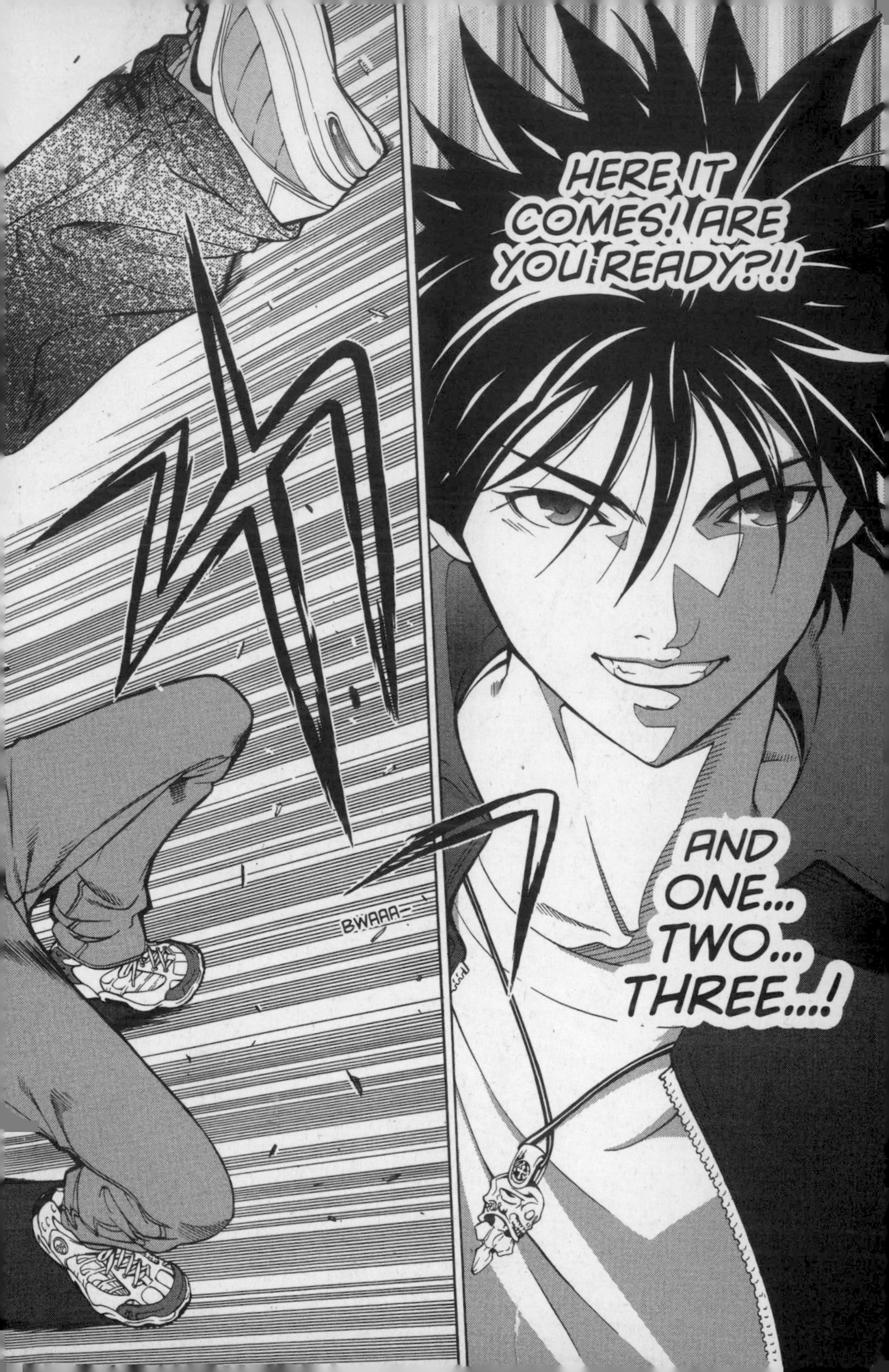
HERE IT COMES! ARE YOU READY?!!
AND ONE... TWO... THREE...!
BWAAA-

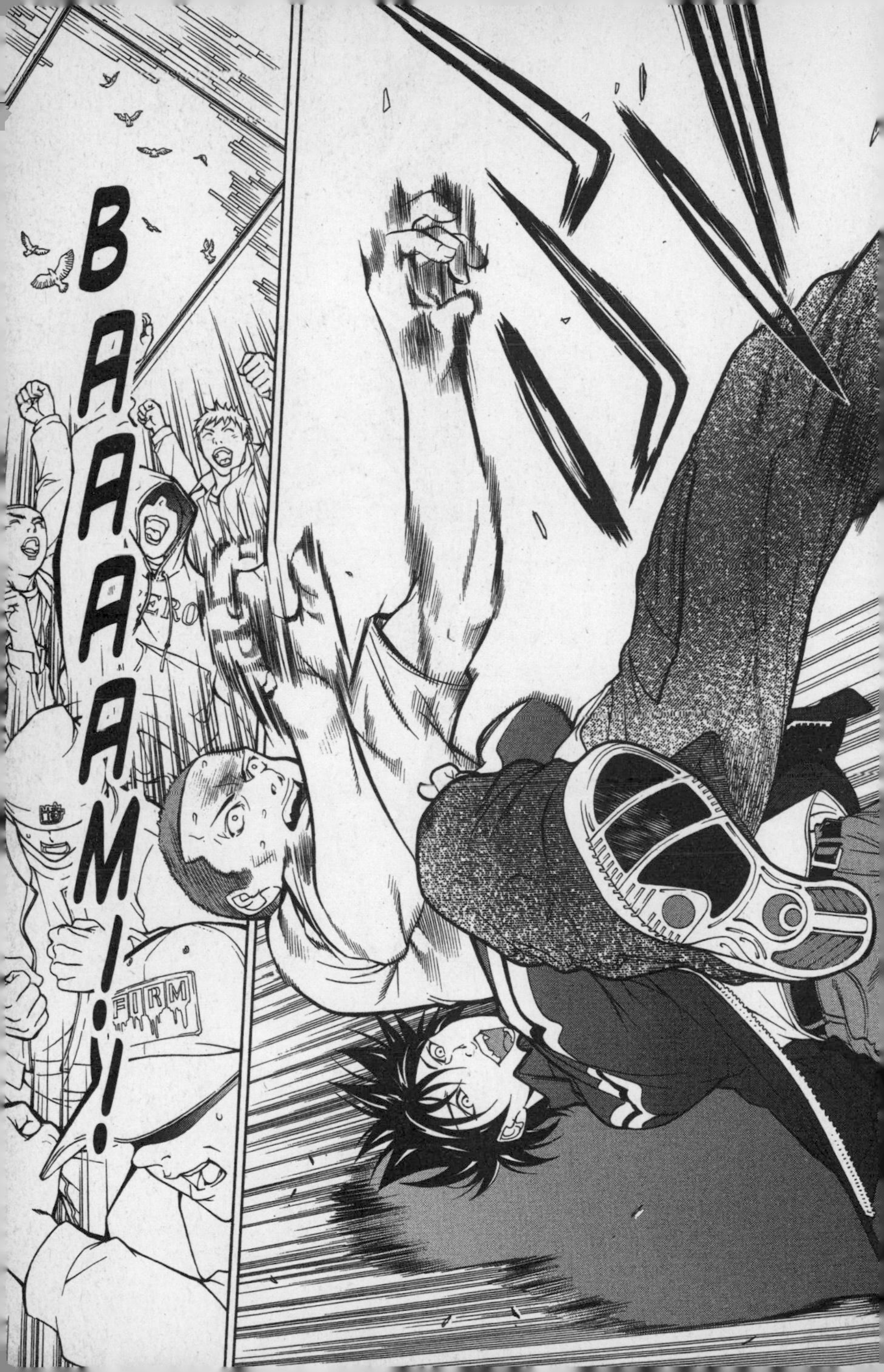
BAAAAM!!
FIRM

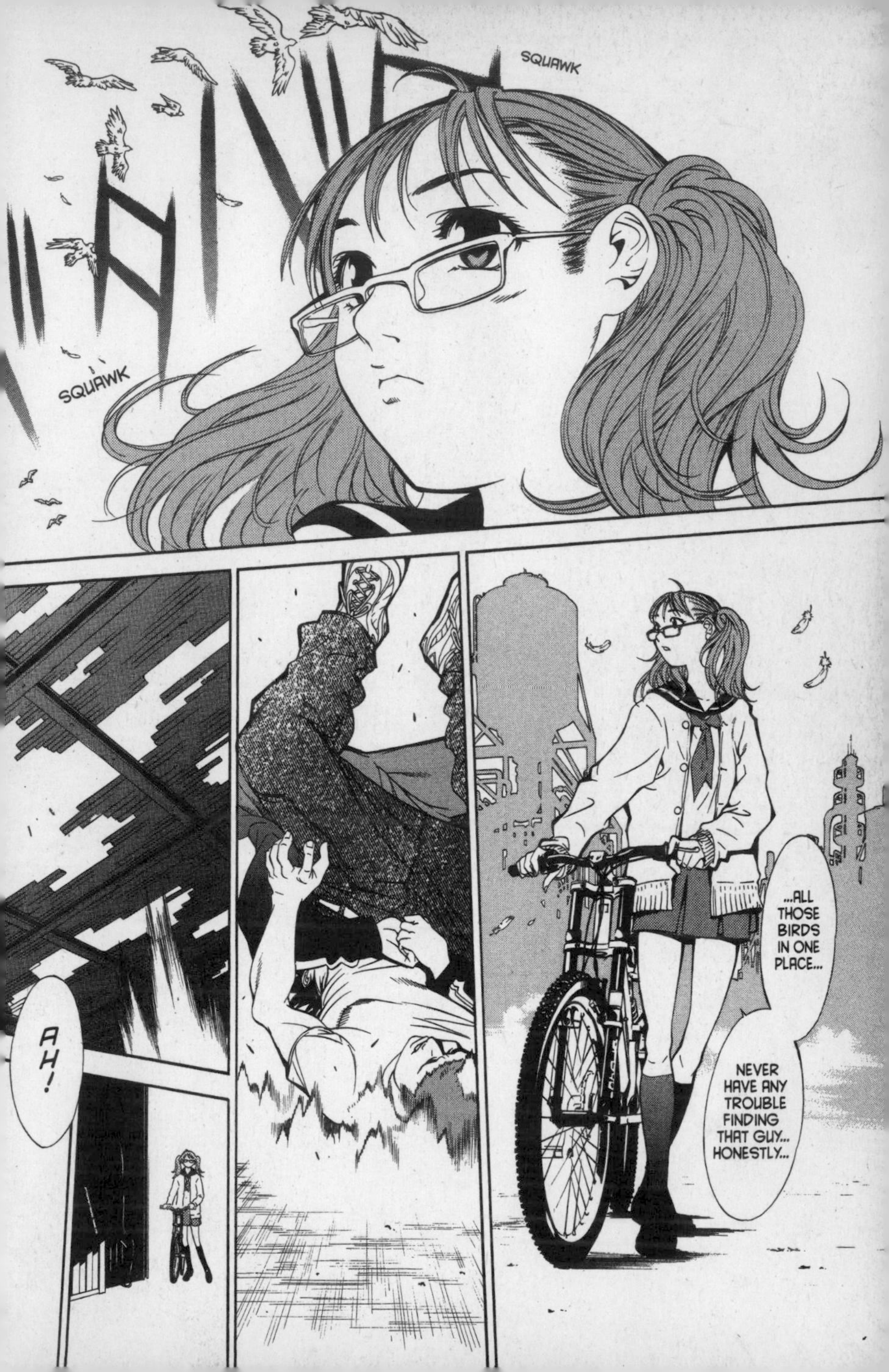
SQUAWK
SQUAWK
...ALL THOSE BIRDS IN ONE PLACE...
NEVER HAVE ANY TROUBLE FINDING THAT GUY... HONESTLY...
AH!

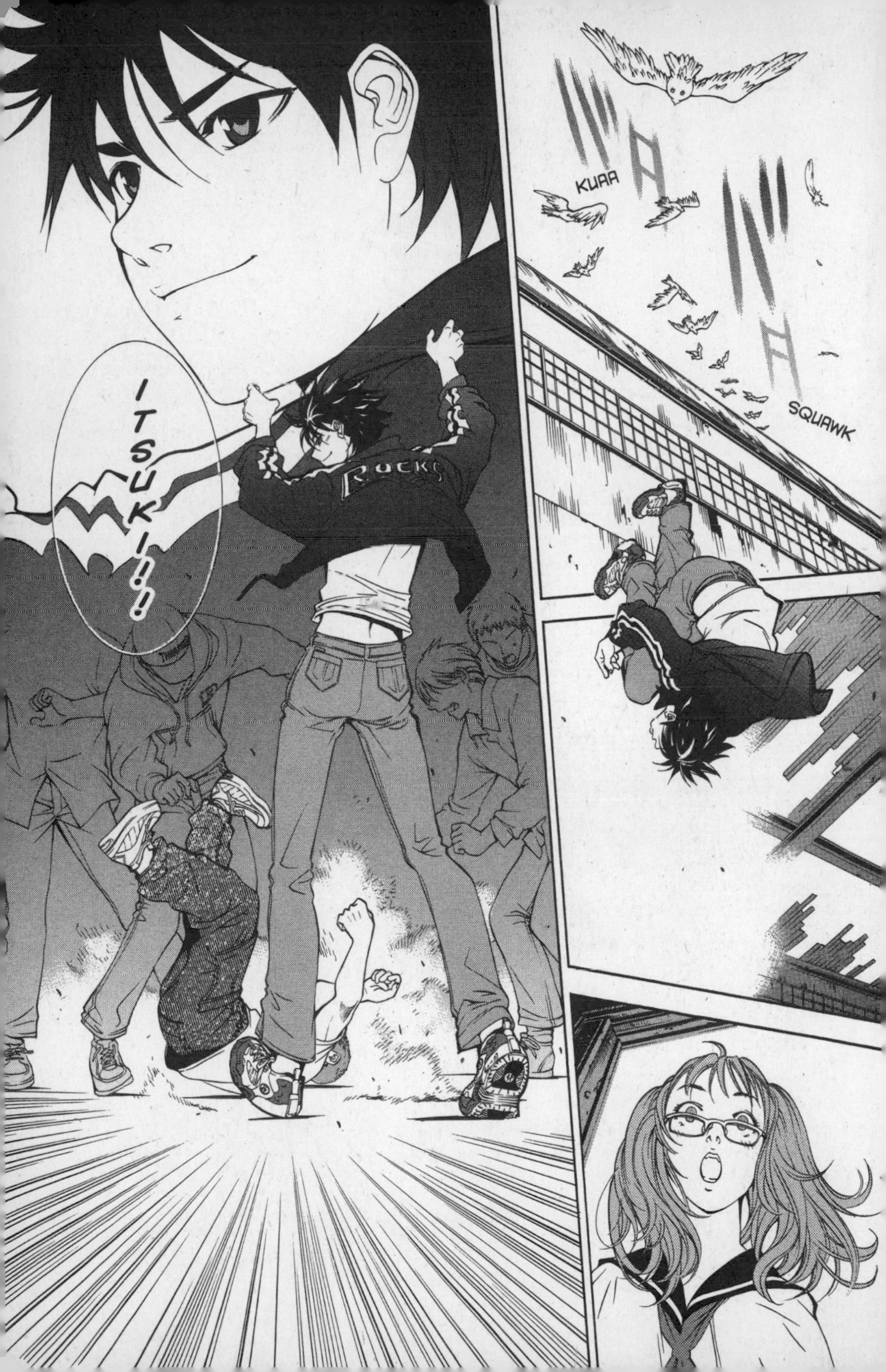
KUAA
SQUAWK
ITSUKI!!!

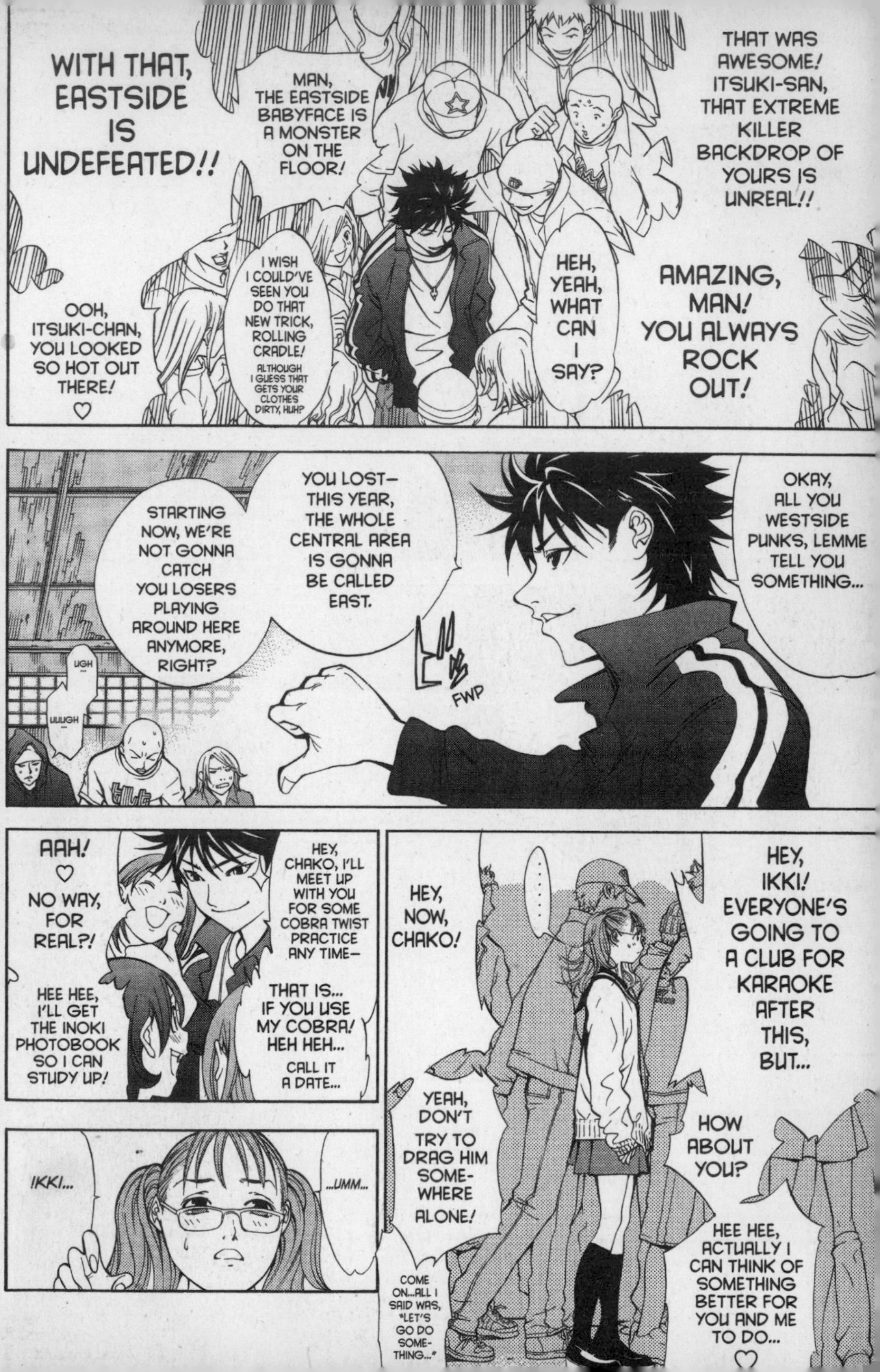
THAT WAS AWESOME! ITSUKI-SAN, THAT EXTREME KILLER BACKDROP OF YOURS IS UNREAL!!
MAN, THE EASTSIDE BABYFACE IS A MONSTER ON THE FLOOR!
WITH THAT, EASTSIDE IS UNDEFEATED!!
AMAZING, MAN! YOU ALWAYS ROCK OUT!
HEH, YEAH, WHAT CAN I SAY?
I WISH I COULD'VE SEEN YOU DO THAT NEW TRICK, ROLLING CRADLE!
ALTHOUGH I GUESS THAT GETS YOUR CLOTHES DIRTY, HUH?
OOH, ITSUKI-CHAN, YOU LOOKED SO HOT OUT THERE! ♡
OKAY, ALL YOU WESTSIDE PUNKS, LEMME TELL YOU SOMETHING...
YOU LOST— THIS YEAR, THE WHOLE CENTRAL AREA IS GONNA BE CALLED EAST.
FWP
STARTING NOW, WE'RE NOT GONNA CATCH YOU LOSERS PLAYING AROUND HERE ANYMORE, RIGHT?
UGH...
UUUGH...
HEY, IKKI! EVERYONE'S GOING TO A CLUB FOR KARAOKE AFTER THIS, BUT...
......
HEY, NOW, CHAKO!
HOW ABOUT YOU?
YEAH, DON'T TRY TO DRAG HIM SOME-WHERE ALONE!
HEE HEE, ACTUALLY I CAN THINK OF SOMETHING BETTER FOR YOU AND ME TO DO... ♡
COME ON...ALL I SAID WAS, "LET'S GO DO SOME-THING..."
HEY, CHAKO, I'LL MEET UP WITH YOU FOR SOME COBRA TWIST PRACTICE ANY TIME—
THAT IS... IF YOU USE MY COBRA! HEH HEH...
CALL IT A DATE...
AAH! ♡
NO WAY, FOR REAL?!
HEE HEE, I'LL GET THE INOKI PHOTOBOOK SO I CAN STUDY UP!
...UMM...
IKKI...

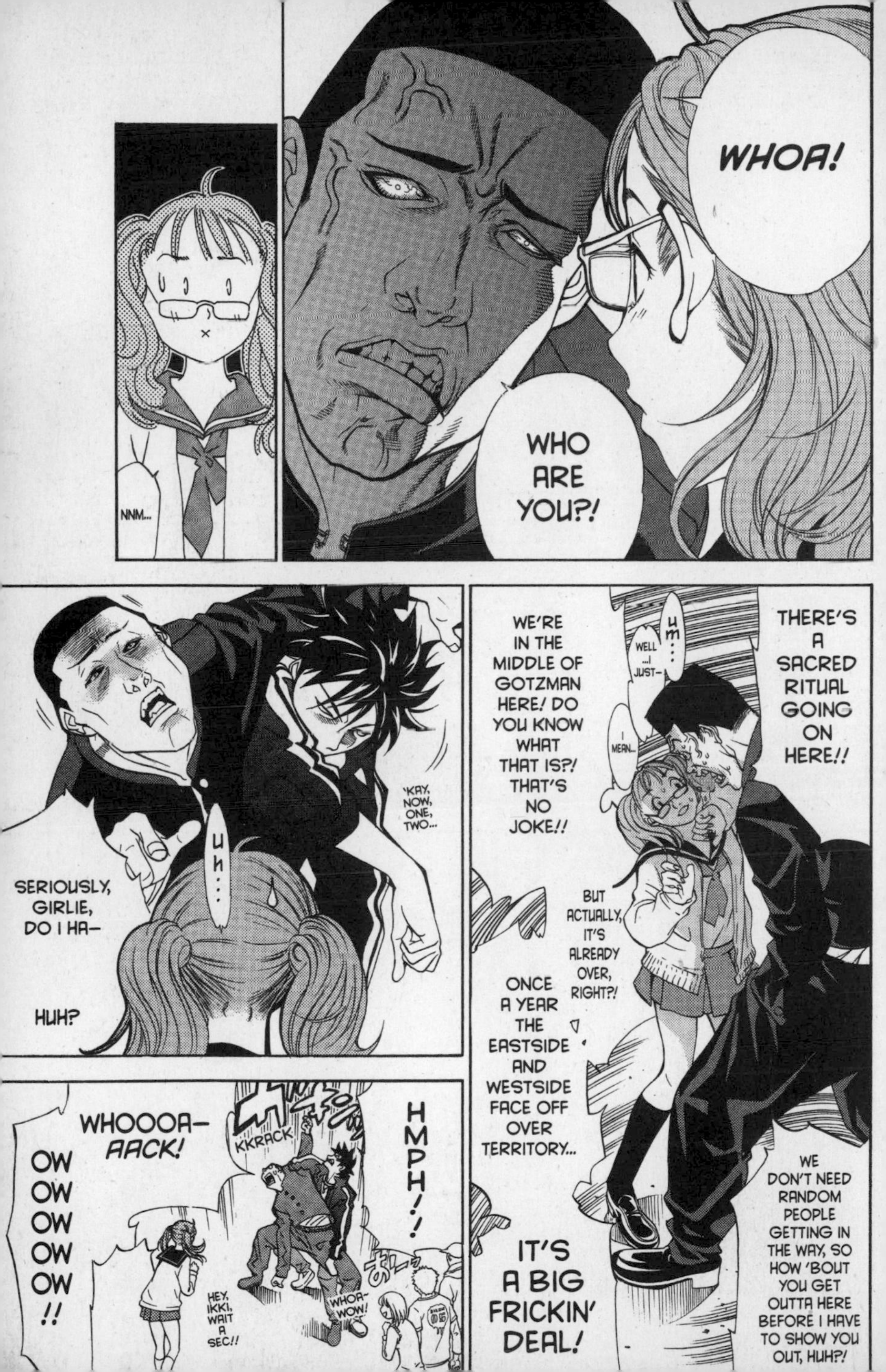
WHOA!
WHO ARE YOU?!
NNM...
THERE'S A SACRED RITUAL GOING ON HERE!!
UM...
WELL ...I JUST-
WE'RE IN THE MIDDLE OF GOTZMAN HERE! DO YOU KNOW WHAT THAT IS?! THAT'S NO JOKE!!
I MEAN...
BUT ACTUALLY, IT'S ALREADY OVER, RIGHT?!
ONCE A YEAR THE EASTSIDE AND WESTSIDE FACE OFF OVER TERRITORY...
WE DON'T NEED RANDOM PEOPLE GETTING IN THE WAY, SO HOW 'BOUT YOU GET OUTTA HERE BEFORE I HAVE TO SHOW YOU OUT, HUH?!
IT'S A BIG FRICKIN' DEAL!
'KAY, NOW, ONE, TWO...
UH...
SERIOUSLY, GIRLIE, DO I HA-
HUH?
HMPH!!
KKRACK
WHOOOA-AACK!
OW OW OW OW OW!!
WHOA-WOW!
HEY, IKKI, WAIT A SEC!!

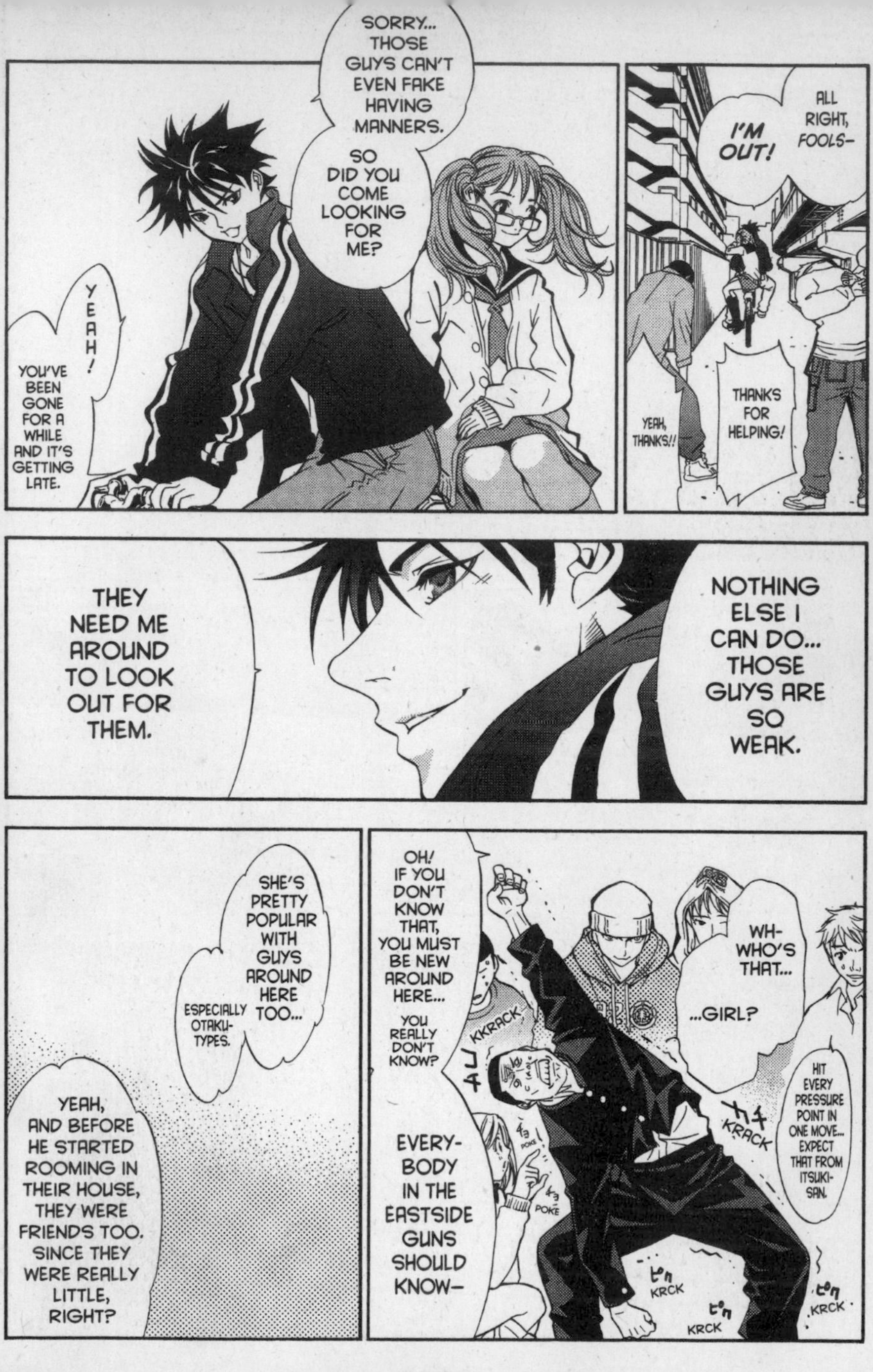
ALL RIGHT, FOOLS—
I'M OUT!
THANKS FOR HELPING!
YEAH, THANKS!!
SORRY... THOSE GUYS CAN'T EVEN FAKE HAVING MANNERS.
SO DID YOU COME LOOKING FOR ME?
YEAH!
YOU'VE BEEN GONE FOR A WHILE AND IT'S GETTING LATE.
NOTHING ELSE I CAN DO... THOSE GUYS ARE SO WEAK.
THEY NEED ME AROUND TO LOOK OUT FOR THEM.
WH-WHO'S THAT...
...GIRL?
OH! IF YOU DON'T KNOW THAT, YOU MUST BE NEW AROUND HERE...
YOU REALLY DON'T KNOW?
KKRACK
HIT EVERY PRESSURE POINT IN ONE MOVE... EXPECT THAT FROM ITSUKI-SAN.
KRACK
POKE
POKE
EVERY-BODY IN THE EASTSIDE GUNS SHOULD KNOW—
KRCK
KRCK
KRCK
SHE'S PRETTY POPULAR WITH GUYS AROUND HERE TOO...
ESPECIALLY OTAKU-TYPES.
YEAH, AND BEFORE HE STARTED ROOMING IN THEIR HOUSE, THEY WERE FRIENDS TOO. SINCE THEY WERE REALLY LITTLE, RIGHT?

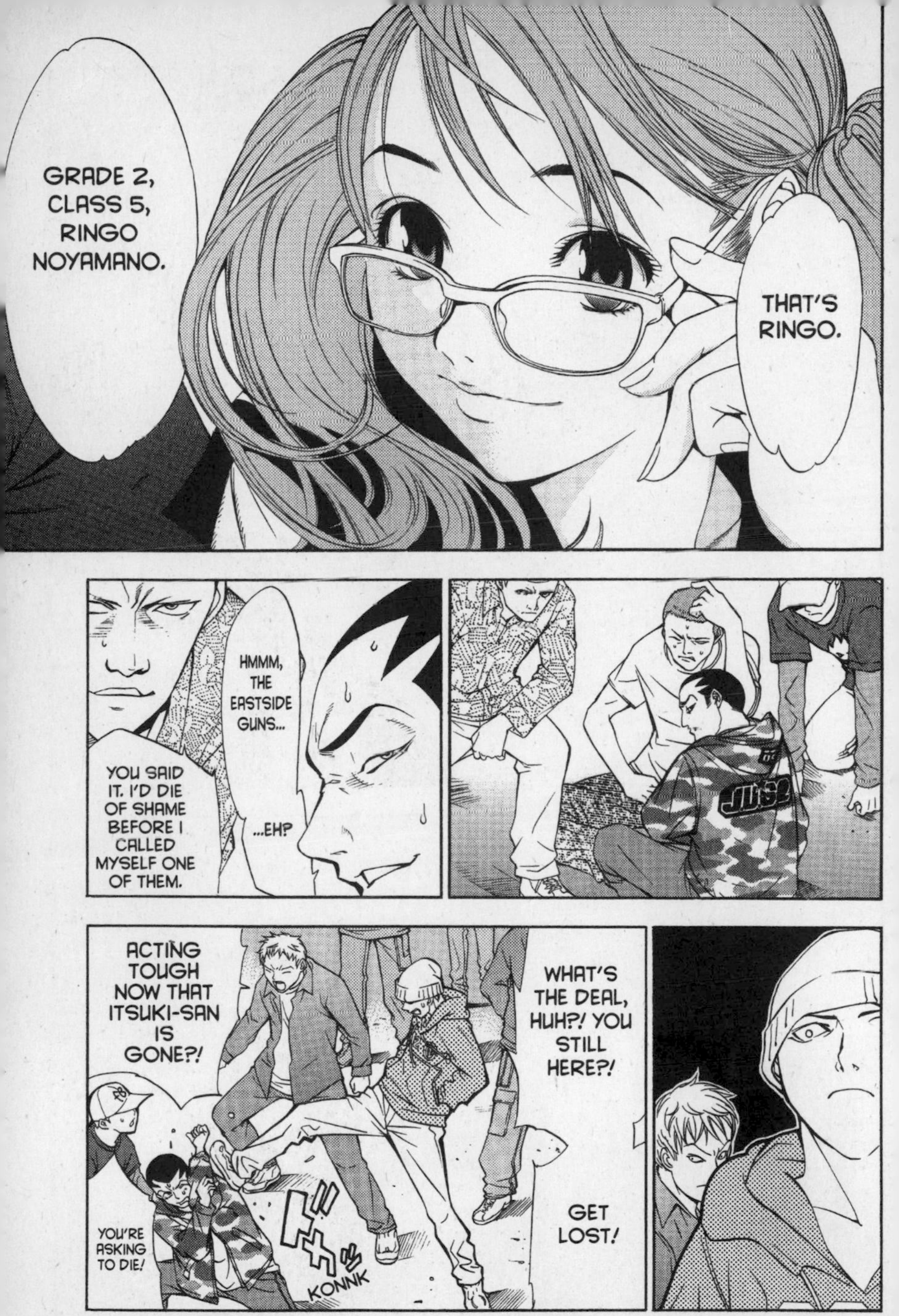
THAT'S RINGO.
GRADE 2, CLASS 5, RINGO NOYAMANO.
HMMM, THE EASTSIDE GUNS...
YOU SAID IT. I'D DIE OF SHAME BEFORE I CALLED MYSELF ONE OF THEM.
...EH?
WHAT'S THE DEAL, HUH?! YOU STILL HERE?!
ACTING TOUGH NOW THAT ITSUKI-SAN IS GONE?!
GET LOST!
KONNK
YOU'RE ASKING TO DIE!

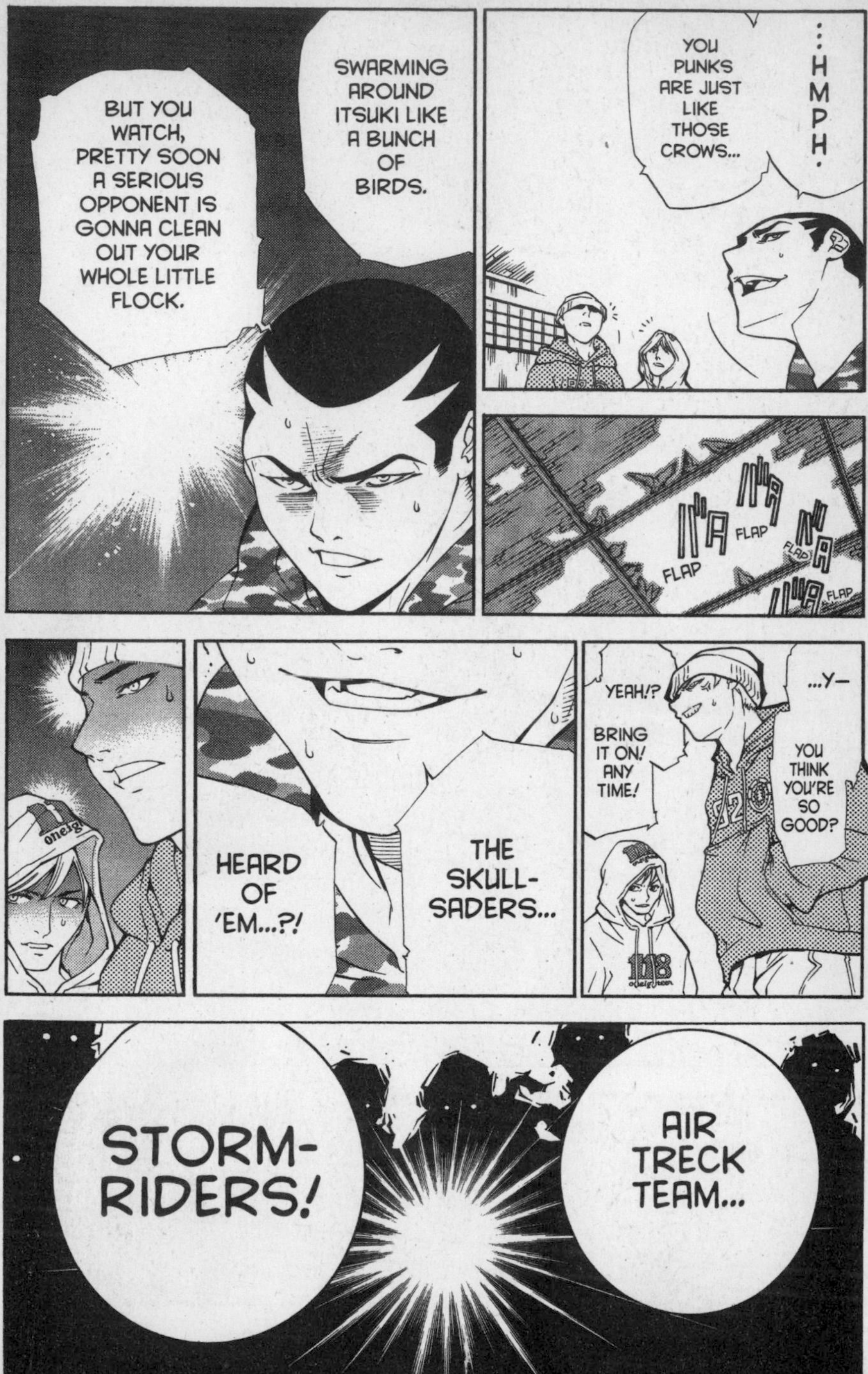
...HMPH.
YOU PUNKS ARE JUST LIKE THOSE CROWS...
FLAP
FLAP
FLAP
FLAP
SWARMING AROUND ITSUKI LIKE A BUNCH OF BIRDS.
BUT YOU WATCH, PRETTY SOON A SERIOUS OPPONENT IS GONNA CLEAN OUT YOUR WHOLE LITTLE FLOCK.
...Y—
YOU THINK YOU'RE SO GOOD?
YEAH!?
BRING IT ON! ANY TIME!
THE SKULL-SADERS...
HEARD OF 'EM...?!
AIR TRECK TEAM...
STORM-RIDERS!

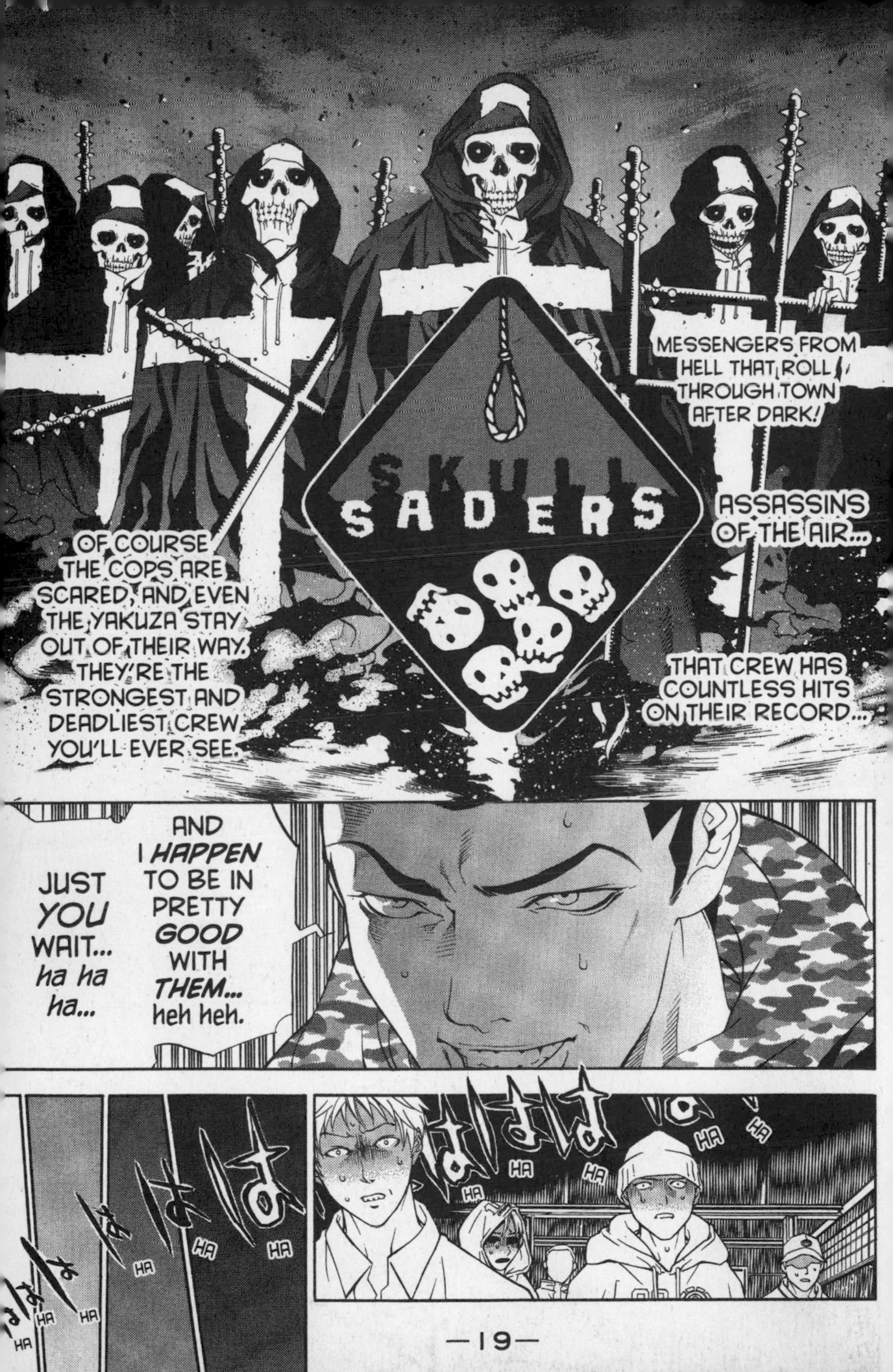
MESSENGERS FROM HELL THAT ROLL THROUGH TOWN AFTER DARK!
ASSASSINS OF THE AIR...
THAT CREW HAS COUNTLESS HITS ON THEIR RECORD...
SKULL SADERS
OF COURSE THE COPS ARE SCARED, AND EVEN THE YAKUZA STAY OUT OF THEIR WAY. THEY'RE THE STRONGEST AND DEADLIEST CREW YOU'LL EVER SEE.
AND I *HAPPEN* TO BE IN PRETTY *GOOD* WITH *THEM*... heh heh.
JUST *YOU* WAIT... ha ha ha...
HA HA HA HA HA
HA HA HA HA HA HA

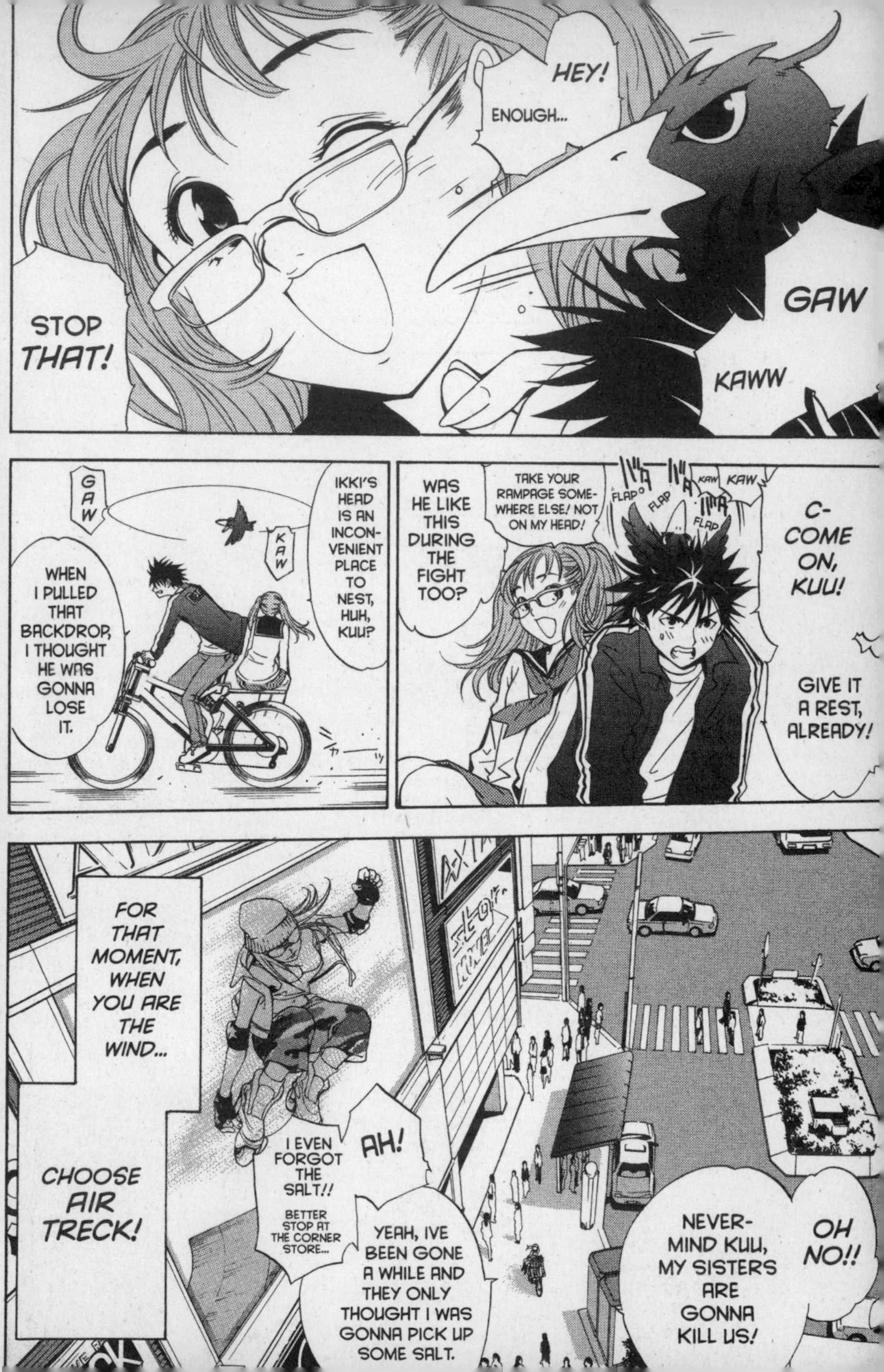
HEY!
ENOUGH...
GAW
KAWW
STOP THAT!
C-COME ON, KUU!
GIVE IT A REST, ALREADY!
KAW KAW
FLAP FLAP FLAP
TAKE YOUR RAMPAGE SOME-WHERE ELSE! NOT ON MY HEAD!
WAS HE LIKE THIS DURING THE FIGHT TOO?
IKKI'S HEAD IS AN INCON-VENIENT PLACE TO NEST, HUH, KUU?
KAW
GAW
WHEN I PULLED THAT BACKDROP, I THOUGHT HE WAS GONNA LOSE IT.
OH NO!!
NEVER-MIND KUU, MY SISTERS ARE GONNA KILL US!
YEAH, IVE BEEN GONE A WHILE AND THEY ONLY THOUGHT I WAS GONNA PICK UP SOME SALT.
AH!
I EVEN FORGOT THE SALT!!
BETTER STOP AT THE CORNER STORE...
FOR THAT MOMENT, WHEN YOU ARE THE WIND...
CHOOSE AIR TRECK!

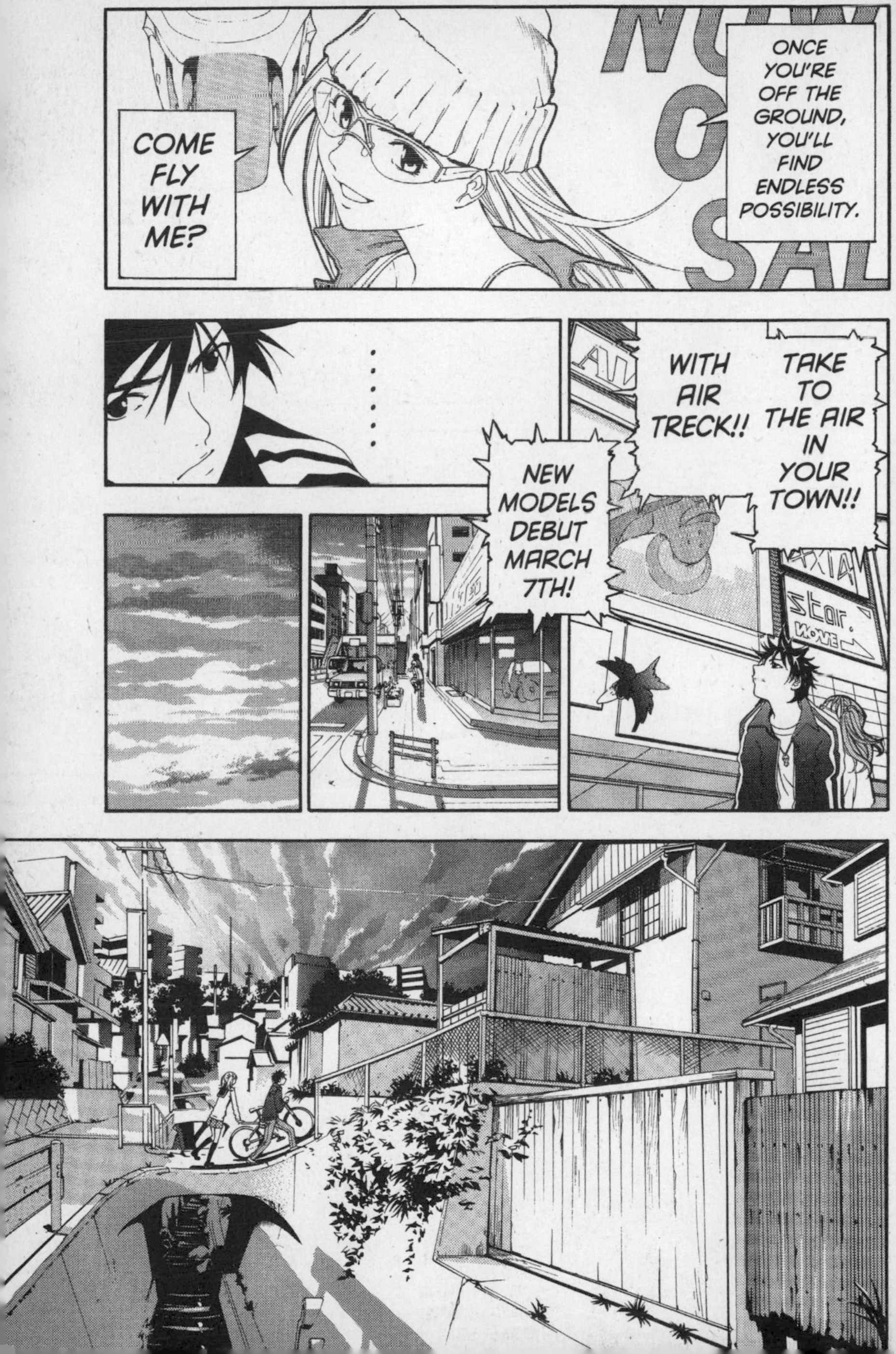
ONCE YOU'RE OFF THE GROUND, YOU'LL FIND ENDLESS POSSIBILITY.
COME FLY WITH ME?
TAKE TO THE AIR IN YOUR TOWN!!
WITH AIR TRECK!!
NEW MODELS DEBUT MARCH 7TH!
......

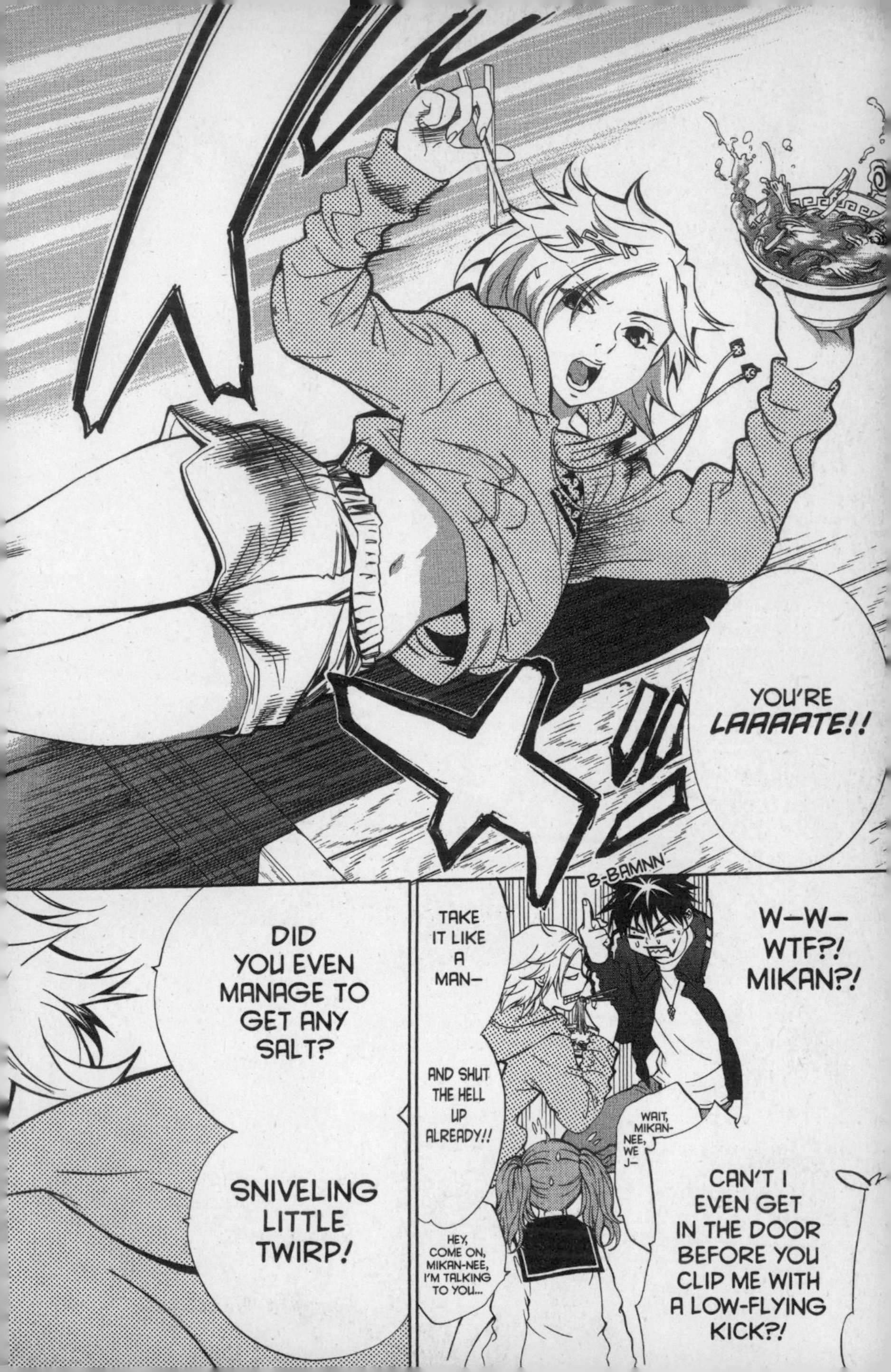
YOU'RE LAAAATE!!
B-BAMNN
W—W—WTF?! MIKAN?!
TAKE IT LIKE A MAN—
AND SHUT THE HELL UP ALREADY!!
WAIT, MIKAN-NEE, WE J—
CAN'T I EVEN GET IN THE DOOR BEFORE YOU CLIP ME WITH A LOW-FLYING KICK?!
HEY, COME ON, MIKAN-NEE, I'M TALKING TO YOU...
DID YOU EVEN MANAGE TO GET ANY SALT?
SNIVELING LITTLE TWIRP!

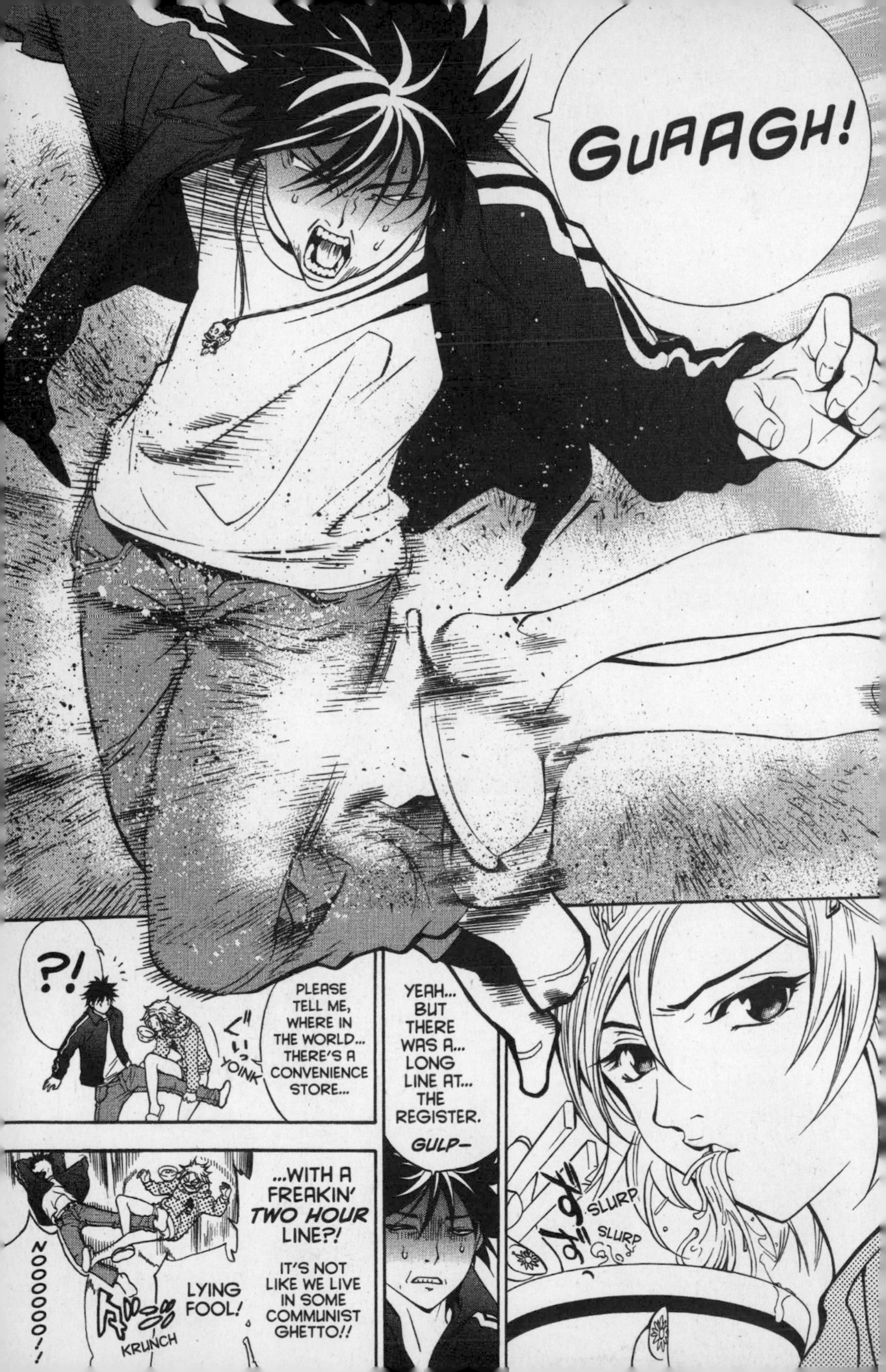

GUAAGH!
SLURP
SLURP
YEAH... BUT THERE WAS A... LONG LINE AT... THE REGISTER.
GULP—
?!
PLEASE TELL ME, WHERE IN THE WORLD... THERE'S A CONVENIENCE STORE...
YOINK
...WITH A FREAKIN' TWO HOUR LINE?!
IT'S NOT LIKE WE LIVE IN SOME COMMUNIST GHETTO!!
LYING FOOL!
KRUNCH
NOOOOOOO!!

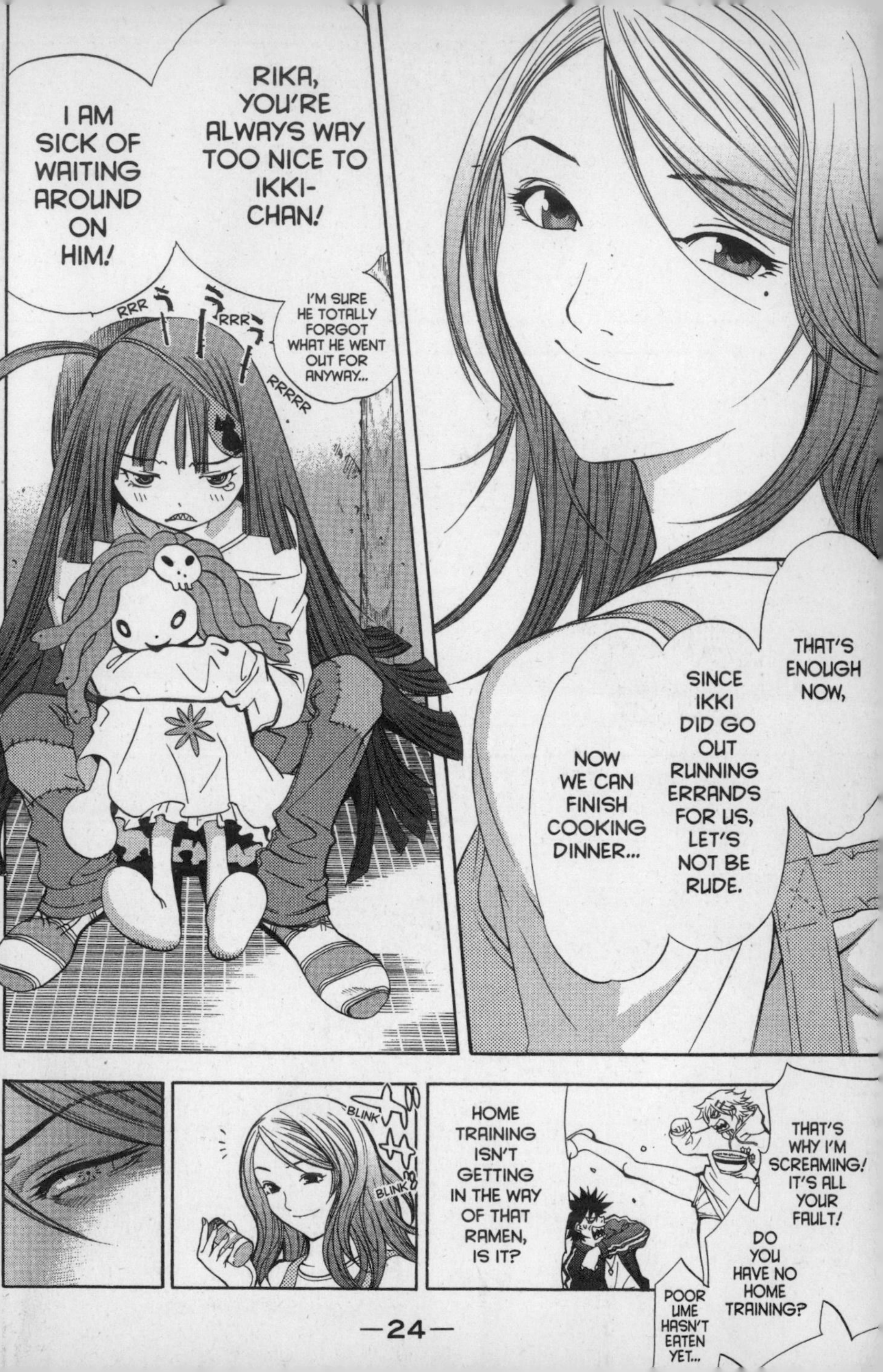

THAT'S ENOUGH NOW,
SINCE IKKI DID GO OUT RUNNING ERRANDS FOR US, LET'S NOT BE RUDE.
NOW WE CAN FINISH COOKING DINNER...
RIKA, YOU'RE ALWAYS WAY TOO NICE TO IKKI-CHAN!
I AM SICK OF WAITING AROUND ON HIM!
RRR
RRR
I'M SURE HE TOTALLY FORGOT WHAT HE WENT OUT FOR ANYWAY...
RRRRR
THAT'S WHY I'M SCREAMING! IT'S ALL YOUR FAULT!
DO YOU HAVE NO HOME TRAINING?
POOR UME HASN'T EATEN YET...
HOME TRAINING ISN'T GETTING IN THE WAY OF THAT RAMEN, IS IT?
BLINK
BLINK

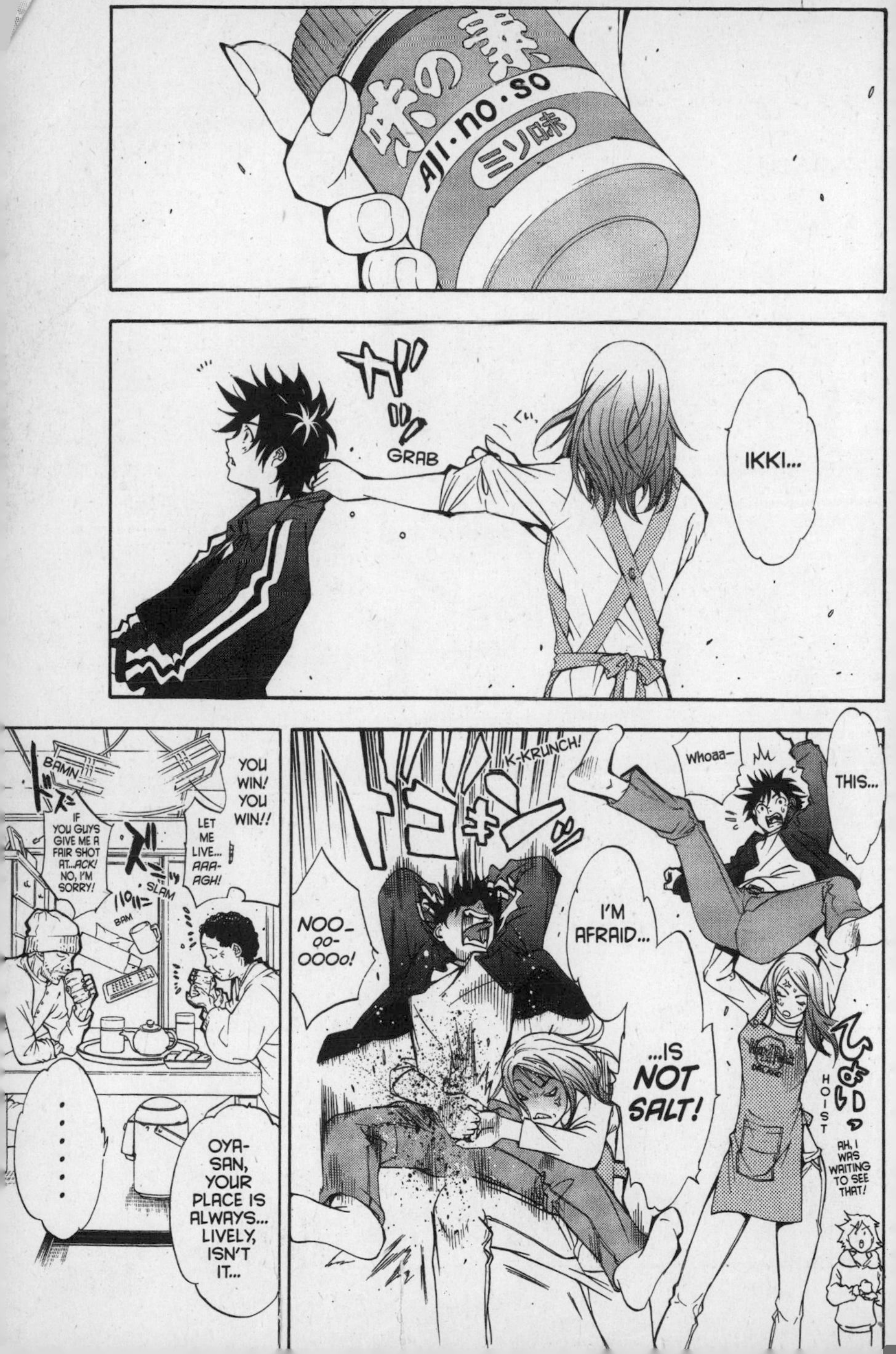
味の素
AJI·no·SO
ミソ味
IKKI...
GRAB
THIS...
Whoaa-
K-KRUNCH!
I'M AFRAID...
...IS NOT SALT!
NOO-oo-OOOo!
HOIST
AH, I WAS WAITING TO SEE THAT!
YOU WIN! YOU WIN!!
LET ME LIVE... AAAAGH!
BAMN
IF YOU GUYS GIVE ME A FAIR SHOT AT...ACK! NO, I'M SORRY!
SLAM
BAM
OYA-SAN, YOUR PLACE IS ALWAYS... LIVELY, ISN'T IT...
......

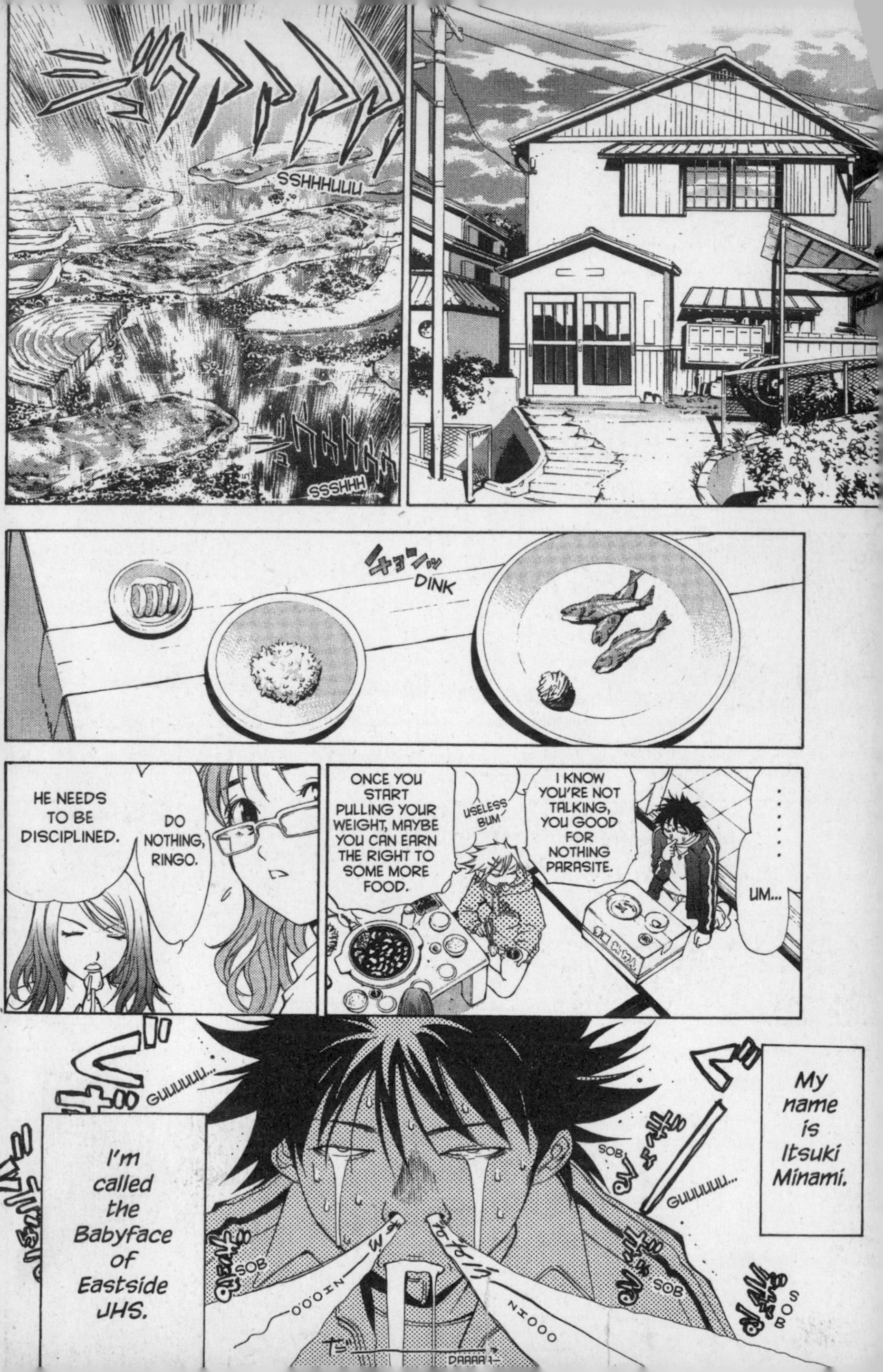
SSHHHUUU
SSSHHH
DINK
......
UM...
I KNOW YOU'RE NOT TALKING, YOU GOOD FOR NOTHING PARASITE.
USELESS BUM
ONCE YOU START PULLING YOUR WEIGHT, MAYBE YOU CAN EARN THE RIGHT TO SOME MORE FOOD.
DO NOTHING, RINGO.
HE NEEDS TO BE DISCIPLINED.
My name is Itsuki Minami.
GUUUUUU...
SOB
GUUUUUU...
SOB
SOB
I'm called the Babyface of Eastside JHS.
SOB
DAAAAA

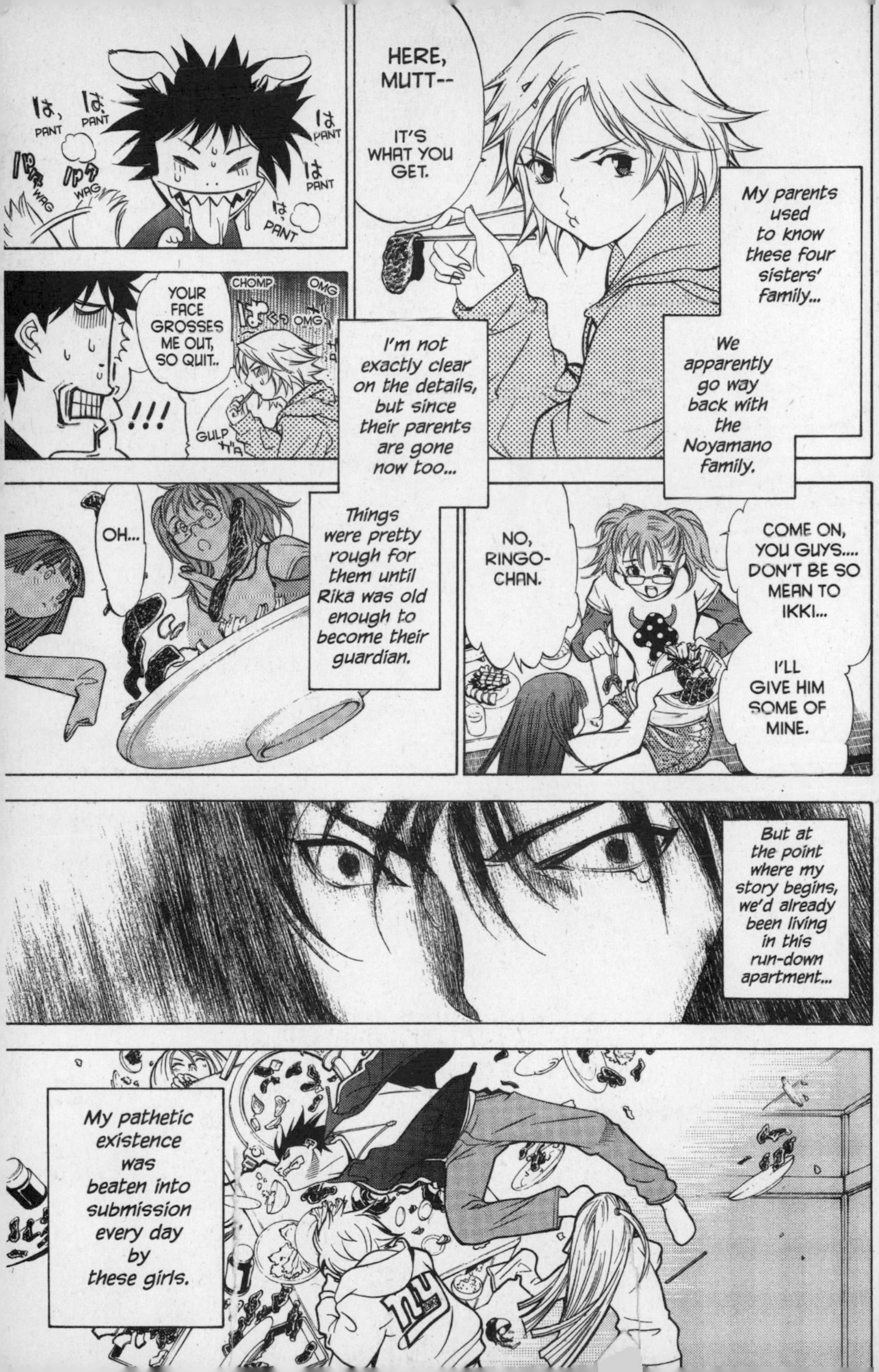
HERE, MUTT--
IT'S WHAT YOU GET.
My parents used to know these four sisters' family...
We apparently go way back with the Noyamano family.
I'm not exactly clear on the details, but since their parents are gone now too...
PANT
PANT
PANT
PANT
PANT
WAG
WAG
CHOMP
OMG
OMG
YOUR FACE GROSSES ME OUT, SO QUIT..
!!!
GULP
COME ON, YOU GUYS.... DON'T BE SO MEAN TO IKKI...
I'LL GIVE HIM SOME OF MINE.
NO, RINGO-CHAN.
Things were pretty rough for them until Rika was old enough to become their guardian.
OH...
But at the point where my story begins, we'd already been living in this run-down apartment...
My pathetic existence was beaten into submission every day by these girls.

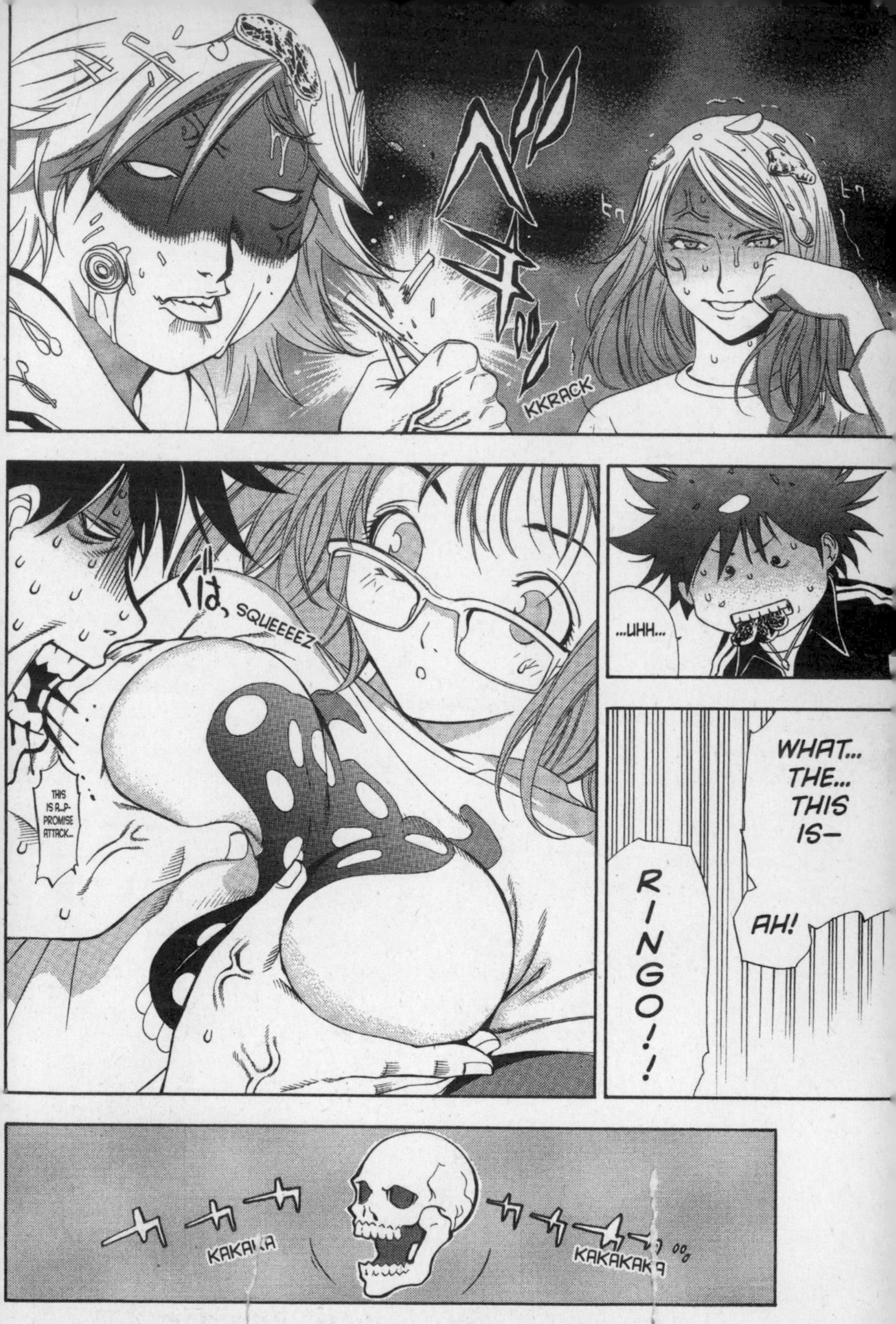
KKRACK
...UHH...
WHAT... THE... THIS IS—
RINGO!!
AH!
SQUEEEEZ
THIS IS A...P-PROMISE ATTACK...
KAKAKA
KAKAKAKA

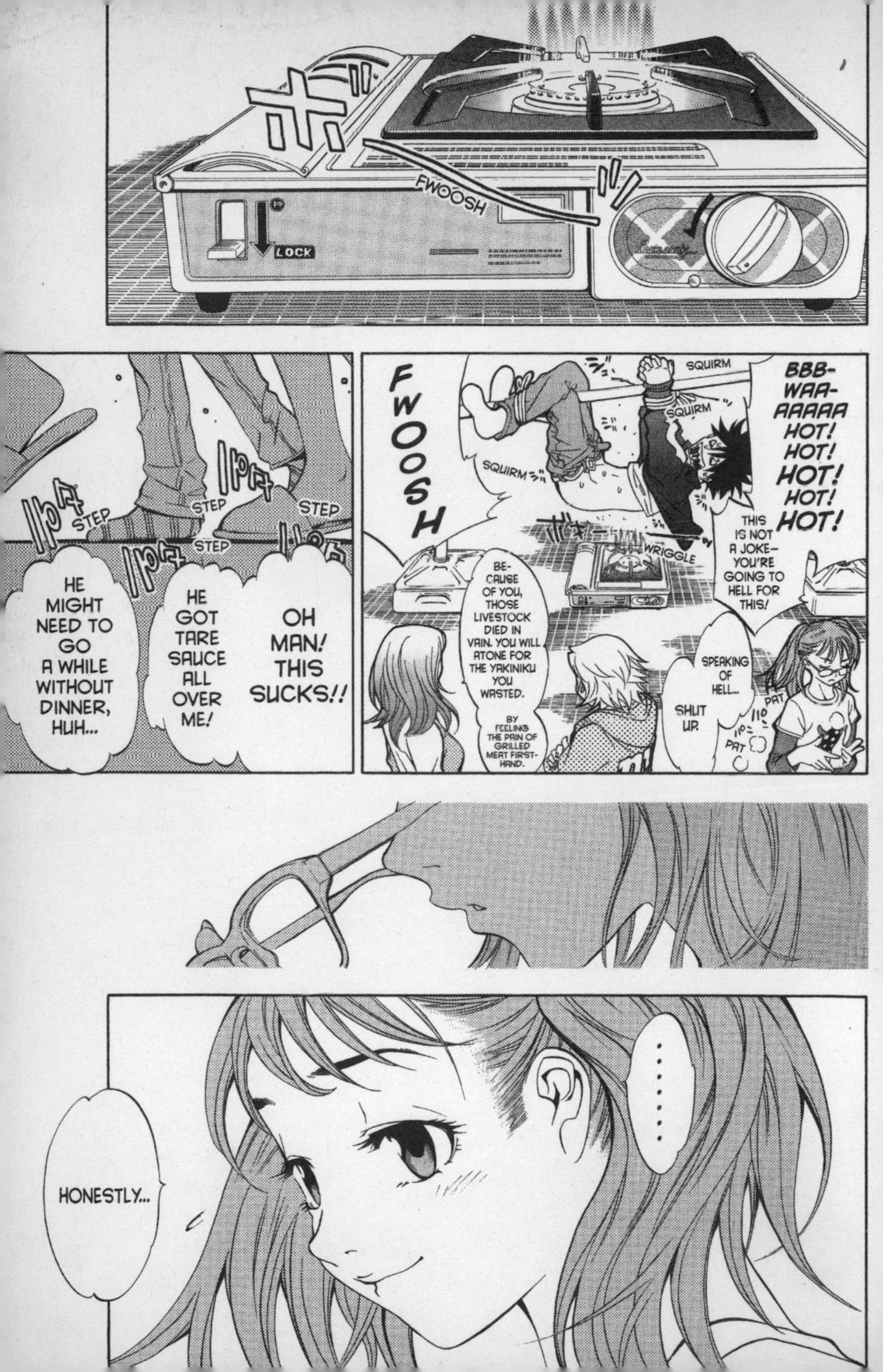
FWOOSH
BBB-WAA-AAAAA HOT! HOT! HOT! HOT! HOT!
SQUIRM
SQUIRM
FWOOSH
SQUIRM
WRIGGLE
THIS IS NOT A JOKE—YOU'RE GOING TO HELL FOR THIS!
SPEAKING OF HELL...
SHUT UP.
PAT
PAT
BE-CAUSE OF YOU, THOSE LIVESTOCK DIED IN VAIN. YOU WILL ATONE FOR THE YAKINIKU YOU WASTED.
BY FEELING THE PAIN OF GRILLED MEAT FIRST-HAND.
STEP
STEP
STEP
STEP
OH MAN! THIS SUCKS!!
HE GOT TARE SAUCE ALL OVER ME!
HE MIGHT NEED TO GO A WHILE WITHOUT DINNER, HUH...
......
HONESTLY...

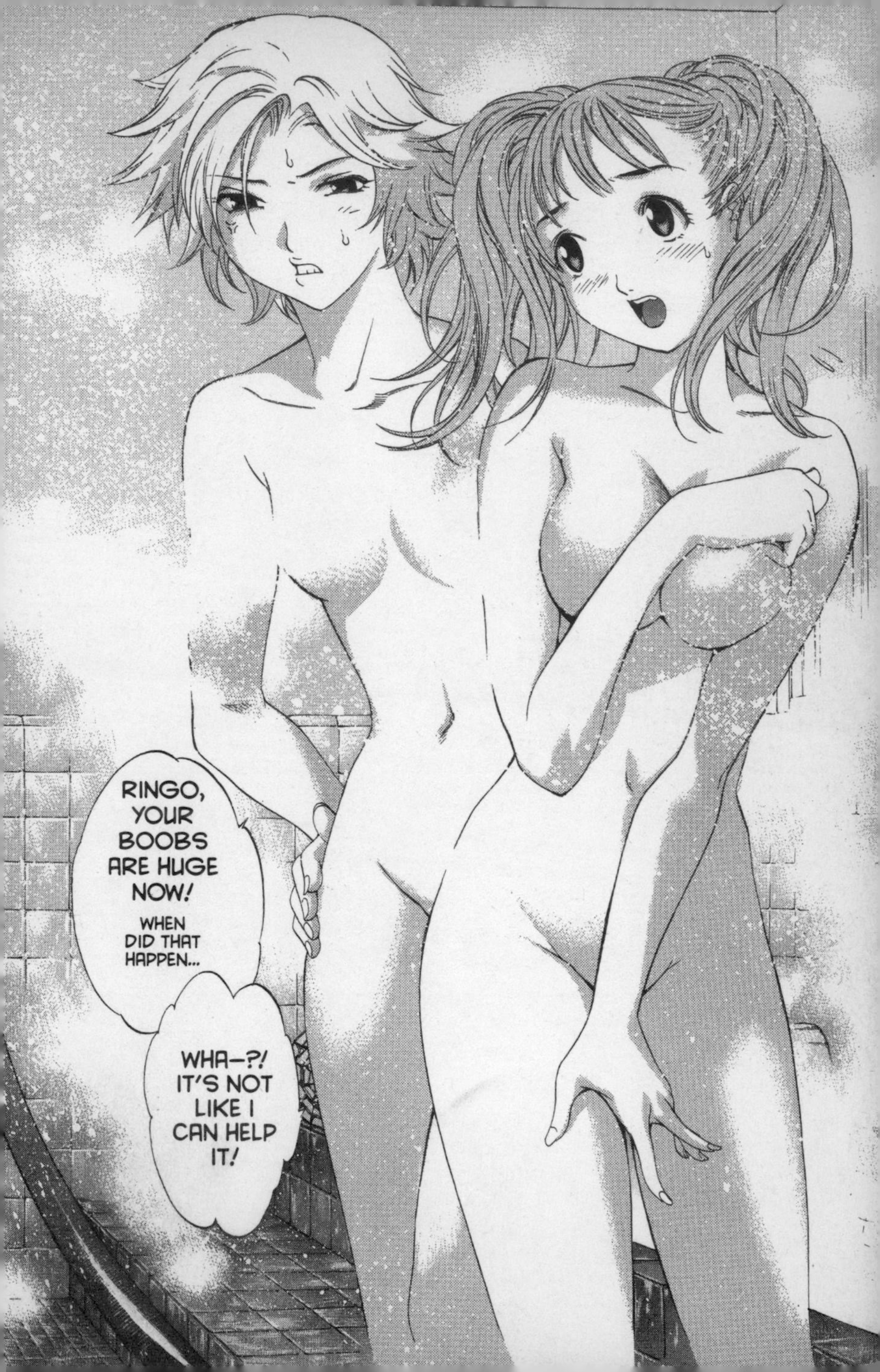
RINGO, YOUR BOOBS ARE HUGE NOW!
WHEN DID THAT HAPPEN...
WHA-?! IT'S NOT LIKE I CAN HELP IT!

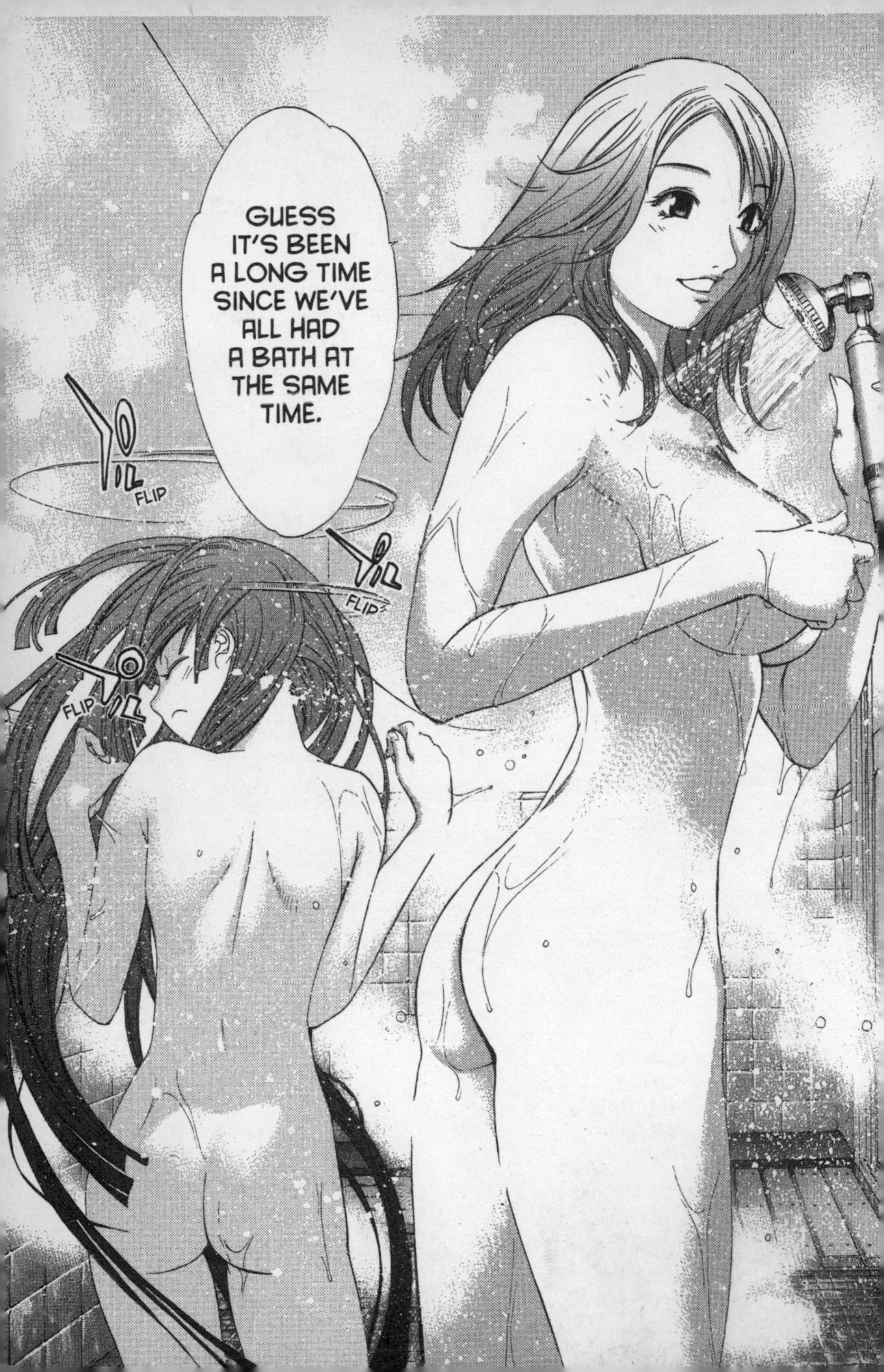
GUESS IT'S BEEN A LONG TIME SINCE WE'VE ALL HAD A BATH AT THE SAME TIME.
FLIP
FLIP
FLIP

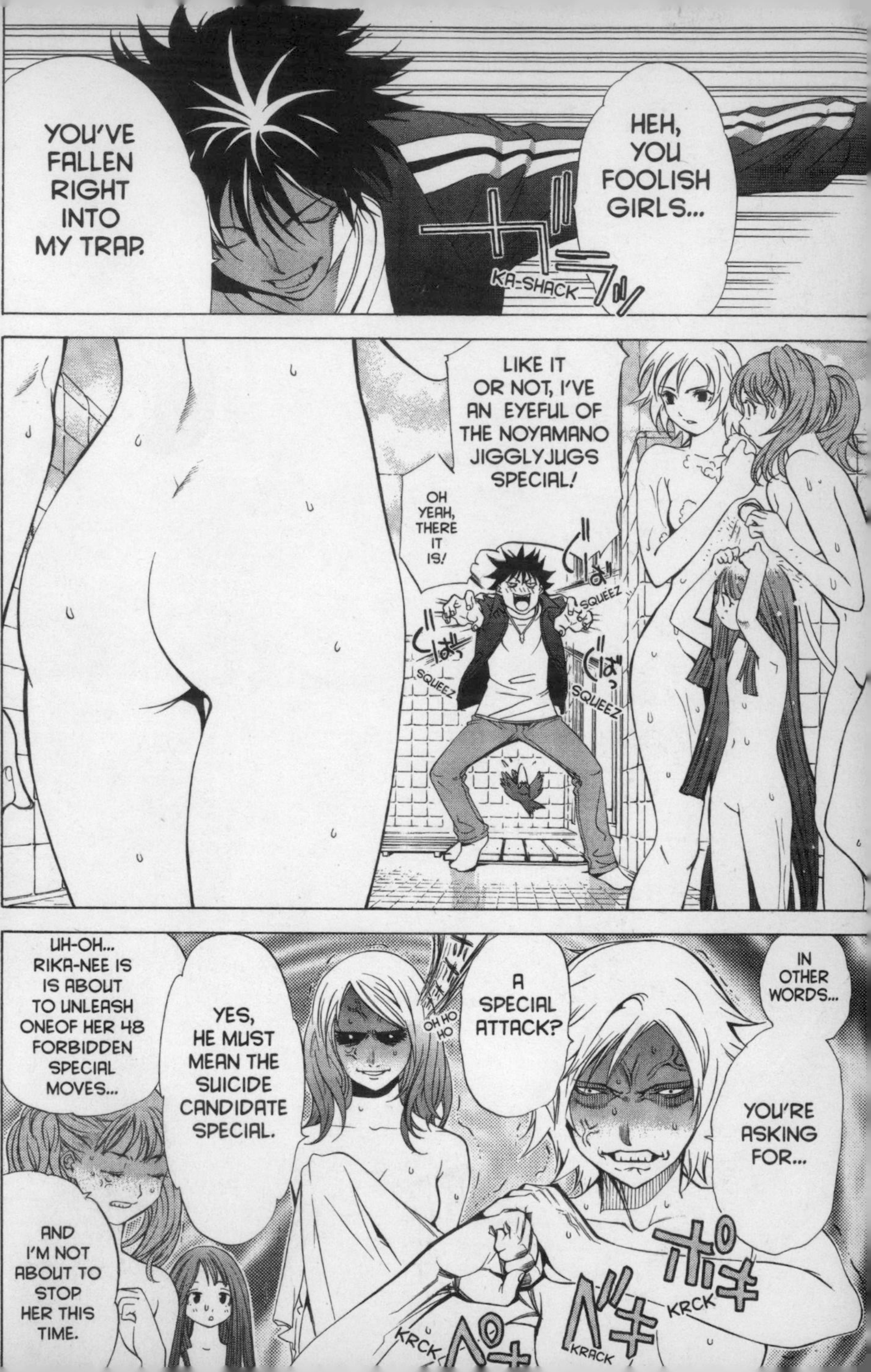
HEH, YOU FOOLISH GIRLS...
KA-SHACK
YOU'VE FALLEN RIGHT INTO MY TRAP.
LIKE IT OR NOT, I'VE AN EYEFUL OF THE NOYAMANO JIGGLYJUGS SPECIAL!
SQUEEZ
SQUEEZ
OH YEAH, THERE IT IS!
SQUEEZ
IN OTHER WORDS...
YOU'RE ASKING FOR...
A SPECIAL ATTACK?
OH HO HO
YES, HE MUST MEAN THE SUICIDE CANDIDATE SPECIAL.
UH-OH... RIKA-NEE IS IS ABOUT TO UNLEASH ONEOF HER 48 FORBIDDEN SPECIAL MOVES...
AND I'M NOT ABOUT TO STOP HER THIS TIME.
KRCK
KRACK
KRCK

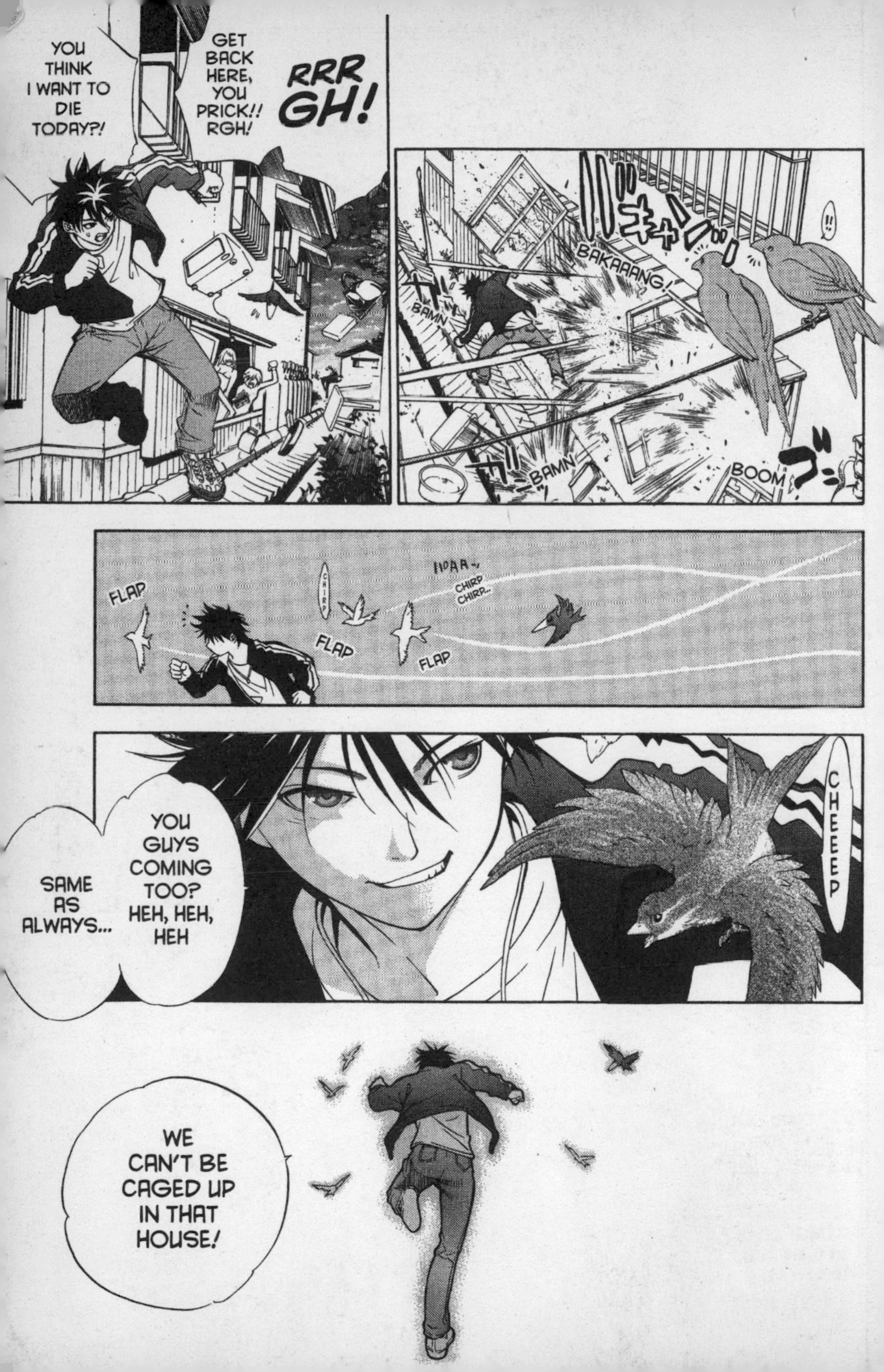
!!
BAKAAAANG!
BAMN
BAMN
BOOM
RRR GH!
GET BACK HERE, YOU PRICK!! RGH!
YOU THINK I WANT TO DIE TODAY?!
CHIRP CHIRP...
FLAP
FLAP
CHIRP
FLAP
FLAP
CHEEEEP
YOU GUYS COMING TOO? HEH, HEH, HEH
SAME AS ALWAYS...
WE CAN'T BE CAGED UP IN THAT HOUSE!

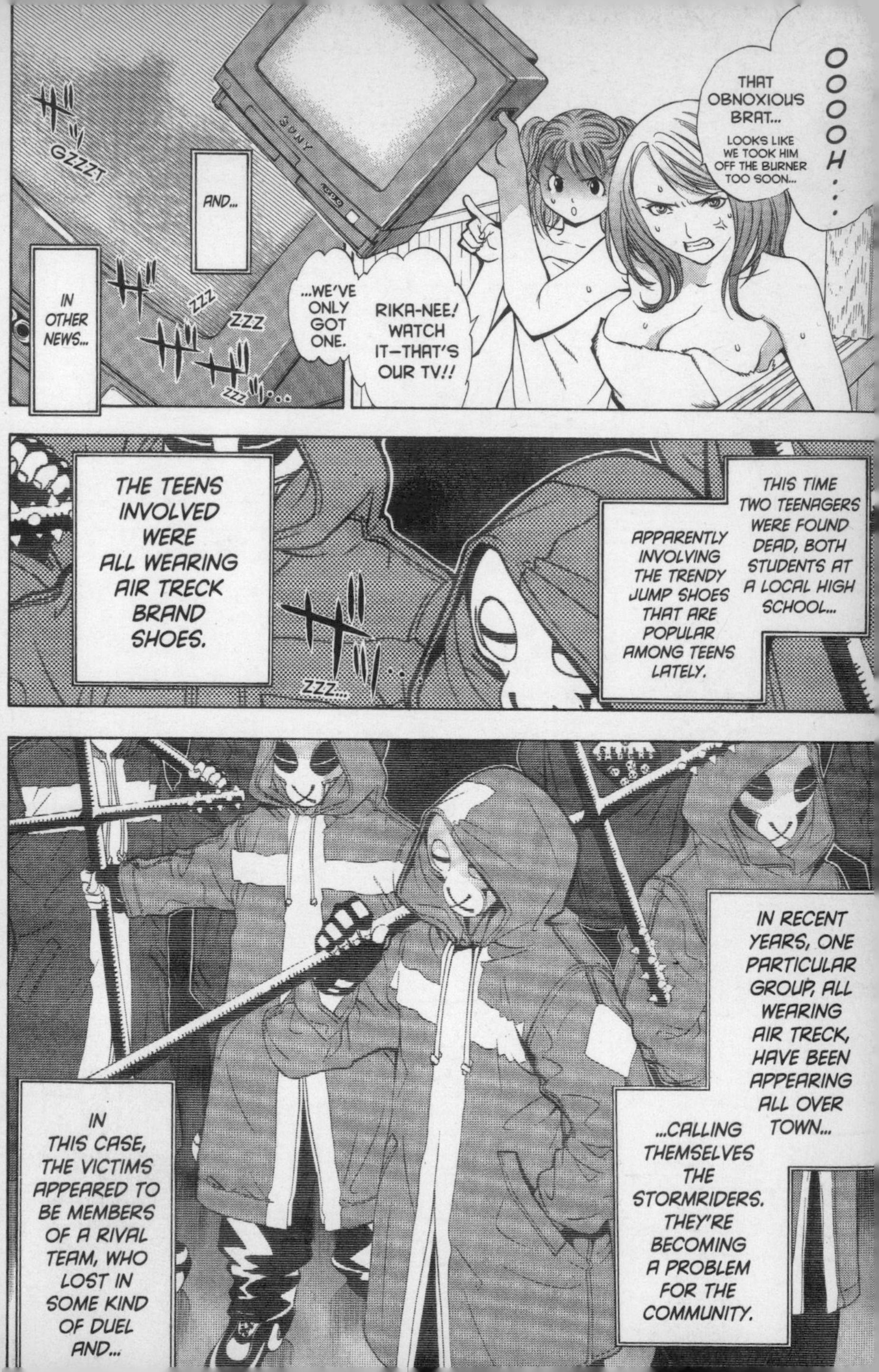
OOOOH...
THAT OBNOXIOUS BRAT...
LOOKS LIKE WE TOOK HIM OFF THE BURNER TOO SOON...
RIKA-NEE! WATCH IT—THAT'S OUR TV!!
...WE'VE ONLY GOT ONE.
GZZZT
AND...
IN OTHER NEWS...
ZZZ
ZZZ
ZZZ
THIS TIME TWO TEENAGERS WERE FOUND DEAD, BOTH STUDENTS AT A LOCAL HIGH SCHOOL...
APPARENTLY INVOLVING THE TRENDY JUMP SHOES THAT ARE POPULAR AMONG TEENS LATELY.
ZZZ...
THE TEENS INVOLVED WERE ALL WEARING AIR TRECK BRAND SHOES.
IN RECENT YEARS, ONE PARTICULAR GROUP, ALL WEARING AIR TRECK, HAVE BEEN APPEARING ALL OVER TOWN...
...CALLING THEMSELVES THE STORMRIDERS. THEY'RE BECOMING A PROBLEM FOR THE COMMUNITY.
IN THIS CASE, THE VICTIMS APPEARED TO BE MEMBERS OF A RIVAL TEAM, WHO LOST IN SOME KIND OF DUEL AND...

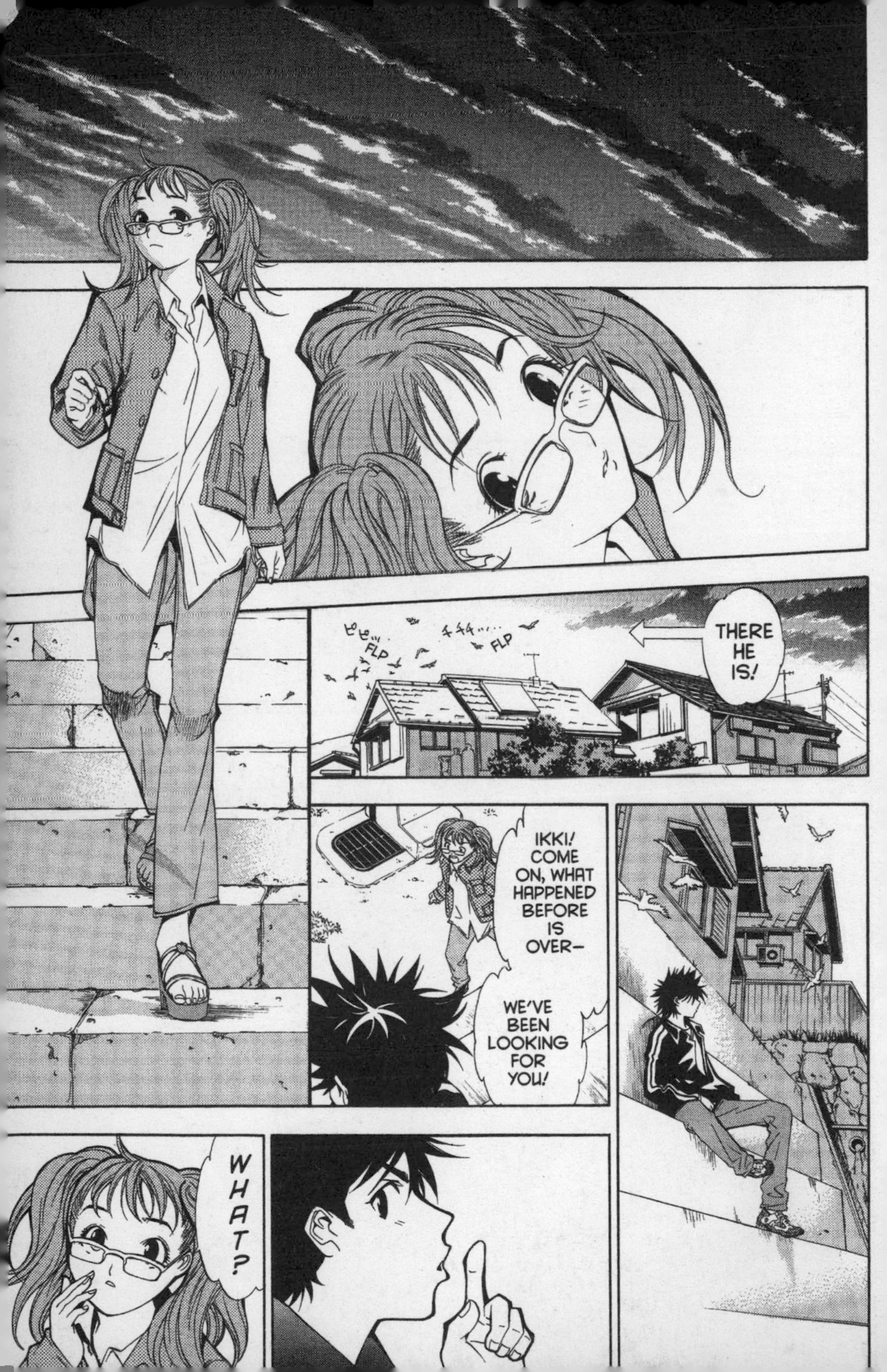
THERE HE IS!
FLP
FLP
IKKI! COME ON, WHAT HAPPENED BEFORE IS OVER—
WE'VE BEEN LOOKING FOR YOU!
WHAT?

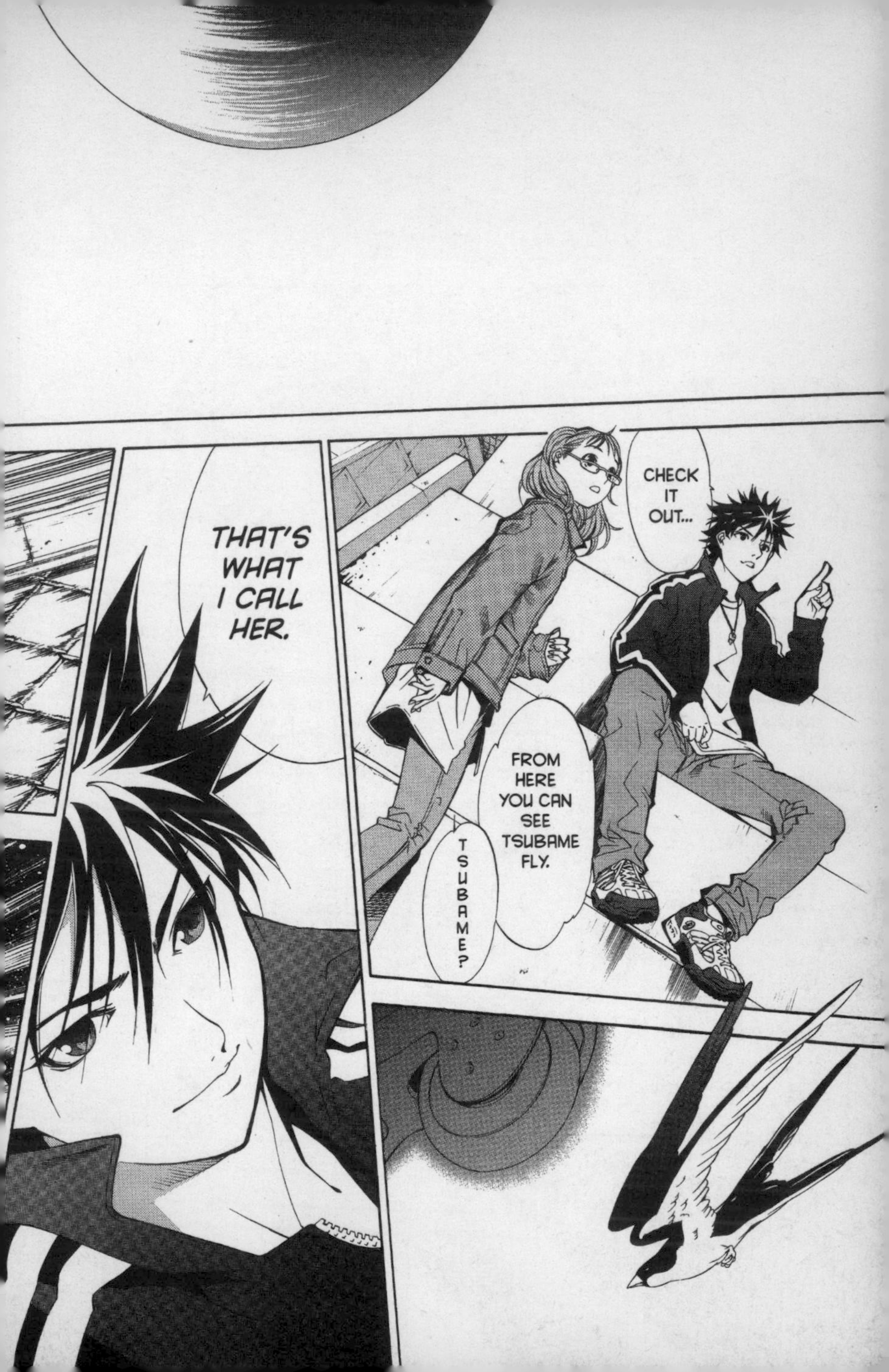
CHECK IT OUT...
FROM HERE YOU CAN SEE TSUBAME FLY.
TSUBAME?
THAT'S WHAT I CALL HER.

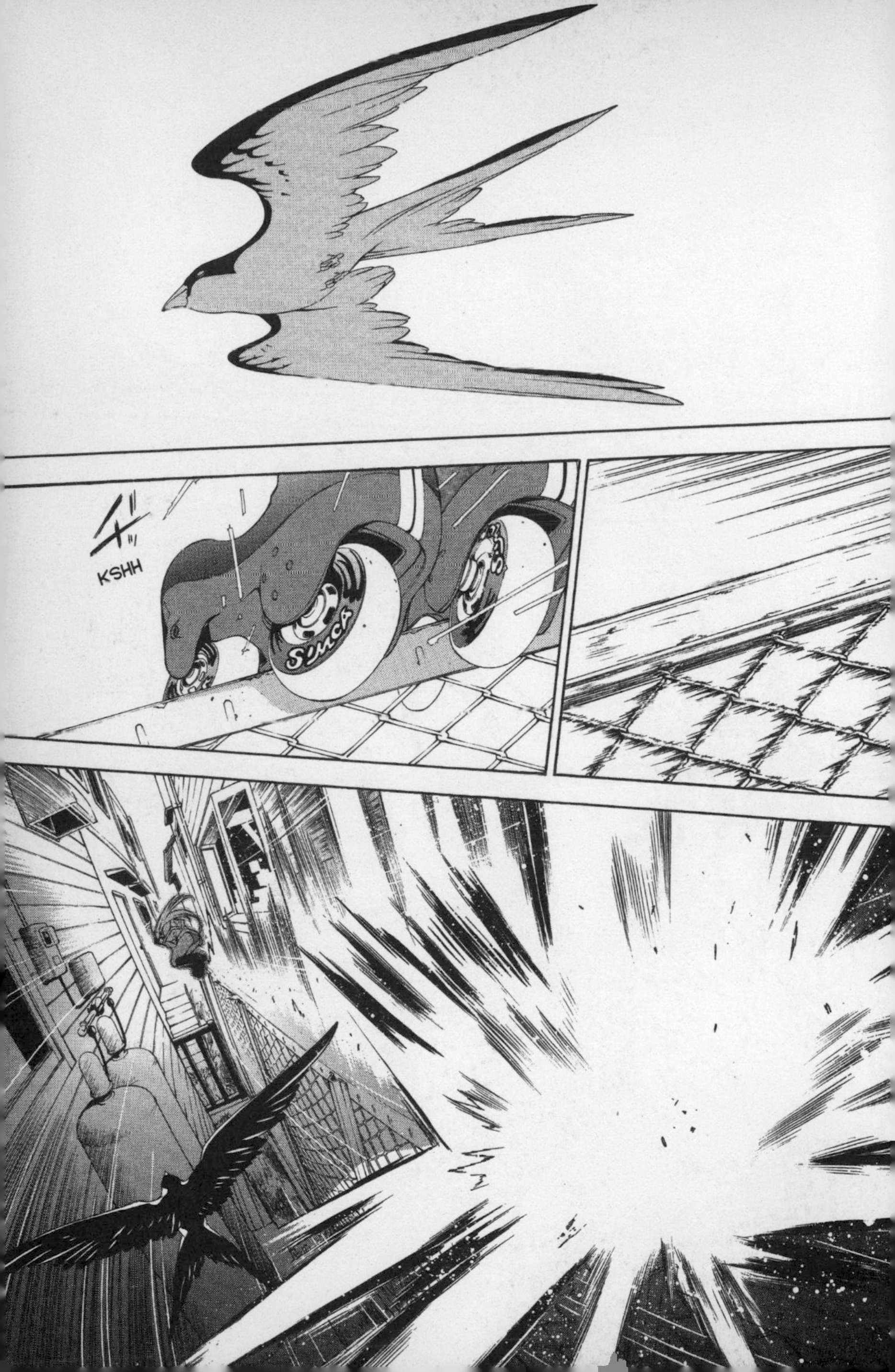
KSHH

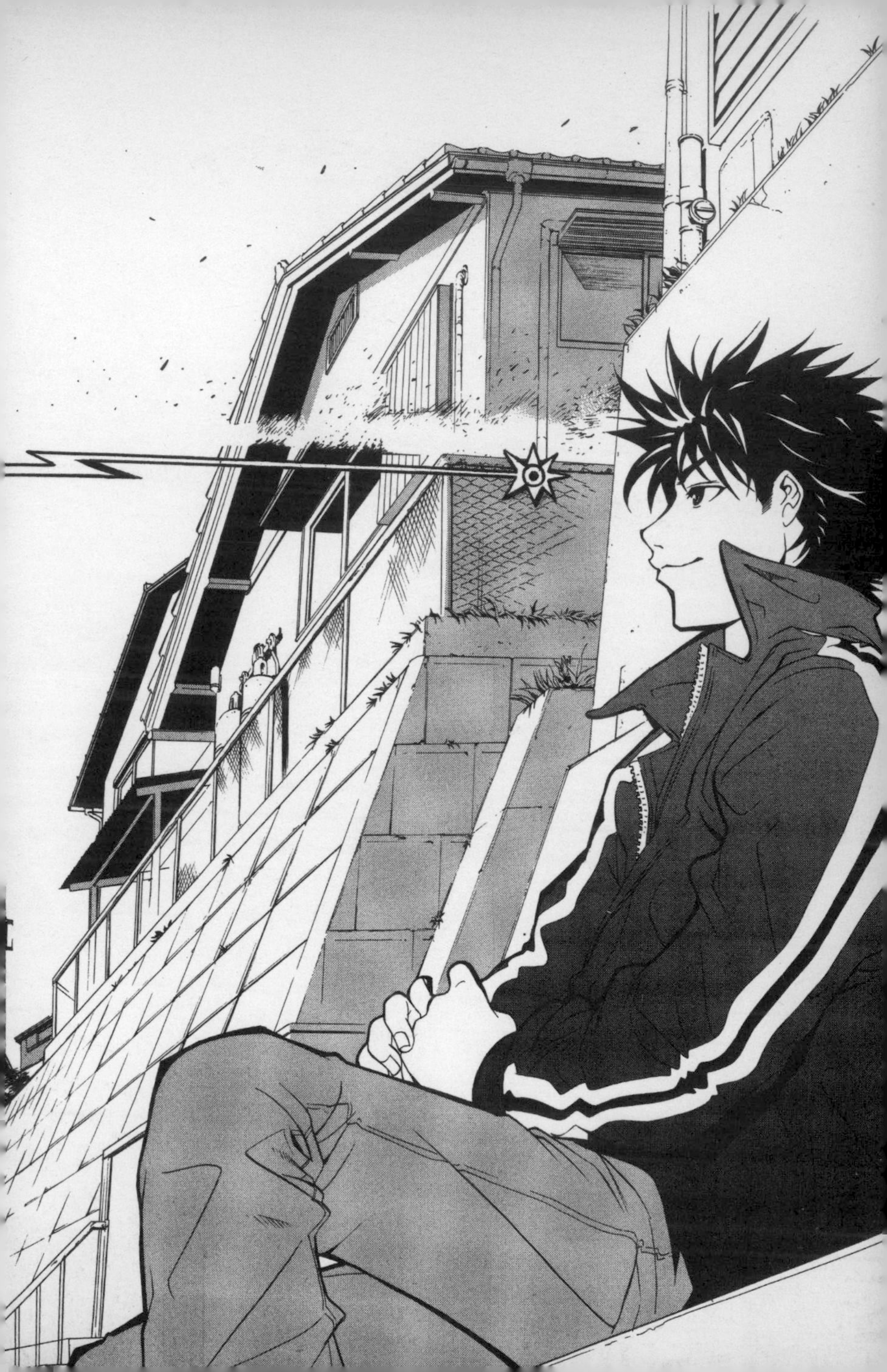

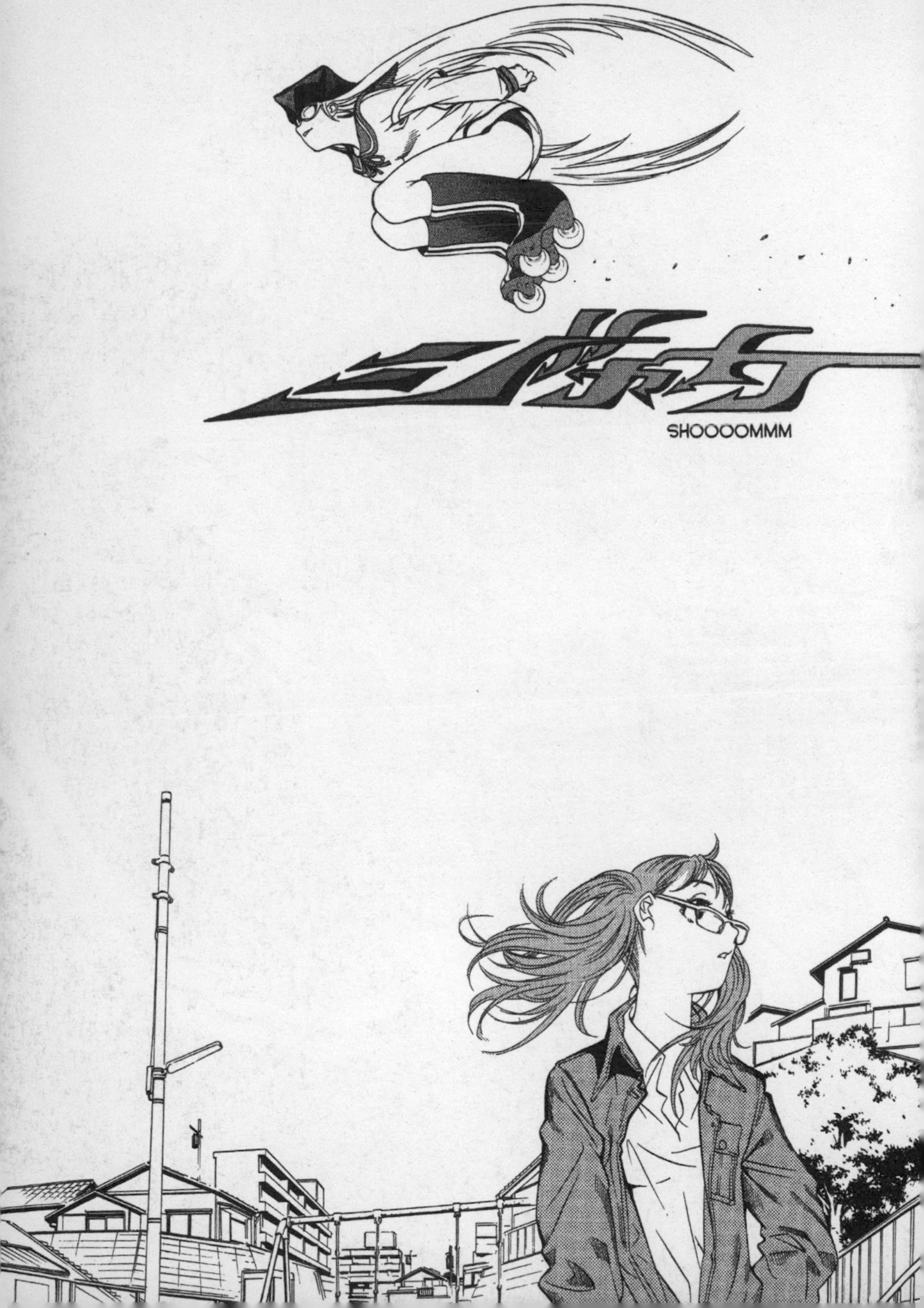
SHOOOOMMM

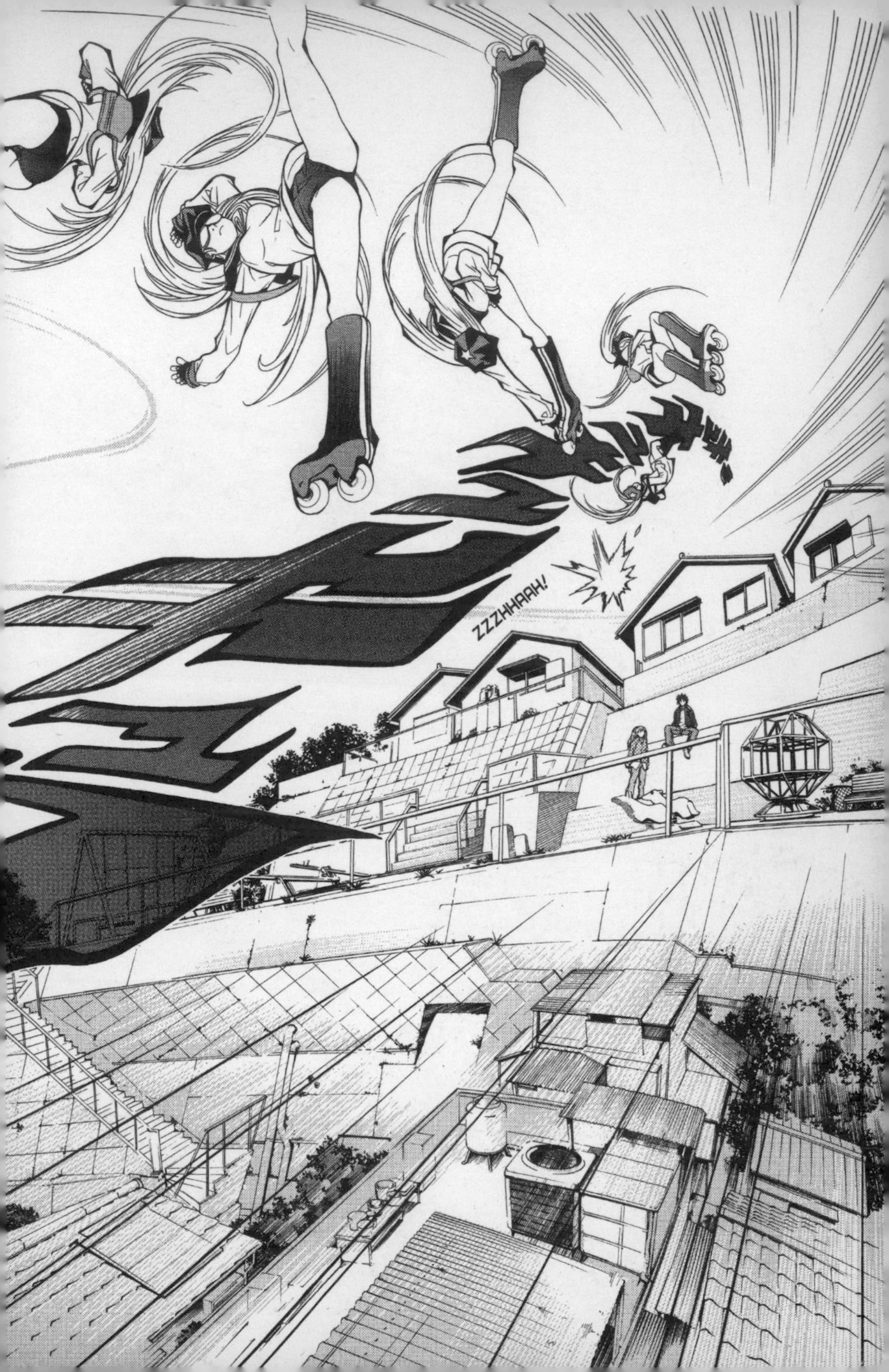
ZZZHHAAH!

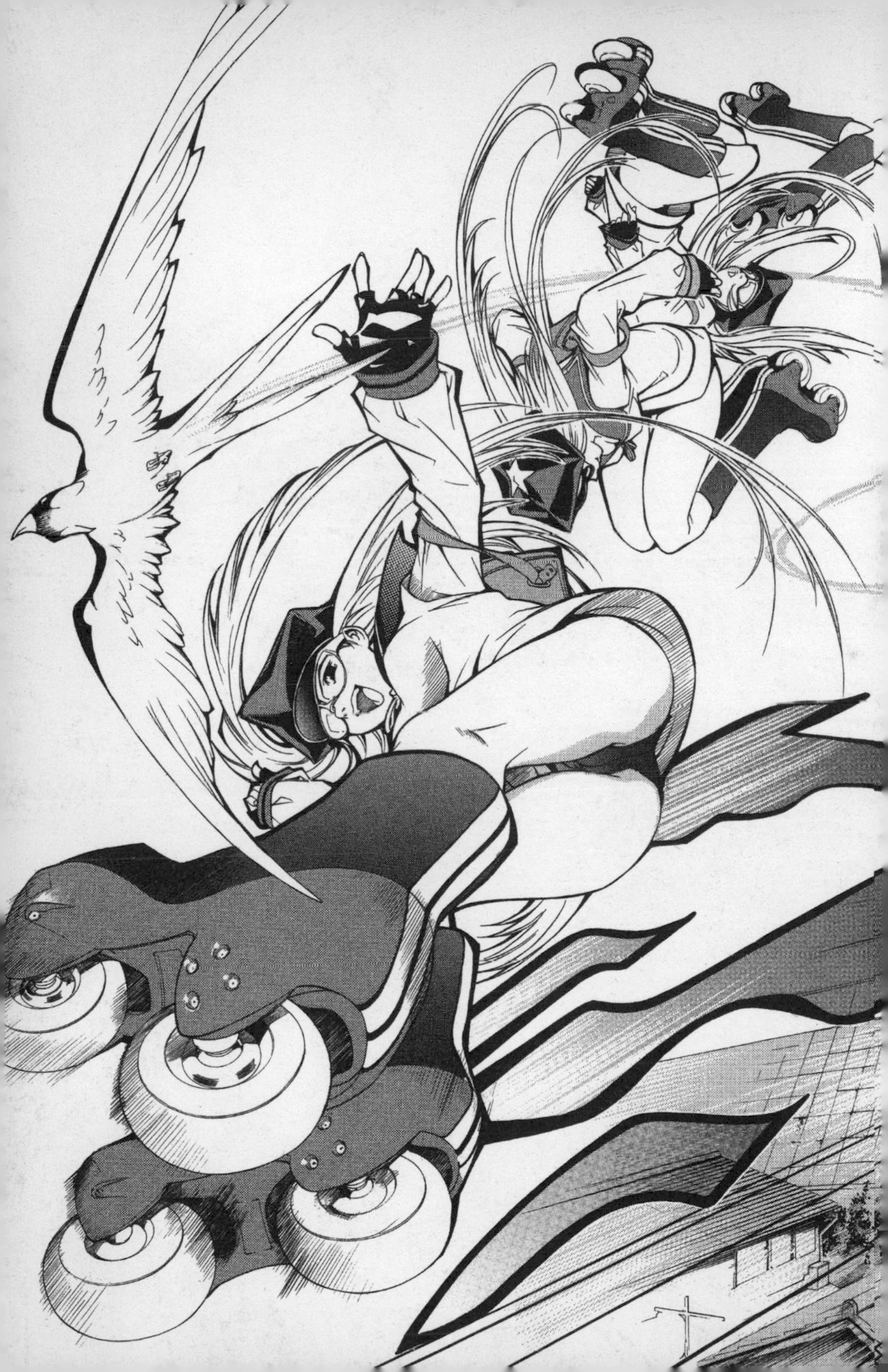

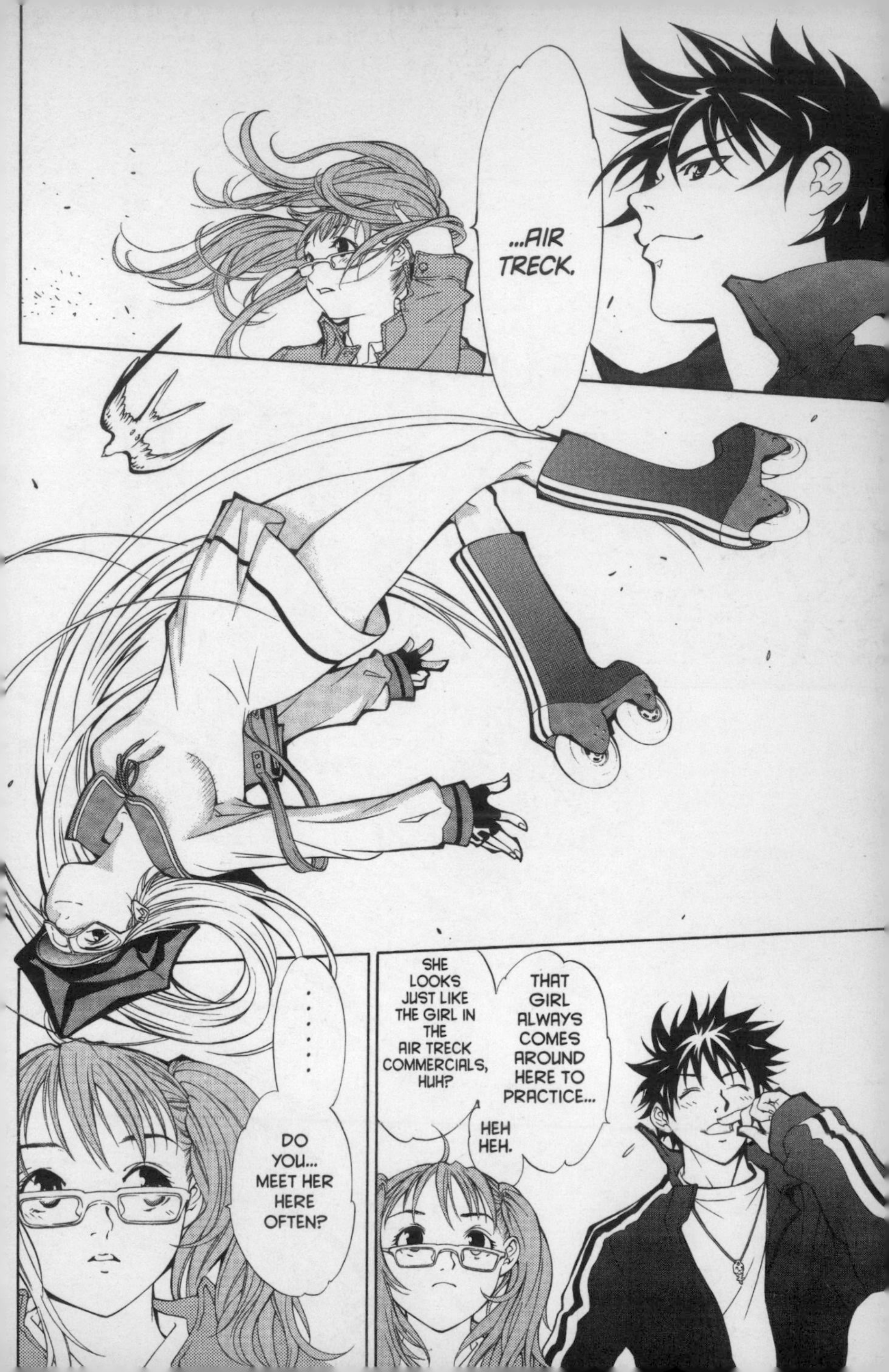
...AIR TRECK.
THAT GIRL ALWAYS COMES AROUND HERE TO PRACTICE...
SHE LOOKS JUST LIKE THE GIRL IN THE AIR TRECK COMMERCIALS, HUH?
HEH HEH.
......
DO YOU... MEET HER HERE OFTEN?

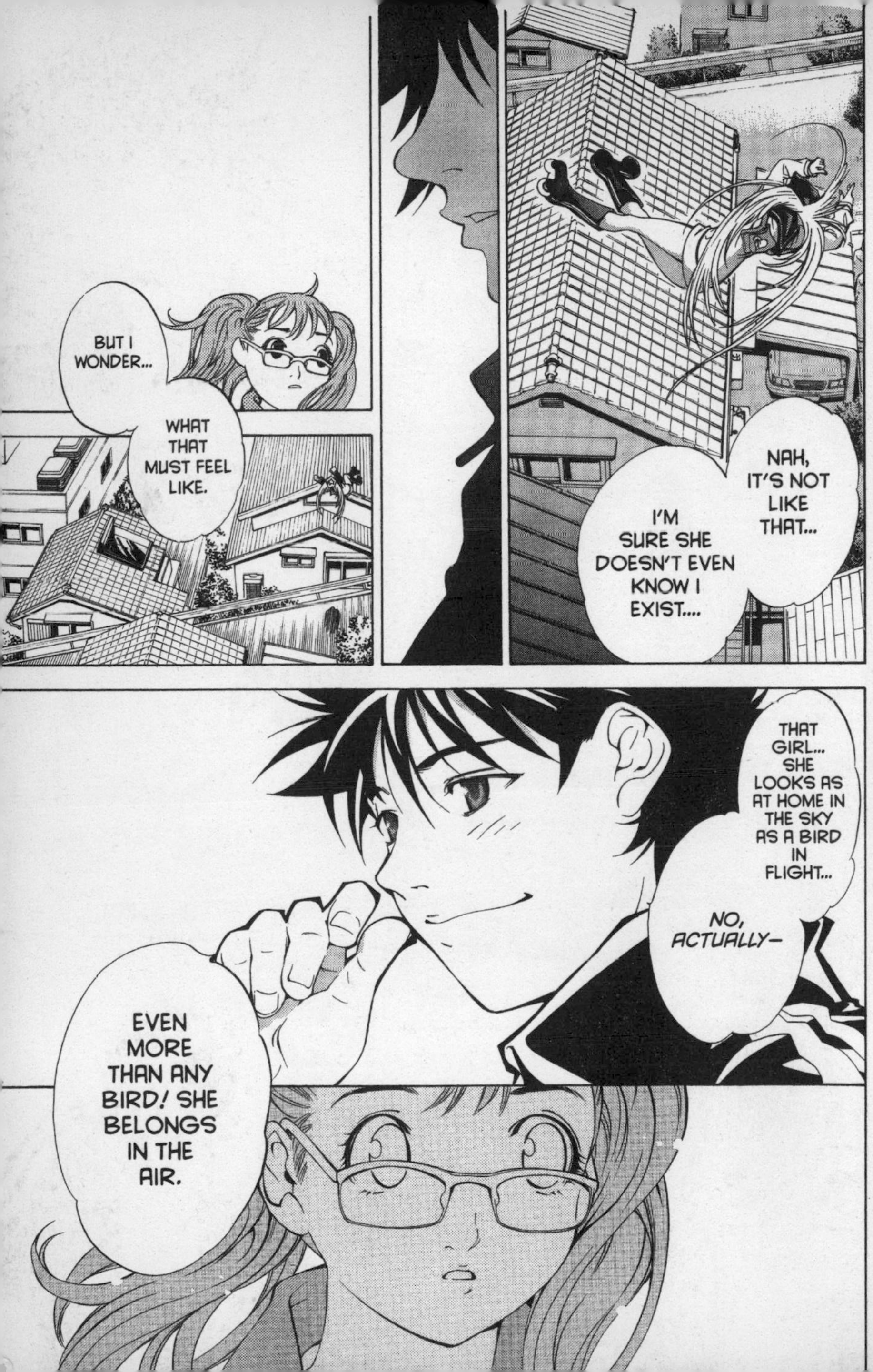
NAH, IT'S NOT LIKE THAT...
I'M SURE SHE DOESN'T EVEN KNOW I EXIST....
BUT I WONDER...
WHAT THAT MUST FEEL LIKE.
THAT GIRL... SHE LOOKS AS AT HOME IN THE SKY AS A BIRD IN FLIGHT...
NO, ACTUALLY—
EVEN MORE THAN ANY BIRD! SHE BELONGS IN THE AIR.

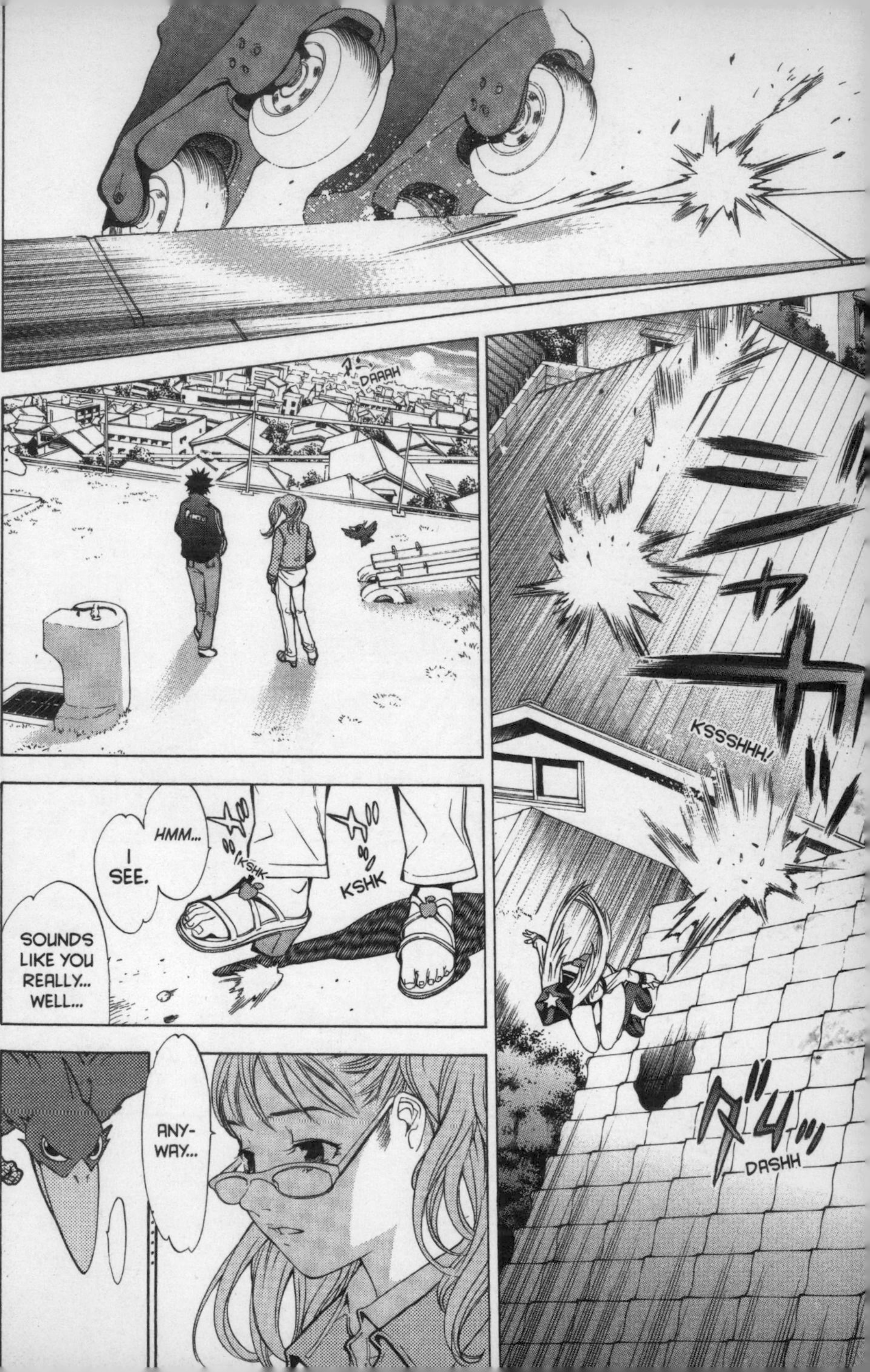
KSSSHHH!
DASHH
DAAAH
HMM...
I SEE.
KSHK
KSHK
SOUNDS LIKE YOU REALLY... WELL...
ANY-WAY...

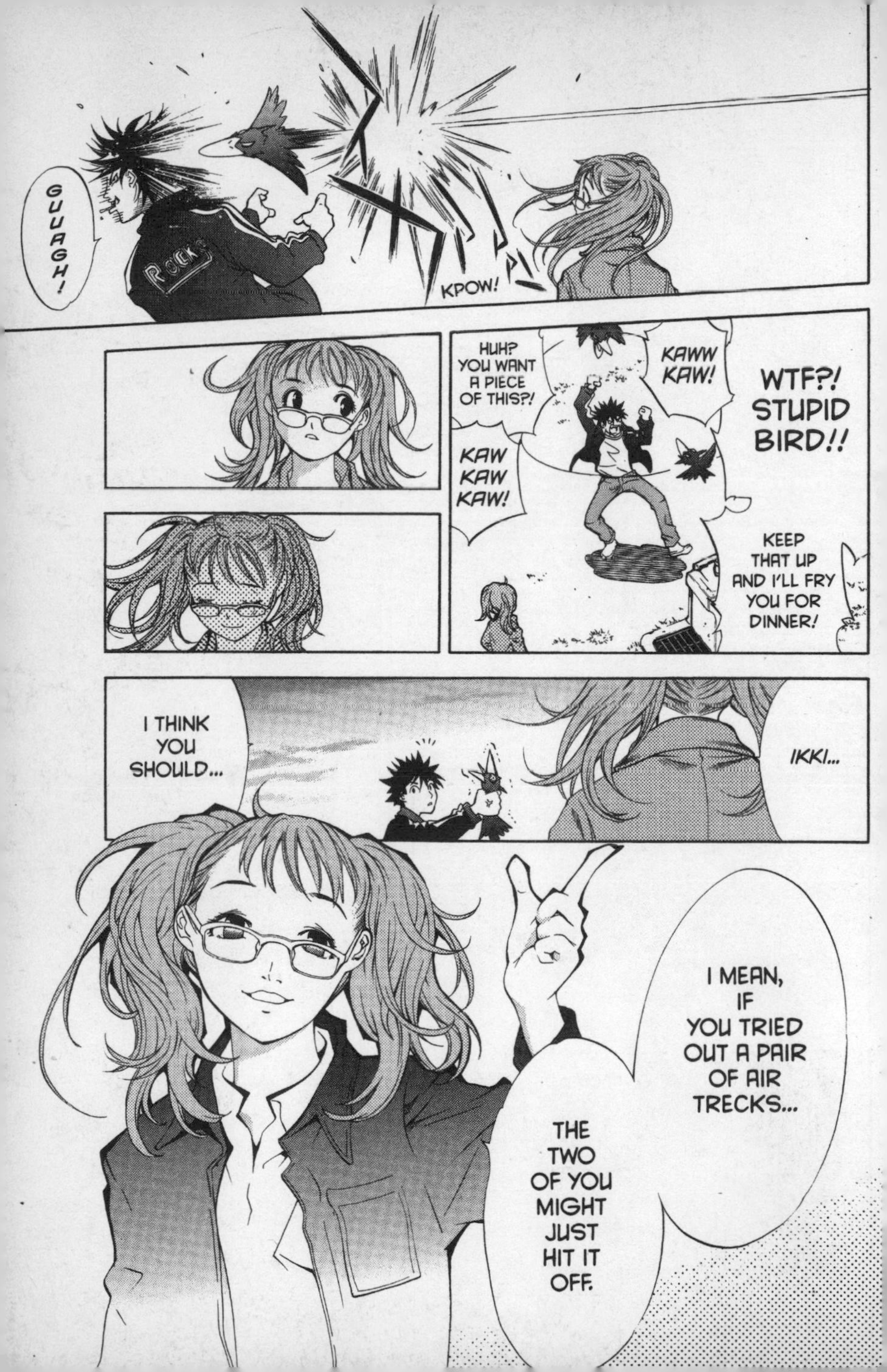
KPOW!
GUUAGH!
WTF?! STUPID BIRD!!
KAWW KAW!
HUH? YOU WANT A PIECE OF THIS?!
KAW KAW KAW!
KEEP THAT UP AND I'LL FRY YOU FOR DINNER!
IKKI...
I THINK YOU SHOULD...
I MEAN, IF YOU TRIED OUT A PAIR OF AIR TRECKS...
THE TWO OF YOU MIGHT JUST HIT IT OFF.

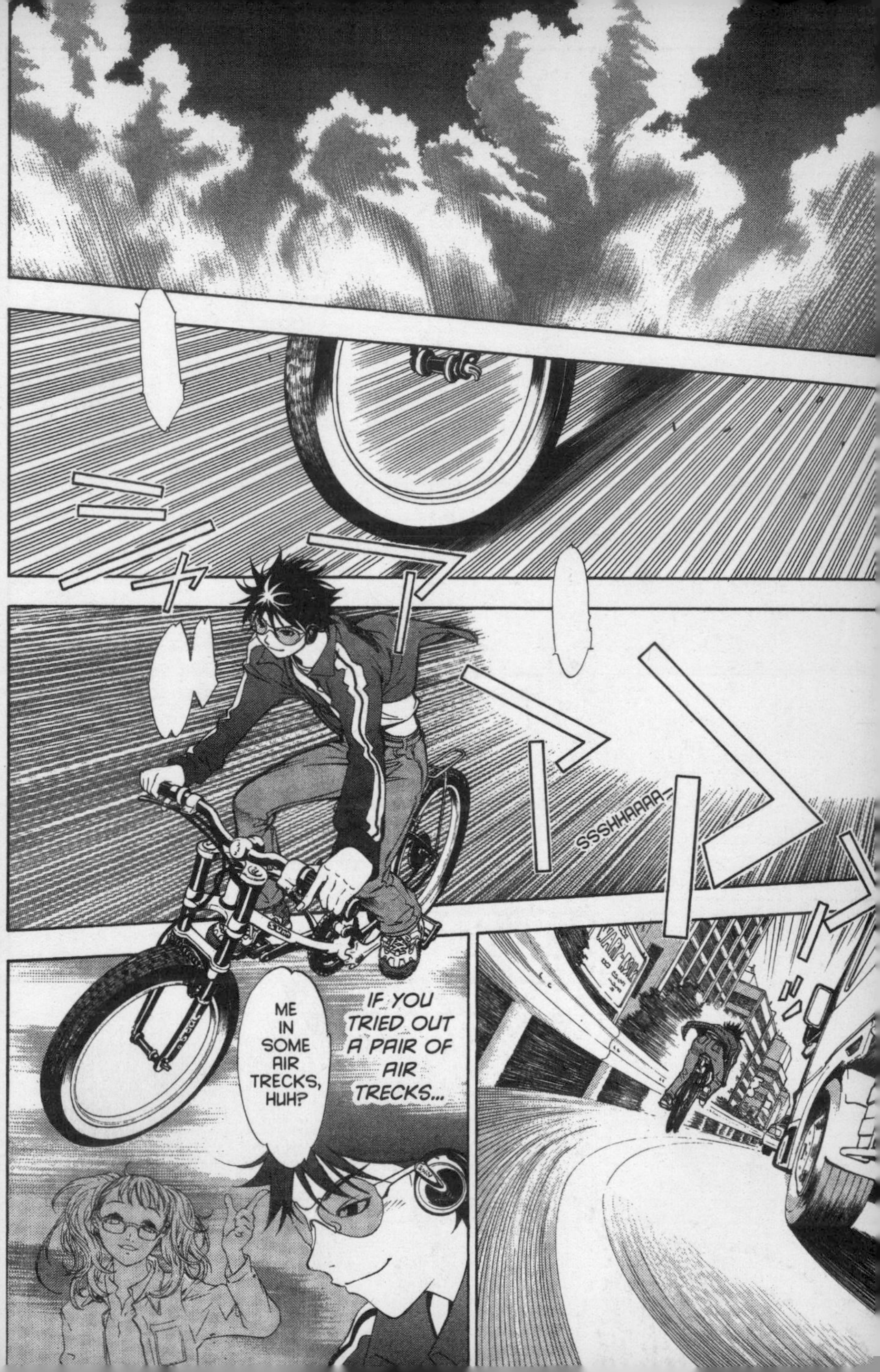
SSSHHAAAA=
IF YOU TRIED OUT A PAIR OF AIR TRECKS...
ME IN SOME AIR TRECKS, HUH?

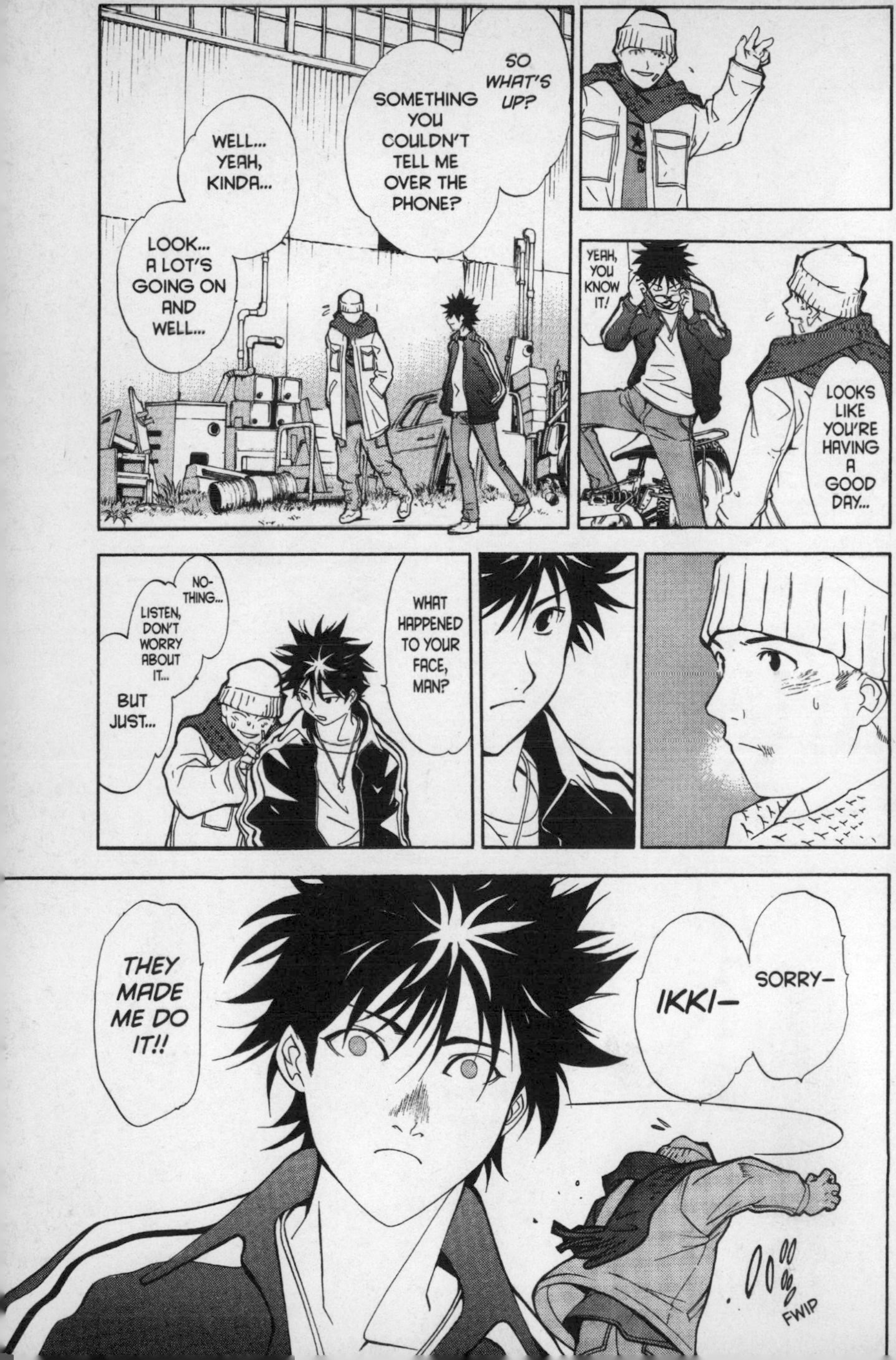
LOOKS LIKE YOU'RE HAVING A GOOD DAY...
YEAH, YOU KNOW IT!
SO WHAT'S UP?
SOMETHING YOU COULDN'T TELL ME OVER THE PHONE?
WELL... YEAH, KINDA...
LOOK... A LOT'S GOING ON AND WELL...
WHAT HAPPENED TO YOUR FACE, MAN?
NO-THING... LISTEN, DON'T WORRY ABOUT IT...
BUT JUST...
SORRY-
IKKI-
THEY MADE ME DO IT!!
FWIP

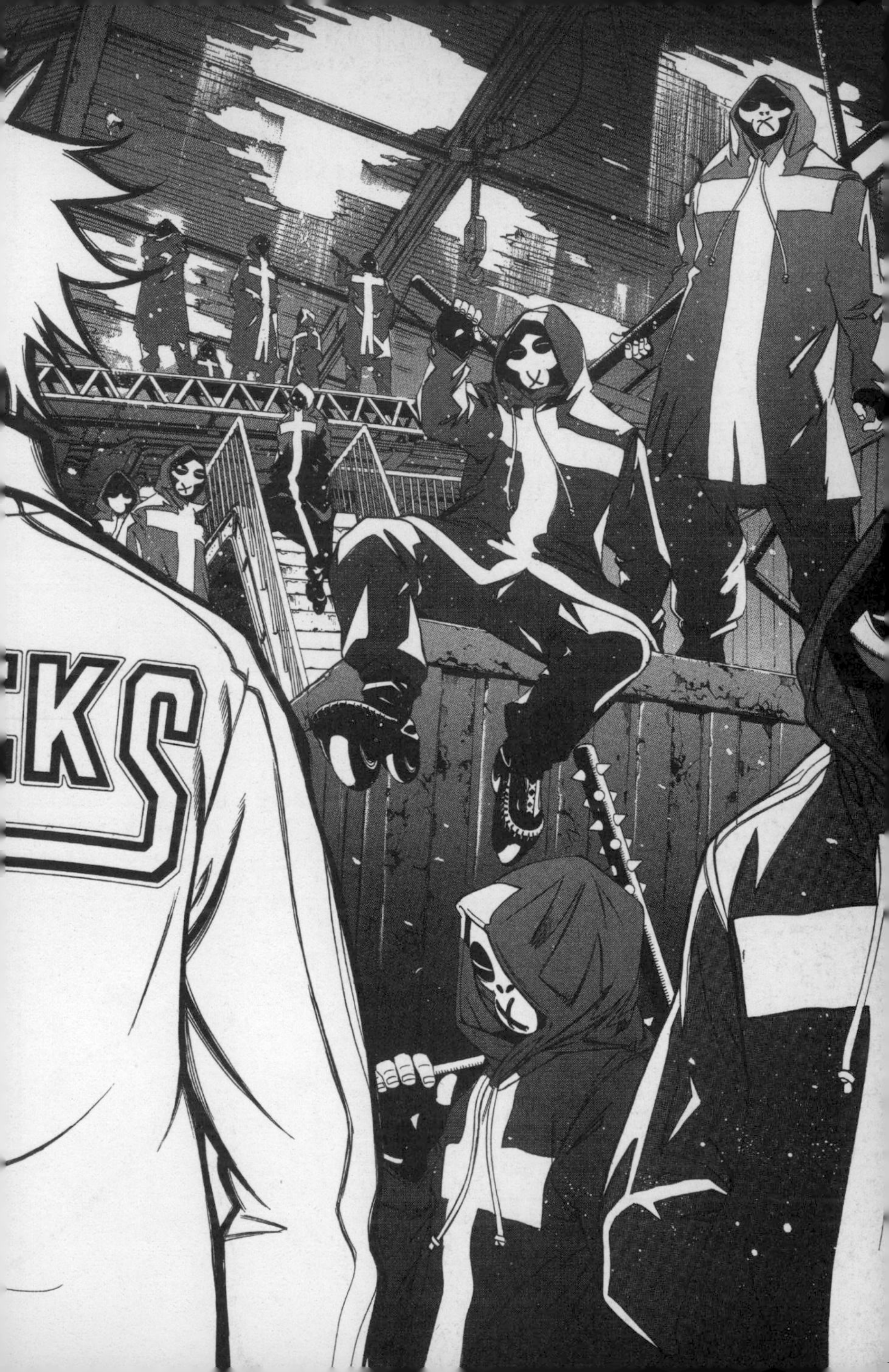
EKS

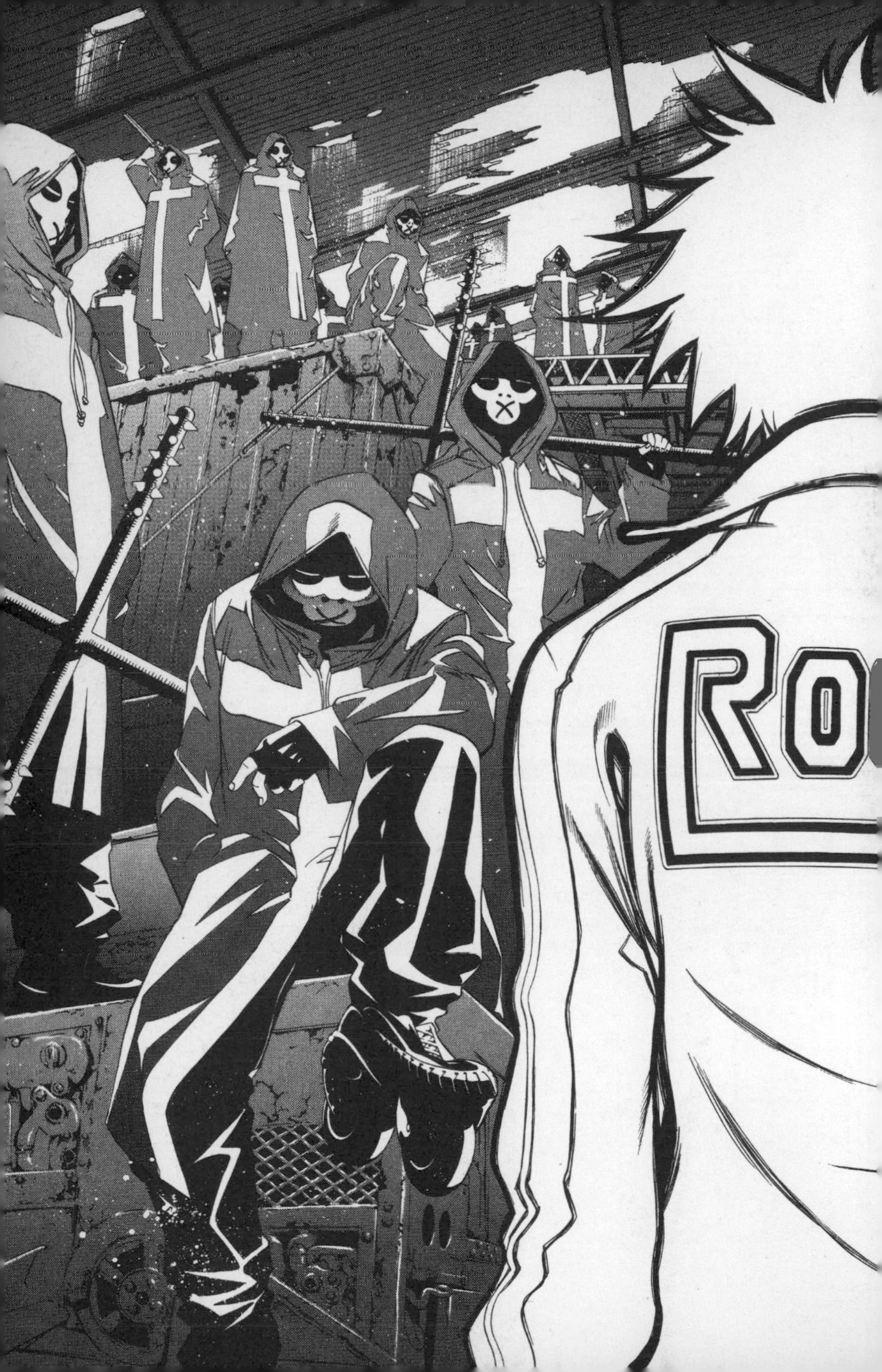
Ro

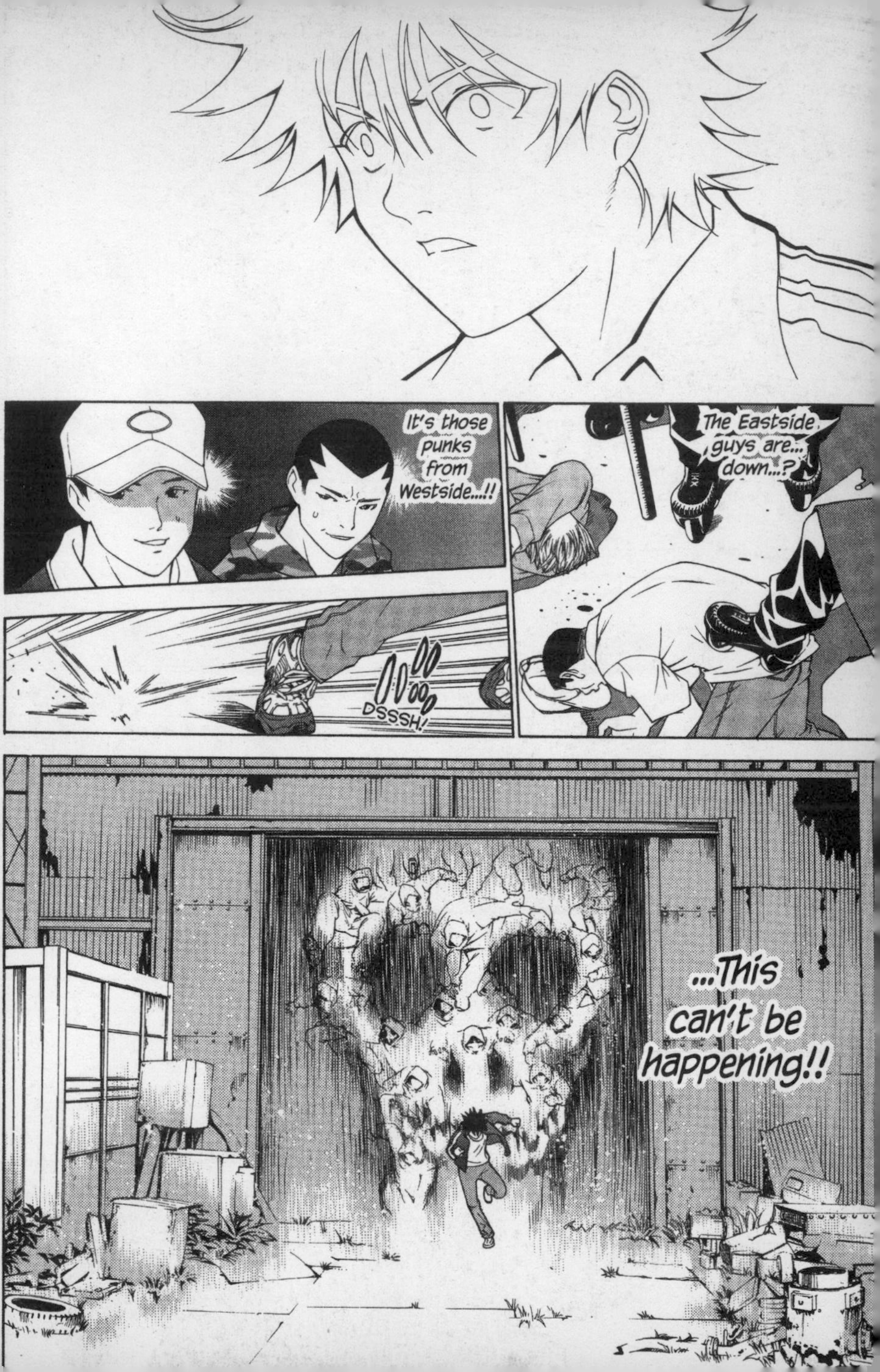
The Eastside guys are... down...?
It's those punks from Westside...!!
DSSSH!
...This can't be happening!!

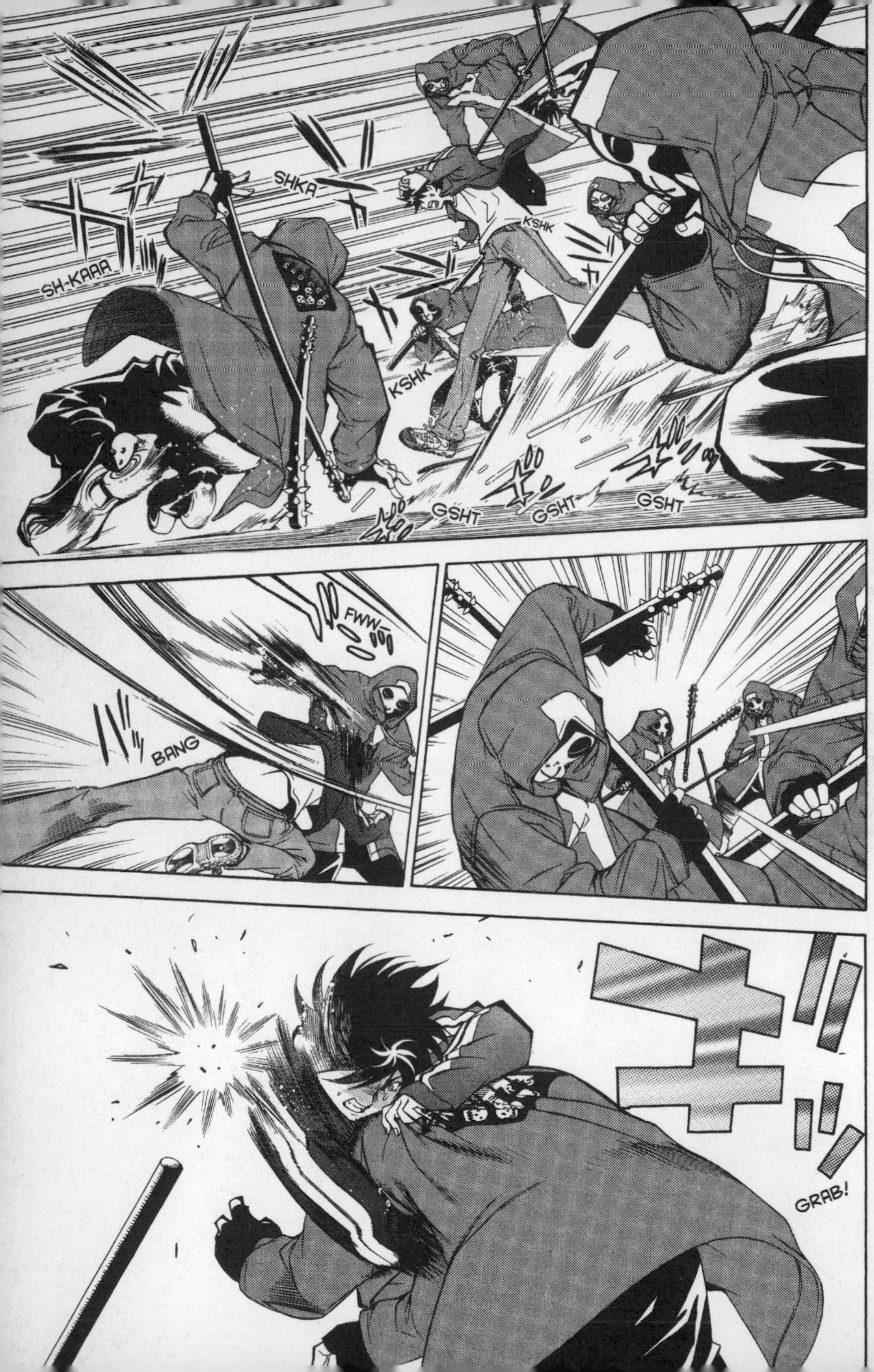
KSHK
SHKA
SH-KAAA
KSHK
GSHT
GSHT
GSHT
FWW
BANG
GRAB!

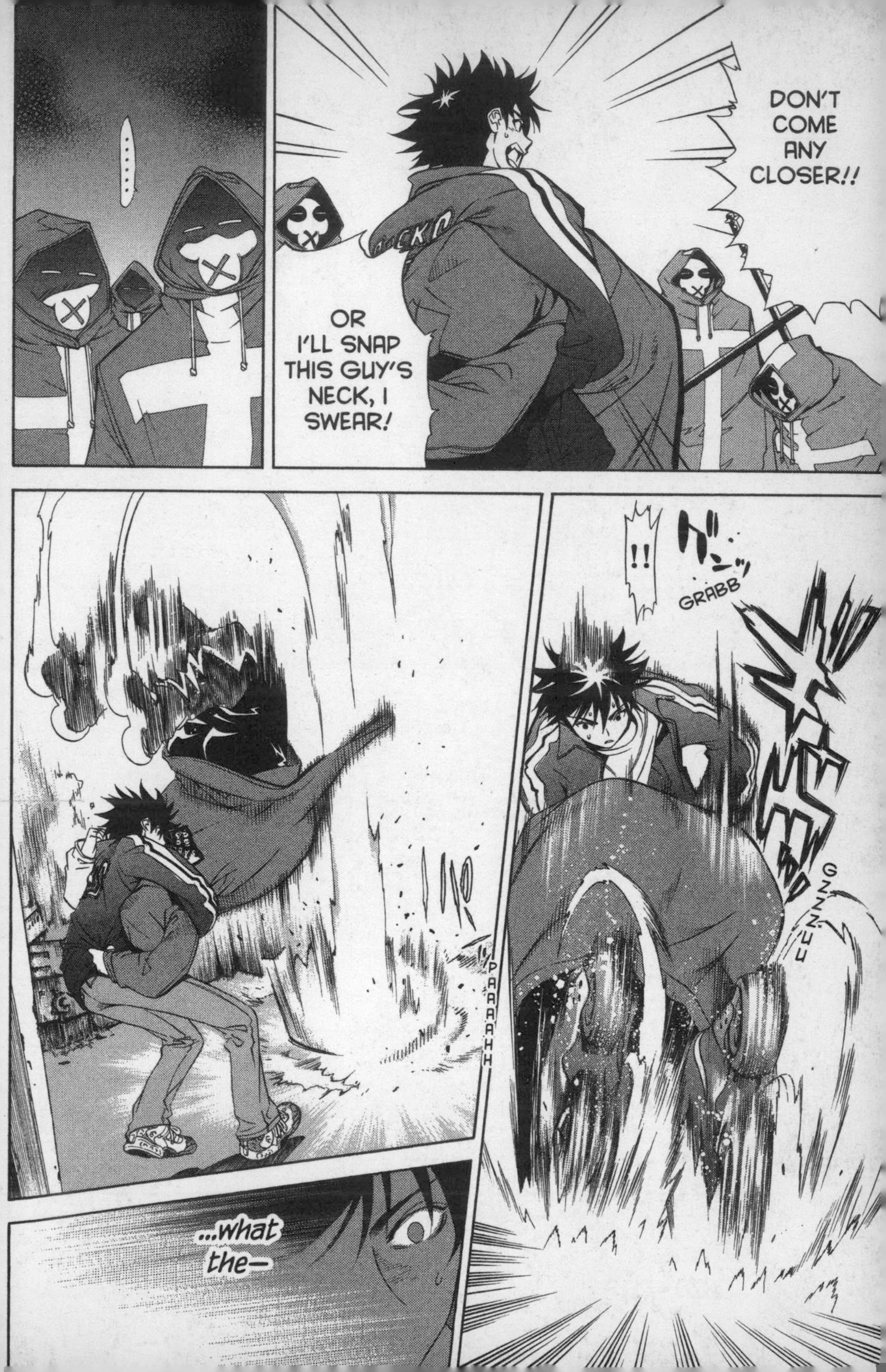
DON'T COME ANY CLOSER!!
OR I'LL SNAP THIS GUY'S NECK, I SWEAR!
......
!!
GRABB
GZZZUU
PAAAAHH
...what the—

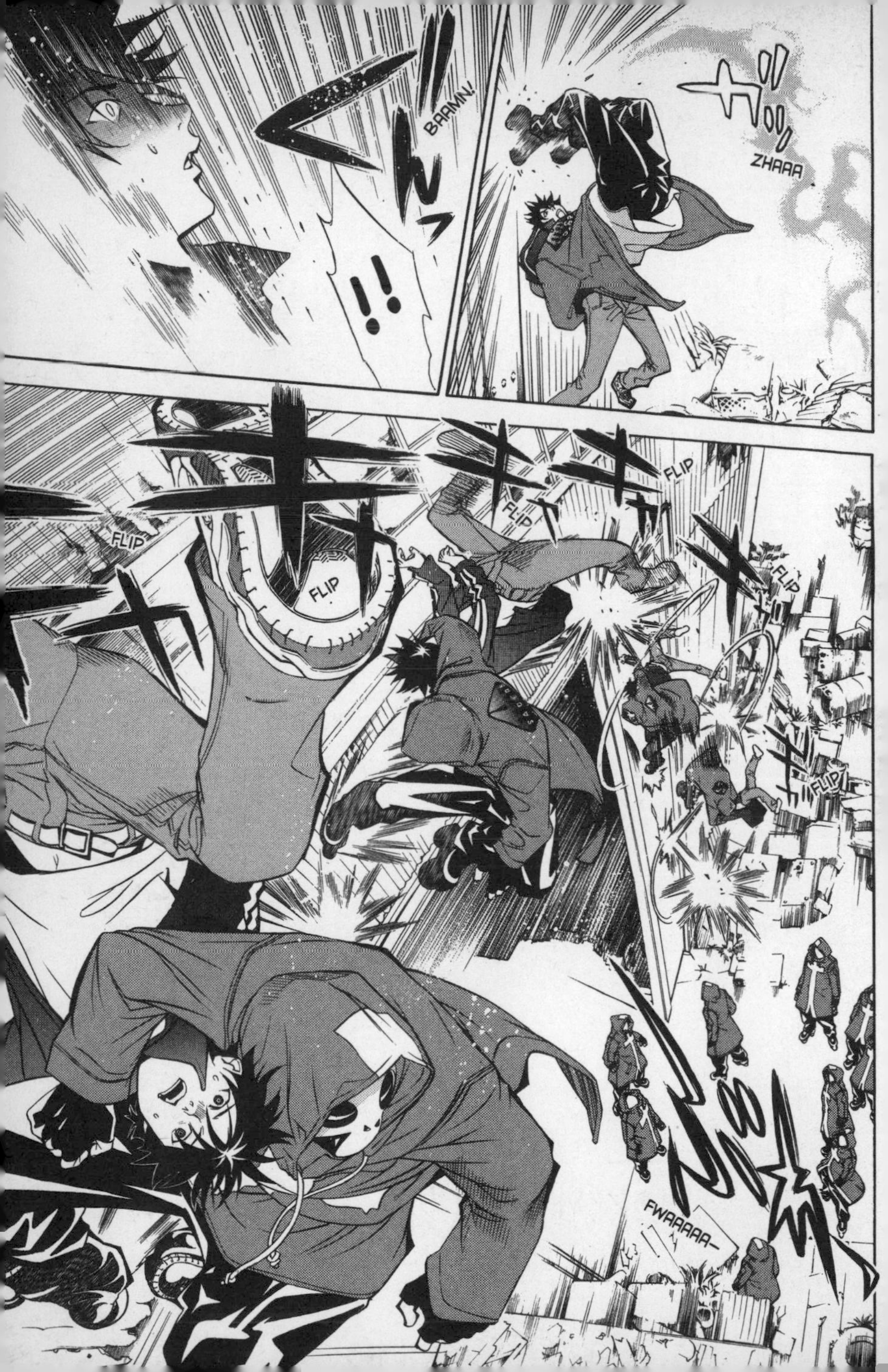

ZHAAA
BAAMN!
!!
FLIP
FLIP
FLIP
FLIP
FLIP
FLIP
FWAAAAA–

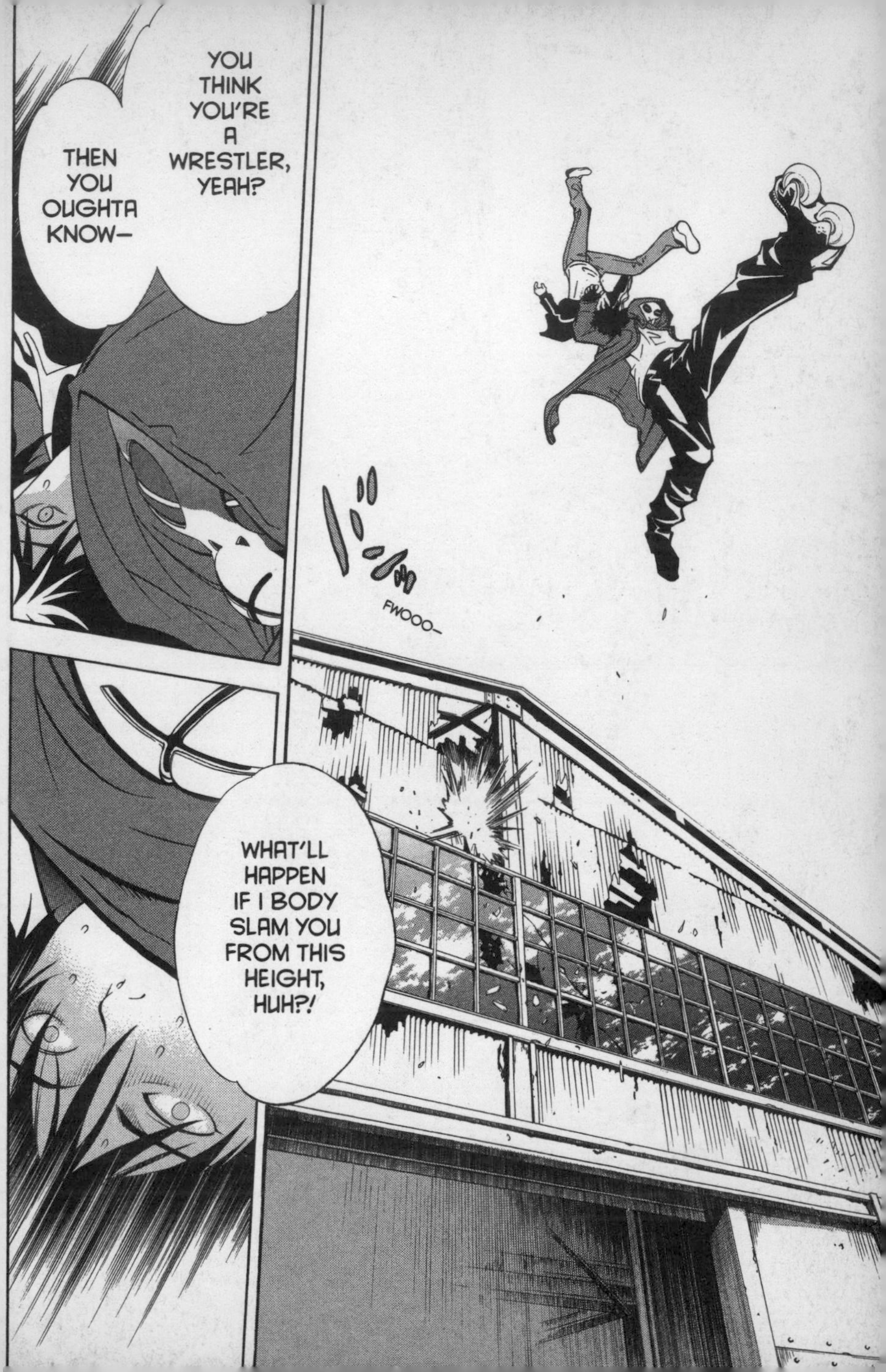
FWOOO-
YOU THINK YOU'RE A WRESTLER, YEAH?
THEN YOU OUGHTA KNOW-
WHAT'LL HAPPEN IF I BODY SLAM YOU FROM THIS HEIGHT, HUH?!

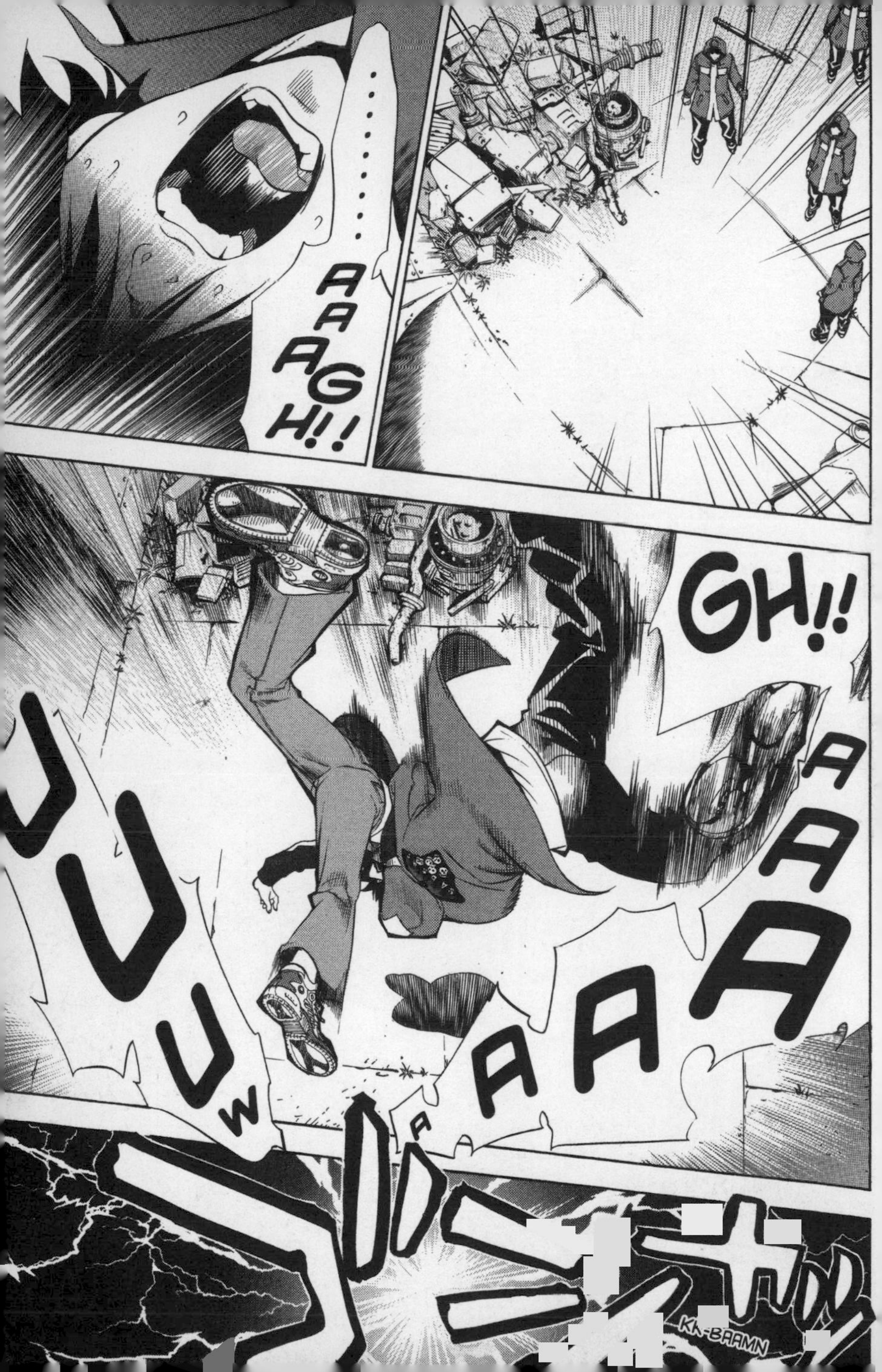

......
AAAAGH!!
UUUWAAAAAAAAAAGH!!
KA-BAAMN

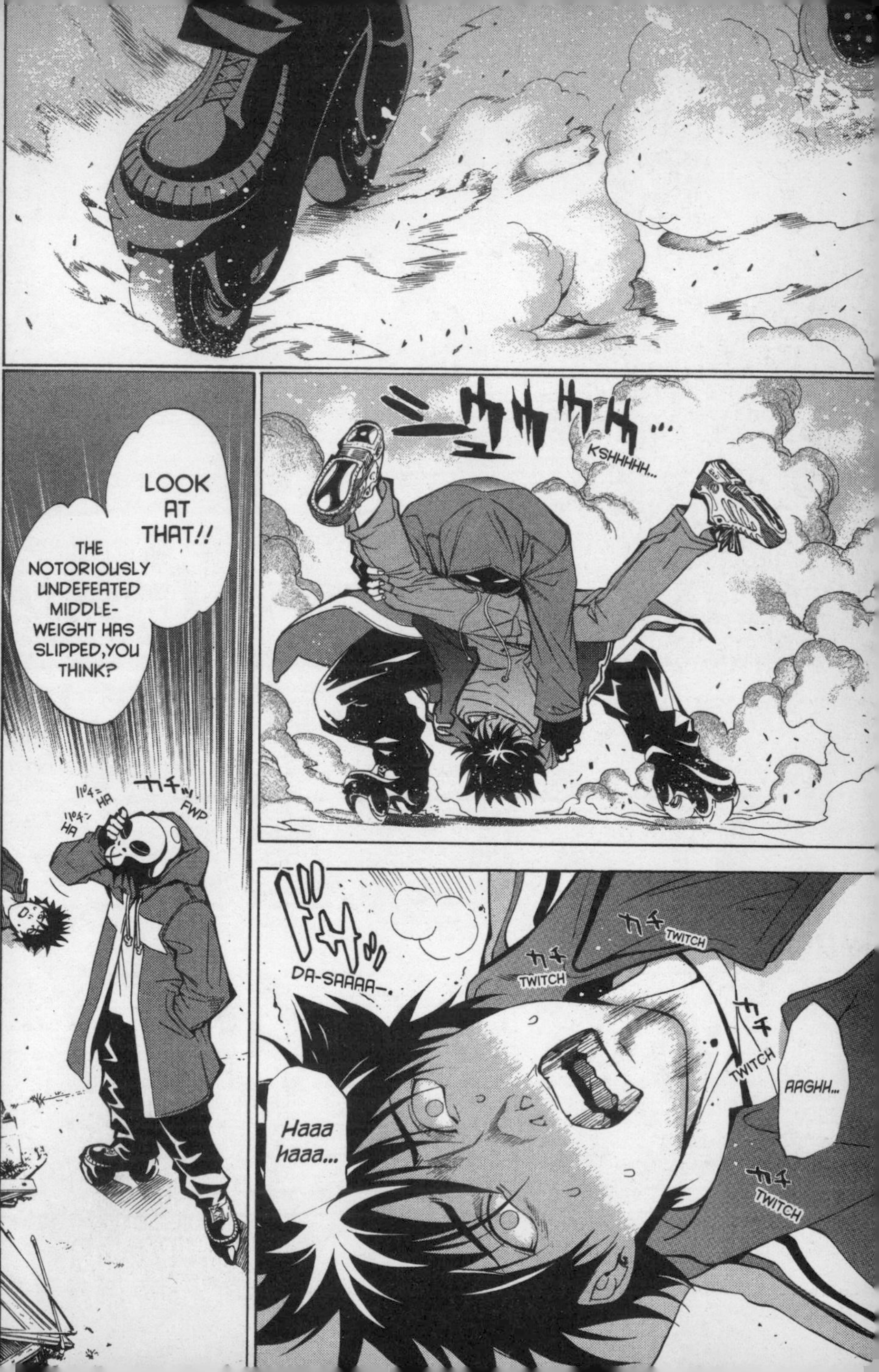
KSHHHHH...
DA-SAAAA-.
TWITCH
TWITCH
TWITCH
AAGHH...
Haaa haaa...
TWITCH
LOOK AT THAT!!
THE NOTORIOUSLY UNDEFEATED MIDDLE-WEIGHT HAS SLIPPED, YOU THINK?
HA
HA
FWP

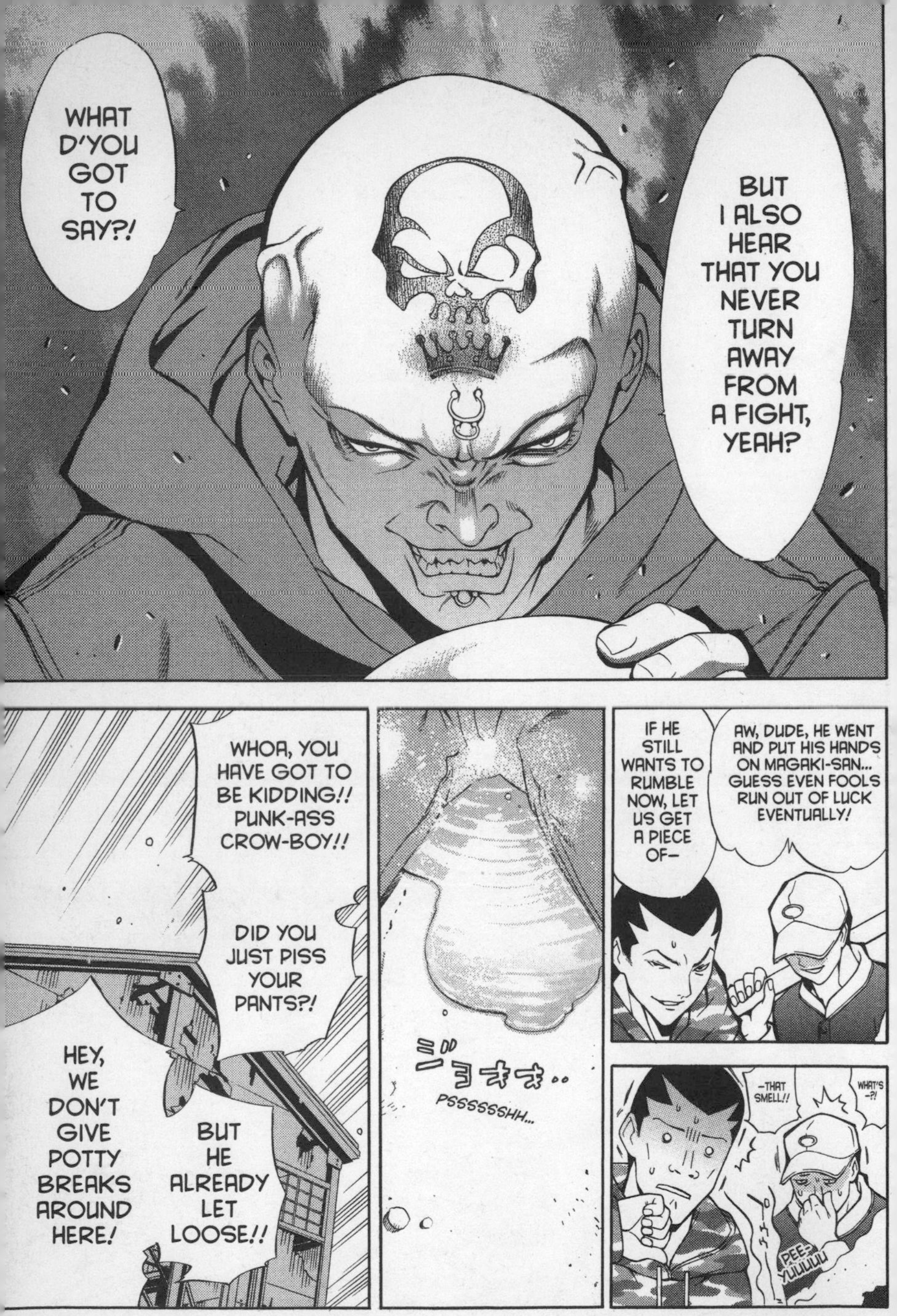
BUT I ALSO HEAR THAT YOU NEVER TURN AWAY FROM A FIGHT, YEAH?
WHAT D'YOU GOT TO SAY?!
AW, DUDE, HE WENT AND PUT HIS HANDS ON MAGAKI-SAN... GUESS EVEN FOOLS RUN OUT OF LUCK EVENTUALLY!
IF HE STILL WANTS TO RUMBLE NOW, LET US GET A PIECE OF—
WHAT'S—?!
—THAT SMELL!!
PEE-YUUUUU
ジョオオ..
PSSSSSSHH...
WHOA, YOU HAVE GOT TO BE KIDDING!! PUNK-ASS CROW-BOY!!
DID YOU JUST PISS YOUR PANTS?!
BUT HE ALREADY LET LOOSE!!
HEY, WE DON'T GIVE POTTY BREAKS AROUND HERE!

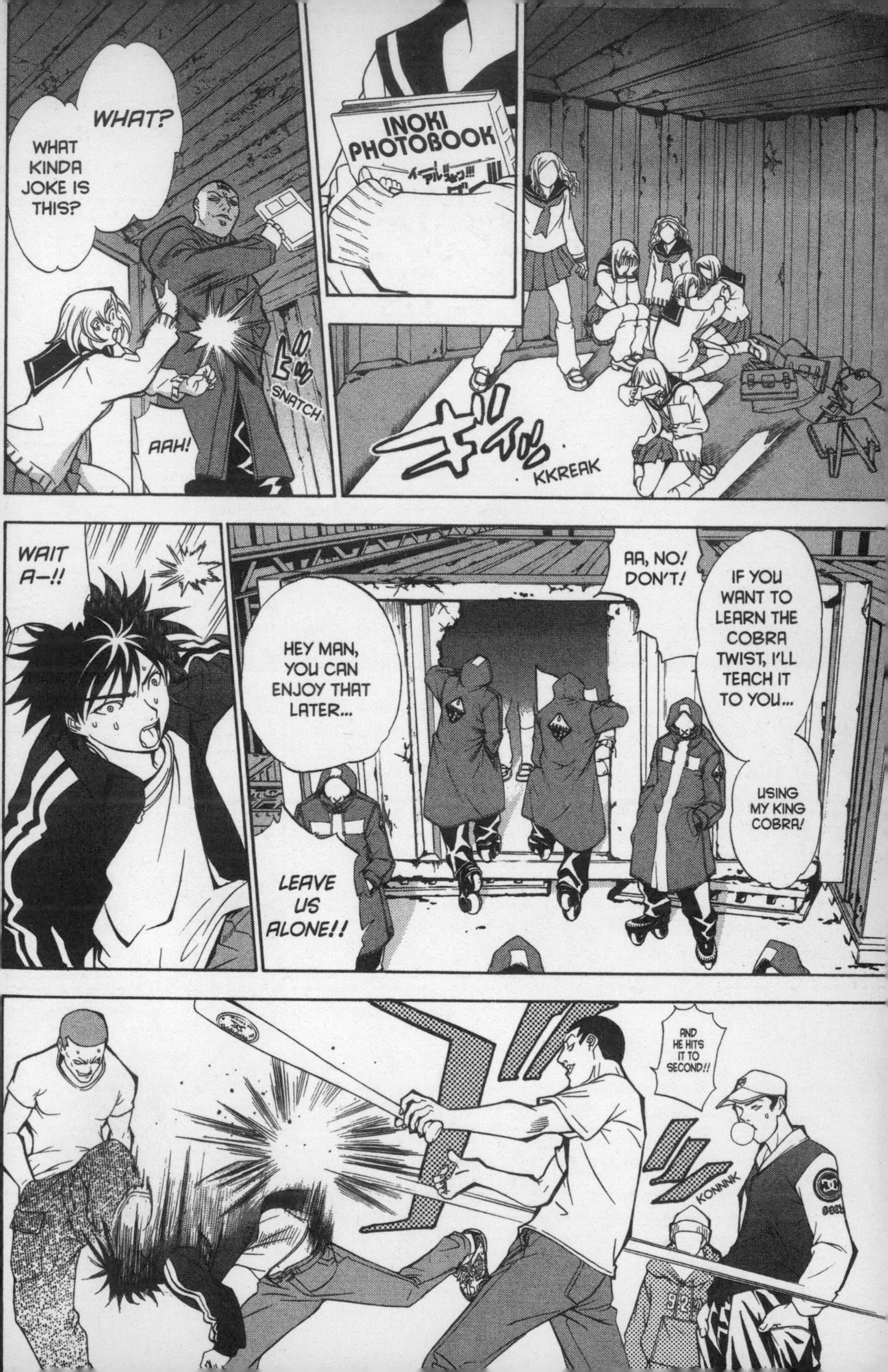
KKREAK
INOKI PHOTOBOOK
WHAT?
WHAT KINDA JOKE IS THIS?
SNATCH
AAH!
IF YOU WANT TO LEARN THE COBRA TWIST, I'LL TEACH IT TO YOU...
AA, NO! DON'T!
USING MY KING COBRA!
HEY MAN, YOU CAN ENJOY THAT LATER...
LEAVE US ALONE!!
WAIT A—!!
AND HE HITS IT TO SECOND!!
KONNNK

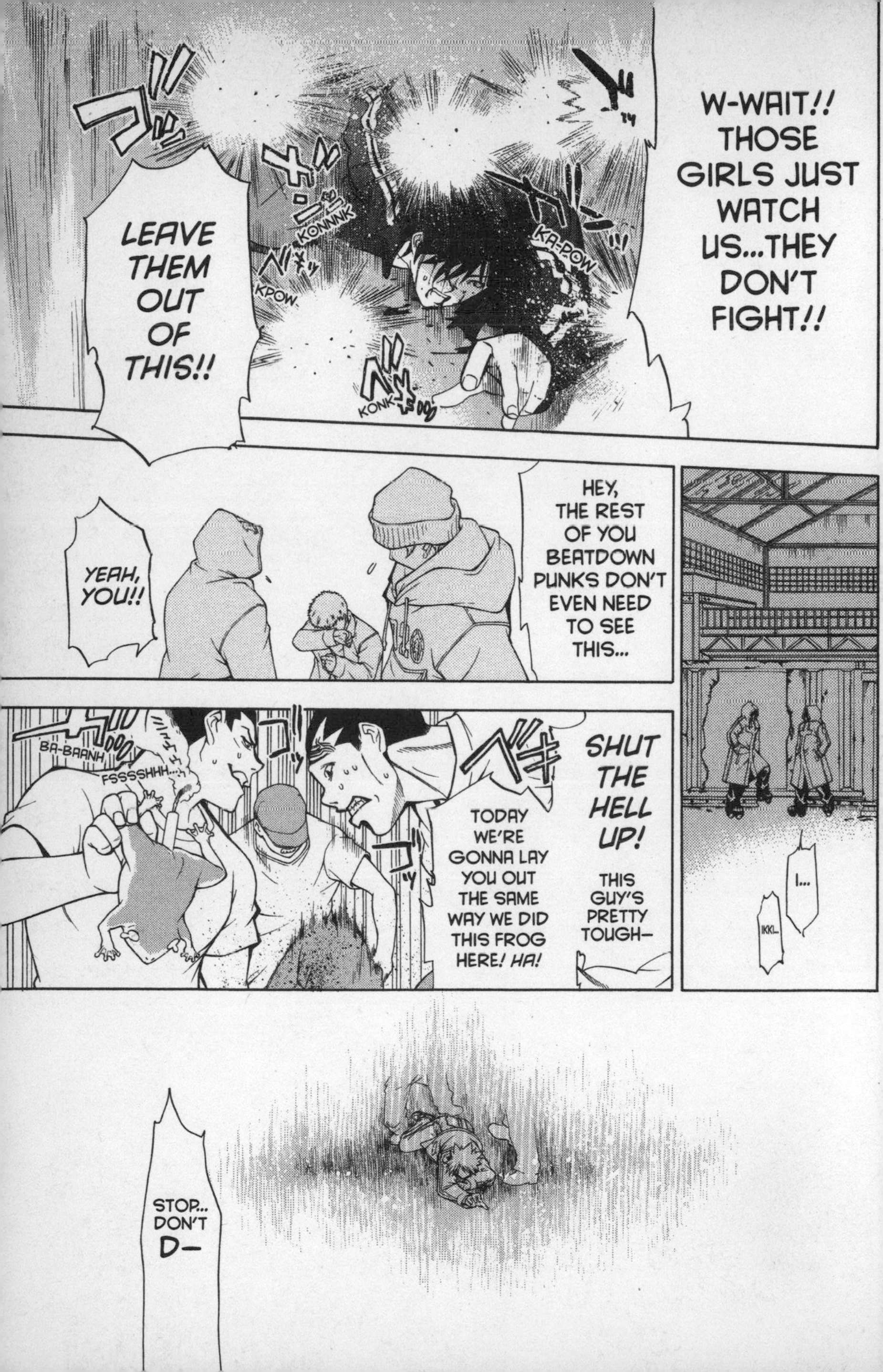
W-WAIT!! THOSE GIRLS JUST WATCH US...THEY DON'T FIGHT!!
KA-POW
KONNNK
KPOW.
KONK
LEAVE THEM OUT OF THIS!!
I...
IKKI...
HEY, THE REST OF YOU BEATDOWN PUNKS DON'T EVEN NEED TO SEE THIS...
YEAH, YOU!!
SHUT THE HELL UP!
THIS GUY'S PRETTY TOUGH—
TODAY WE'RE GONNA LAY YOU OUT THE SAME WAY WE DID THIS FROG HERE! HA!
FSSSSHHH...
BA-BAANH
STOP... DON'T D—

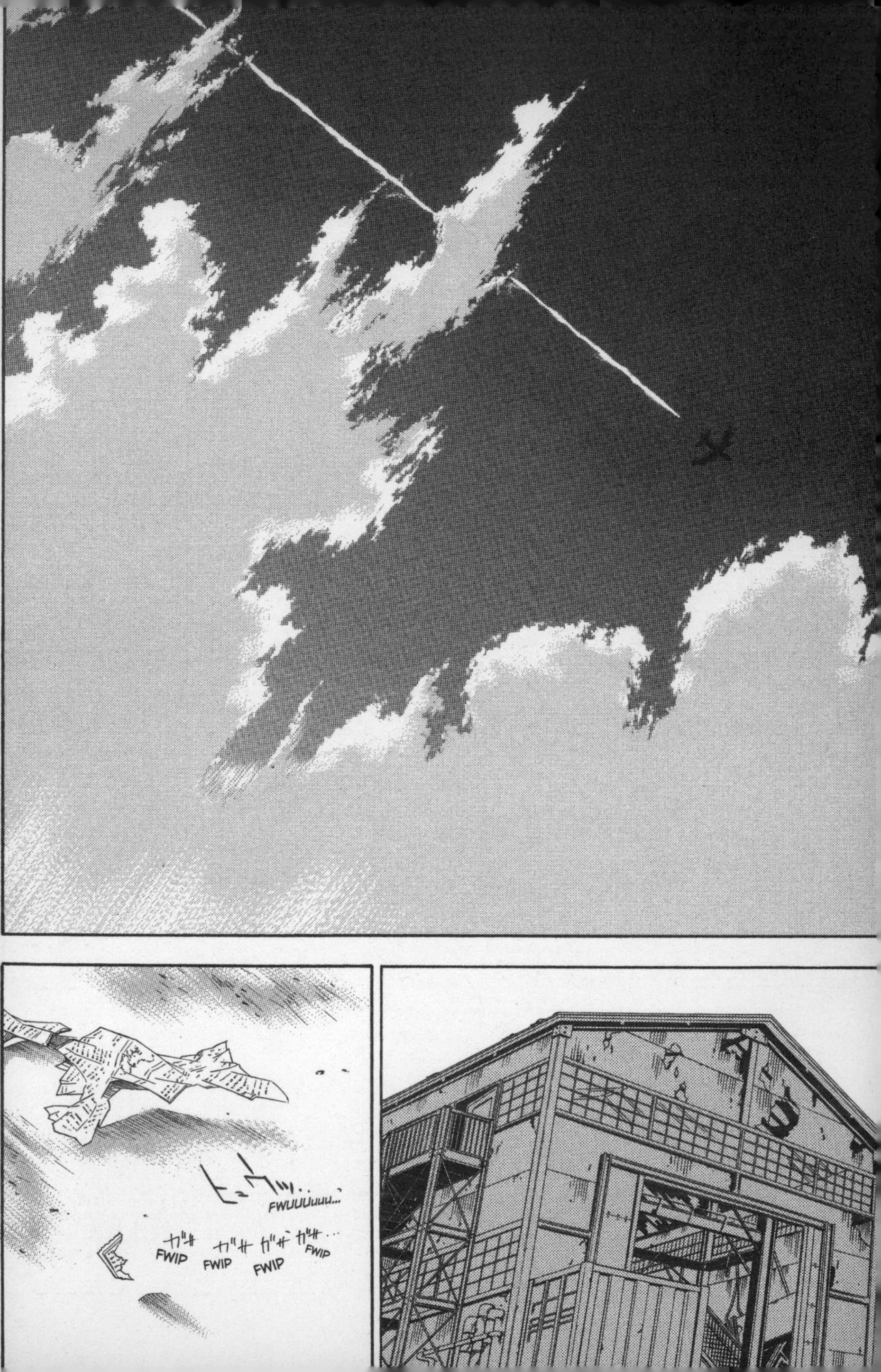
ヒュゥッ..
FWUUUuuu...
ガサ ガサ ガサ ガサ...
FWIP
FWIP
FWIP
FWIP

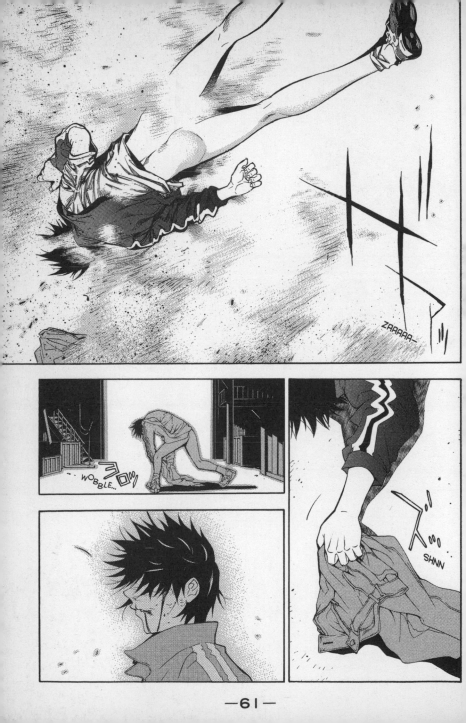

ZRAAAA—

WOBBLE...

SHNN

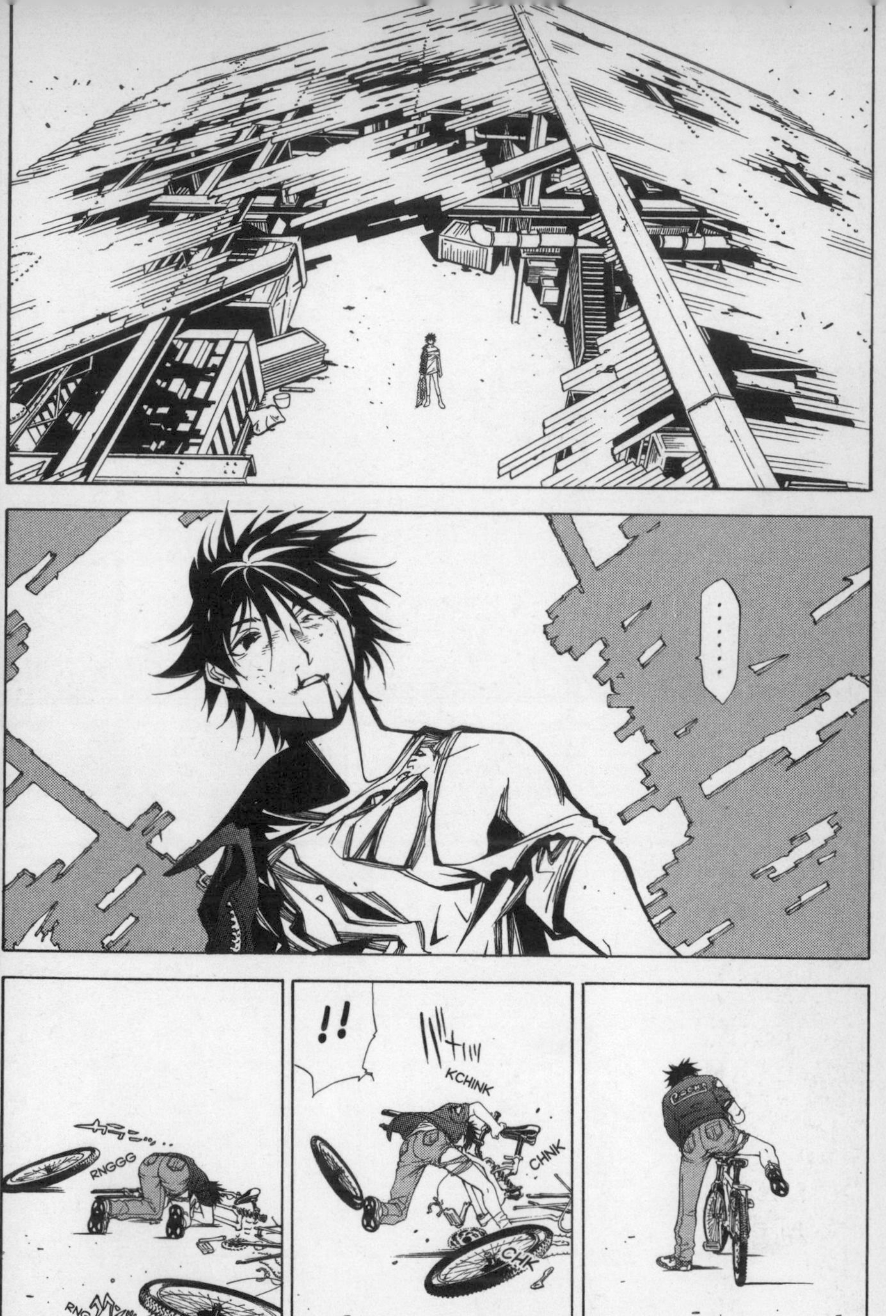
……
!!
KCHINK
CHNK
CHK
RNGGG
RNG
RNG

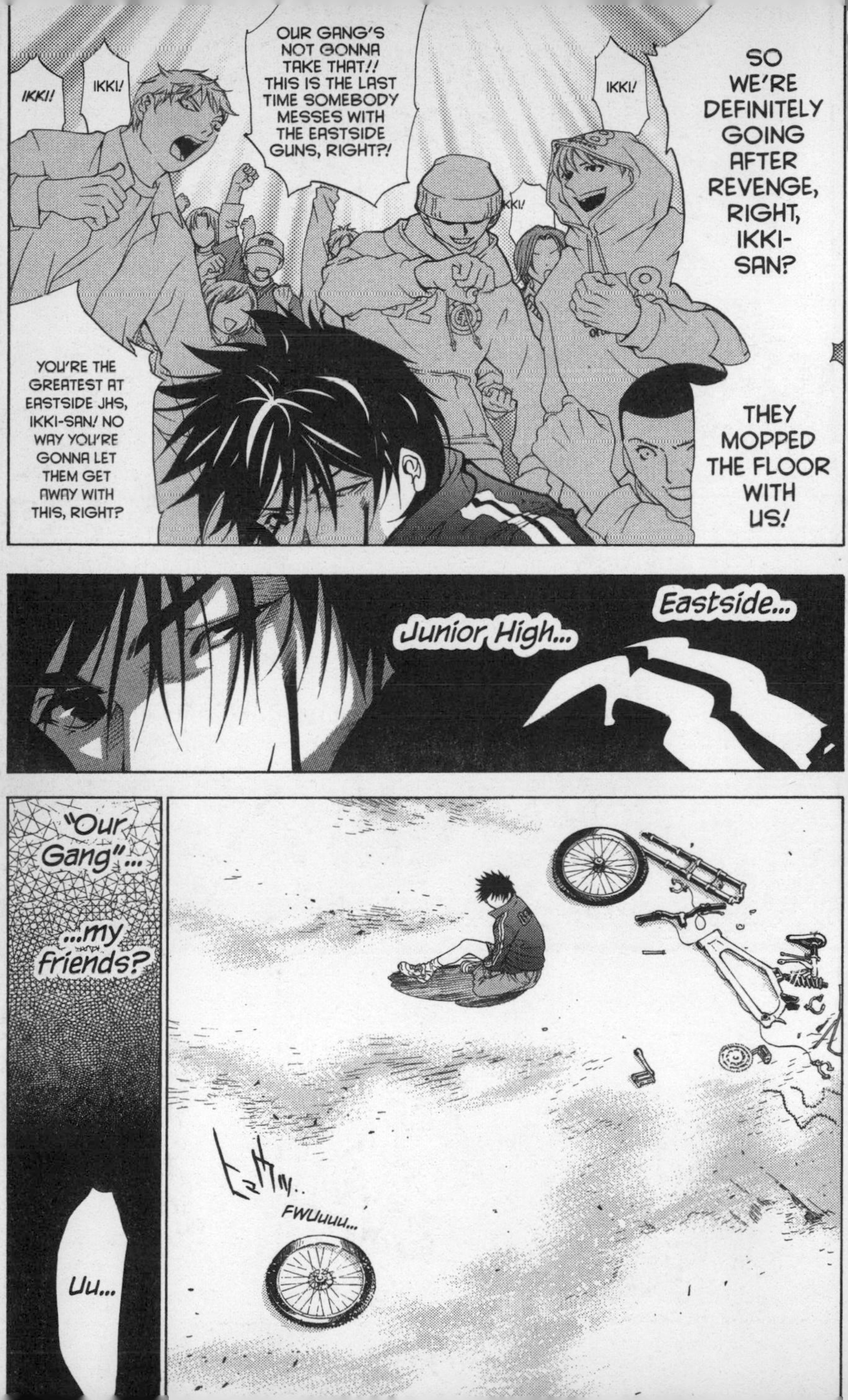
SO WE'RE DEFINITELY GOING AFTER REVENGE, RIGHT, IKKI-SAN?
IKKI!
OUR GANG'S NOT GONNA TAKE THAT!! THIS IS THE LAST TIME SOMEBODY MESSES WITH THE EASTSIDE GUNS, RIGHT?!
IKKI!
IKKI!
THEY MOPPED THE FLOOR WITH US!
YOU'RE THE GREATEST AT EASTSIDE JHS, IKKI-SAN! NO WAY YOU'RE GONNA LET THEM GET AWAY WITH THIS, RIGHT?
Eastside...
Junior High...
FWuuuu...
"Our Gang"...
...my friends?
Uu...

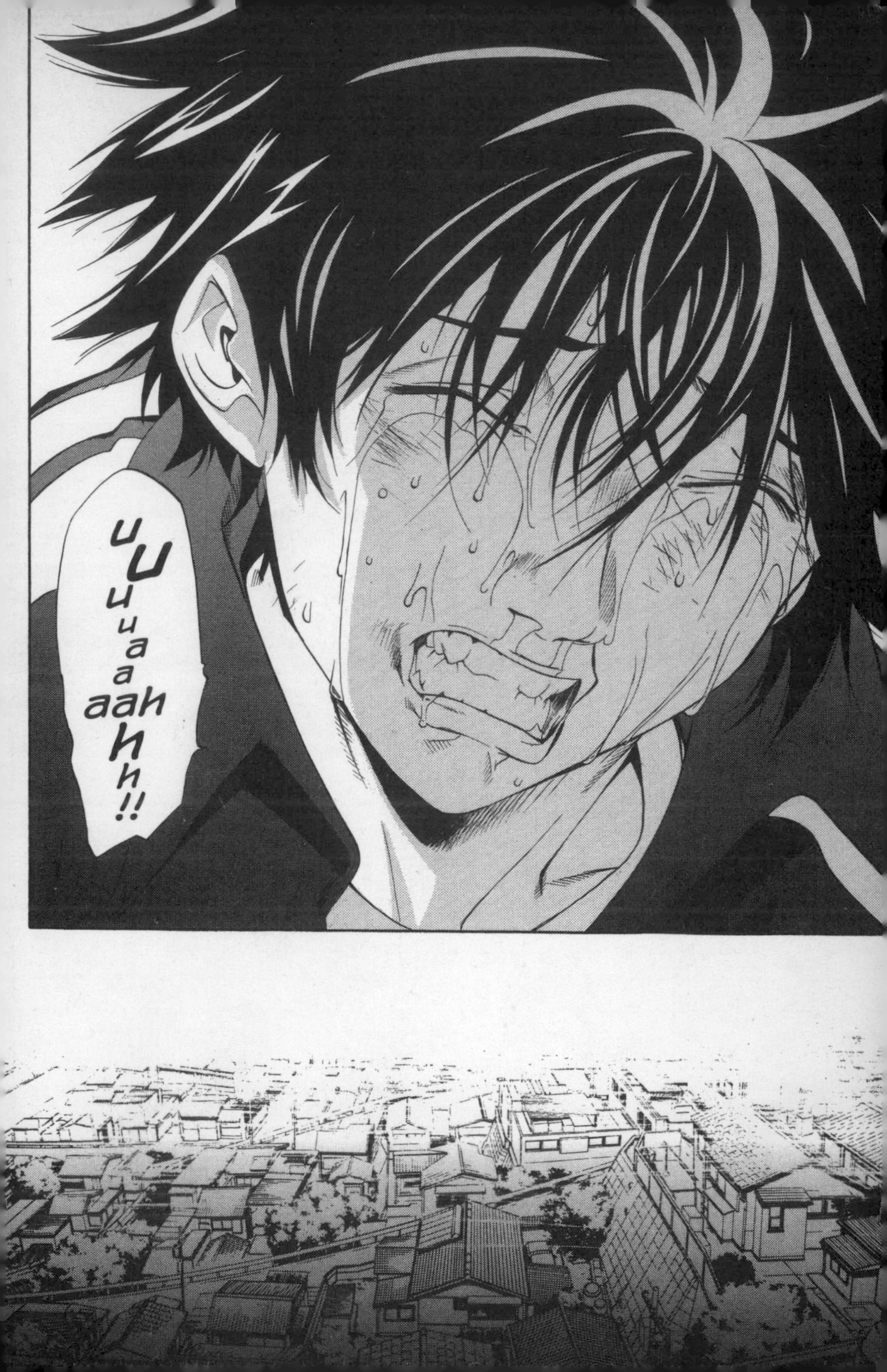
uUuuaaaahHh!!

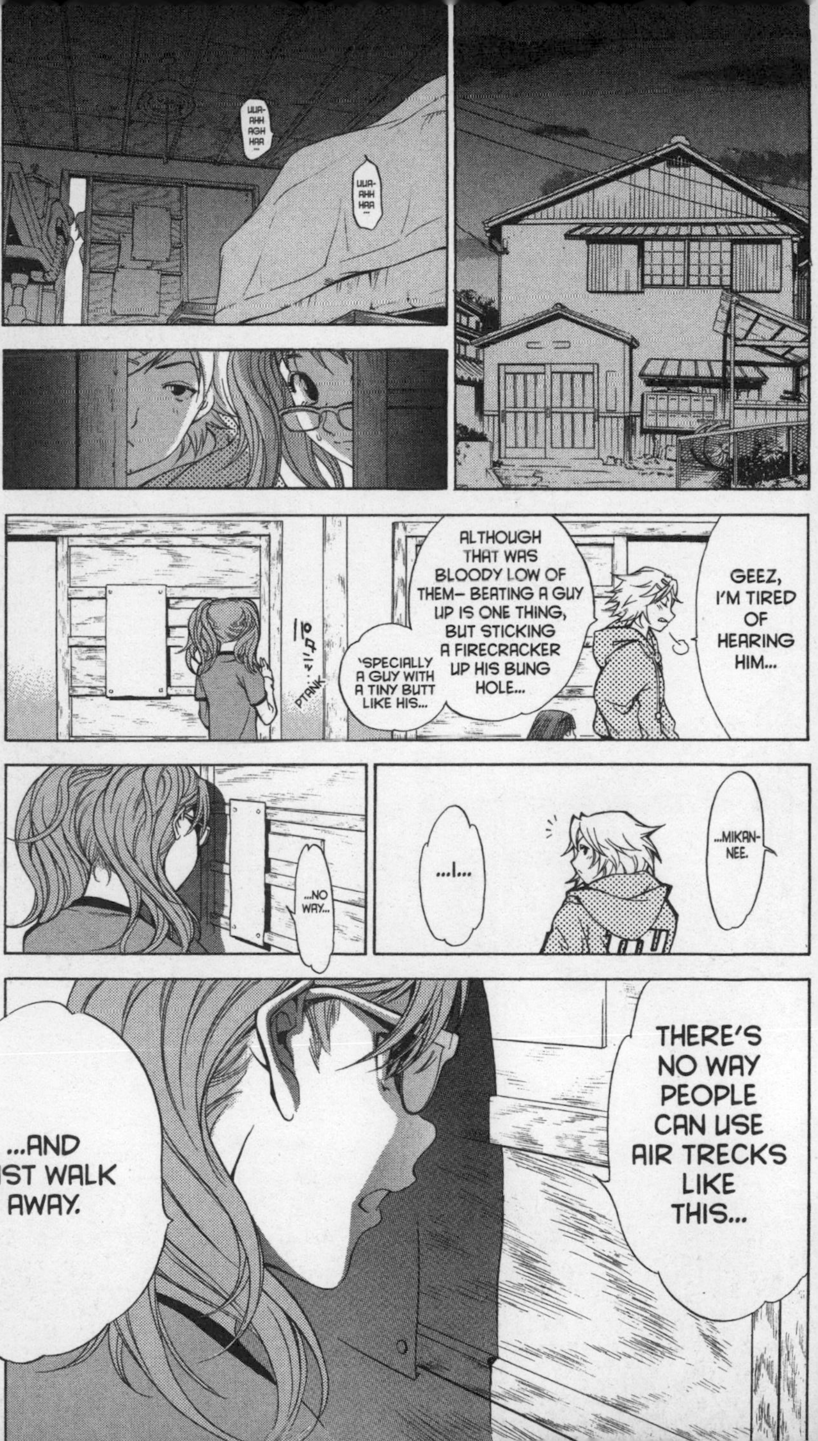
UUA-AHH HAA...
UUA-AHH AGH HAA...
GEEZ, I'M TIRED OF HEARING HIM...
ALTHOUGH THAT WAS BLOODY LOW OF THEM— BEATING A GUY UP IS ONE THING, BUT STICKING A FIRECRACKER UP HIS BUNG HOLE...
'SPECIALLY A GUY WITH A TINY BUTT LIKE HIS...
PTANK
...MIKAN-NEE.
...I...
...NO WAY...
THERE'S NO WAY PEOPLE CAN USE AIR TRECKS LIKE THIS...
...AND JUST WALK AWAY.

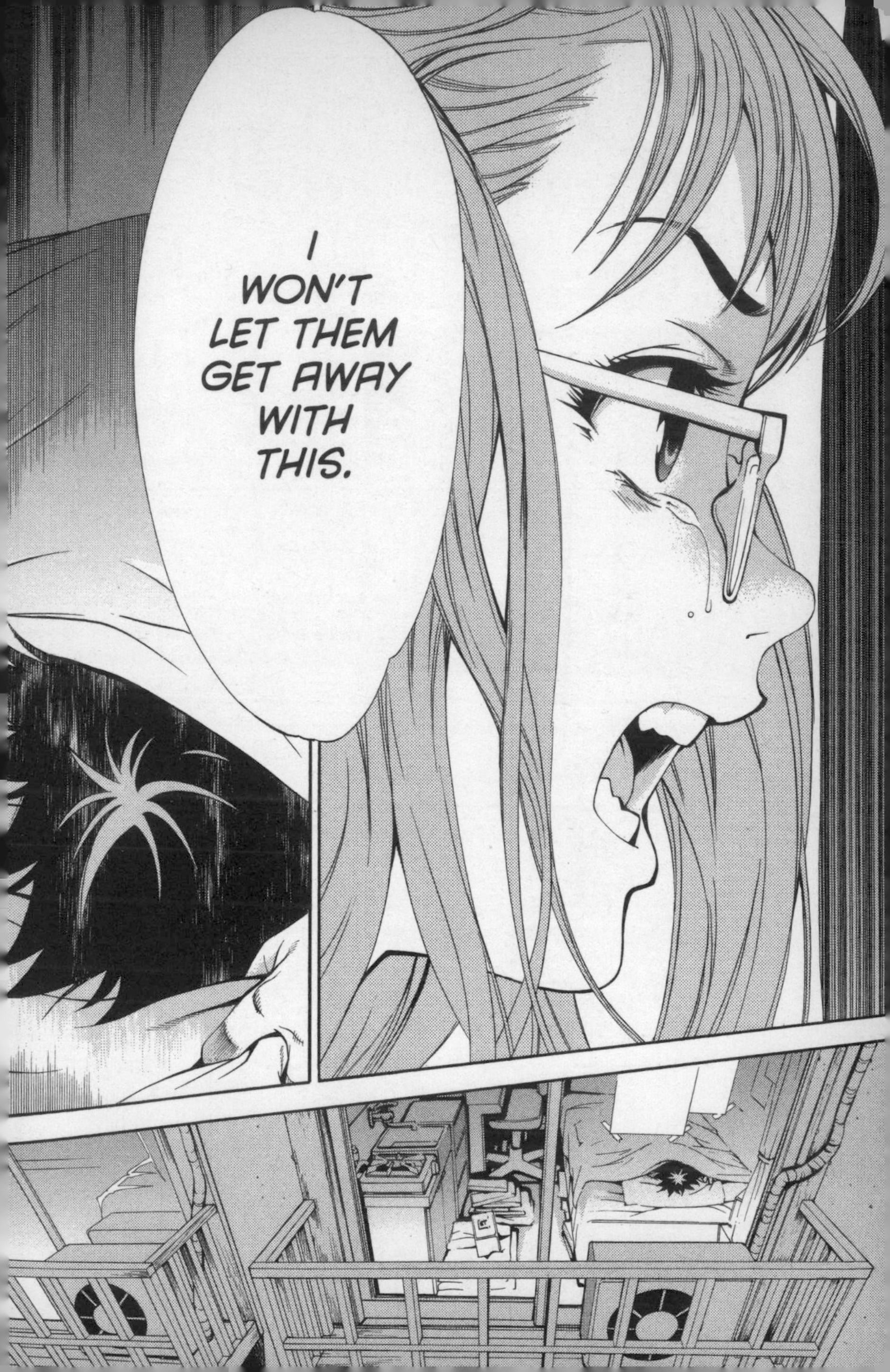
I WON'T LET THEM GET AWAY WITH THIS.

KNOCK
KNOCK

KNOCK
KNOCK

KNOCK
KNOCK

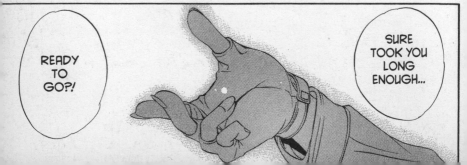

READY
TO
GO?!

SURE
TOOK YOU
LONG
ENOUGH...

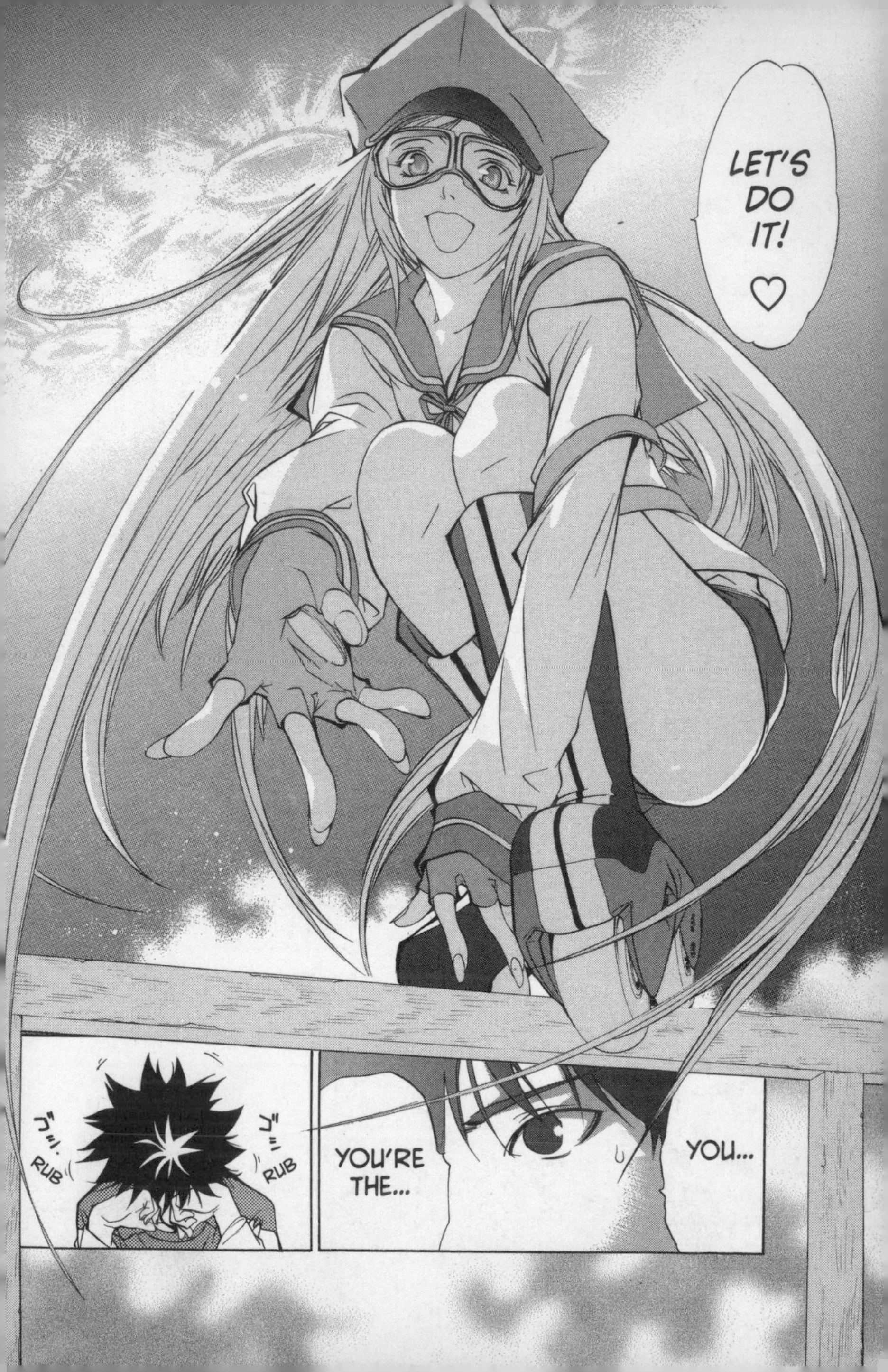
LET'S DO IT! ♡
YOU...
YOU'RE THE...
RUB
RUB

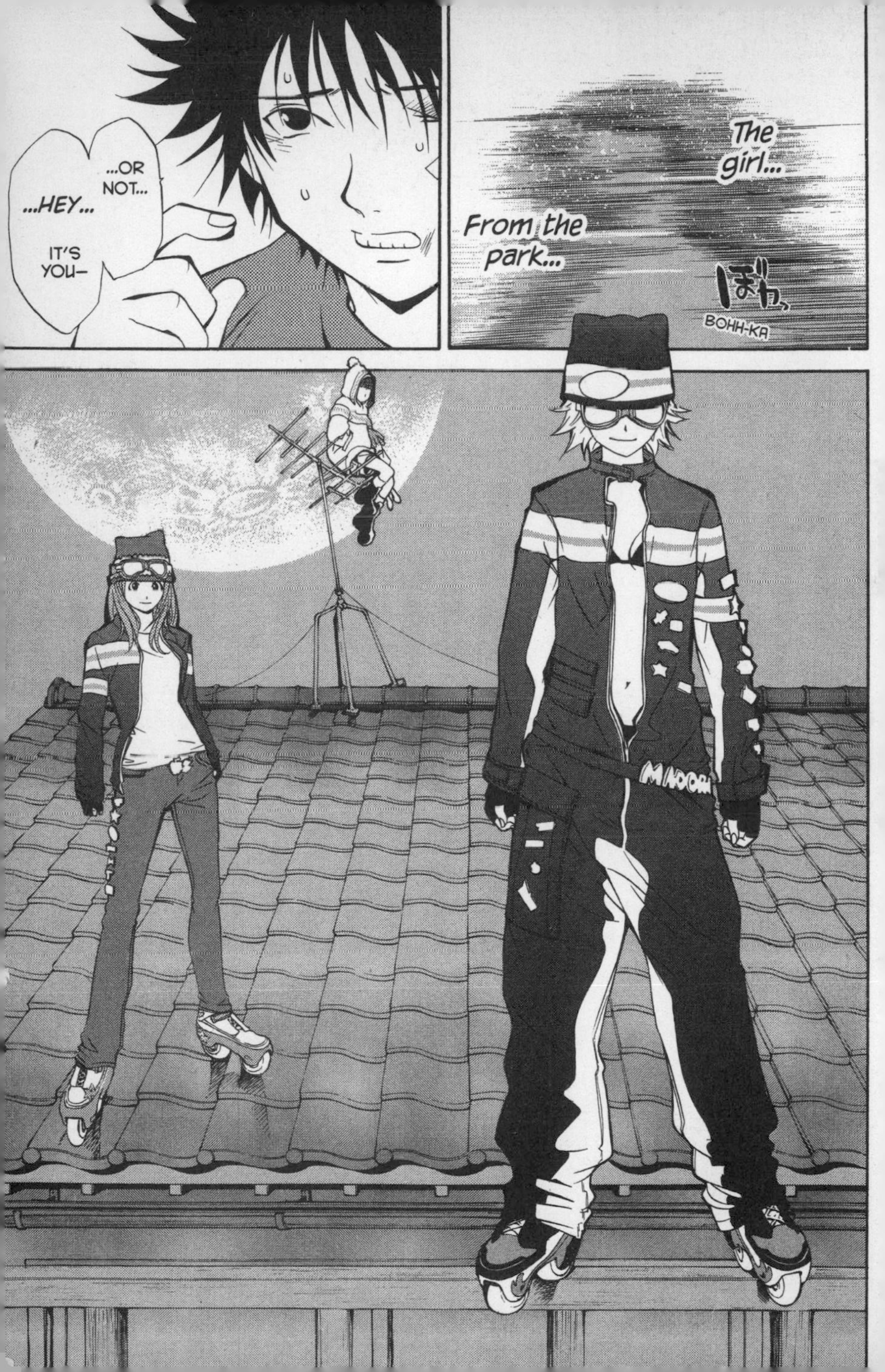
The girl...
From the park...
BOHH-KA
...OR NOT...
...HEY...
IT'S YOU—

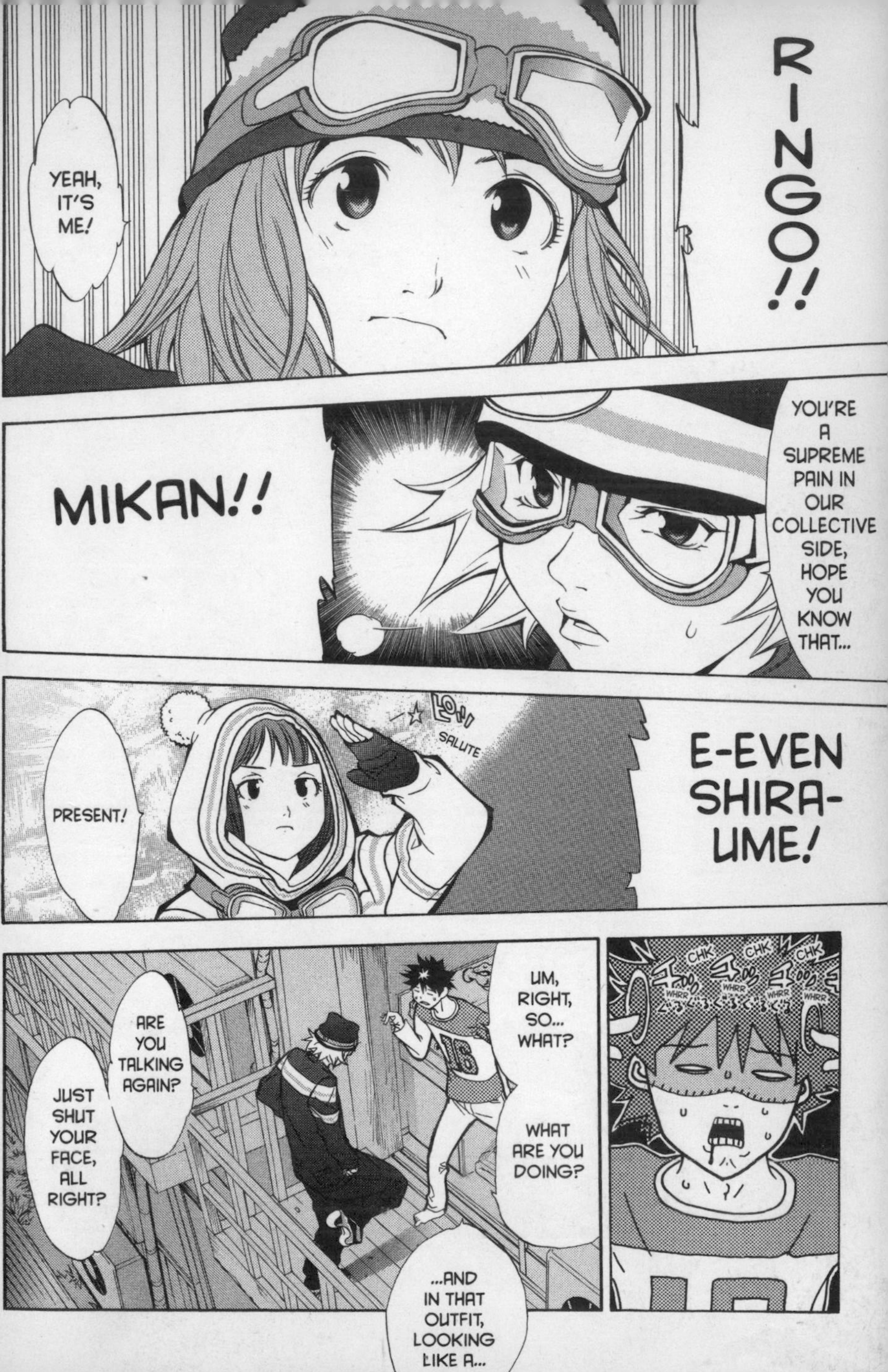
RINGO!!
YEAH, IT'S ME!
YOU'RE A SUPREME PAIN IN OUR COLLECTIVE SIDE, HOPE YOU KNOW THAT...
MIKAN!!
E-EVEN SHIRA-UME!
SALUTE
PRESENT!
CHK CHK CHK
WHRR WHRR WHRR WHRR
UM, RIGHT, SO... WHAT?
WHAT ARE YOU DOING?
...AND IN THAT OUTFIT, LOOKING LIKE A...
ARE YOU TALKING AGAIN?
JUST SHUT YOUR FACE, ALL RIGHT?

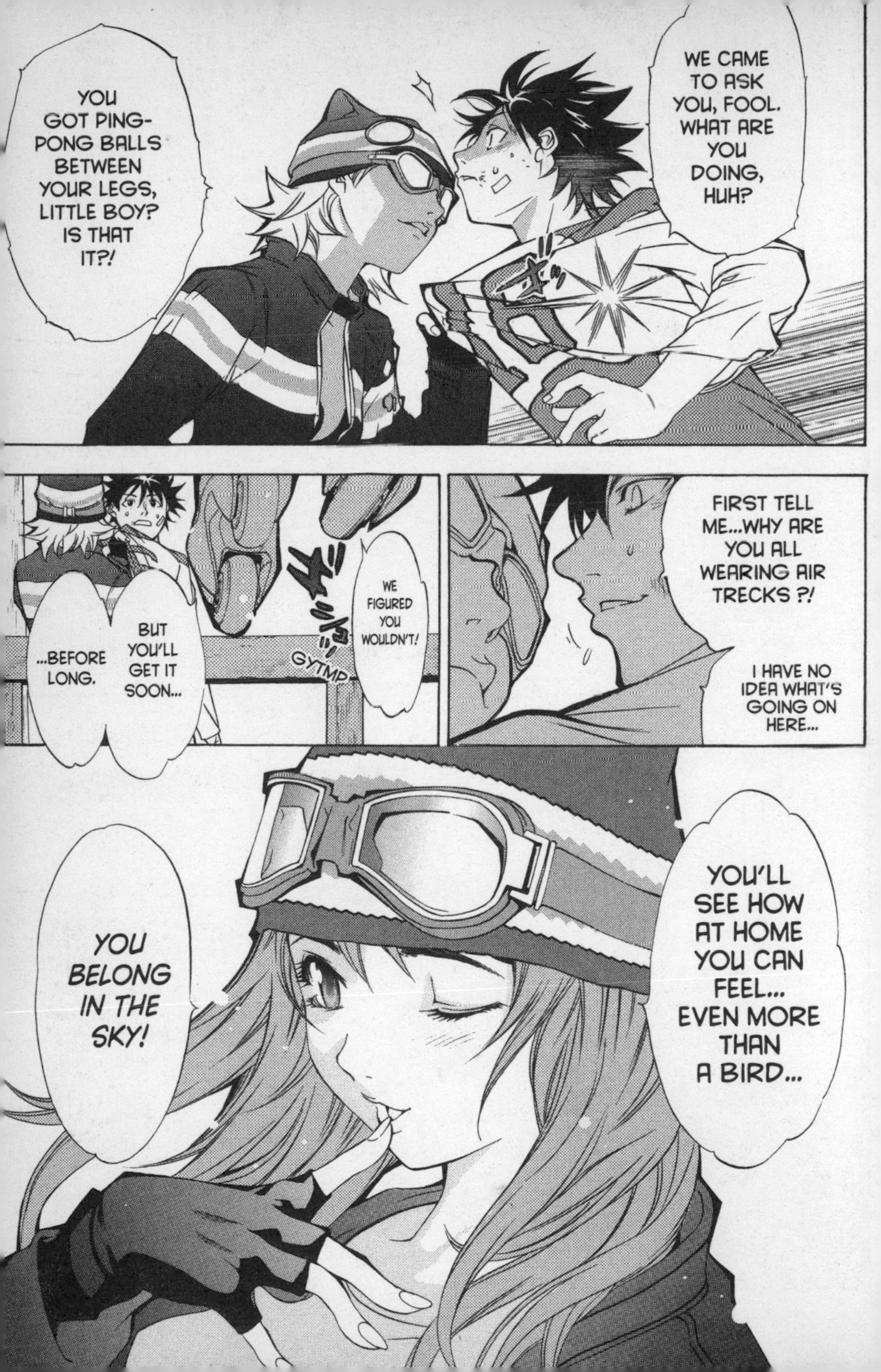
WE CAME TO ASK YOU, FOOL. WHAT ARE YOU DOING, HUH?
YOU GOT PING-PONG BALLS BETWEEN YOUR LEGS, LITTLE BOY? IS THAT IT?!
FIRST TELL ME...WHY ARE YOU ALL WEARING AIR TRECKS ?!
I HAVE NO IDEA WHAT'S GOING ON HERE...
WE FIGURED YOU WOULDN'T!
GYTMP
BUT YOU'LL GET IT SOON...
...BEFORE LONG.
YOU'LL SEE HOW AT HOME YOU CAN FEEL... EVEN MORE THAN A BIRD...
YOU BELONG IN THE SKY!

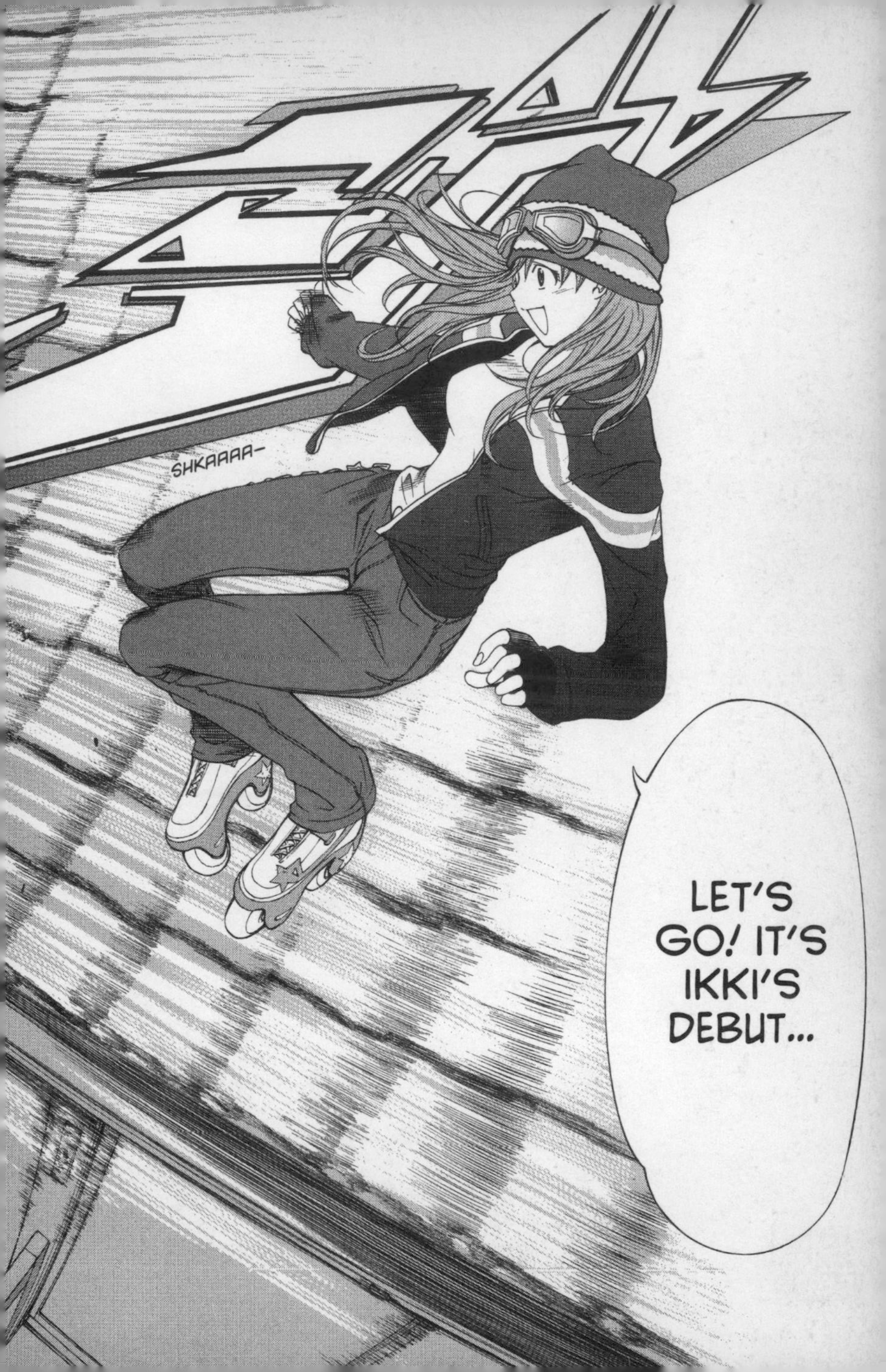
LET'S GO! IT'S IKKI'S DEBUT...
SHKAAAA-

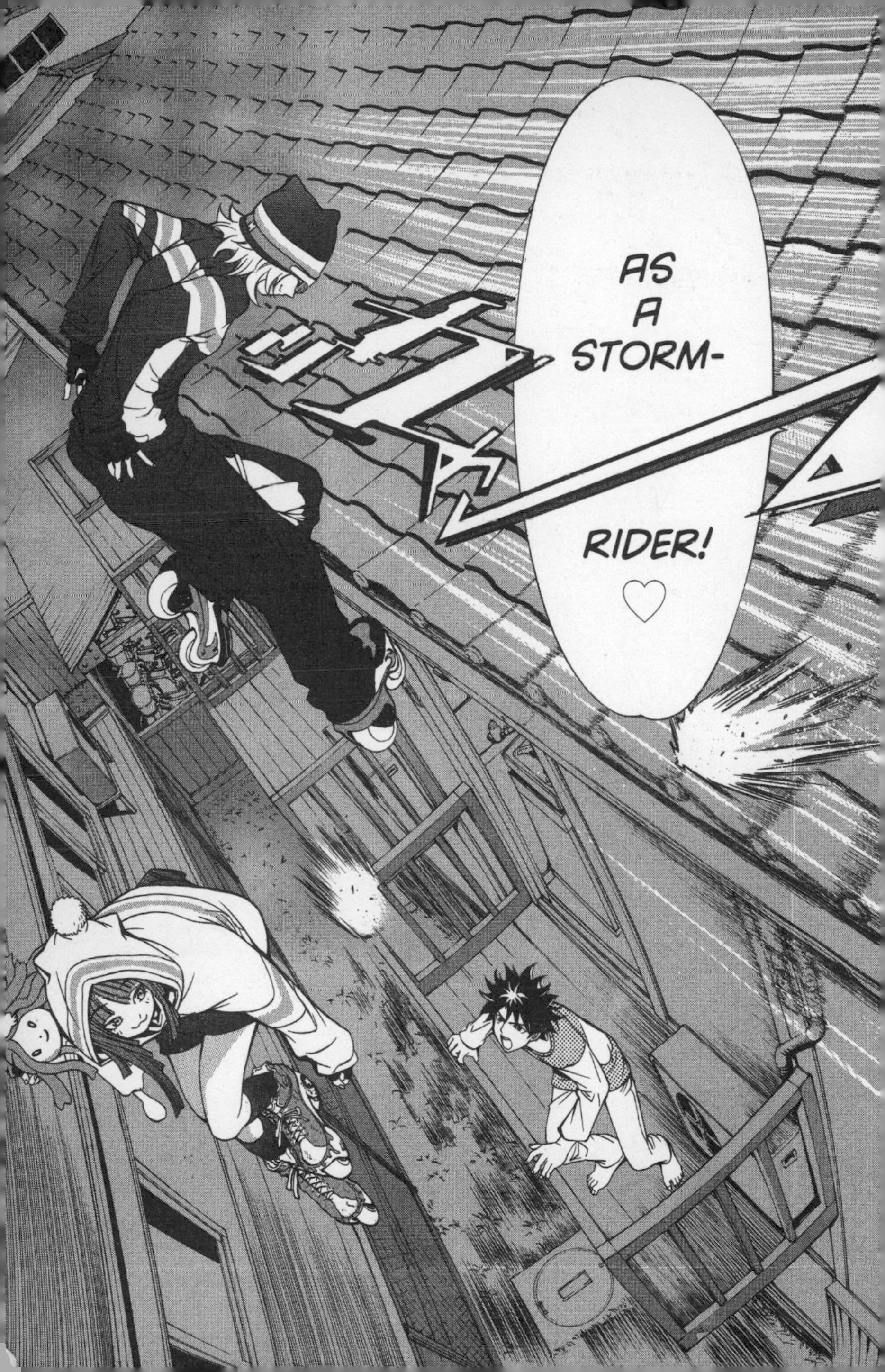
AS A STORM-RIDER! ♡

リアンクカ
GRAWW

ギョエヘぃ
GYOE-
HEI-

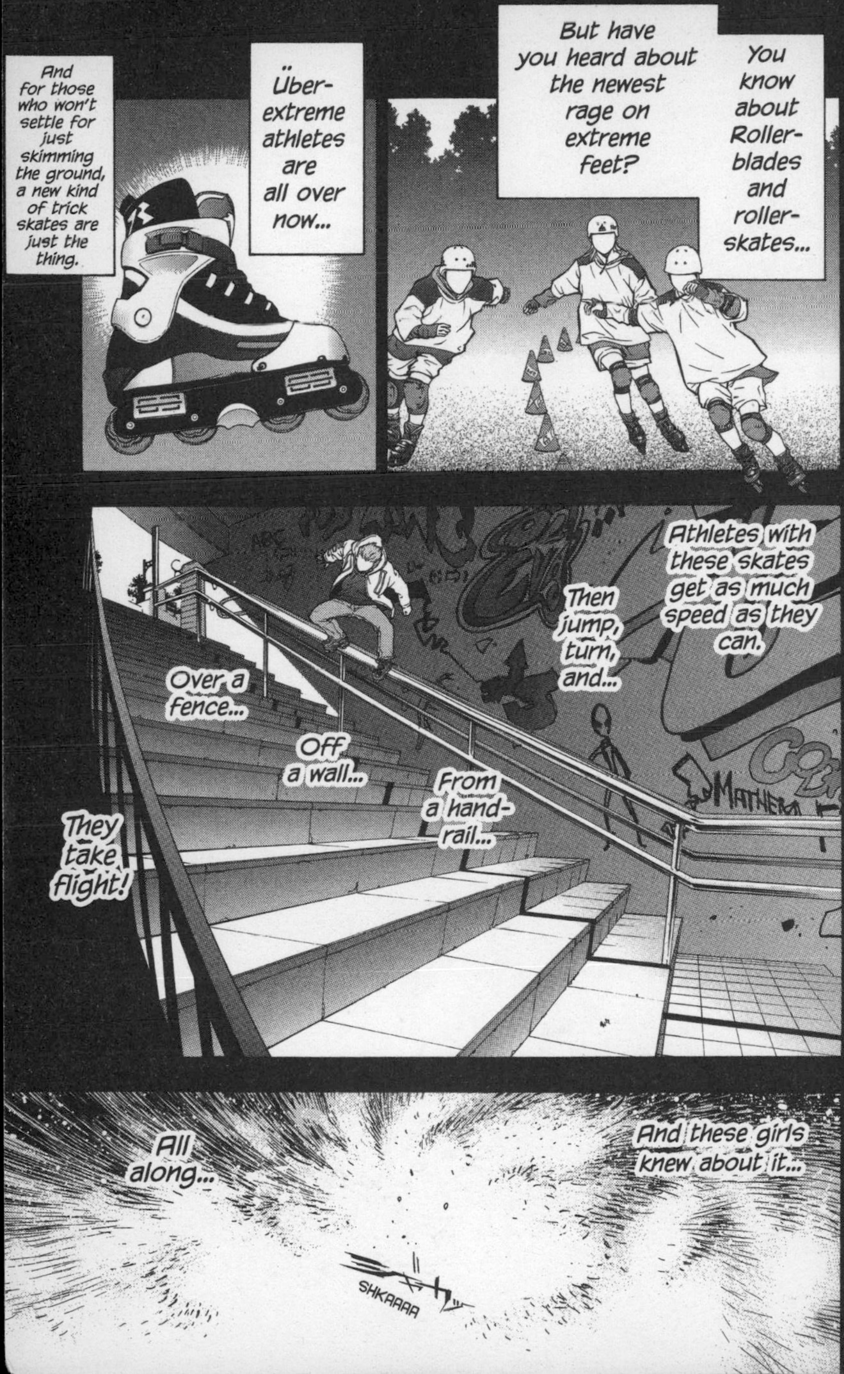
You know about Roller-blades and roller-skates...
But have you heard about the newest rage on extreme feet?
Über-extreme athletes are all over now...
And for those who won't settle for just skimming the ground, a new kind of trick skates are just the thing.
Athletes with these skates get as much speed as they can.
Then jump, turn, and...
Over a fence...
Off a wall...
From a hand-rail...
They take flight!
And these girls knew about it...
All along...
SHKAAAA

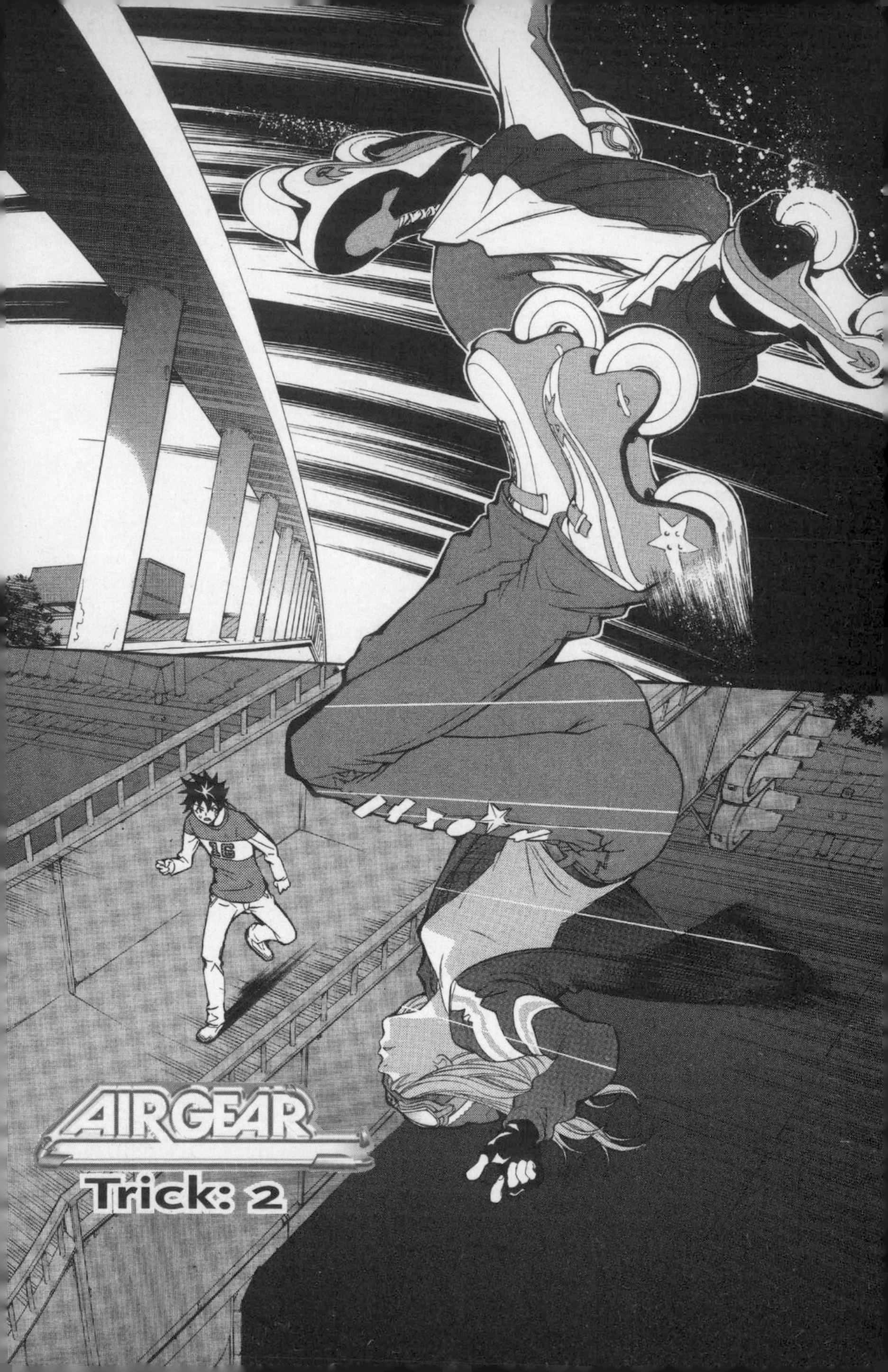
AIRGEAR
Trick: 2

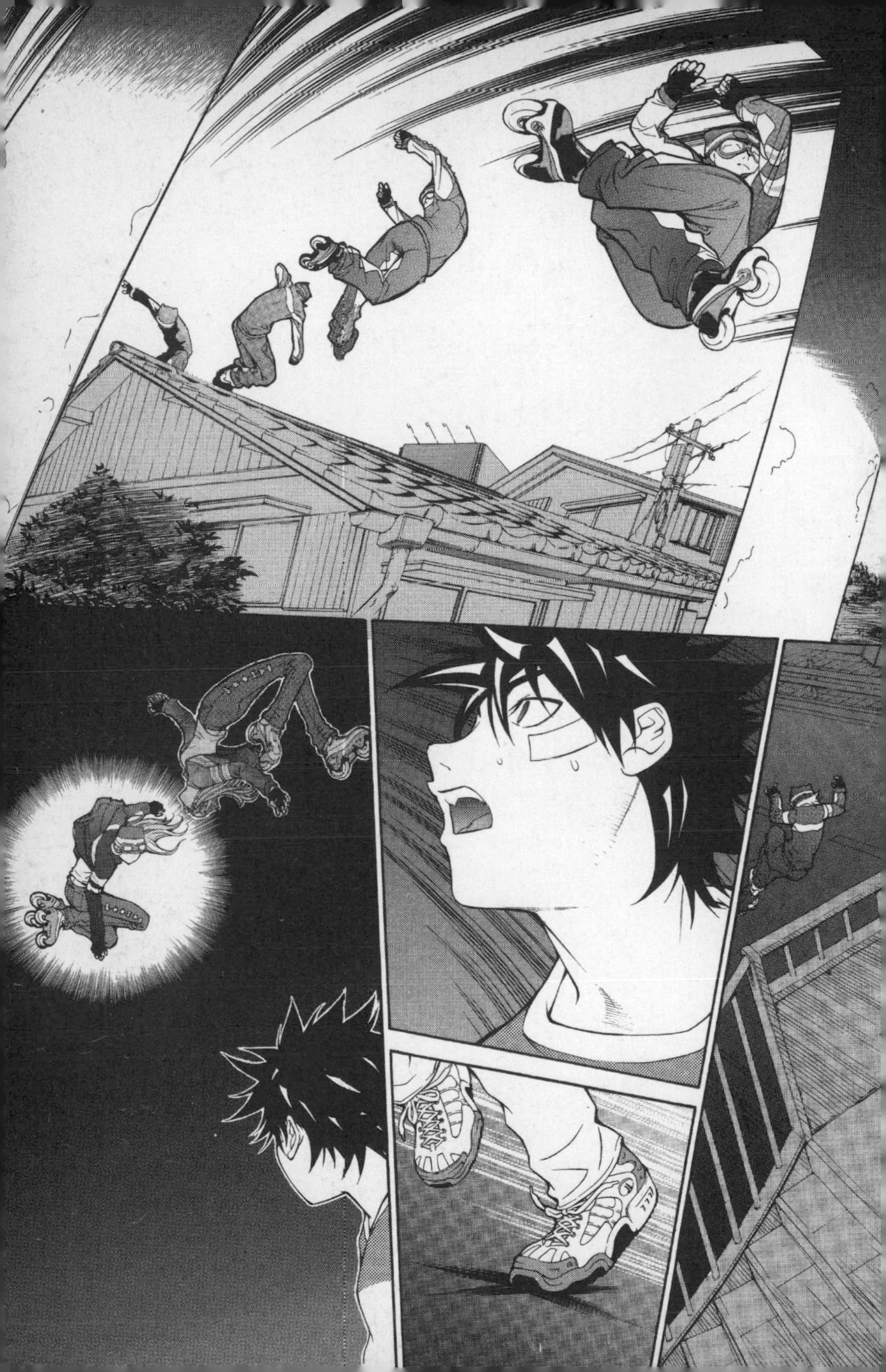

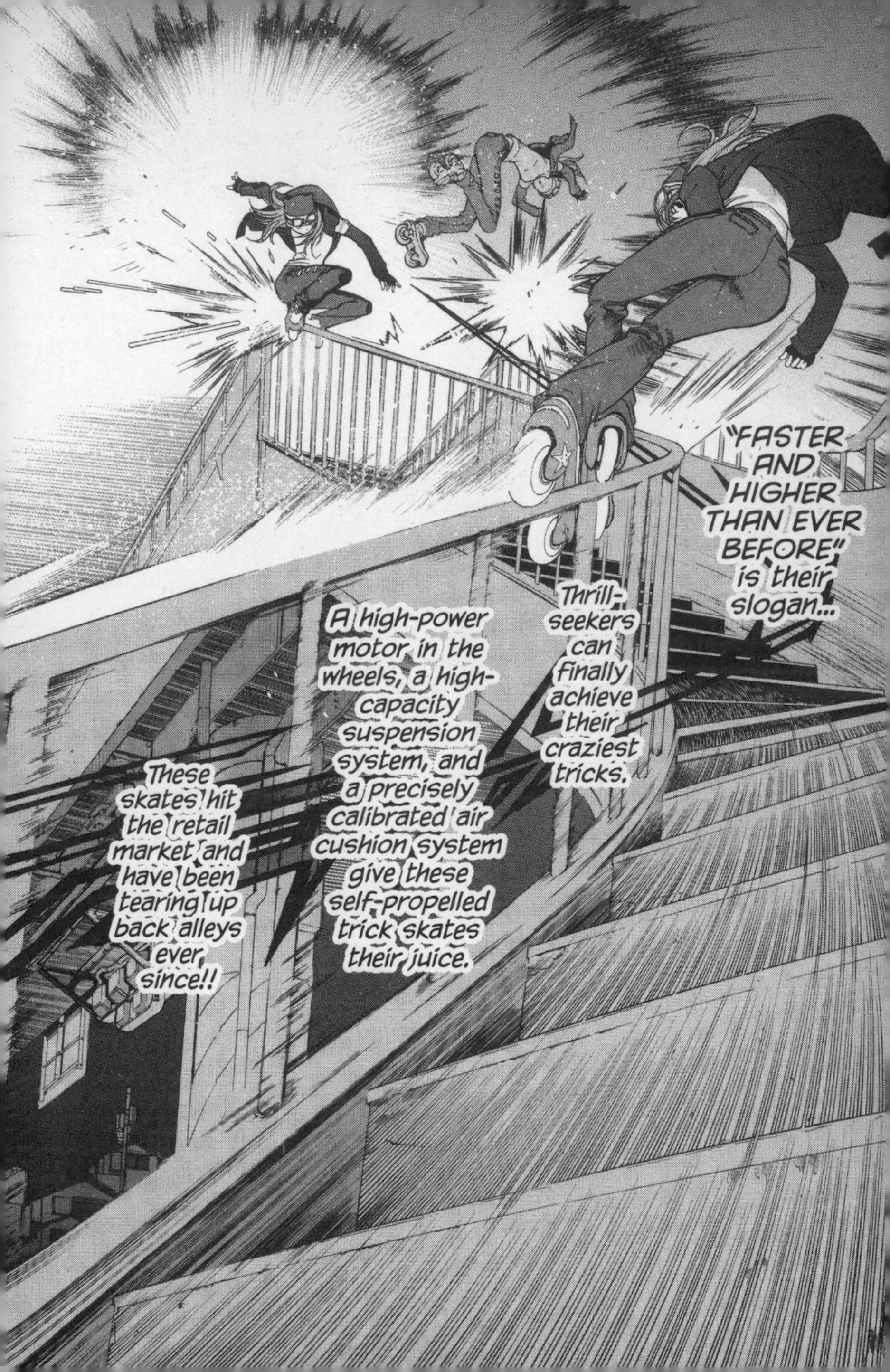
"FASTER AND HIGHER THAN EVER BEFORE" is their slogan...
Thrill-seekers can finally achieve their craziest tricks.
A high-power motor in the wheels, a high-capacity suspension system, and a precisely calibrated air cushion system give these self-propelled trick skates their juice.
These skates hit the retail market and have been tearing up back alleys ever since!!

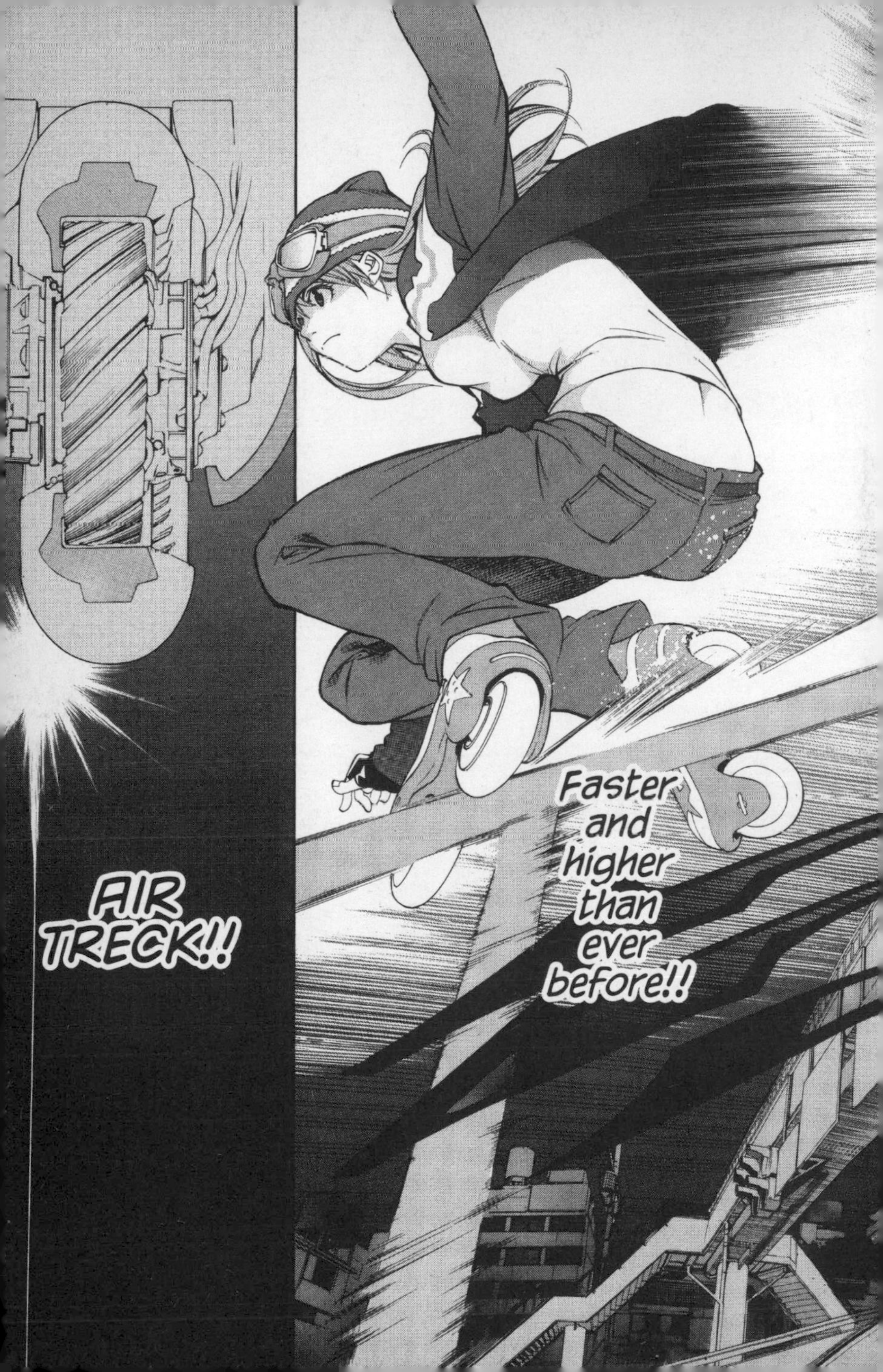
Faster and higher than ever before!!
AIR TRECK!!

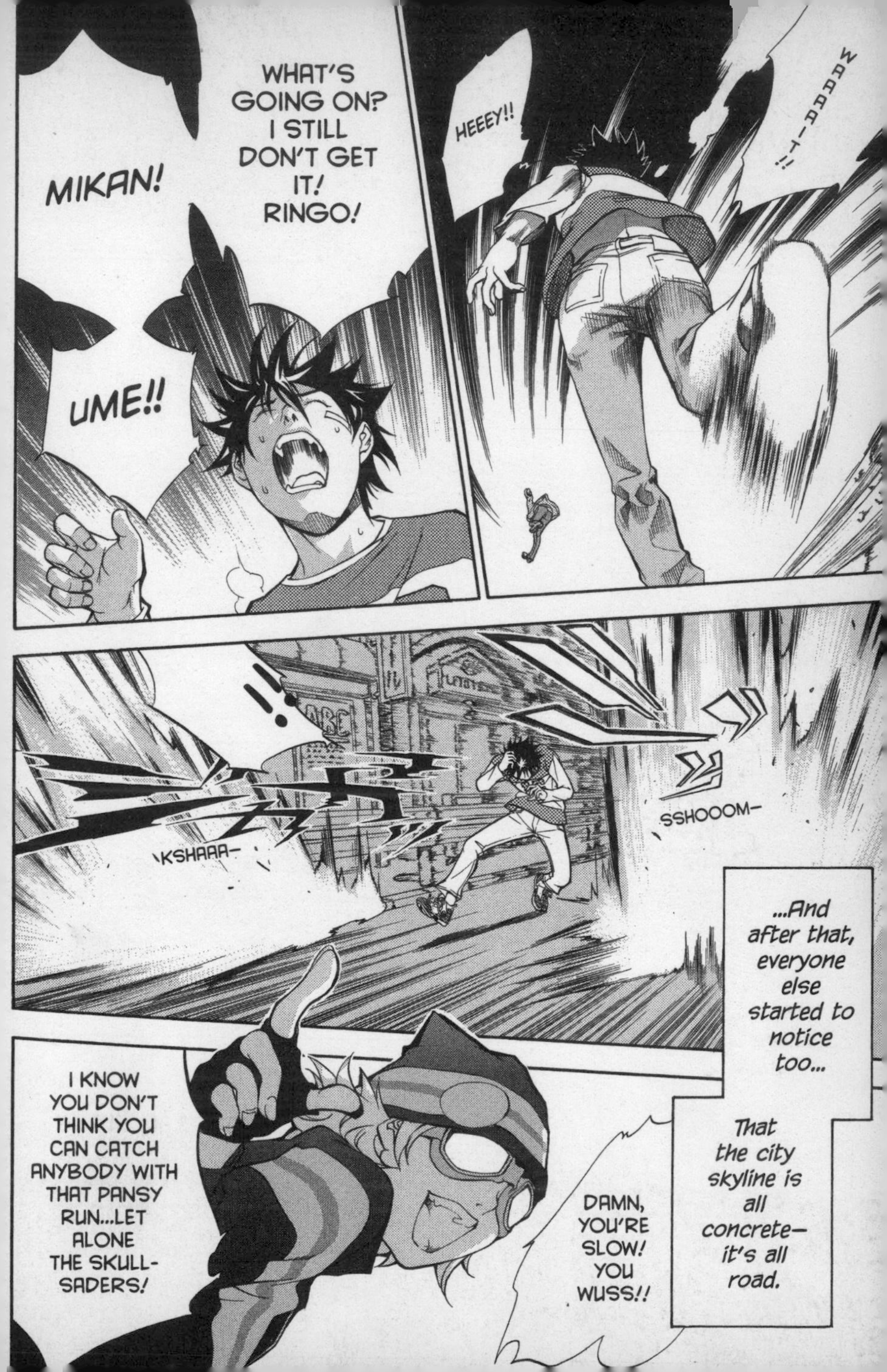
WAAAA-IT!!
HEEEY!!
WHAT'S GOING ON? I STILL DON'T GET IT! RINGO!
MIKAN!
UME!!
SSHOOOM-
!!
KSHAAA-
...And after that, everyone else started to notice too...
That the city skyline is all concrete—it's all road.
DAMN, YOU'RE SLOW! YOU WUSS!!
I KNOW YOU DON'T THINK YOU CAN CATCH ANYBODY WITH THAT PANSY RUN...LET ALONE THE SKULL-SADERS!

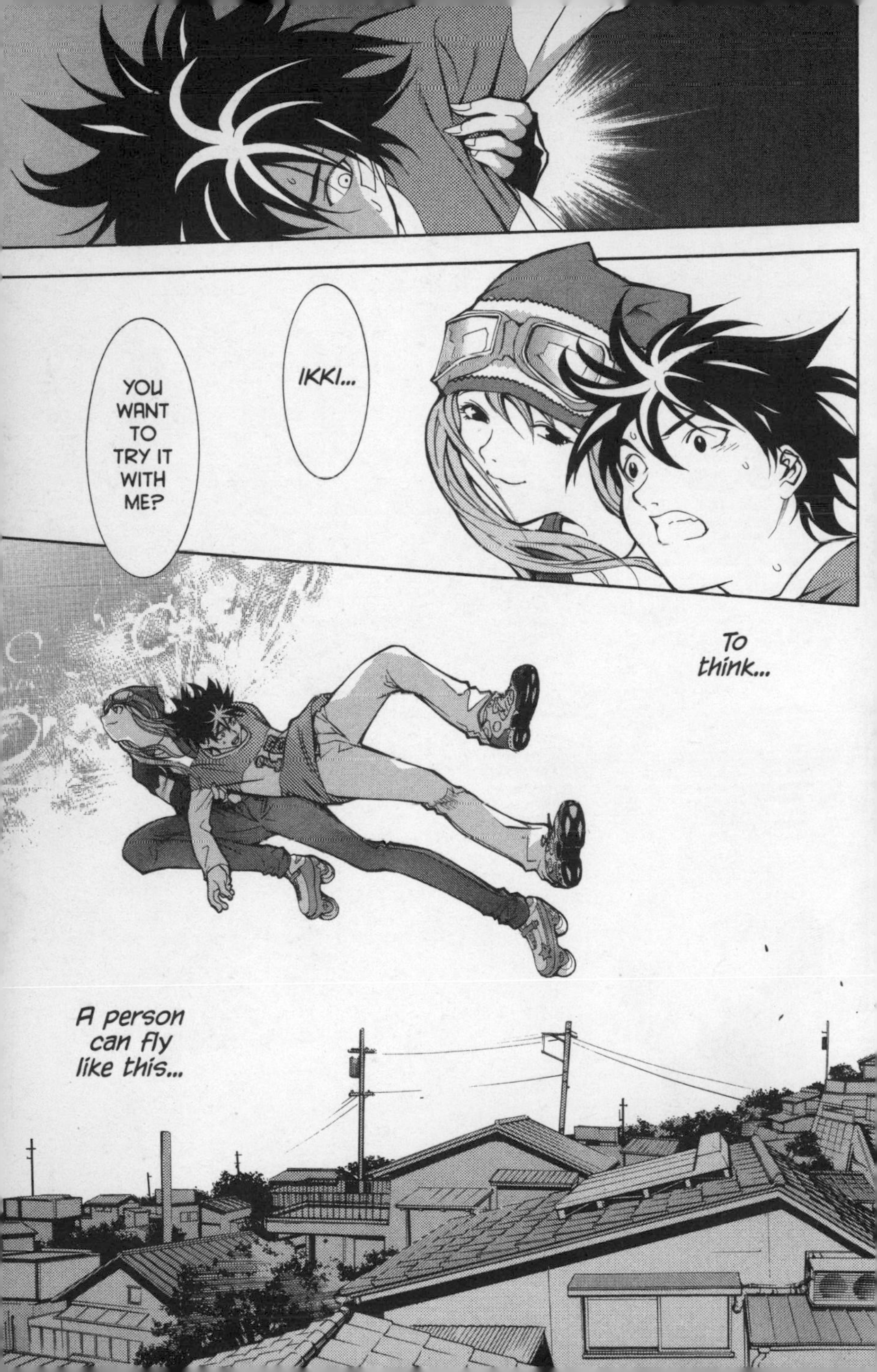
IKKI...
YOU WANT TO TRY IT WITH ME?
To think...
A person can fly like this...

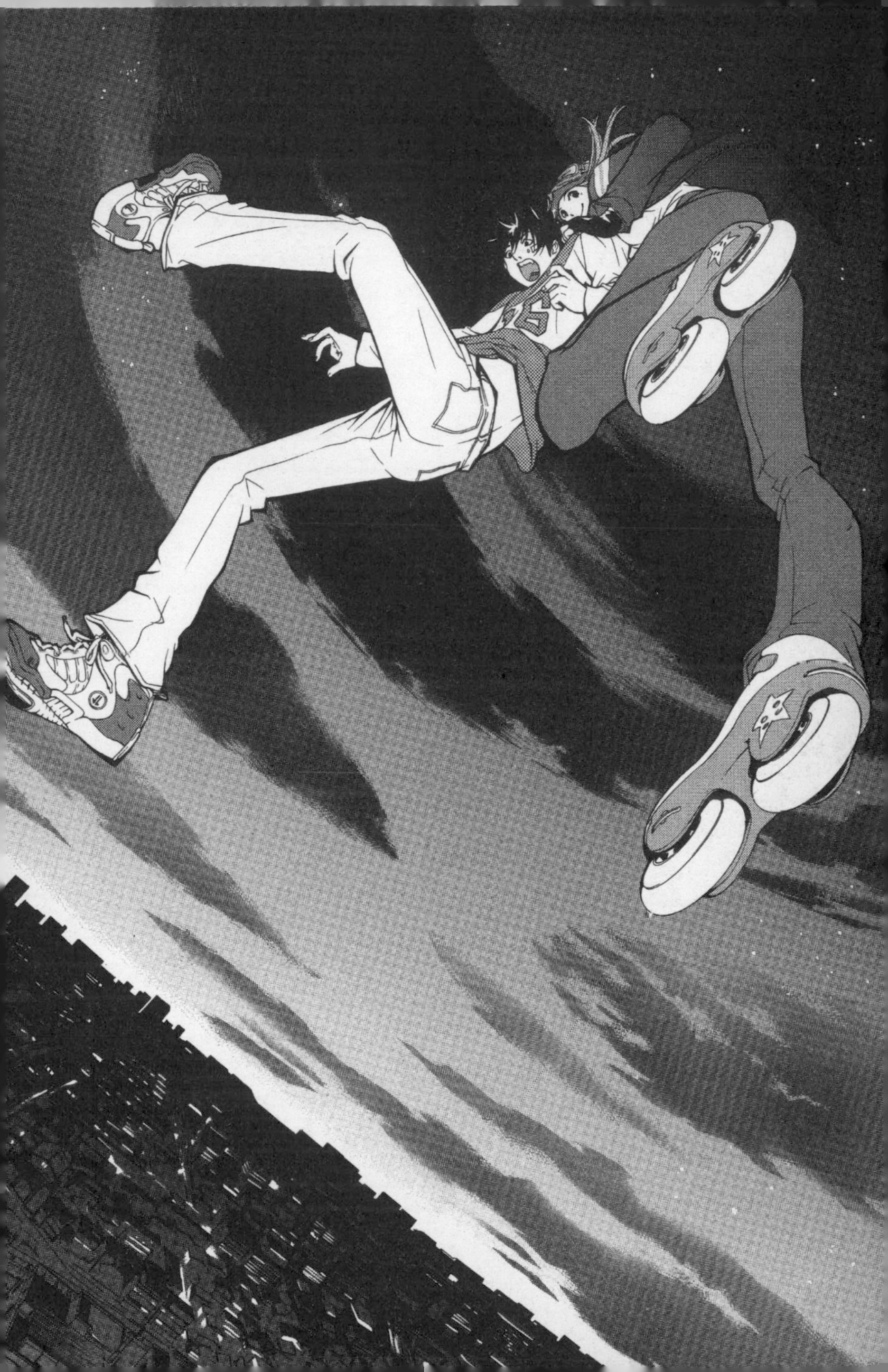

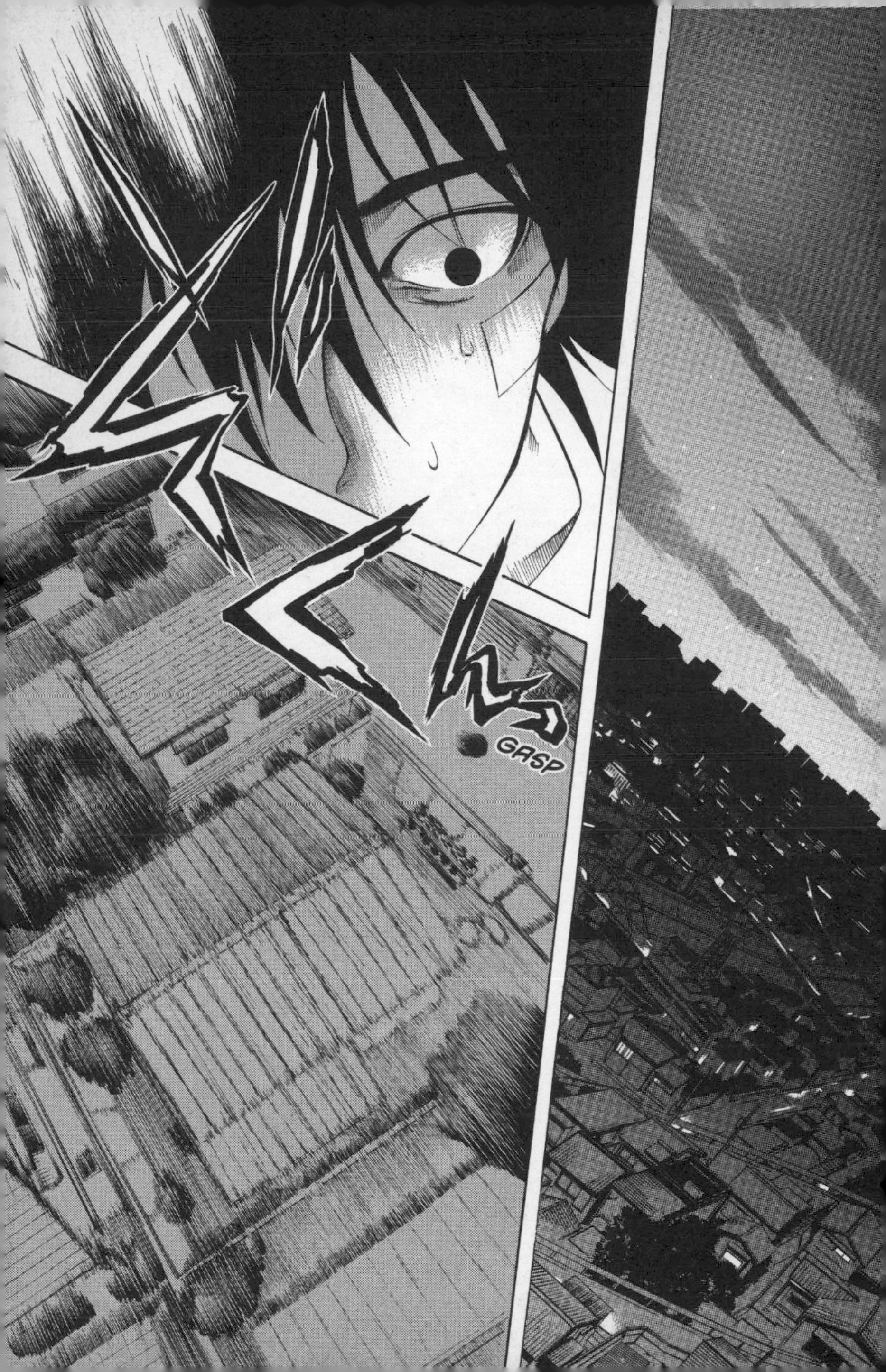
GASP

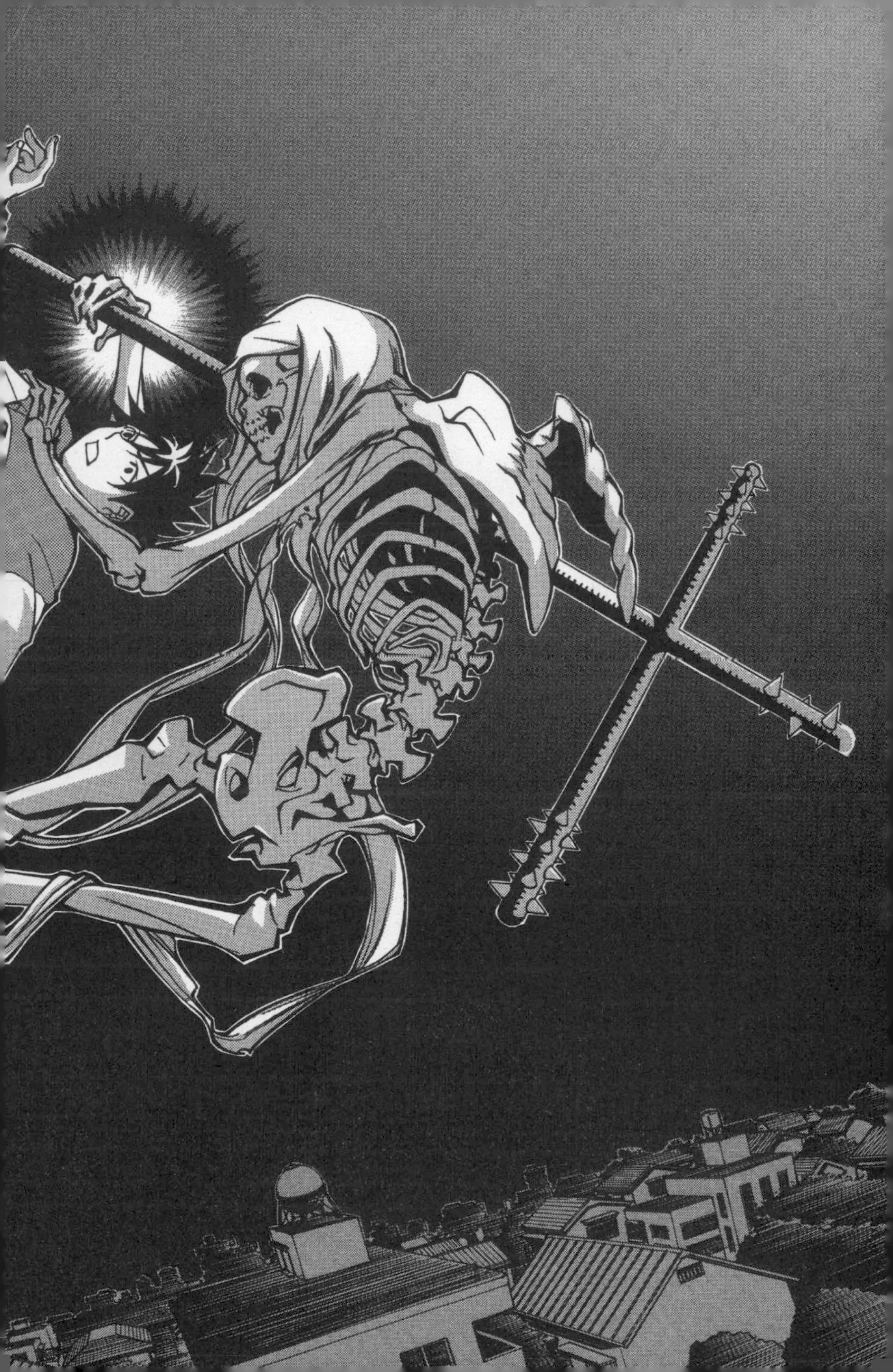

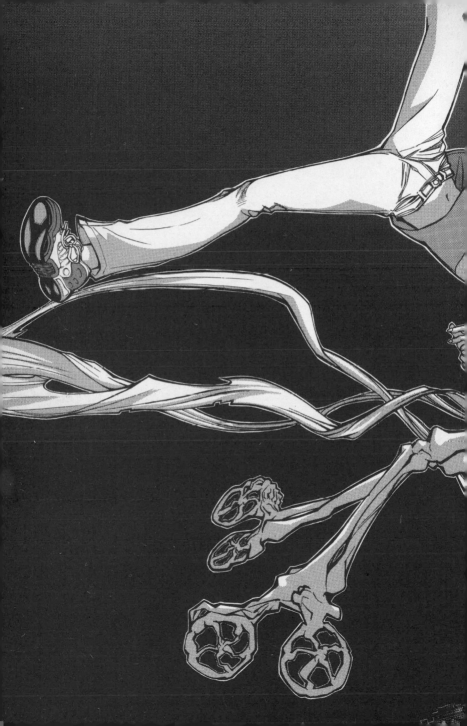

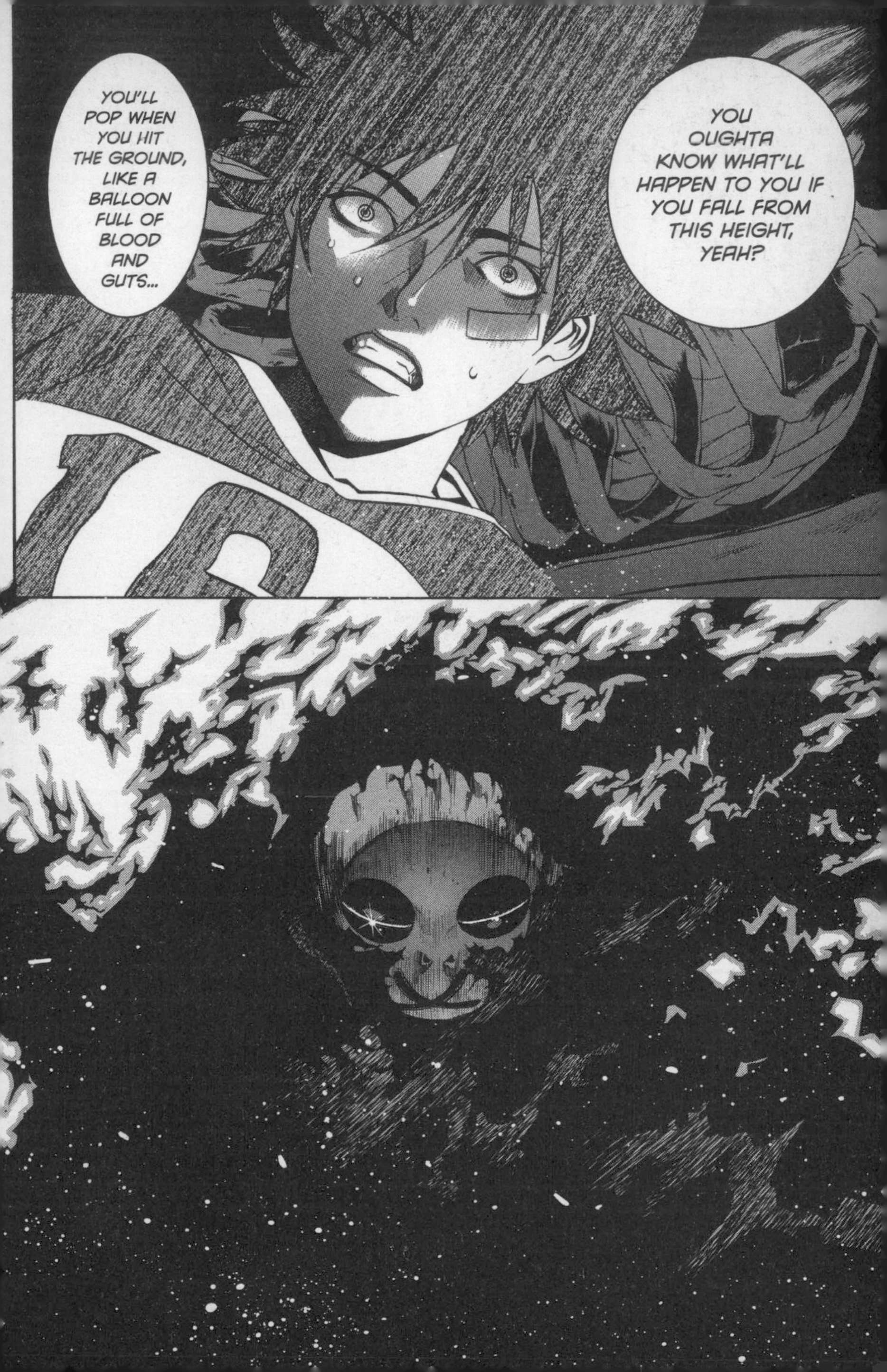
YOU OUGHTA KNOW WHAT'LL HAPPEN TO YOU IF YOU FALL FROM THIS HEIGHT, YEAH?
YOU'LL POP WHEN YOU HIT THE GROUND, LIKE A BALLOON FULL OF BLOOD AND GUTS...

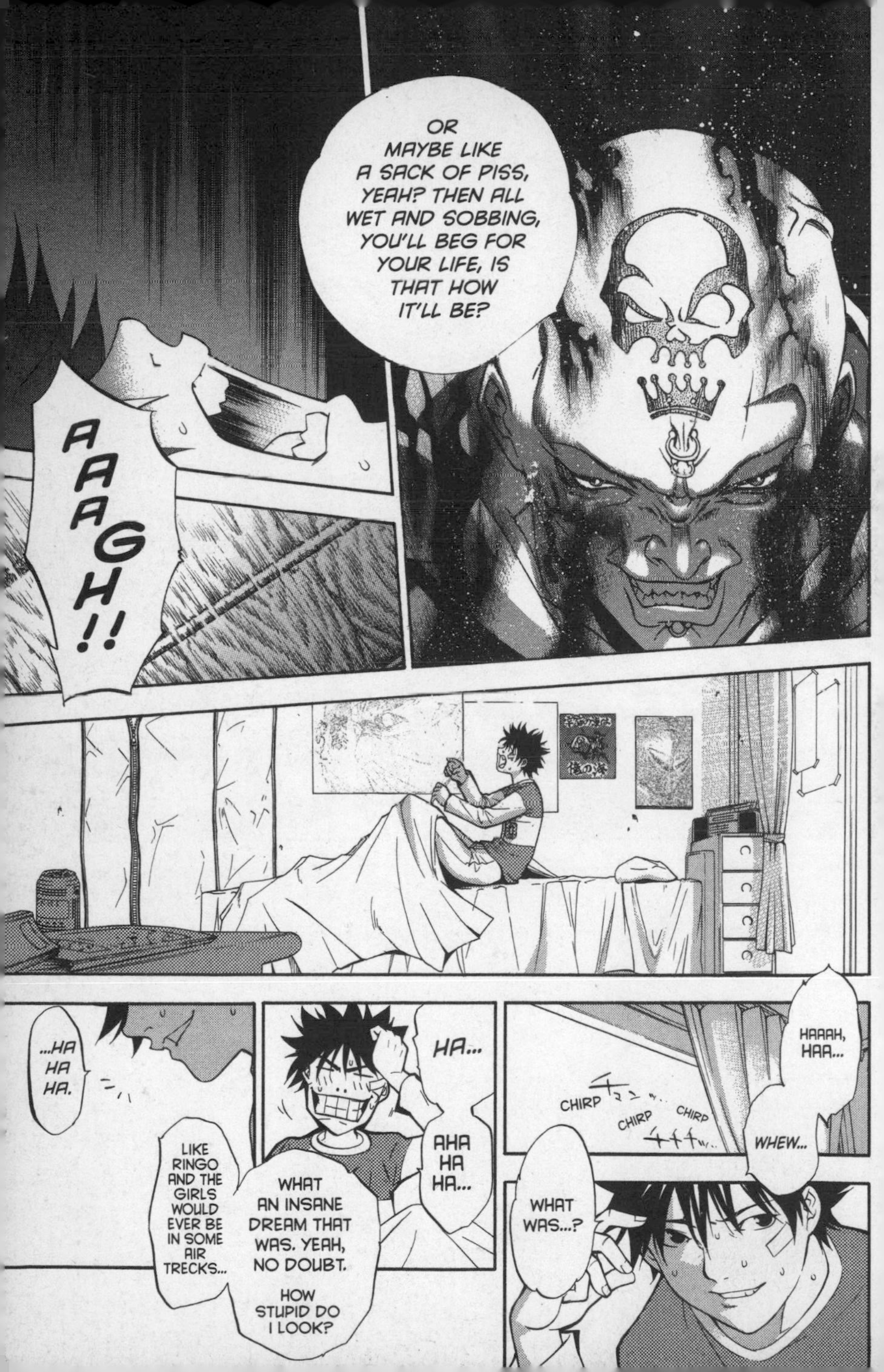
OR MAYBE LIKE A SACK OF PISS, YEAH? THEN ALL WET AND SOBBING, YOU'LL BEG FOR YOUR LIFE, IS THAT HOW IT'LL BE?
AAAGH!!
HAAAH, HAA...
CHIRP
CHIRP
CHIRP
WHEW...
WHAT WAS...?
HA...
AHA HA HA...
WHAT AN INSANE DREAM THAT WAS. YEAH, NO DOUBT.
HOW STUPID DO I LOOK?
...HA HA HA.
LIKE RINGO AND THE GIRLS WOULD EVER BE IN SOME AIR TRECKS...

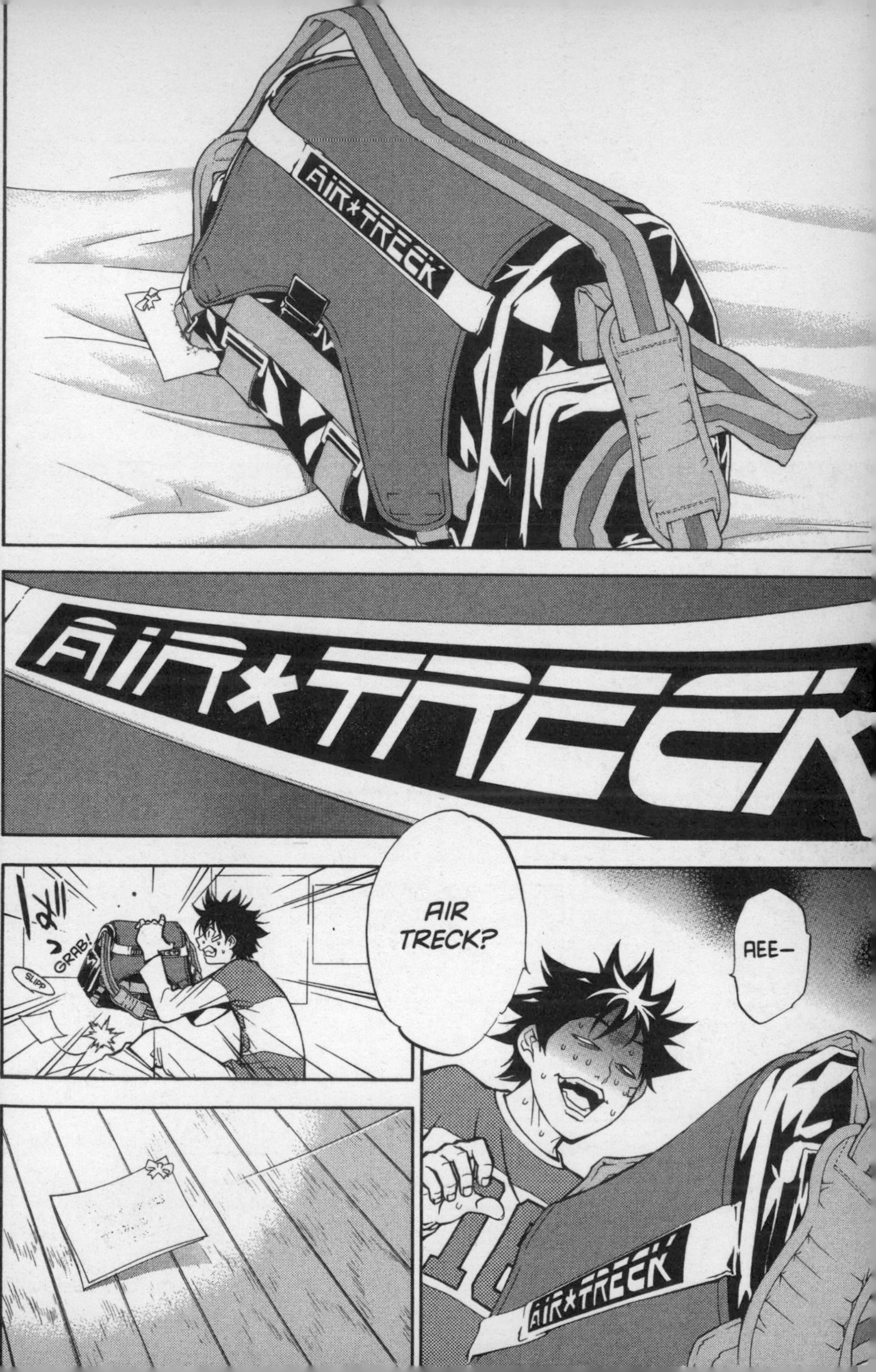
AIR★TRECK
AIR★TRECK
AEE—
AIR TRECK?
AIR★TRECK
GRAB!
SLIPP

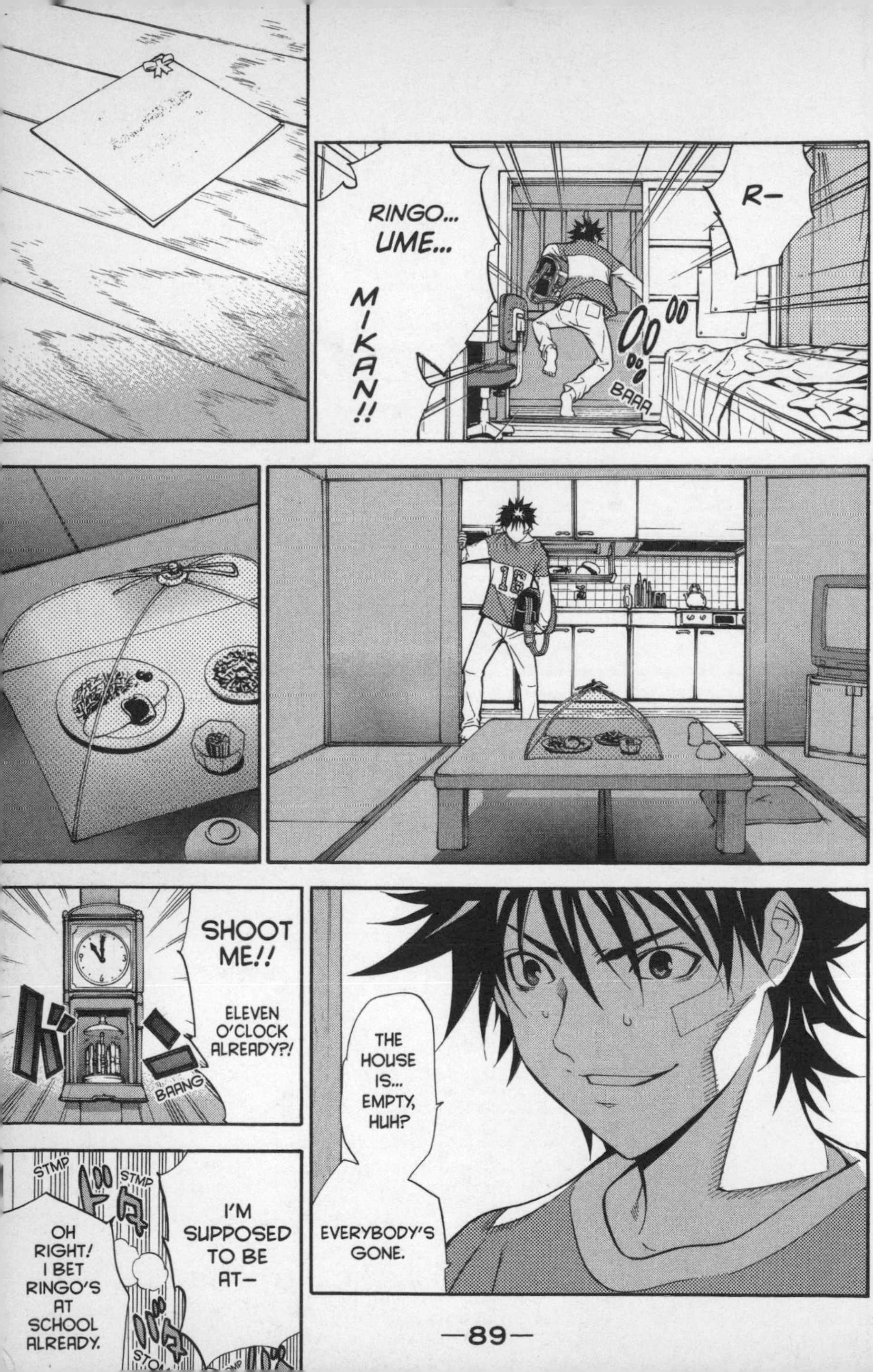
R–
RINGO... UME...
MIKAN!!
BAAA
THE HOUSE IS... EMPTY, HUH?
EVERYBODY'S GONE.
SHOOT ME!!
ELEVEN O'CLOCK ALREADY?!
BAANG
I'M SUPPOSED TO BE AT–
STMP
STMP
OH RIGHT! I BET RINGO'S AT SCHOOL ALREADY.

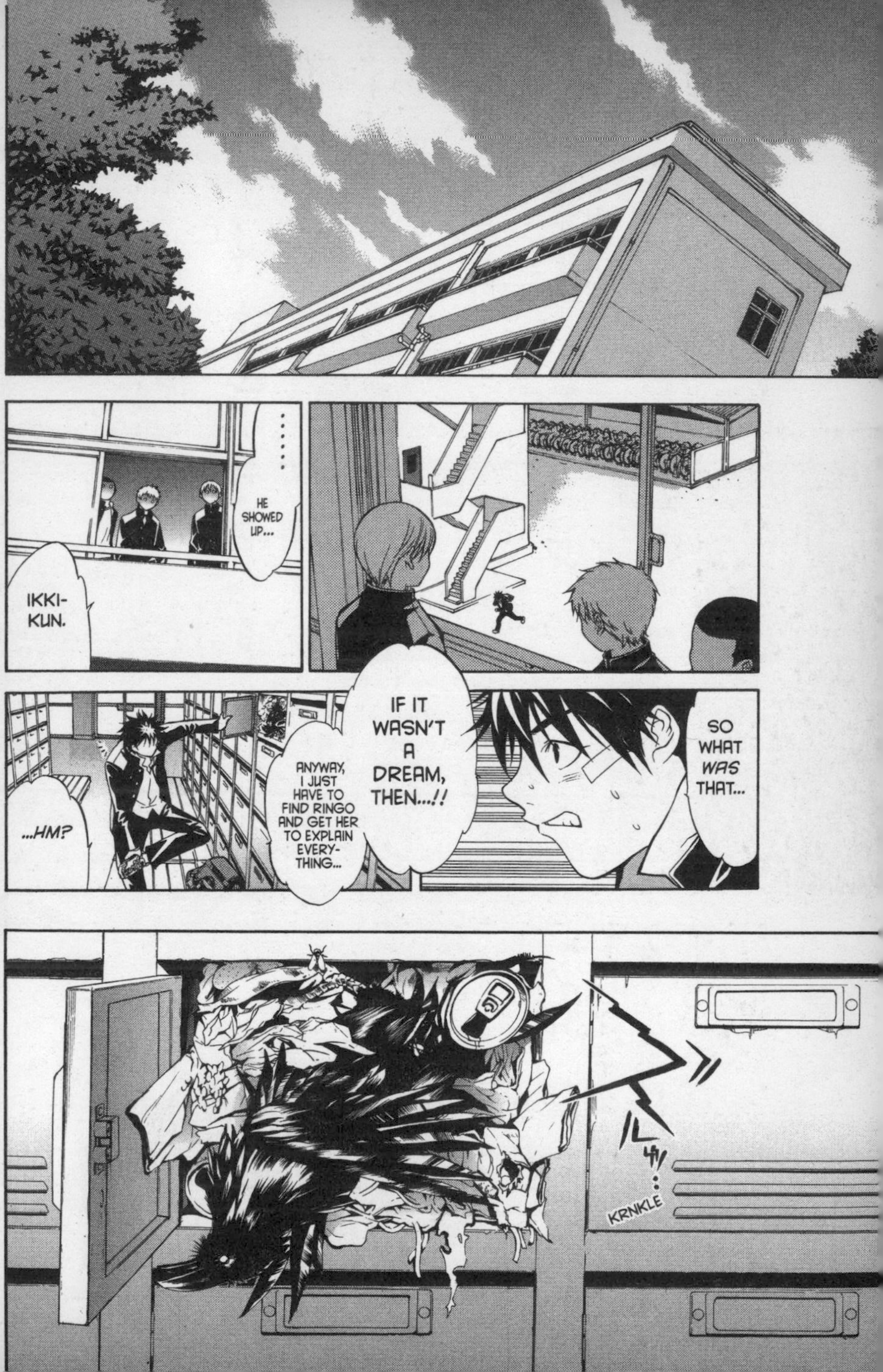
......
HE SHOWED UP...
IKKI-KUN.
SO WHAT *WAS* THAT...
IF IT WASN'T A DREAM, THEN...!!
ANYWAY, I JUST HAVE TO FIND RINGO AND GET HER TO EXPLAIN EVERYTHING...
...HM?
KRNKLE

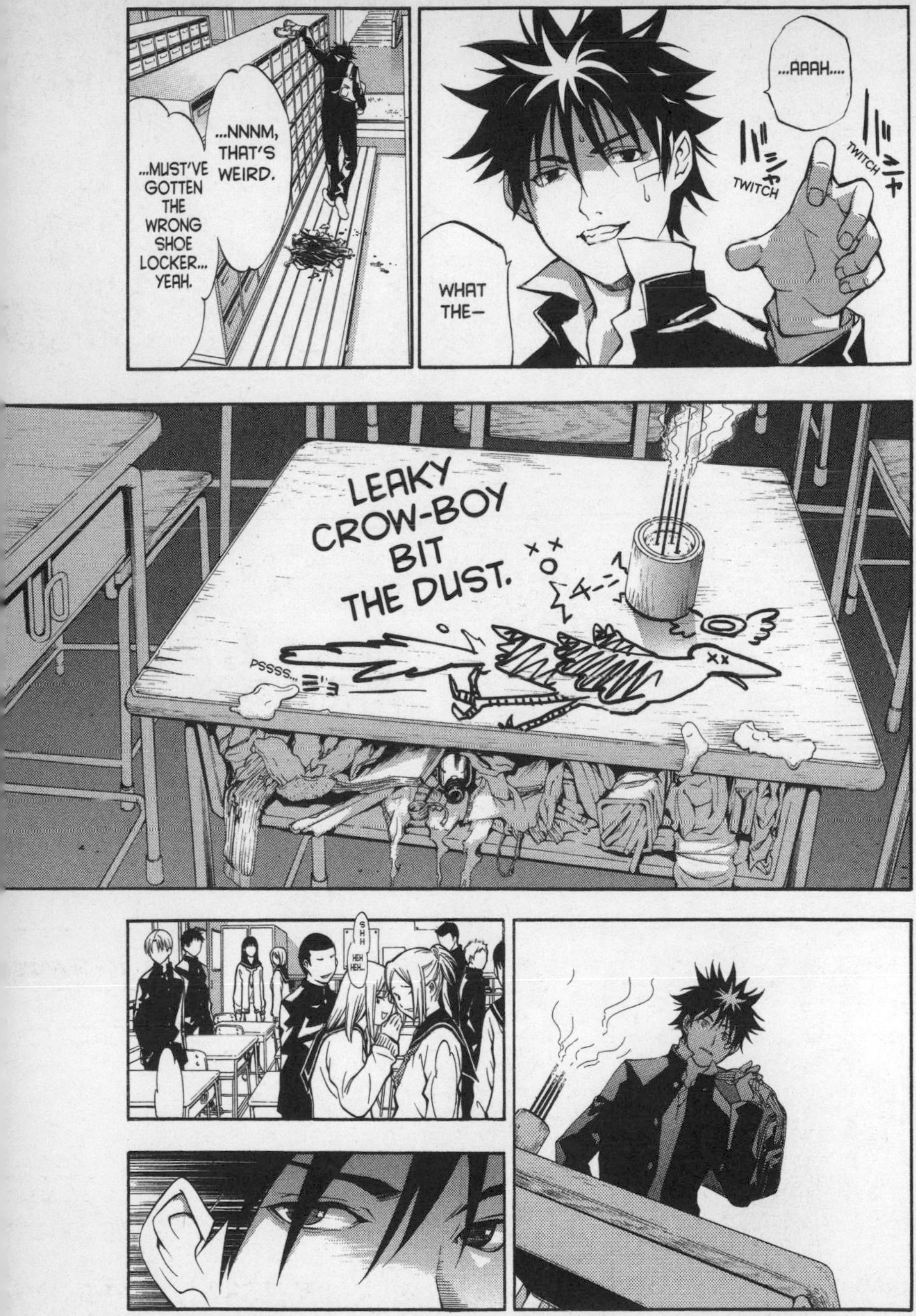
...AAAH....
TWITCH
TWITCH
WHAT THE—
...NNNM, THAT'S WEIRD.
...MUST'VE GOTTEN THE WRONG SHOE LOCKER... YEAH.
LEAKY CROW-BOY BIT THE DUST.
PSSSS...
SHH
HEH HEH.

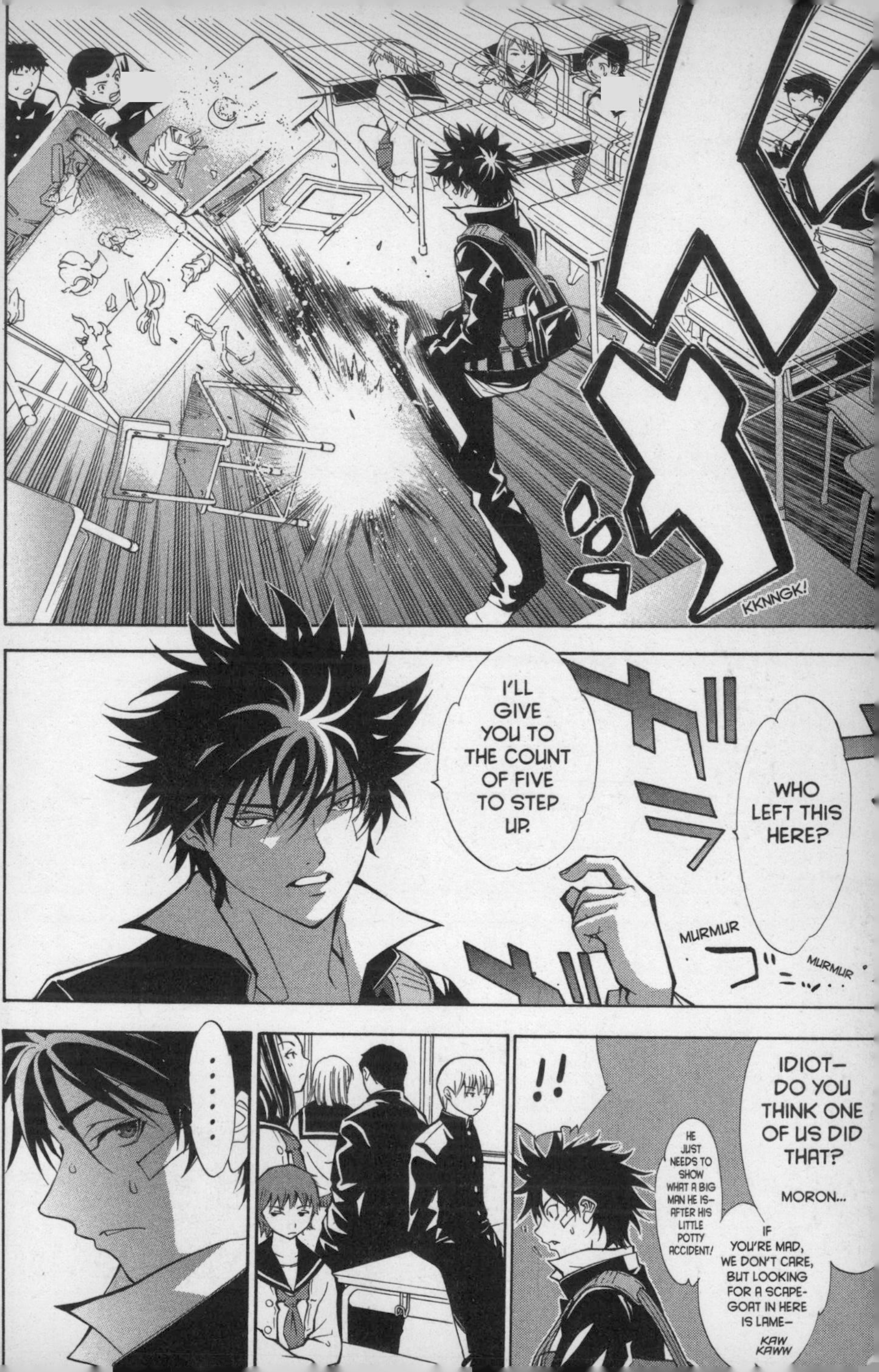
KKNNGK!
WHO LEFT THIS HERE?
I'LL GIVE YOU TO THE COUNT OF FIVE TO STEP UP.
MURMUR
MURMUR
IDIOT— DO YOU THINK ONE OF US DID THAT?
MORON...
HE JUST NEEDS TO SHOW WHAT A BIG MAN HE IS— AFTER HIS LITTLE POTTY ACCIDENT!
IF YOU'RE MAD, WE DON'T CARE, BUT LOOKING FOR A SCAPE-GOAT IN HERE IS LAME—
KAW KAWW
!!
......

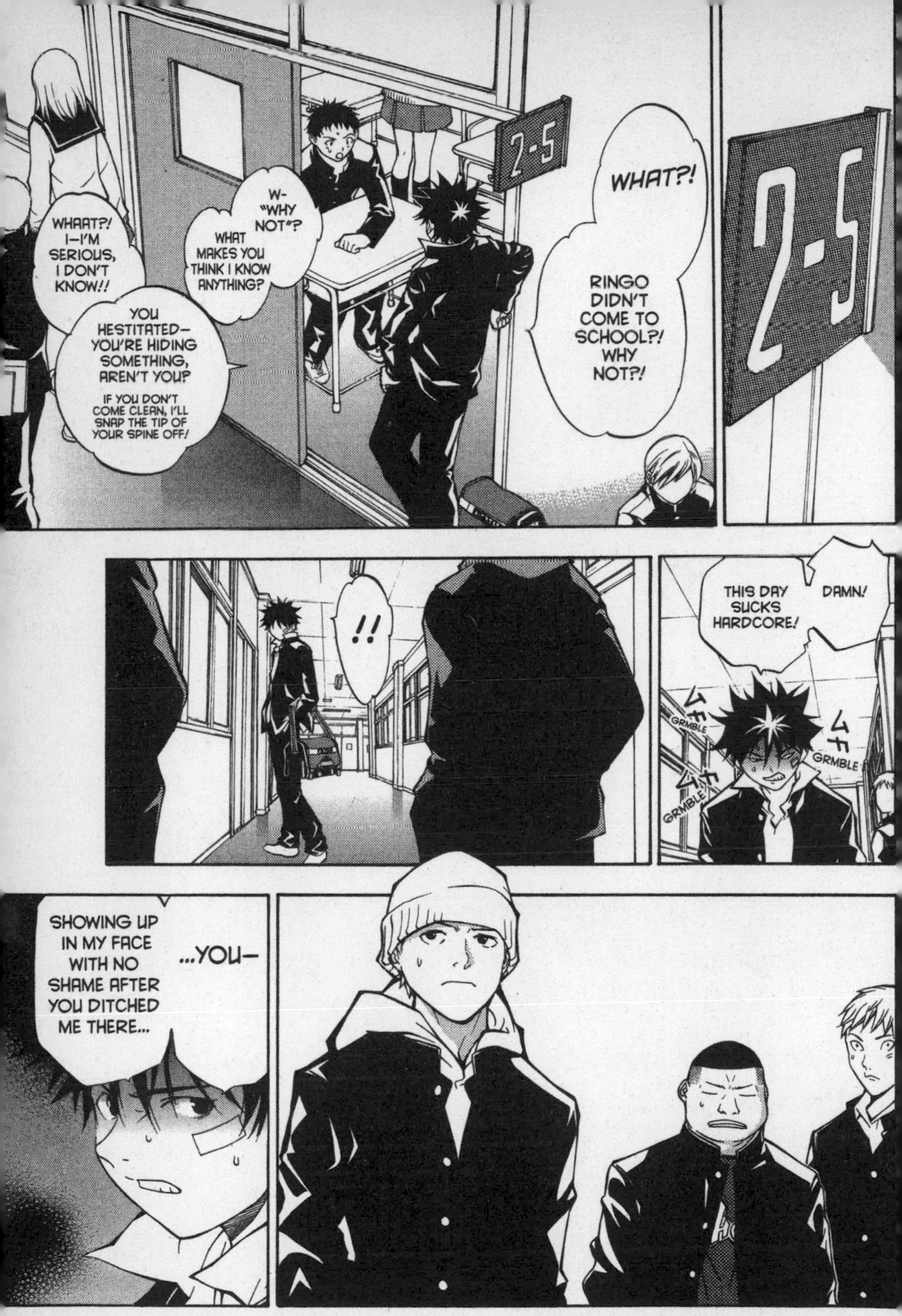
WHAT?!
RINGO DIDN'T COME TO SCHOOL?! WHY NOT?!
W- "WHY NOT"?
WHAT MAKES YOU THINK I KNOW ANYTHING?
YOU HESTITATED— YOU'RE HIDING SOMETHING, AREN'T YOU?
IF YOU DON'T COME CLEAN, I'LL SNAP THE TIP OF YOUR SPINE OFF!
WHAAT?! I—I'M SERIOUS, I DON'T KNOW!!
DAMN!
THIS DAY SUCKS HARDCORE!
GRMBLE
GRMBLE
GRMBLE
!!
...YOU—
SHOWING UP IN MY FACE WITH NO SHAME AFTER YOU DITCHED ME THERE...

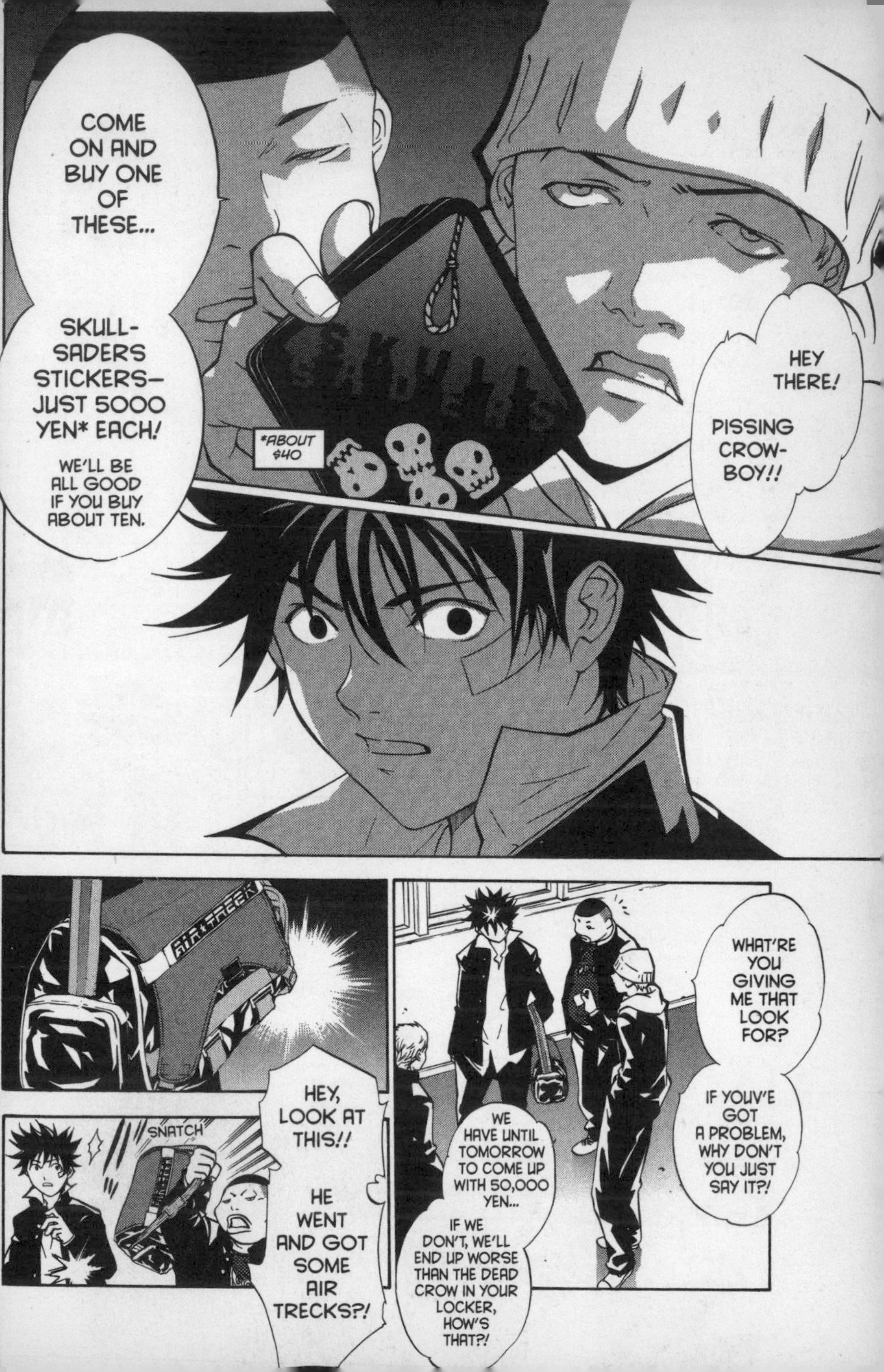
HEY THERE!
PISSING CROW-BOY!!
COME ON AND BUY ONE OF THESE...
SKULL-SADERS STICKERS—JUST 5000 YEN* EACH!
*ABOUT $40
WE'LL BE ALL GOOD IF YOU BUY ABOUT TEN.
WHAT'RE YOU GIVING ME THAT LOOK FOR?
IF YOUV'E GOT A PROBLEM, WHY DON'T YOU JUST SAY IT?!
WE HAVE UNTIL TOMORROW TO COME UP WITH 50,000 YEN...
IF WE DON'T, WE'LL END UP WORSE THAN THE DEAD CROW IN YOUR LOCKER, HOW'S THAT?!
SNATCH
HEY, LOOK AT THIS!!
HE WENT AND GOT SOME AIR TRECKS?!

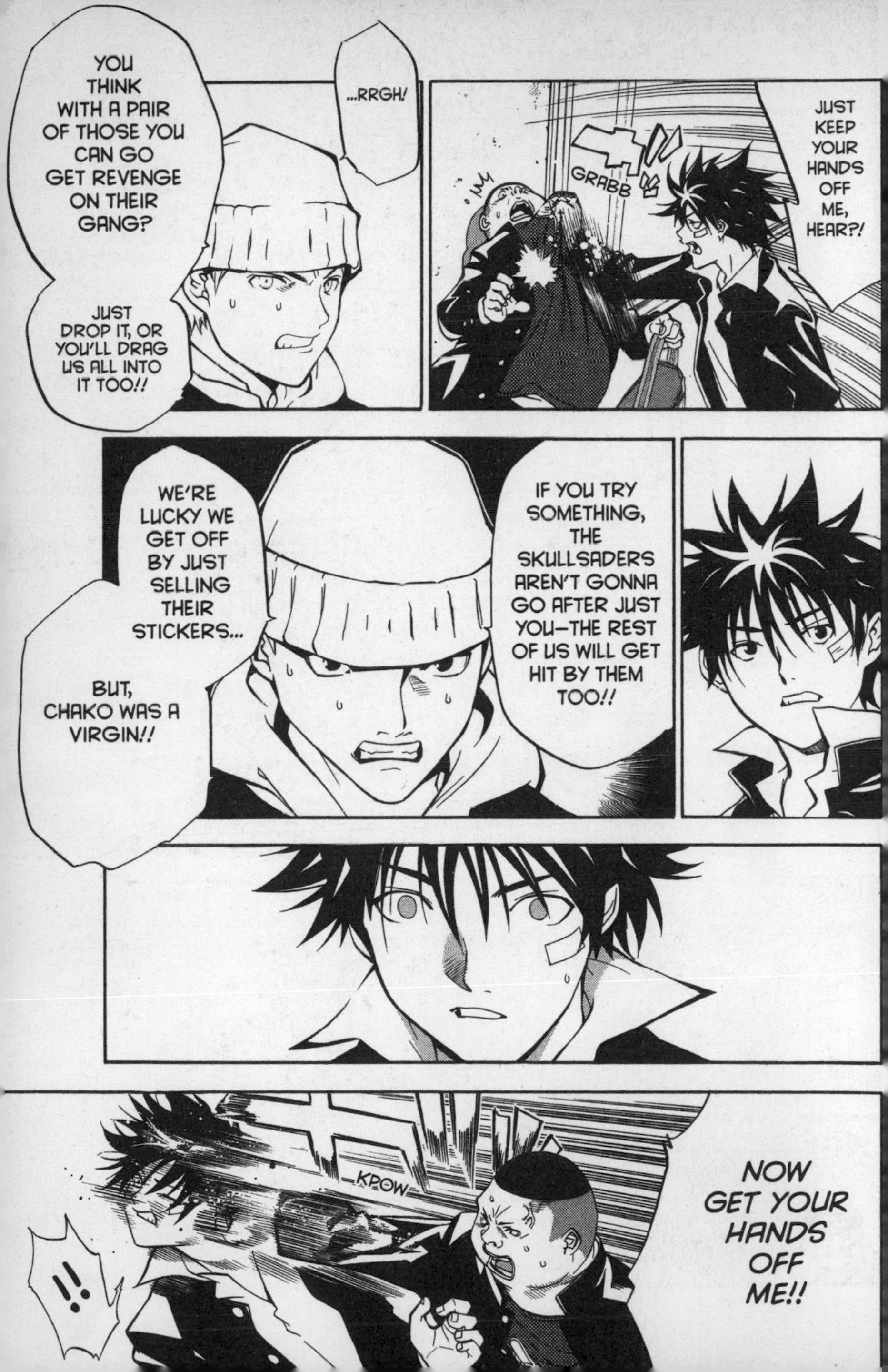
JUST KEEP YOUR HANDS OFF ME, HEAR?!
GRABB
...RRGH!
YOU THINK WITH A PAIR OF THOSE YOU CAN GO GET REVENGE ON THEIR GANG?
JUST DROP IT, OR YOU'LL DRAG US ALL INTO IT TOO!!
IF YOU TRY SOMETHING, THE SKULLSADERS AREN'T GONNA GO AFTER JUST YOU—THE REST OF US WILL GET HIT BY THEM TOO!!
WE'RE LUCKY WE GET OFF BY JUST SELLING THEIR STICKERS...
BUT, CHAKO WAS A VIRGIN!!
NOW GET YOUR HANDS OFF ME!!
KPOW
!!

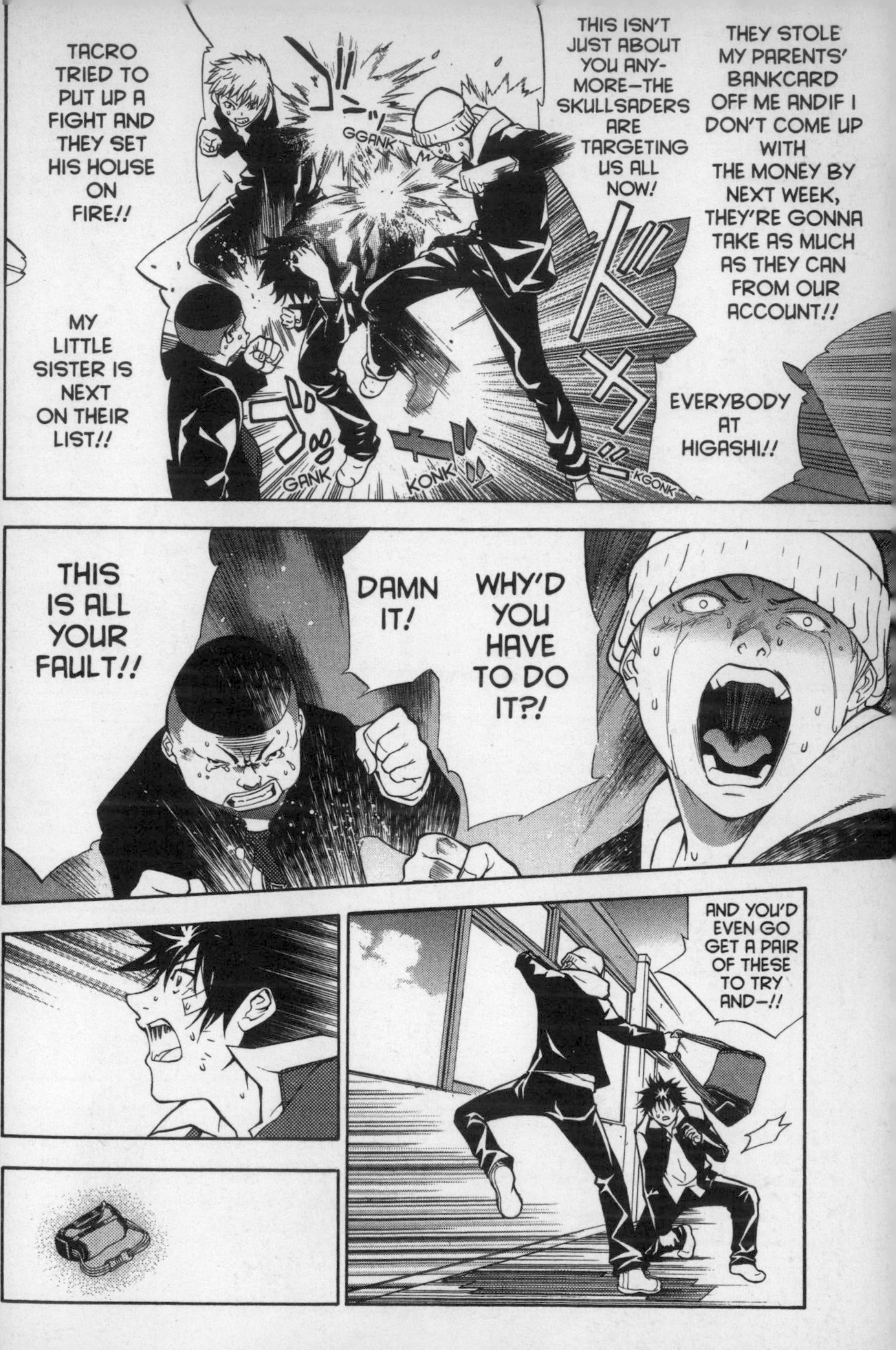
THEY STOLE MY PARENTS' BANKCARD OFF ME ANDIF I DON'T COME UP WITH THE MONEY BY NEXT WEEK, THEY'RE GONNA TAKE AS MUCH AS THEY CAN FROM OUR ACCOUNT!!
THIS ISN'T JUST ABOUT YOU ANY-MORE—THE SKULLSADERS ARE TARGETING US ALL NOW!
TACRO TRIED TO PUT UP A FIGHT AND THEY SET HIS HOUSE ON FIRE!!
GGANK
EVERYBODY AT HIGASHI!!
MY LITTLE SISTER IS NEXT ON THEIR LIST!!
KGONK
KONK
GANK
WHY'D YOU HAVE TO DO IT?!
DAMN IT!
THIS IS ALL YOUR FAULT!!
AND YOU'D EVEN GO GET A PAIR OF THESE TO TRY AND—!!

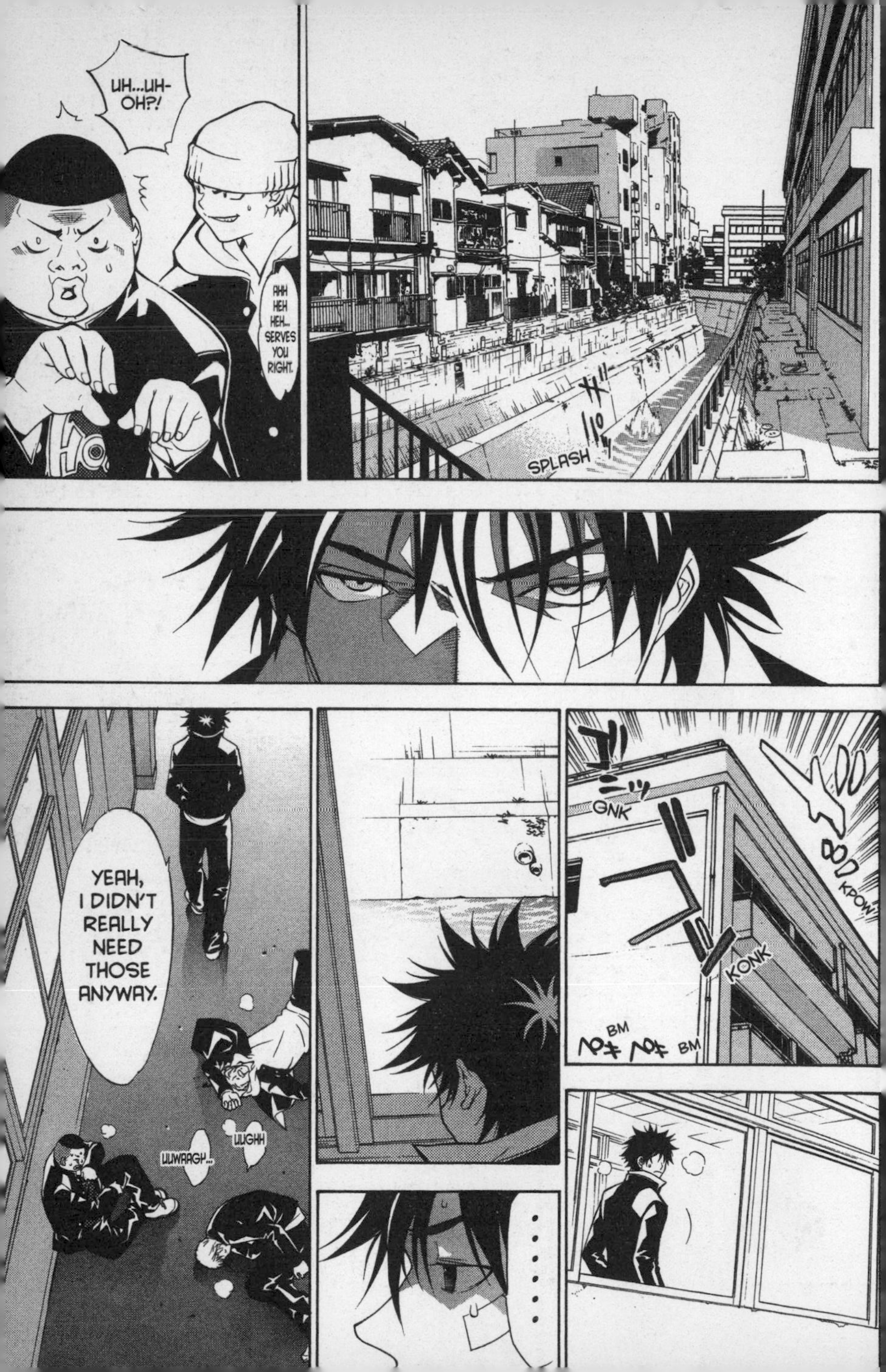
SPLASH
UH...UH-OH?!
AHH HEH HEH... SERVES YOU RIGHT.
GONK
KPOW
KONK
BM BM
......
YEAH, I DIDN'T REALLY NEED THOSE ANYWAY.
UUGHH
UUWAAGH...

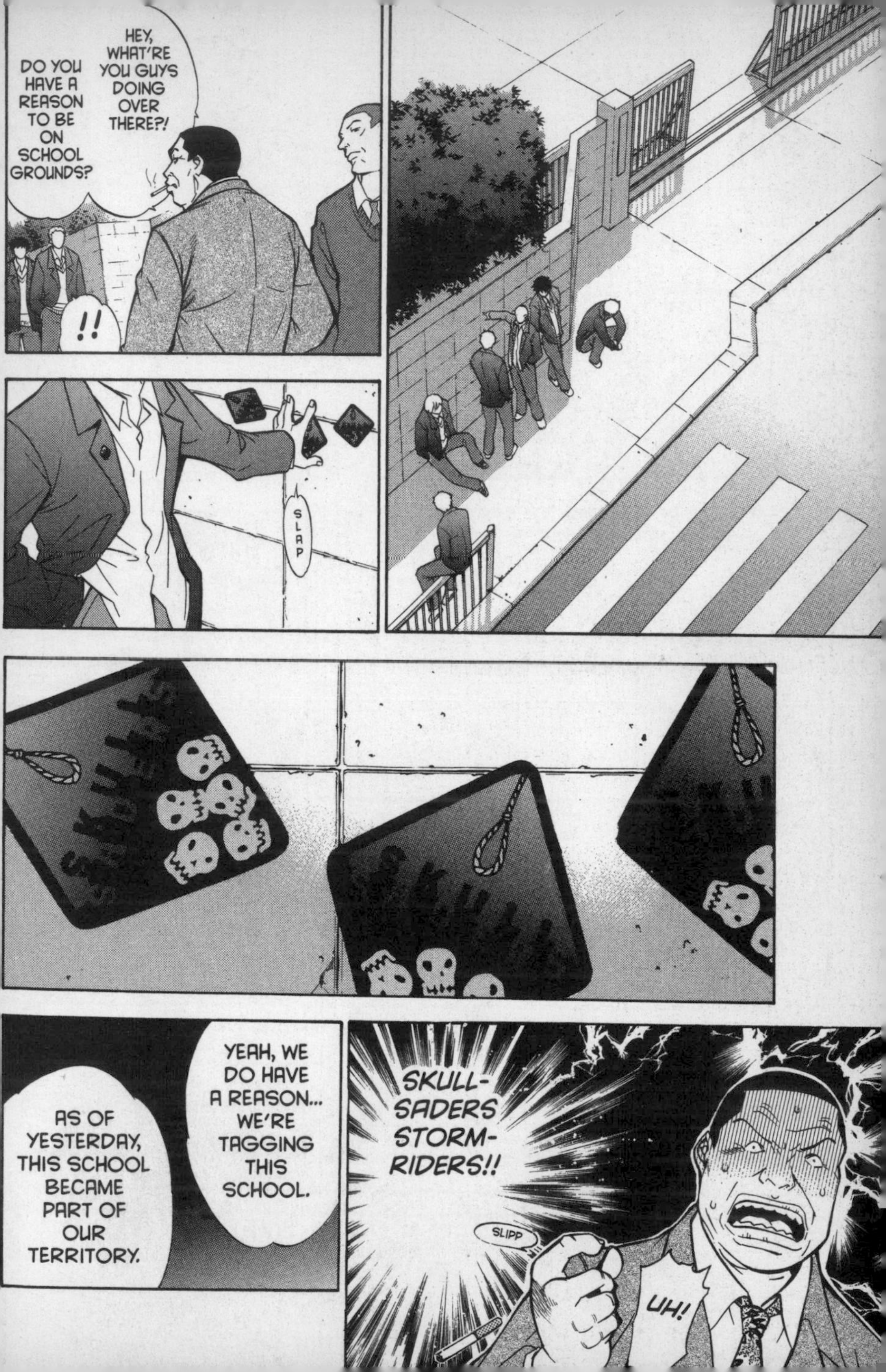
HEY, WHAT'RE YOU GUYS DOING OVER THERE?!
DO YOU HAVE A REASON TO BE ON SCHOOL GROUNDS?
!!
SLAP
YEAH, WE DO HAVE A REASON... WE'RE TAGGING THIS SCHOOL.
AS OF YESTERDAY, THIS SCHOOL BECAME PART OF OUR TERRITORY.
SKULL-SADERS STORM-RIDERS!!
SLIPP
UH!

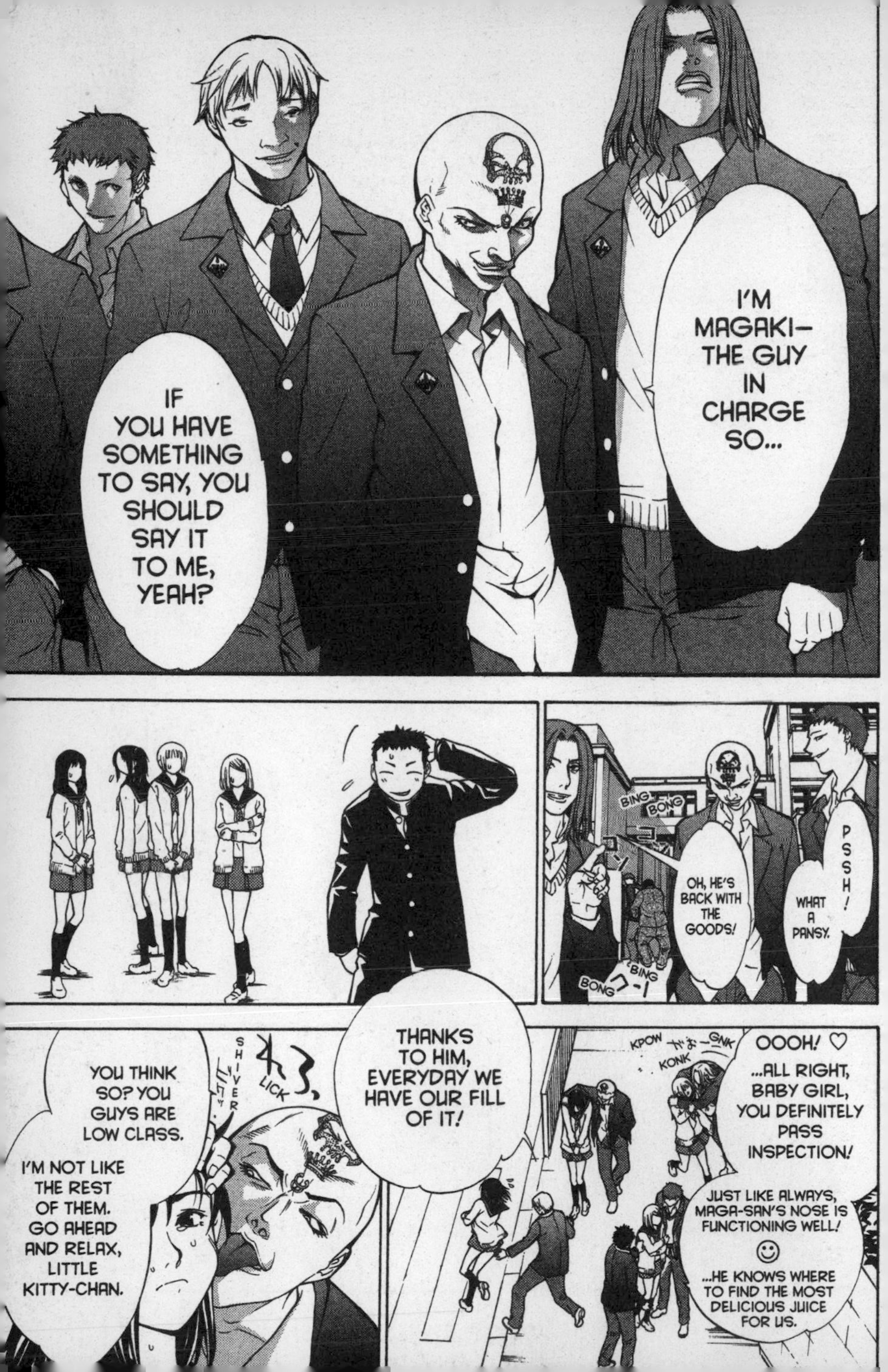

I'M MAGAKI— THE GUY IN CHARGE SO...
IF YOU HAVE SOMETHING TO SAY, YOU SHOULD SAY IT TO ME, YEAH?
PSSH! WHAT A PANSY.
BING BONG
OH, HE'S BACK WITH THE GOODS!
BING BONG
OOOH! ♡ ...ALL RIGHT, BABY GIRL, YOU DEFINITELY PASS INSPECTION!
GNK
KPOW
KONK
JUST LIKE ALWAYS, MAGA-SAN'S NOSE IS FUNCTIONING WELL! ☺ ...HE KNOWS WHERE TO FIND THE MOST DELICIOUS JUICE FOR US.
THANKS TO HIM, EVERYDAY WE HAVE OUR FILL OF IT!
LICK
SHIVER
YOU THINK SO? YOU GUYS ARE LOW CLASS.
I'M NOT LIKE THE REST OF THEM. GO AHEAD AND RELAX, LITTLE KITTY-CHAN.

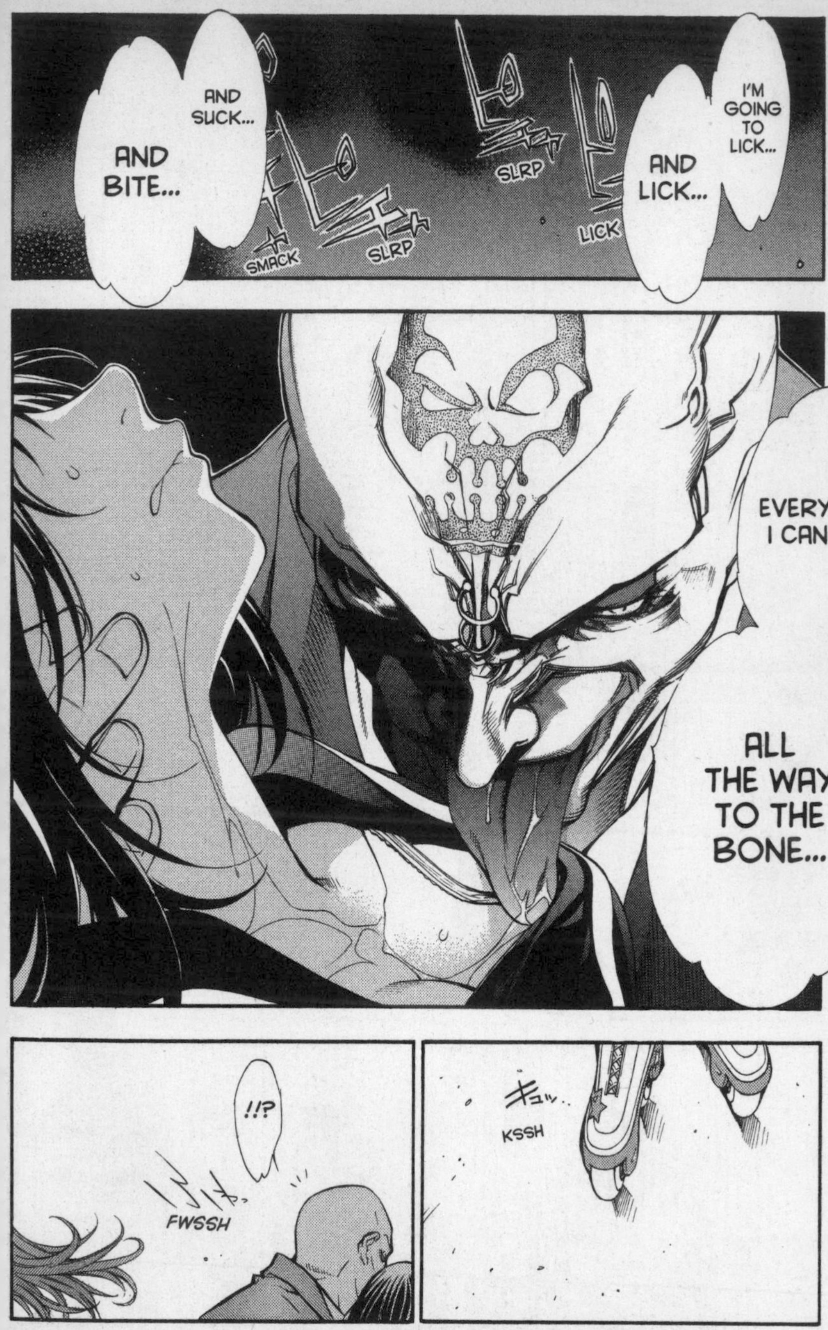
I'M GOING TO LICK...
AND LICK...
LICK
SLRP
SLRP
SMACK
AND SUCK...
AND BITE...
EVERYTHING I CAN SEE...
ALL THE WAY TO THE BONE...
KSSH
!!?
FWSSH

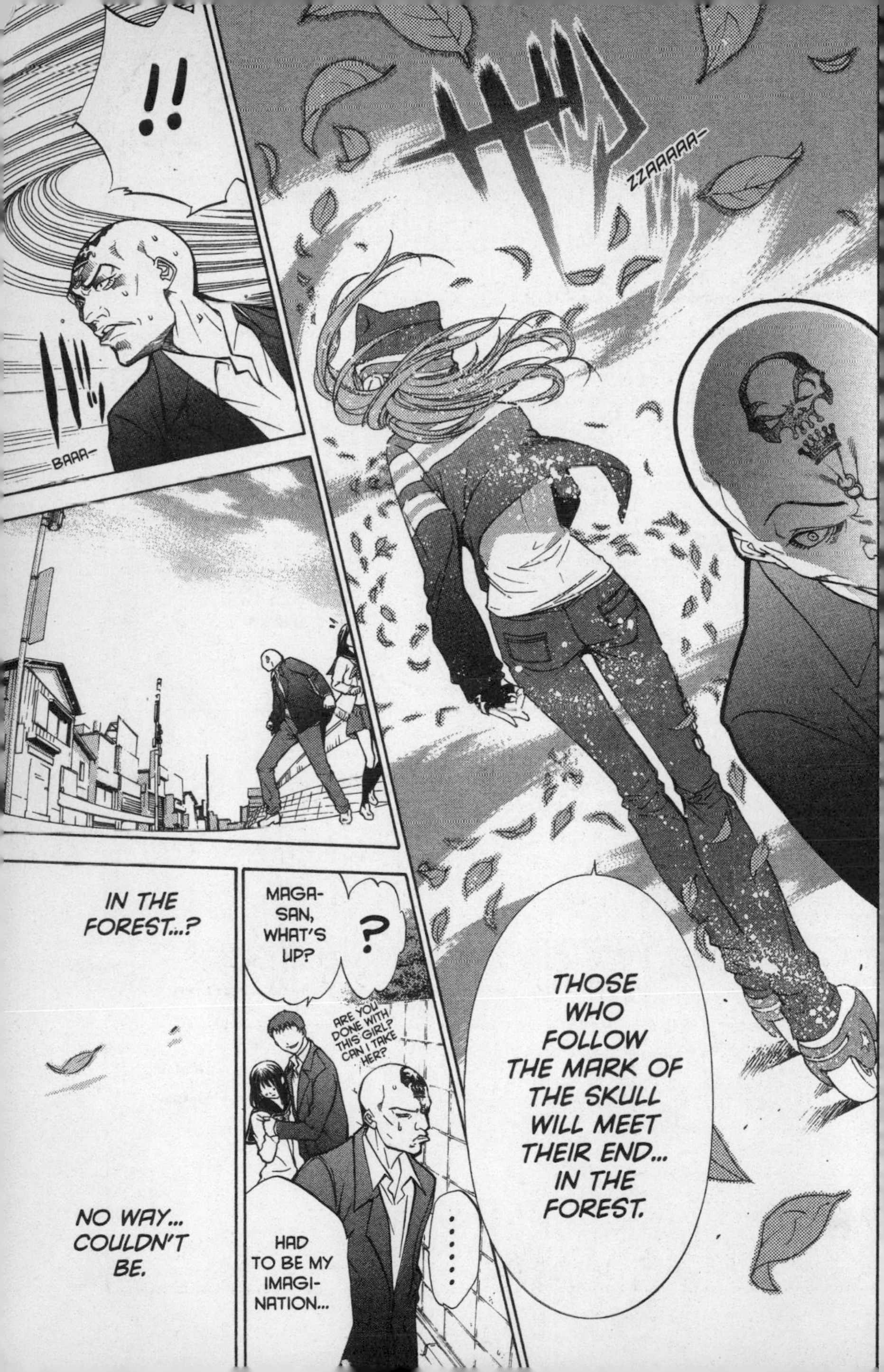
ZZAAAAAA-
THOSE WHO FOLLOW THE MARK OF THE SKULL WILL MEET THEIR END... IN THE FOREST.
!!
BAAA-
MAGA-SAN, WHAT'S UP?
?
ARE YOU DONE WITH THIS GIRL? CAN I TAKE HER?
......
HAD TO BE MY IMAGINATION...
IN THE FOREST...?
NO WAY... COULDN'T BE.

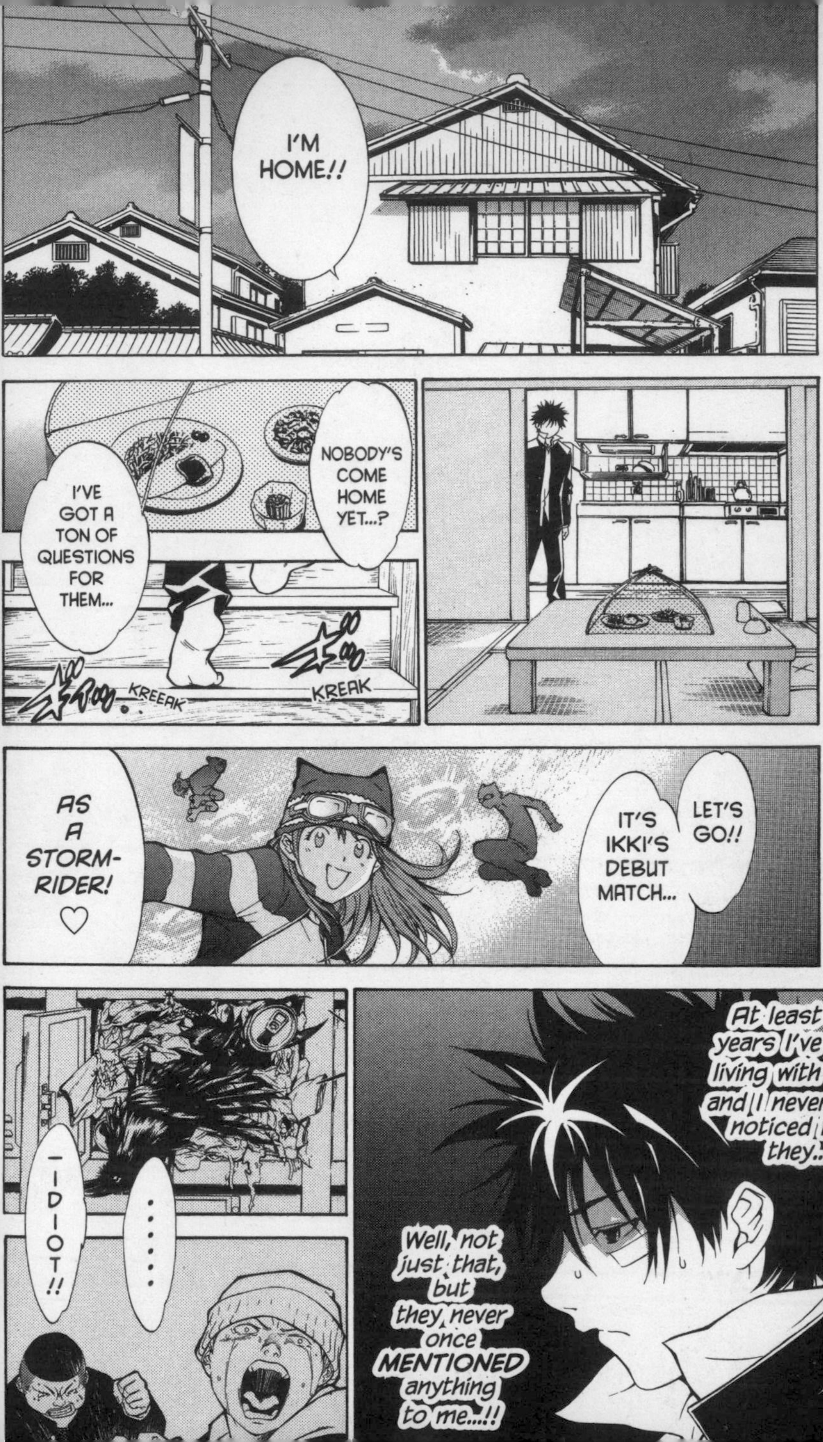
I'M HOME!!
NOBODY'S COME HOME YET...?
I'VE GOT A TON OF QUESTIONS FOR THEM...
KREAK
KREEAK
LET'S GO!!
IT'S IKKI'S DEBUT MATCH...
AS A STORM-RIDER! ♡
At least ten years I've been living with them and I never once noticed that they...
Well, not just that, but they never once MENTIONED anything to me...!!
......
—IDIOT!!

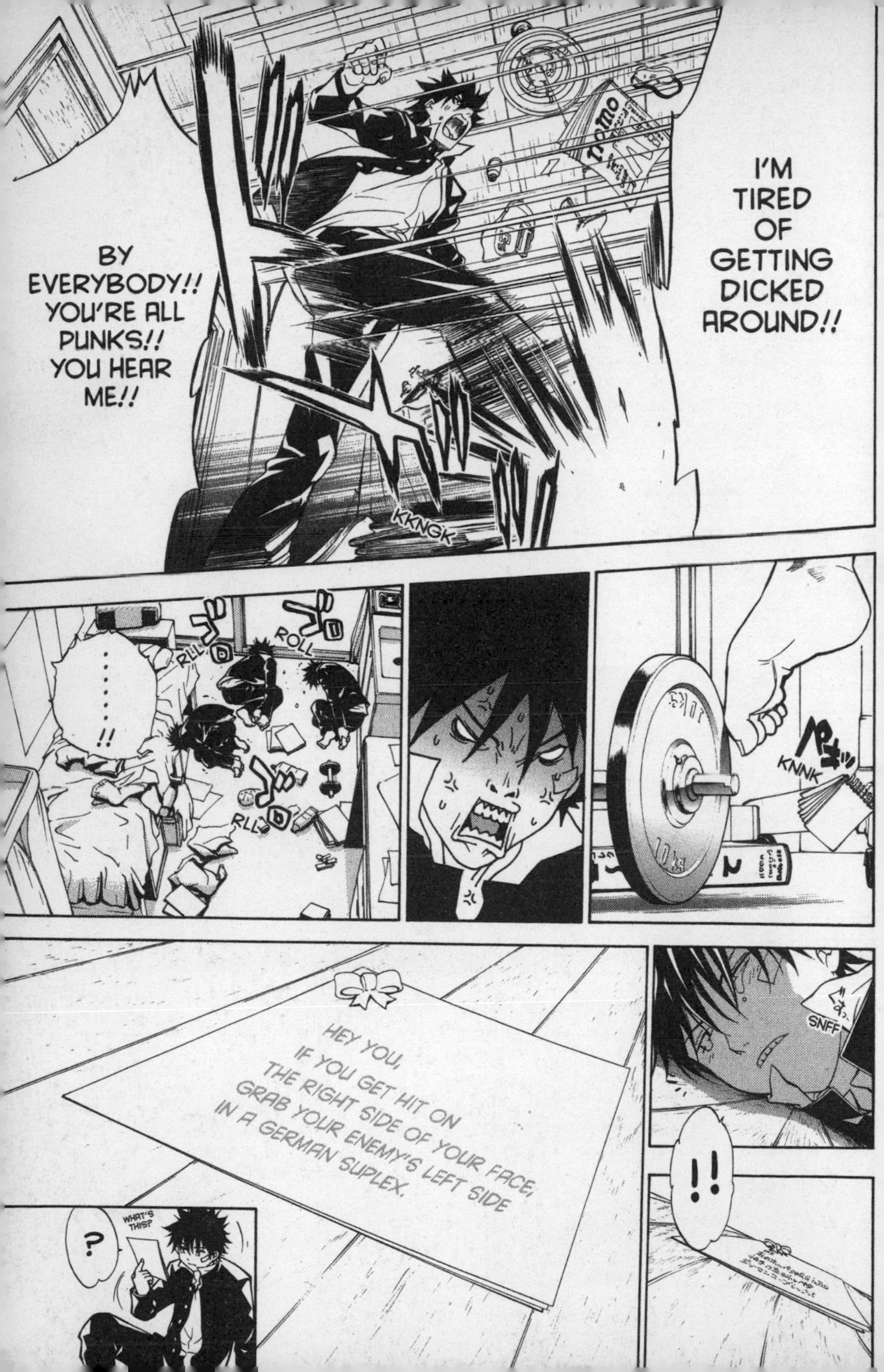
I'M TIRED OF GETTING DICKED AROUND!!
BY EVERYBODY!! YOU'RE ALL PUNKS!! YOU HEAR ME!!
KKNGK
KNNK
ROLL
RLL
RLL
......!!
SNFF
!!
HEY YOU,
IF YOU GET HIT ON
THE RIGHT SIDE OF YOUR FACE,
GRAB YOUR ENEMY'S LEFT SIDE
IN A GERMAN SUPLEX.
WHAT'S THIS?
?

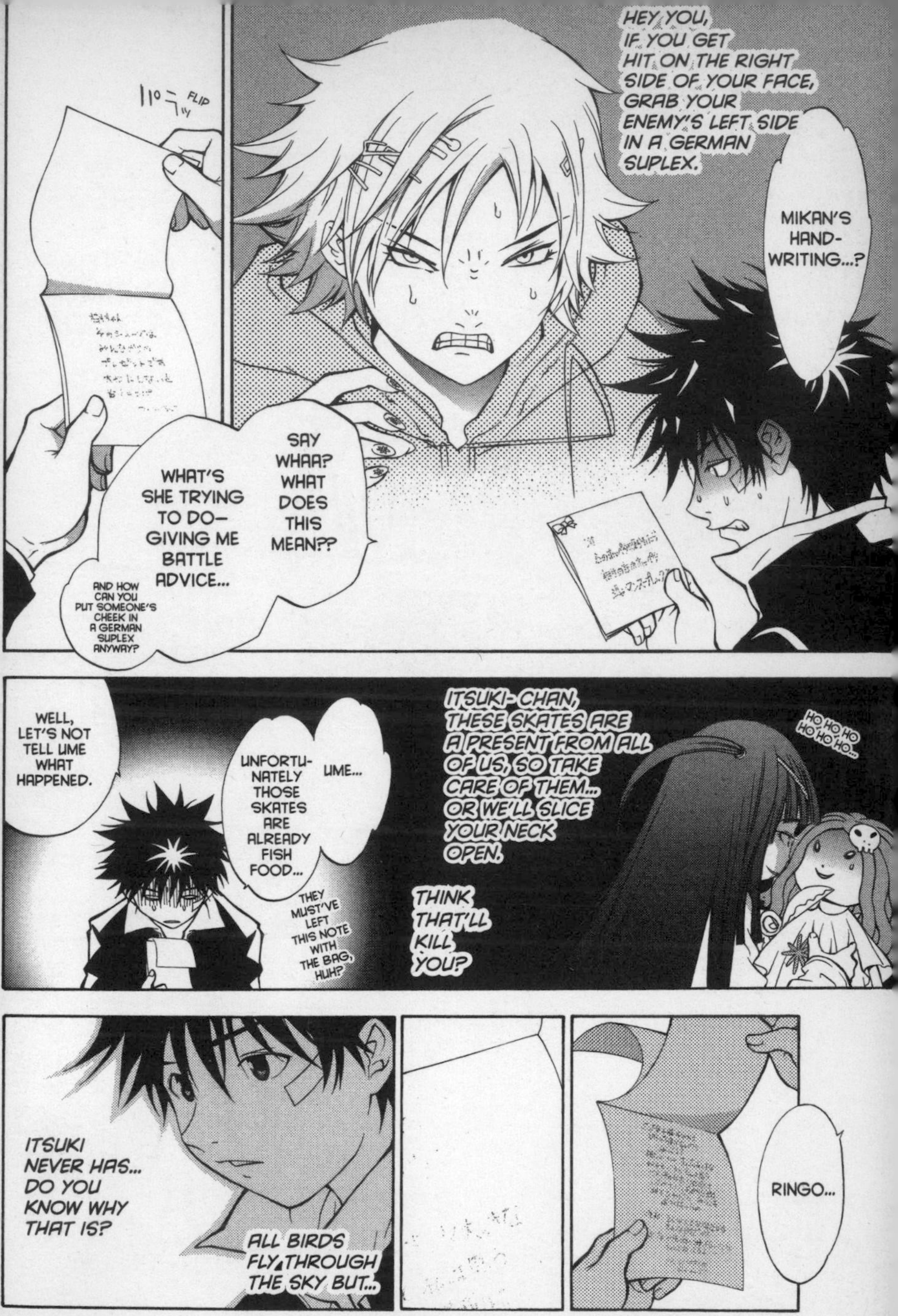
HEY YOU, IF YOU GET HIT ON THE RIGHT SIDE OF YOUR FACE, GRAB YOUR ENEMY'S LEFT SIDE IN A GERMAN SUPLEX.
MIKAN'S HAND-WRITING...?
SAY WHAA? WHAT DOES THIS MEAN??
WHAT'S SHE TRYING TO DO— GIVING ME BATTLE ADVICE...
AND HOW CAN YOU PUT SOMEONE'S CHEEK IN A GERMAN SUPLEX ANYWAY?
FLIP
HO HO HO HO HO HO...
ITSUKI-CHAN, THESE SKATES ARE A PRESENT FROM ALL OF US, SO TAKE CARE OF THEM... OR WE'LL SLICE YOUR NECK OPEN.
THINK THAT'LL KILL YOU?
UME...
UNFORTU-NATELY THOSE SKATES ARE ALREADY FISH FOOD...
THEY MUST'VE LEFT THIS NOTE WITH THE BAG, HUH?
WELL, LET'S NOT TELL UME WHAT HAPPENED.
RINGO...
ALL BIRDS FLY THROUGH THE SKY BUT...
ITSUKI NEVER HAS... DO YOU KNOW WHY THAT IS?

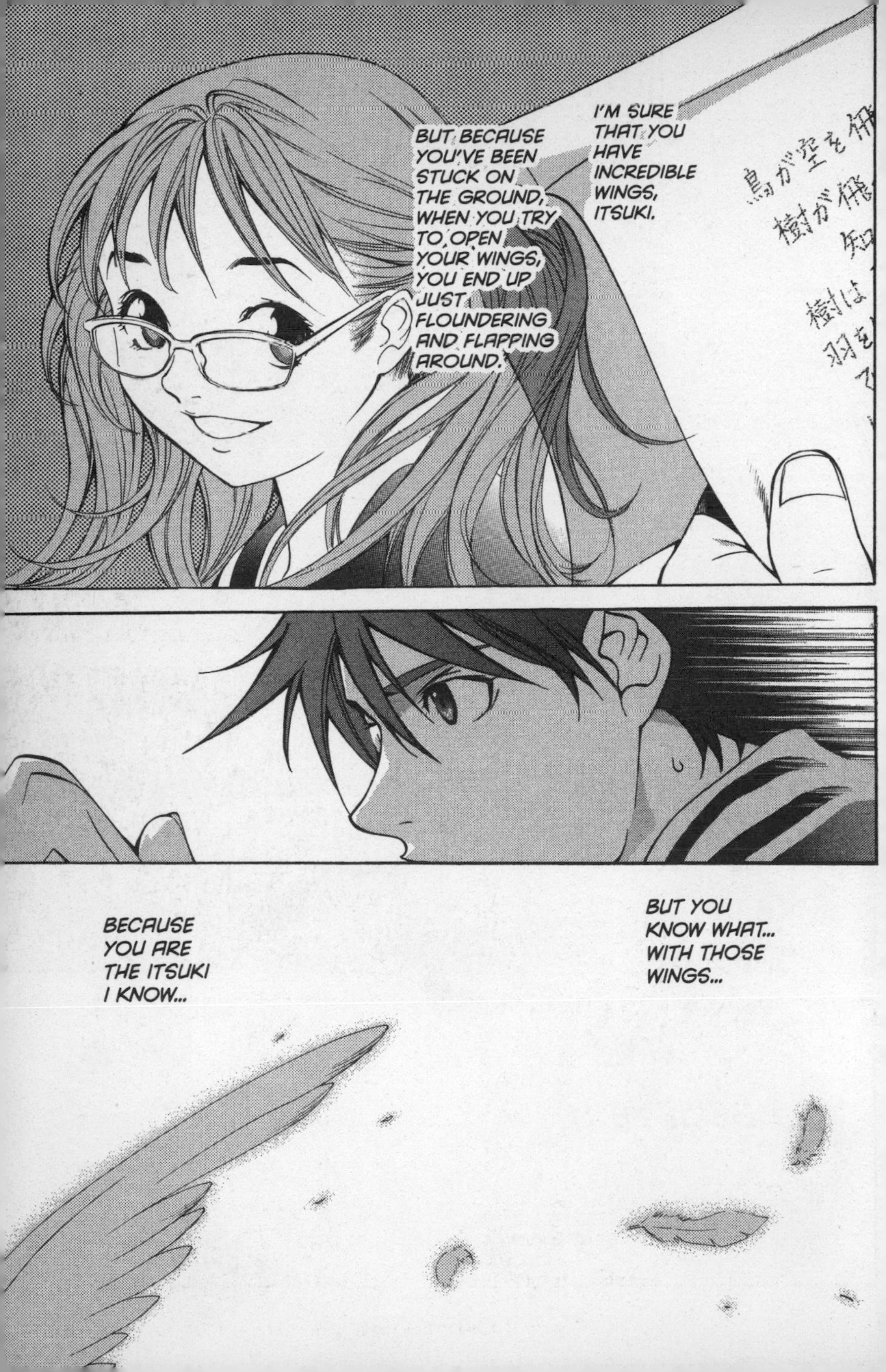
I'M SURE THAT YOU HAVE INCREDIBLE WINGS, ITSUKI.
BUT BECAUSE YOU'VE BEEN STUCK ON THE GROUND, WHEN YOU TRY TO OPEN YOUR WINGS, YOU END UP JUST FLOUNDERING AND FLAPPING AROUND.
BUT YOU KNOW WHAT... WITH THOSE WINGS...
BECAUSE YOU ARE THE ITSUKI I KNOW...

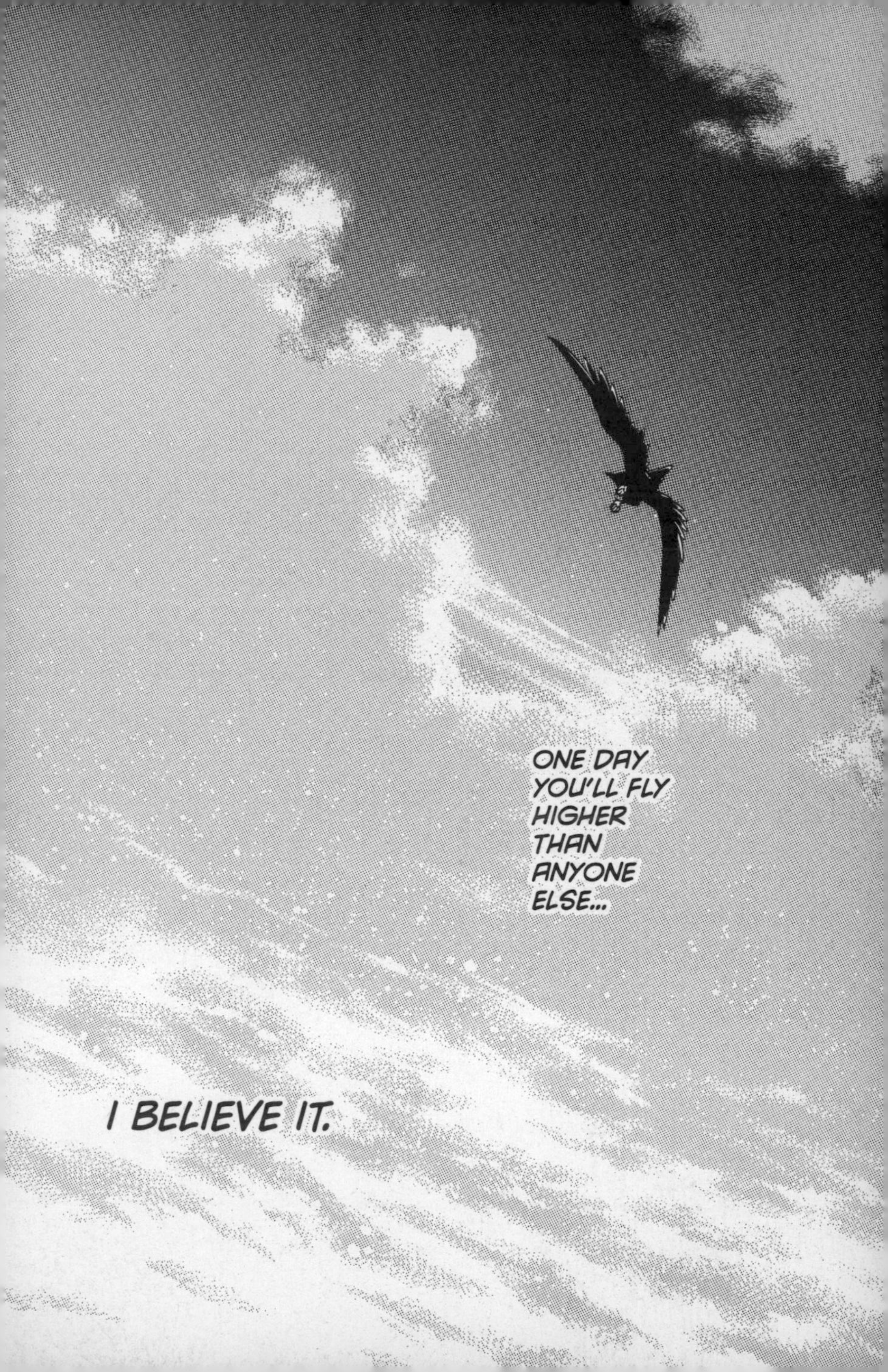
ONE DAY YOU'LL FLY HIGHER THAN ANYONE ELSE...
I BELIEVE IT.

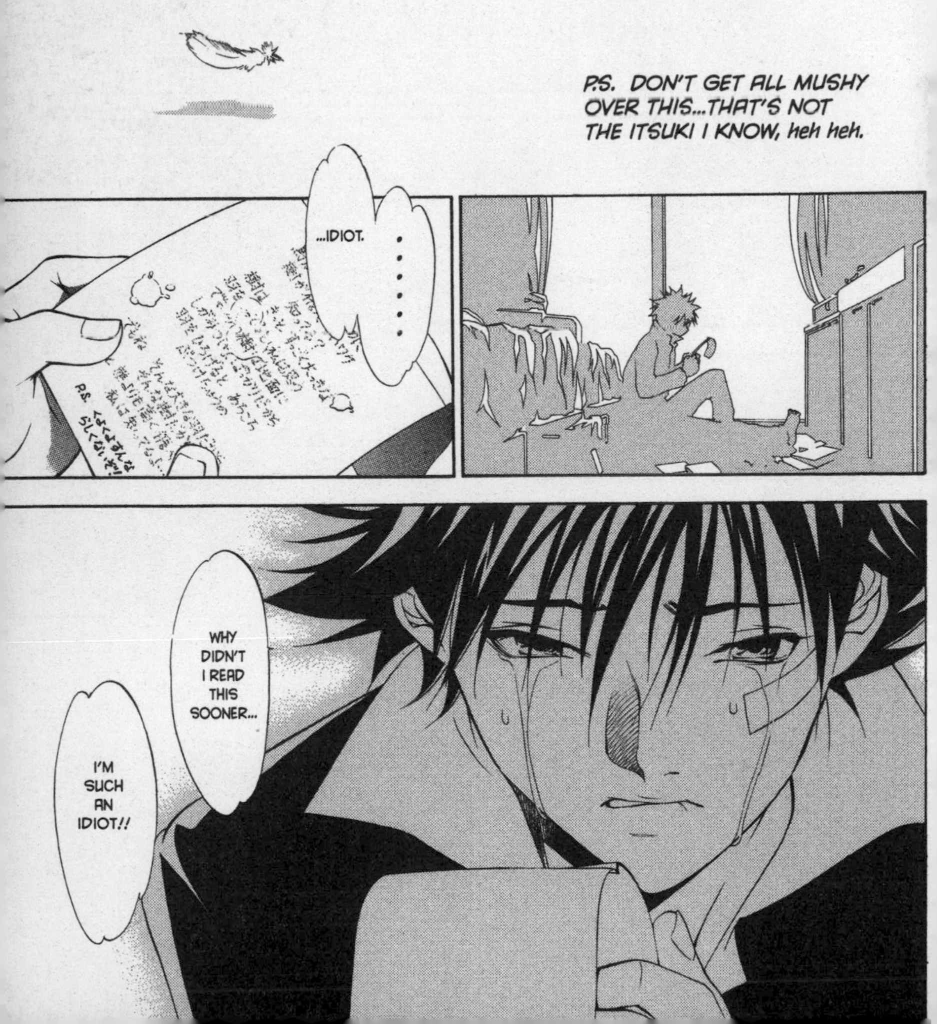
P.S. DON'T GET ALL MUSHY OVER THIS...THAT'S NOT THE ITSUKI I KNOW, heh heh.
...IDIOT.
......
WHY DIDN'T I READ THIS SOONER...
I'M SUCH AN IDIOT!!

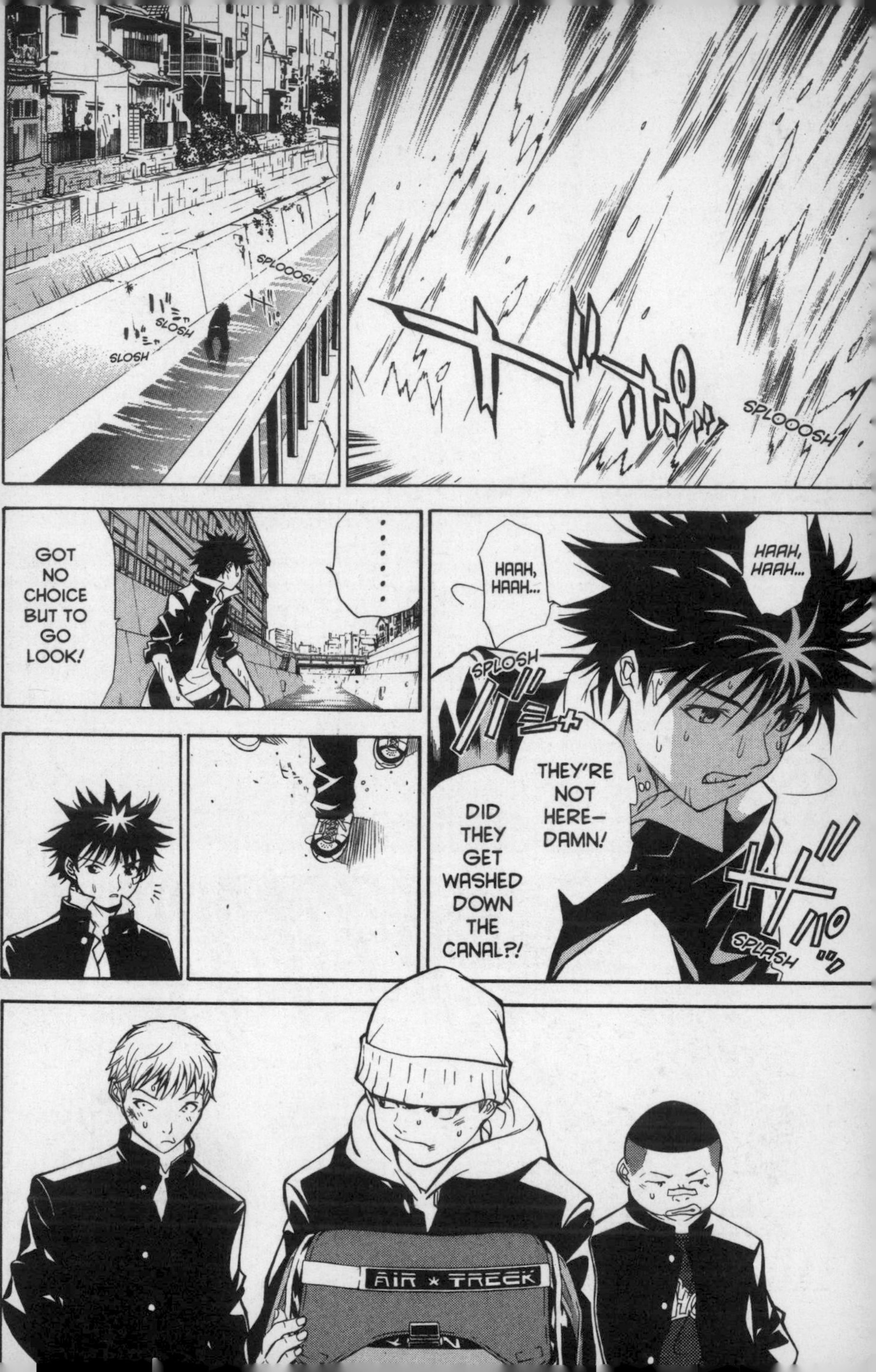
SPLOOOSH
SPLOOOSH
SLOSH
SLOSH
HAAH, HAAH...
HAAH, HAAH...
SPLOSH
THEY'RE NOT HERE— DAMN!
DID THEY GET WASHED DOWN THE CANAL?!
SPLASH
......
GOT NO CHOICE BUT TO GO LOOK!
AIR ★ TRECK

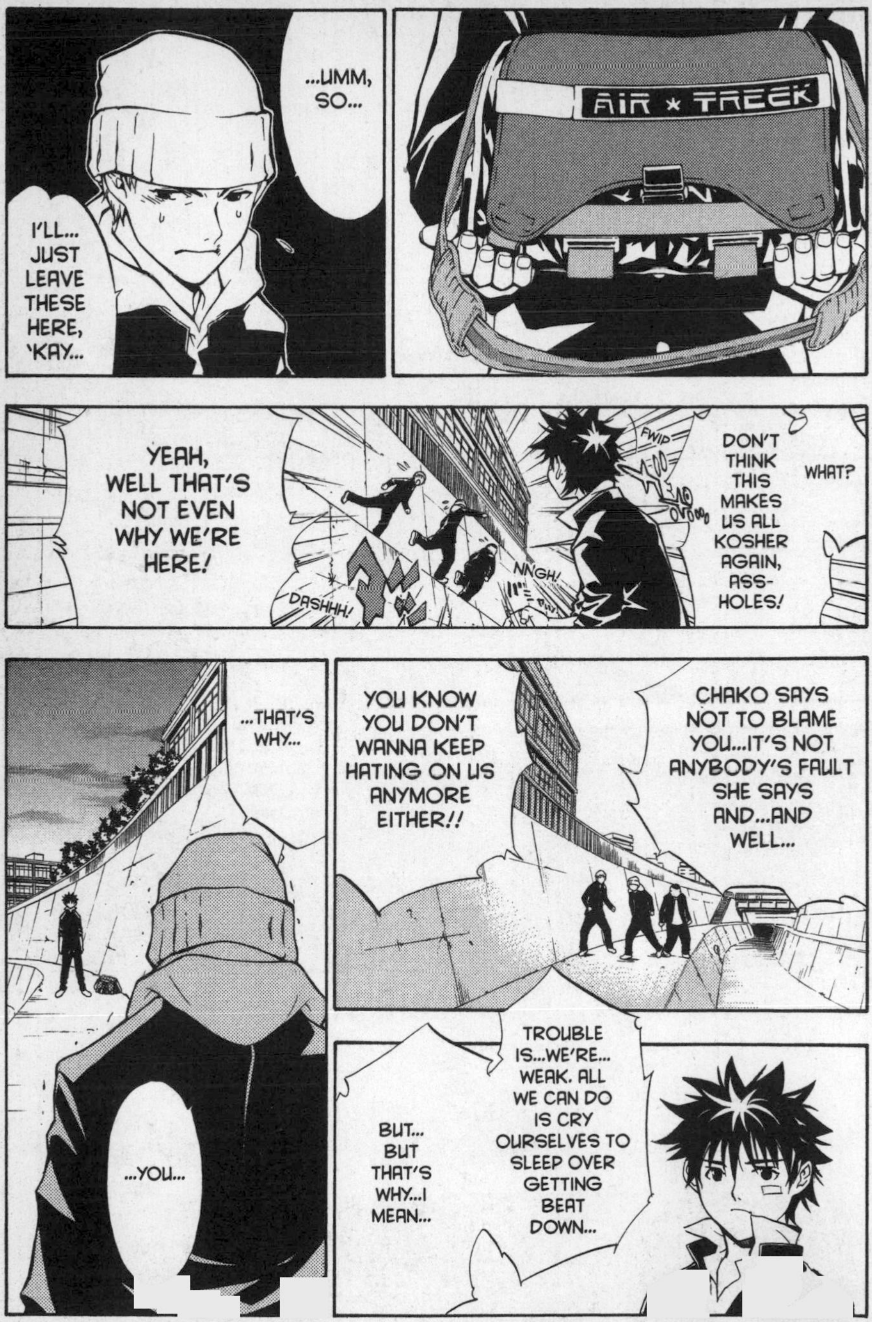
AIR ★ TREEK
...UMM, SO...
I'LL... JUST LEAVE THESE HERE, 'KAY...
WHAT?
DON'T THINK THIS MAKES US ALL KOSHER AGAIN, ASS-HOLES!
FWIP
NNGH!
DASHHH!
YEAH, WELL THAT'S NOT EVEN WHY WE'RE HERE!
CHAKO SAYS NOT TO BLAME YOU...IT'S NOT ANYBODY'S FAULT SHE SAYS AND...AND WELL...
YOU KNOW YOU DON'T WANNA KEEP HATING ON US ANYMORE EITHER!!
TROUBLE IS...WE'RE... WEAK. ALL WE CAN DO IS CRY OURSELVES TO SLEEP OVER GETTING BEAT DOWN...
BUT... BUT THAT'S WHY...I MEAN...
...THAT'S WHY...
...YOU...

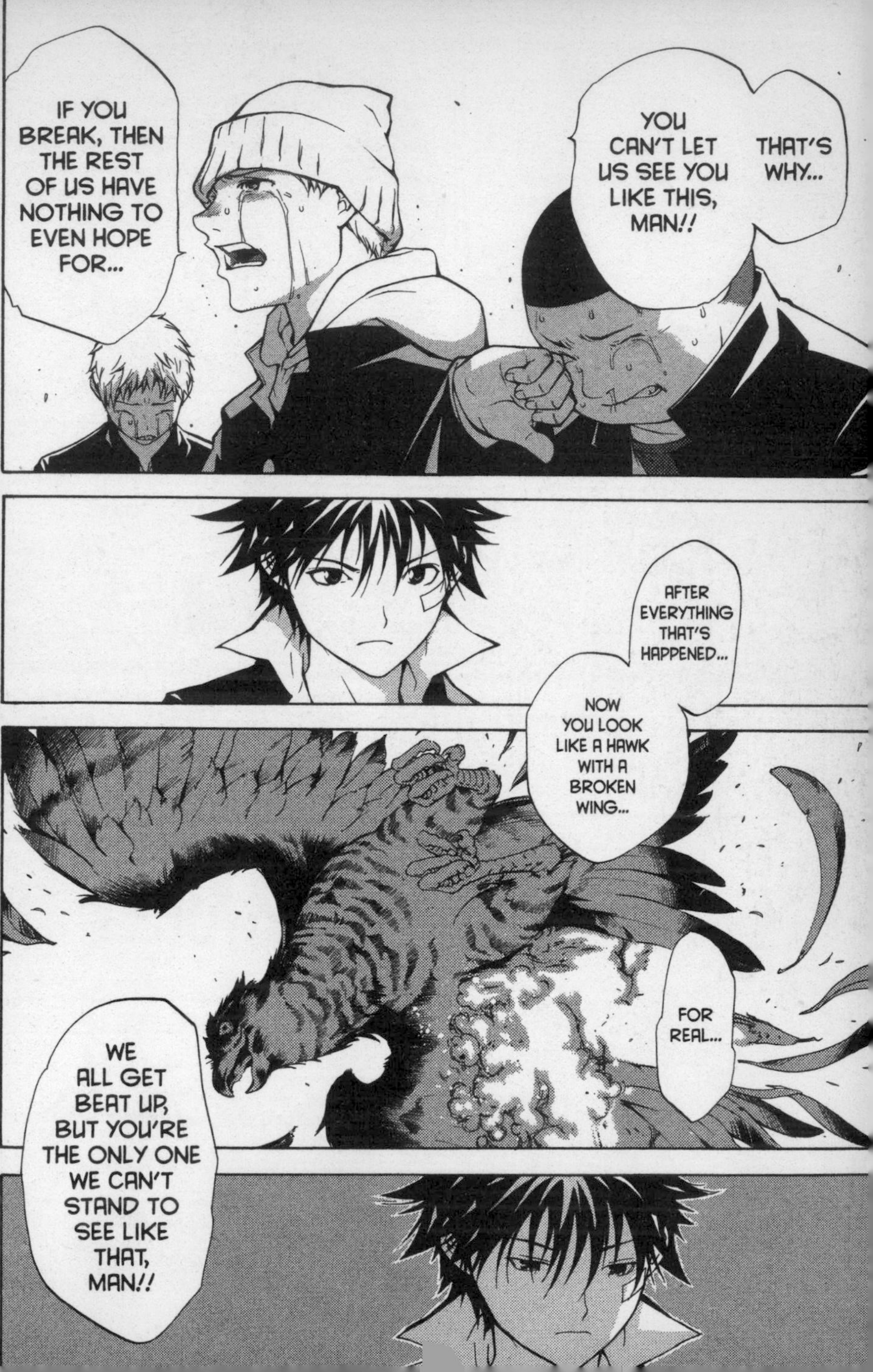
YOU CAN'T LET US SEE YOU LIKE THIS, MAN!! THAT'S WHY...
IF YOU BREAK, THEN THE REST OF US HAVE NOTHING TO EVEN HOPE FOR...
AFTER EVERYTHING THAT'S HAPPENED...
NOW YOU LOOK LIKE A HAWK WITH A BROKEN WING...
FOR REAL...
WE ALL GET BEAT UP, BUT YOU'RE THE ONLY ONE WE CAN'T STAND TO SEE LIKE THAT, MAN!!

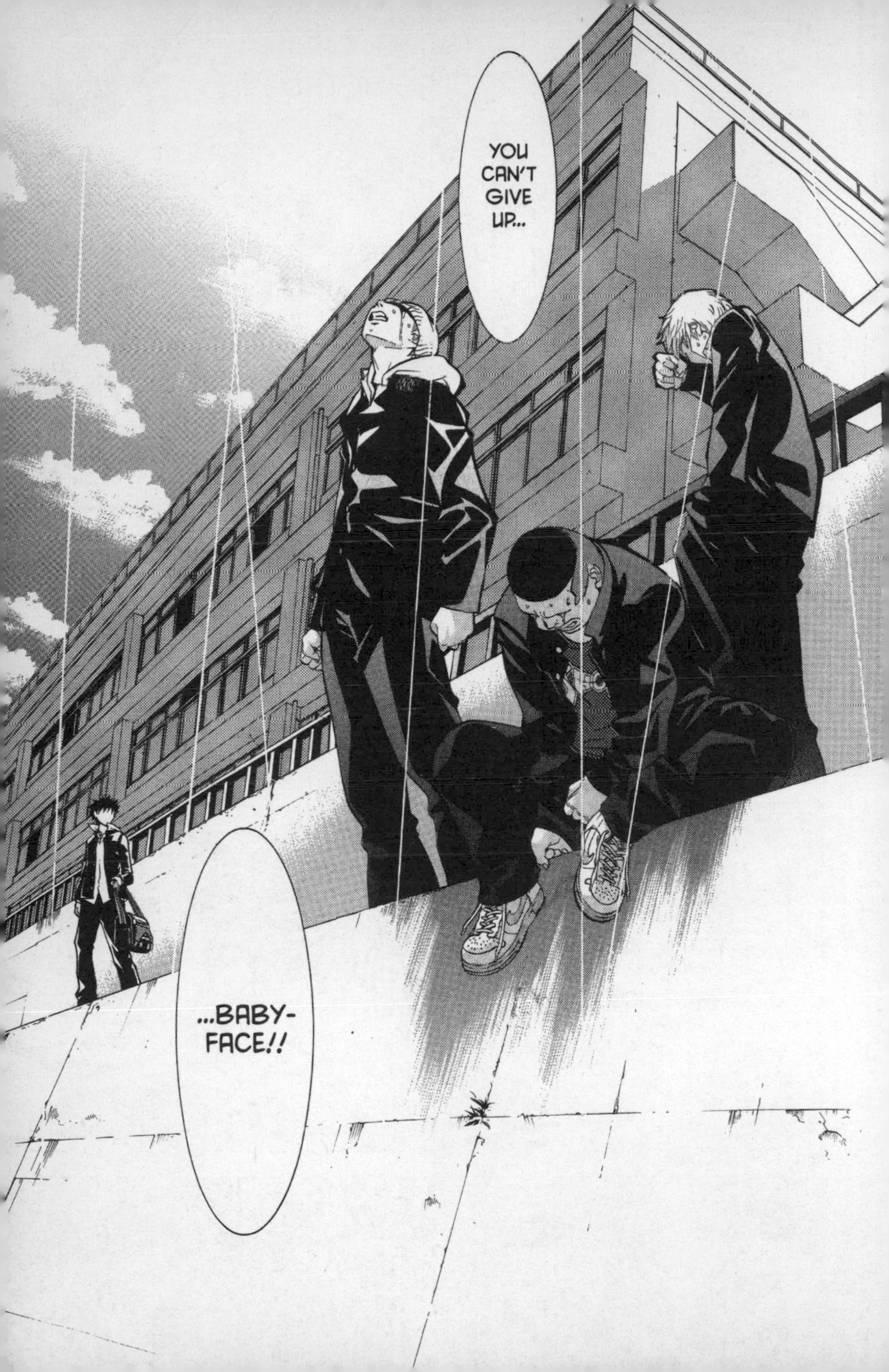
YOU CAN'T GIVE UP...
...BABY-FACE!!

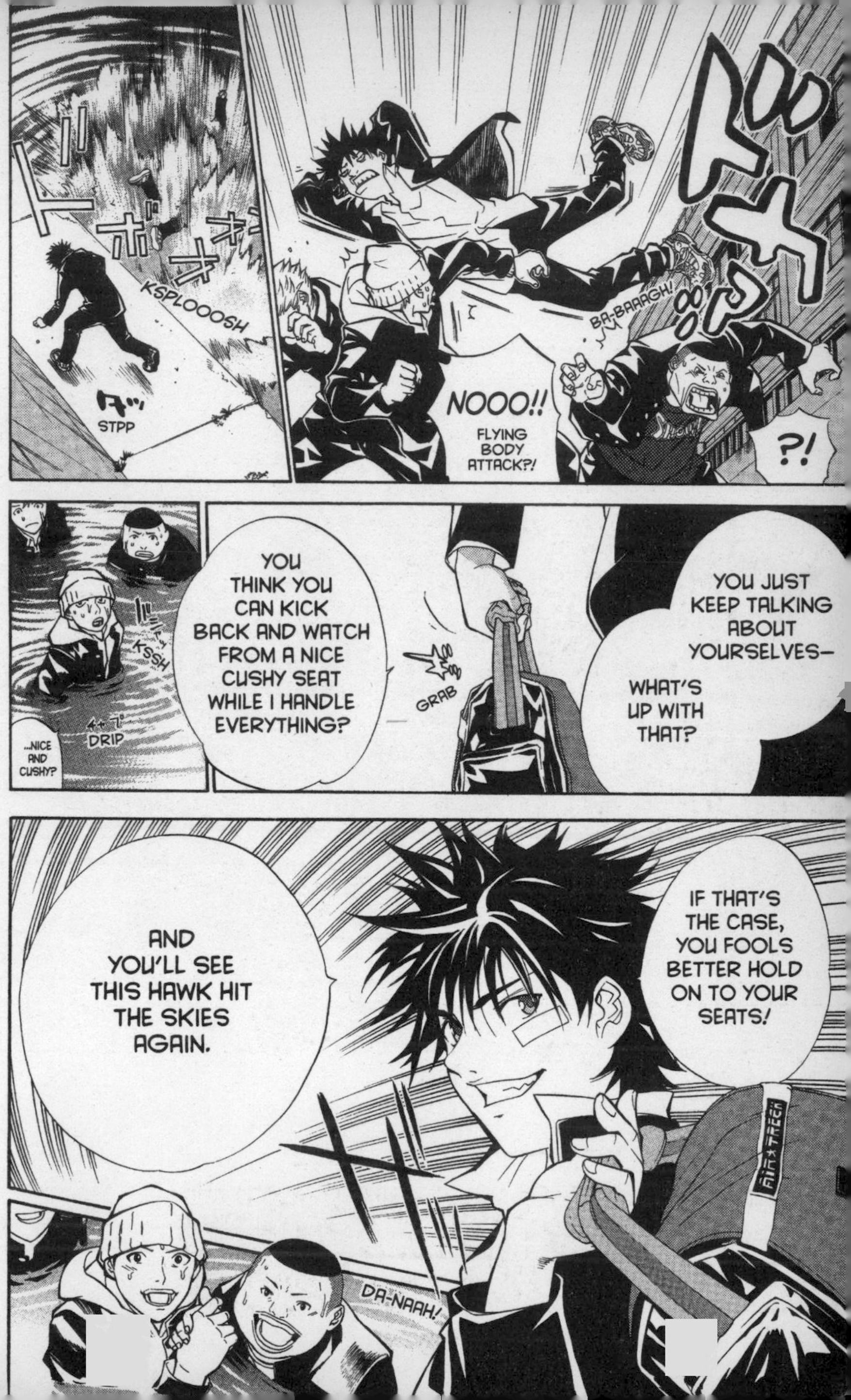
BA-BAAAGH!
?!
NOOO!!
FLYING BODY ATTACK?!
KSPLOOOSH
STPP
YOU JUST KEEP TALKING ABOUT YOURSELVES—
WHAT'S UP WITH THAT?
GRAB
YOU THINK YOU CAN KICK BACK AND WATCH FROM A NICE CUSHY SEAT WHILE I HANDLE EVERYTHING?
KSSH
DRIP
...NICE AND CUSHY?
IF THAT'S THE CASE, YOU FOOLS BETTER HOLD ON TO YOUR SEATS!
AND YOU'LL SEE THIS HAWK HIT THE SKIES AGAIN.
DA-NAAH!

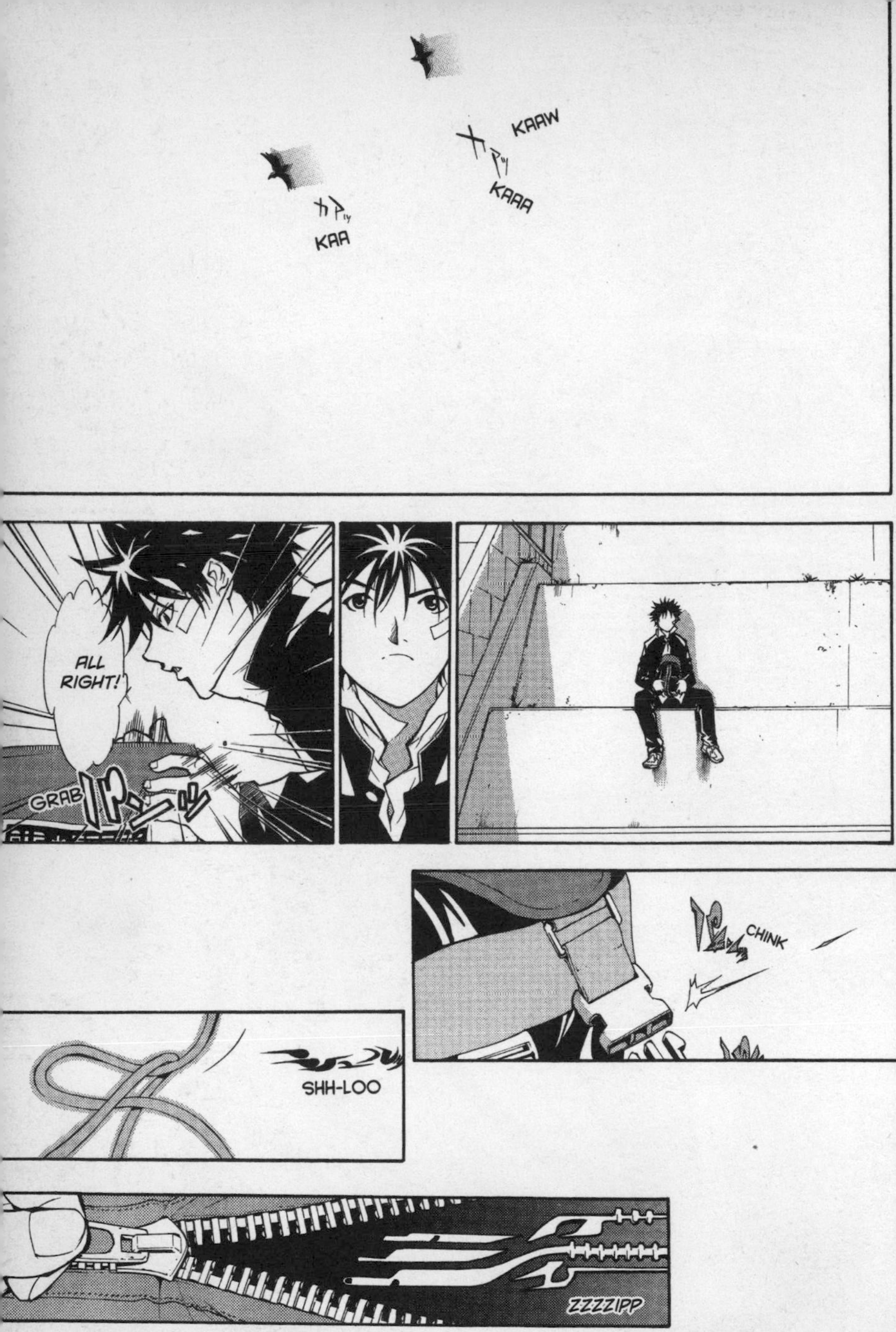
KAAW
KAAA
KAA
ALL RIGHT!
GRAB
CHINK
SHH-LOO
ZZZZIPP

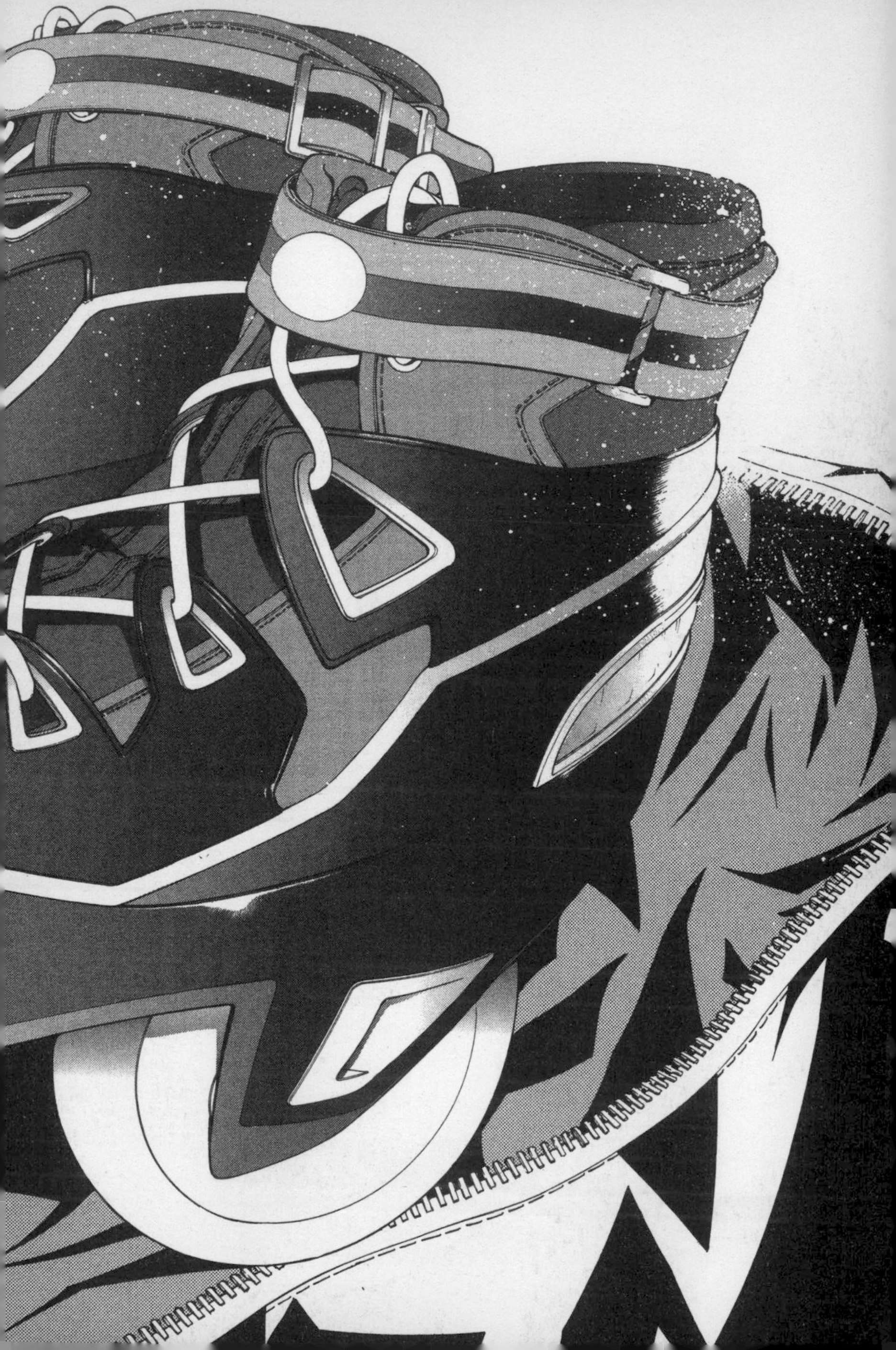

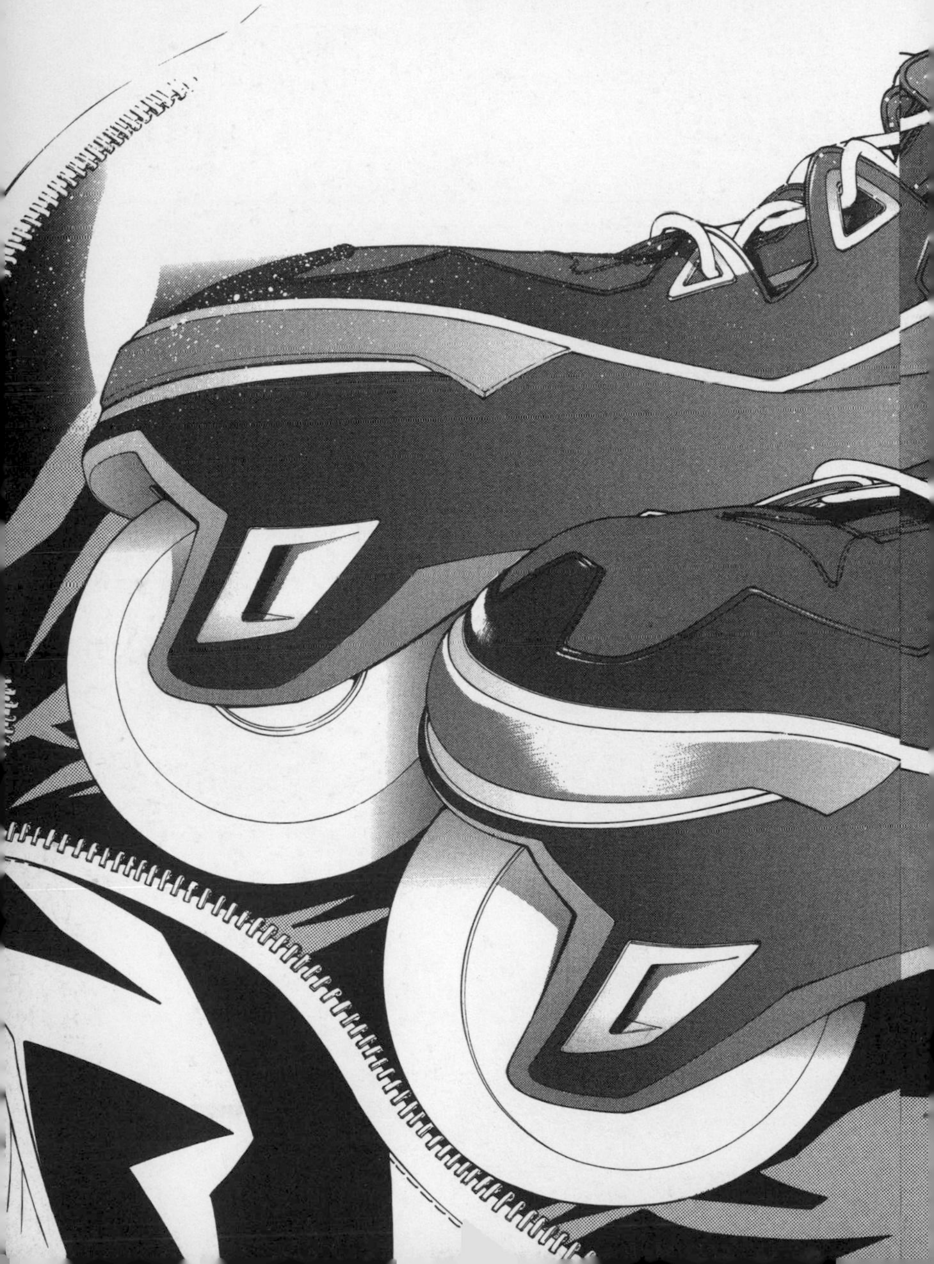

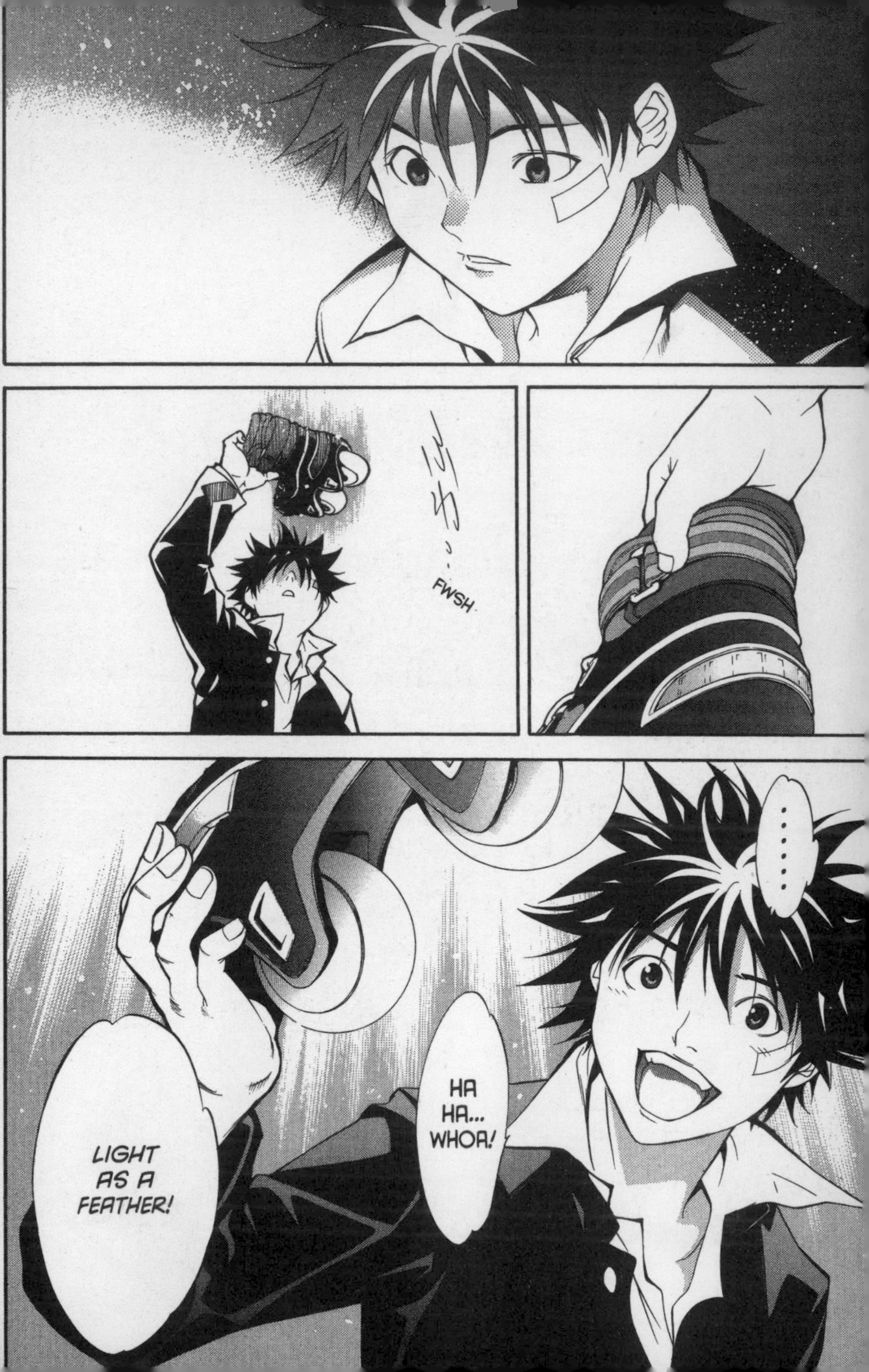
FWSH
......
HA HA... WHOA!
LIGHT AS A FEATHER!

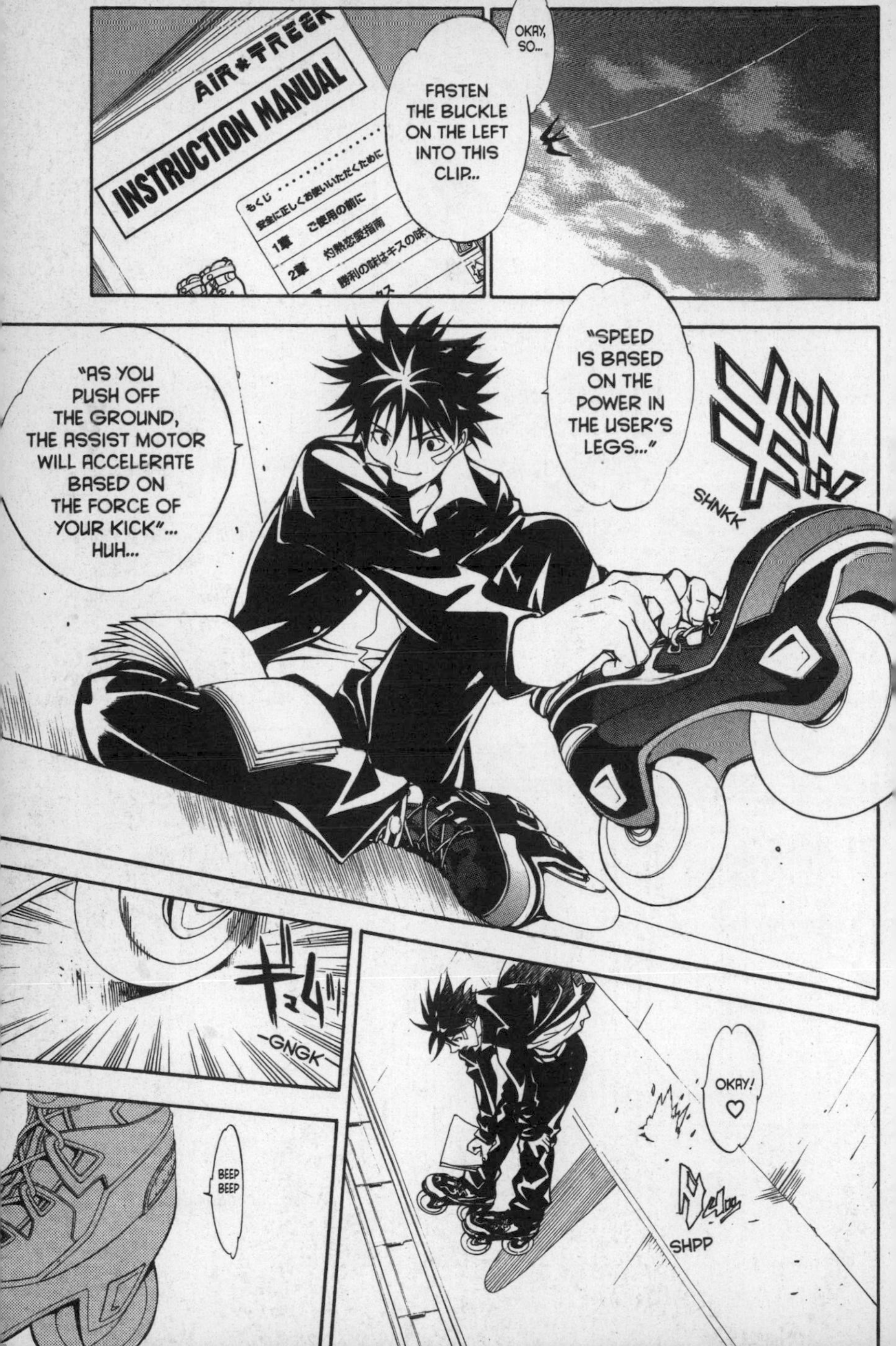
OKAY, SO...
FASTEN THE BUCKLE ON THE LEFT INTO THIS CLIP...
INSTRUCTION MANUAL
もくじ
安全に正しくお使いいただくために
ご使用の前に
1章 灼熱恋愛指南
2章 勝利の味はキスの味
"SPEED IS BASED ON THE POWER IN THE USER'S LEGS..."
SHNKK
"AS YOU PUSH OFF THE GROUND, THE ASSIST MOTOR WILL ACCELERATE BASED ON THE FORCE OF YOUR KICK"... HUH...
OKAY! ♡
SHPP
-GNGK-
BEEP BEEP

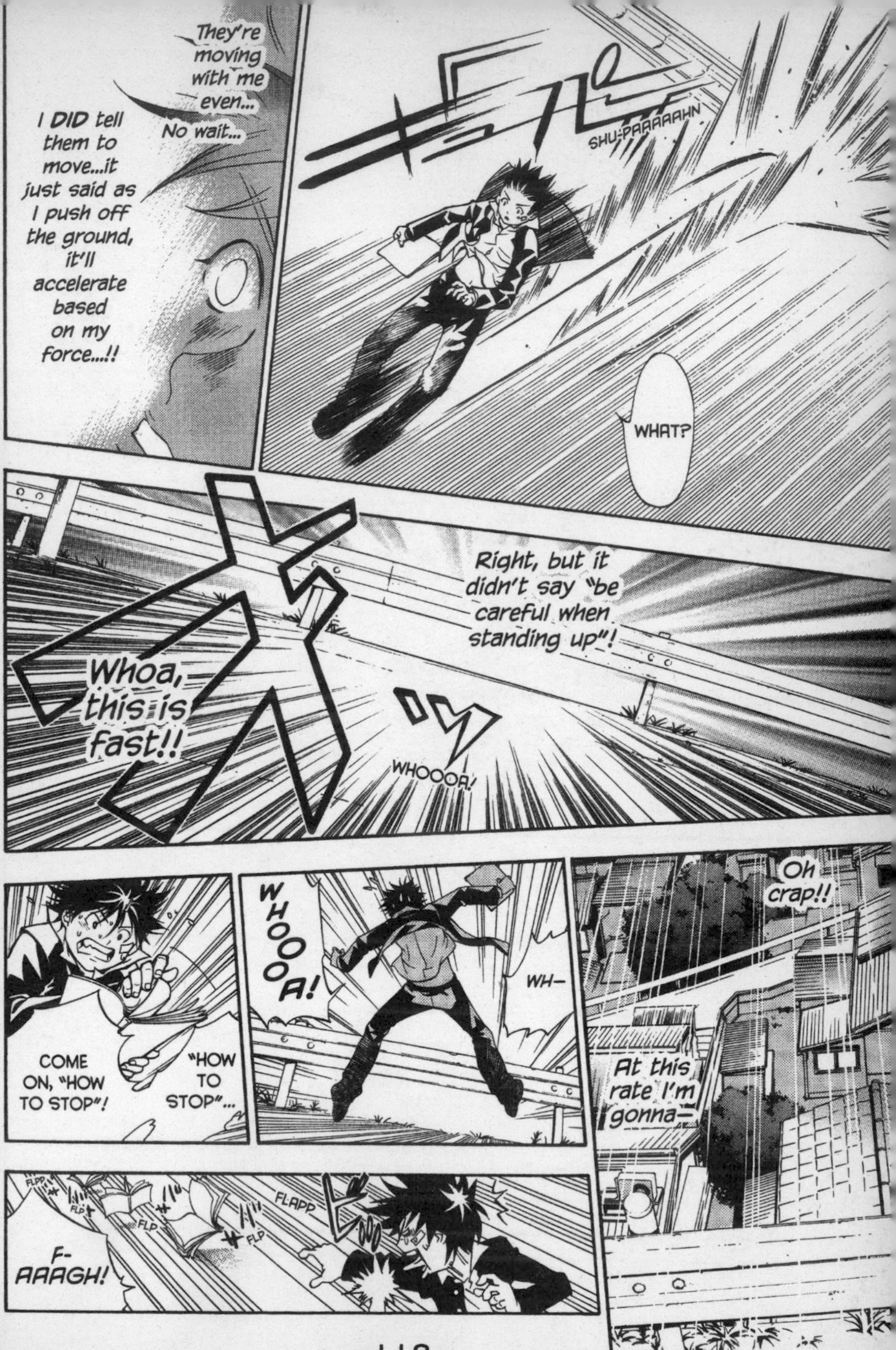
SHU-PAAAAAHN
WHAT?
They're moving with me even... No wait...
I **DID** tell them to move...it just said as I push off the ground, it'll accelerate based on my force...!!
Right, but it didn't say "be careful when standing up"!
Whoa, this is fast!!
WHOOOA!
Oh crap!!
At this rate I'm gonna—
WHOOOA!
WH-
"HOW TO STOP"...
COME ON, "HOW TO STOP"!
FLAPP
FLP
F-AAAGH!

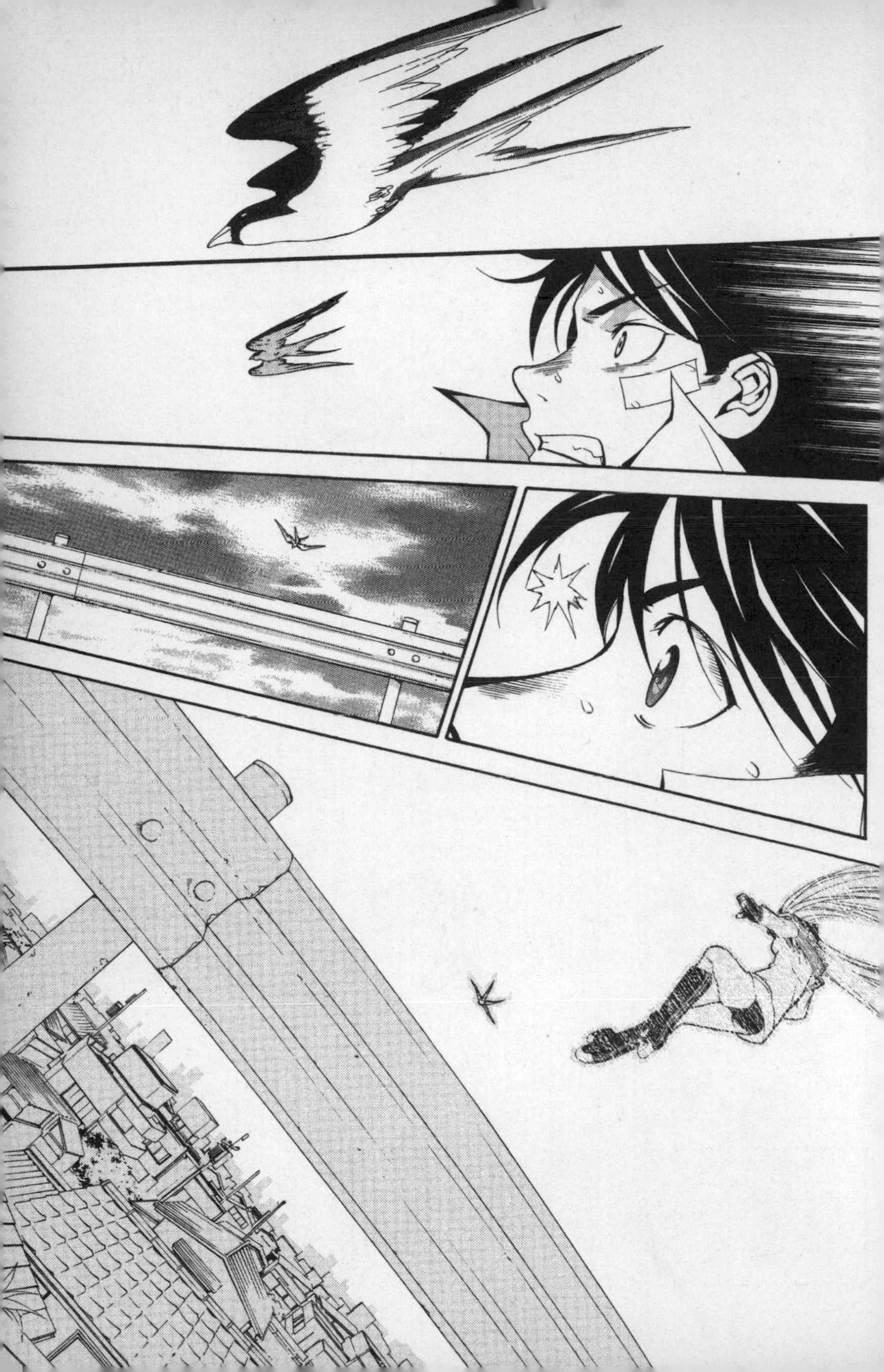

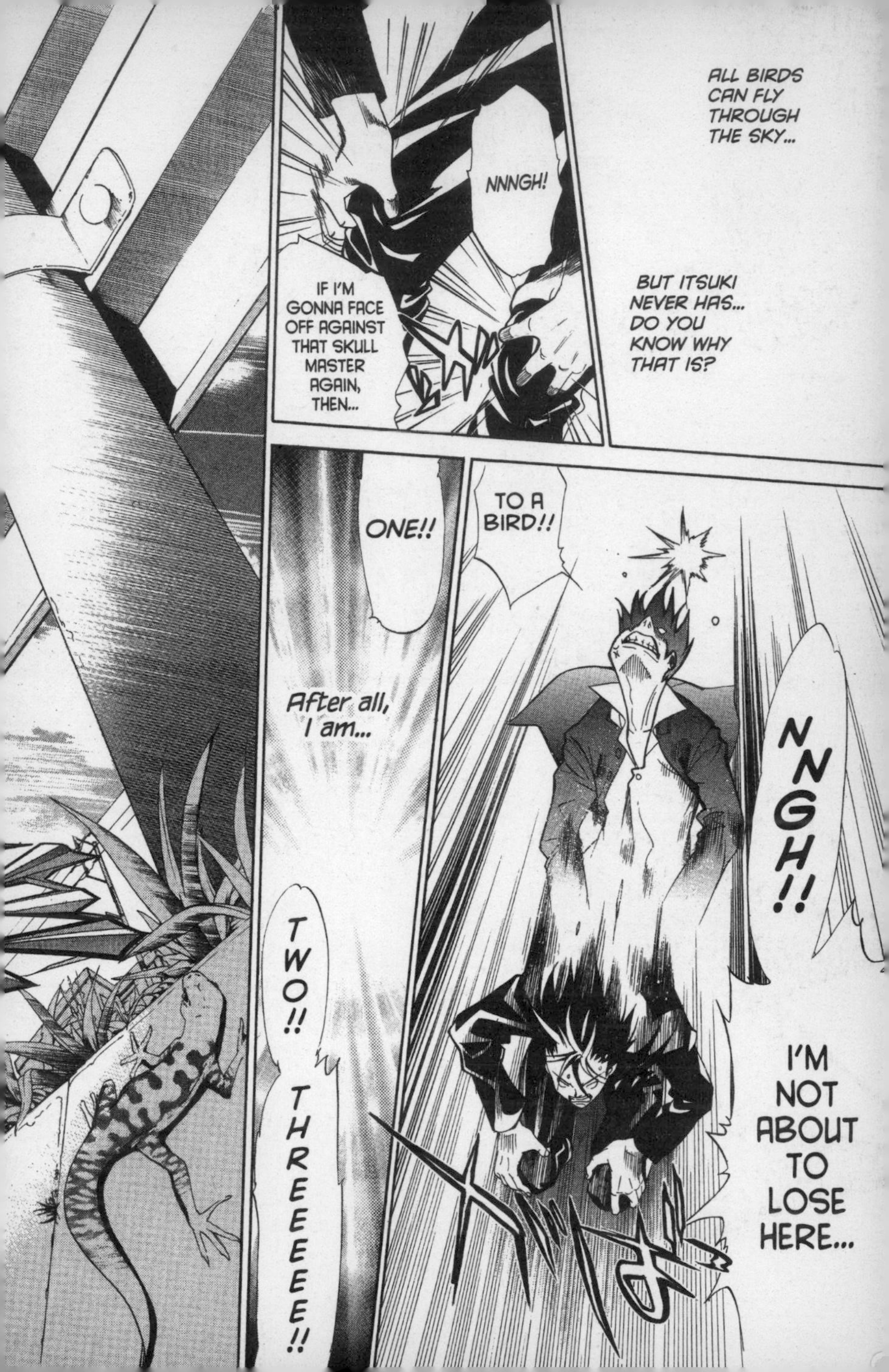
ALL BIRDS CAN FLY THROUGH THE SKY...
BUT ITSUKI NEVER HAS... DO YOU KNOW WHY THAT IS?
NNNGH!
IF I'M GONNA FACE OFF AGAINST THAT SKULL MASTER AGAIN, THEN...
I'M NOT ABOUT TO LOSE HERE...
NNGH!!
TO A BIRD!!
ONE!!
After all, I am...
TWO!!
THREEEEEE!!

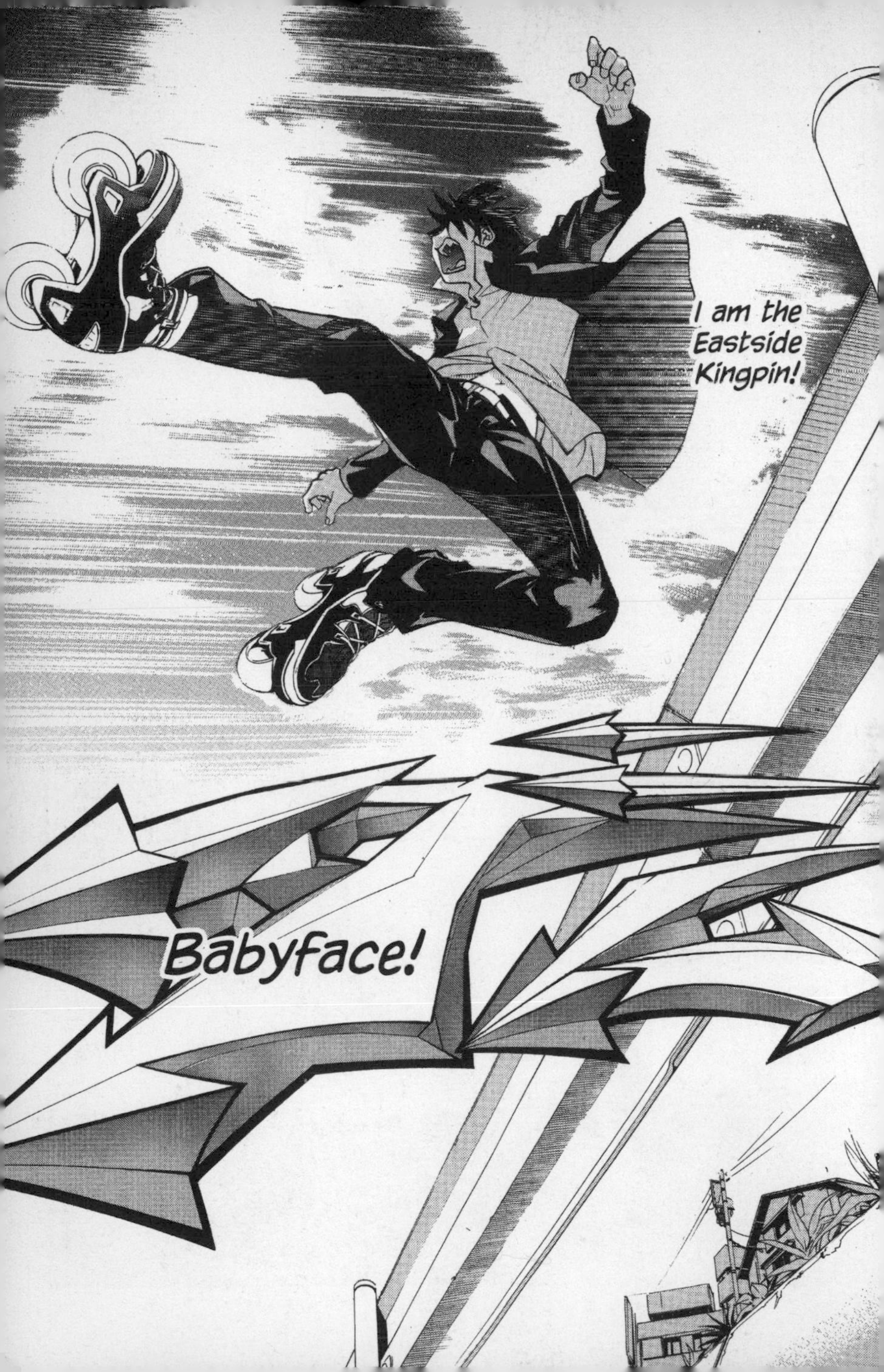
I am the Eastside Kingpin!
Babyface!

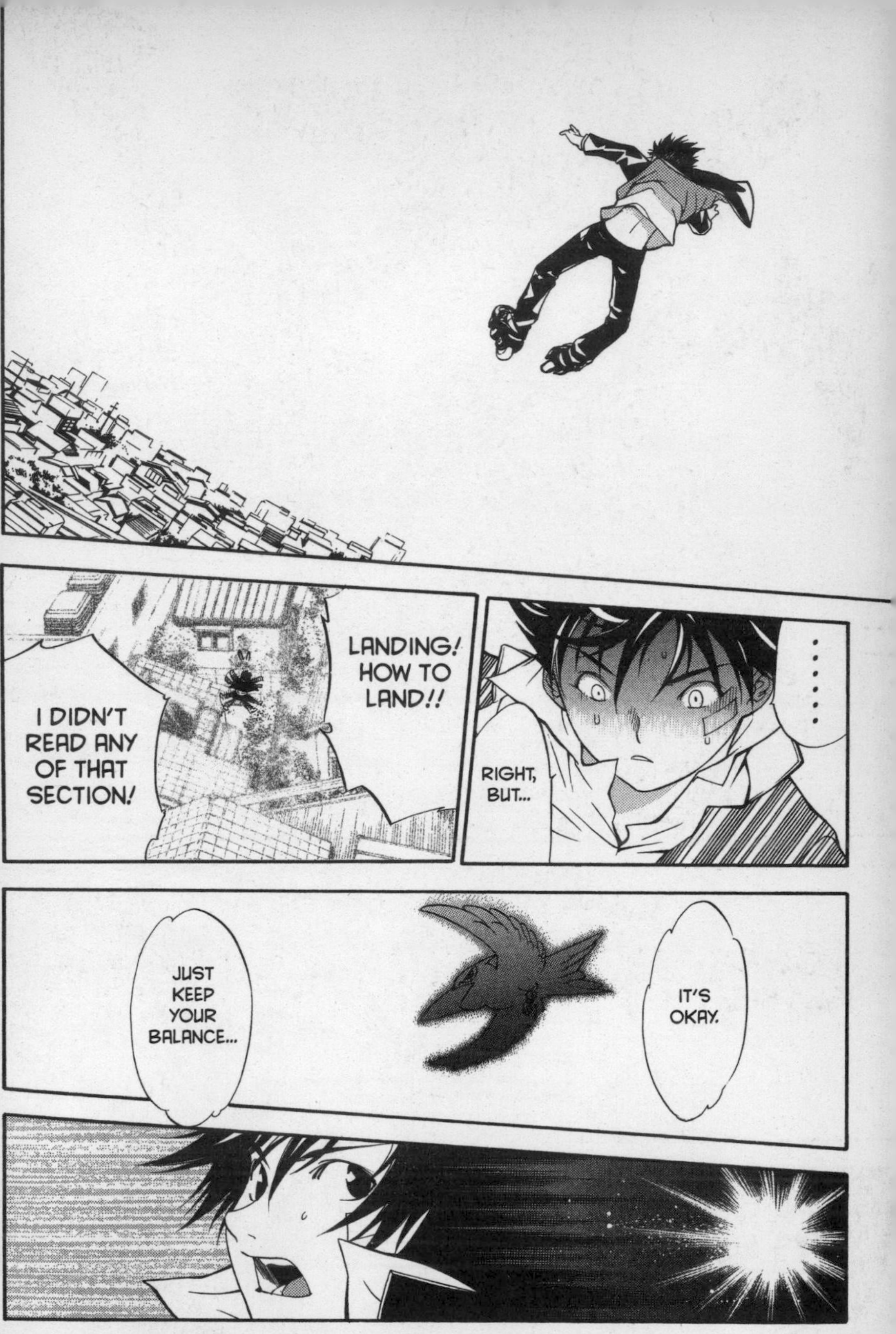
......
RIGHT, BUT...
LANDING! HOW TO LAND!!
I DIDN'T READ ANY OF THAT SECTION!
IT'S OKAY.
JUST KEEP YOUR BALANCE...

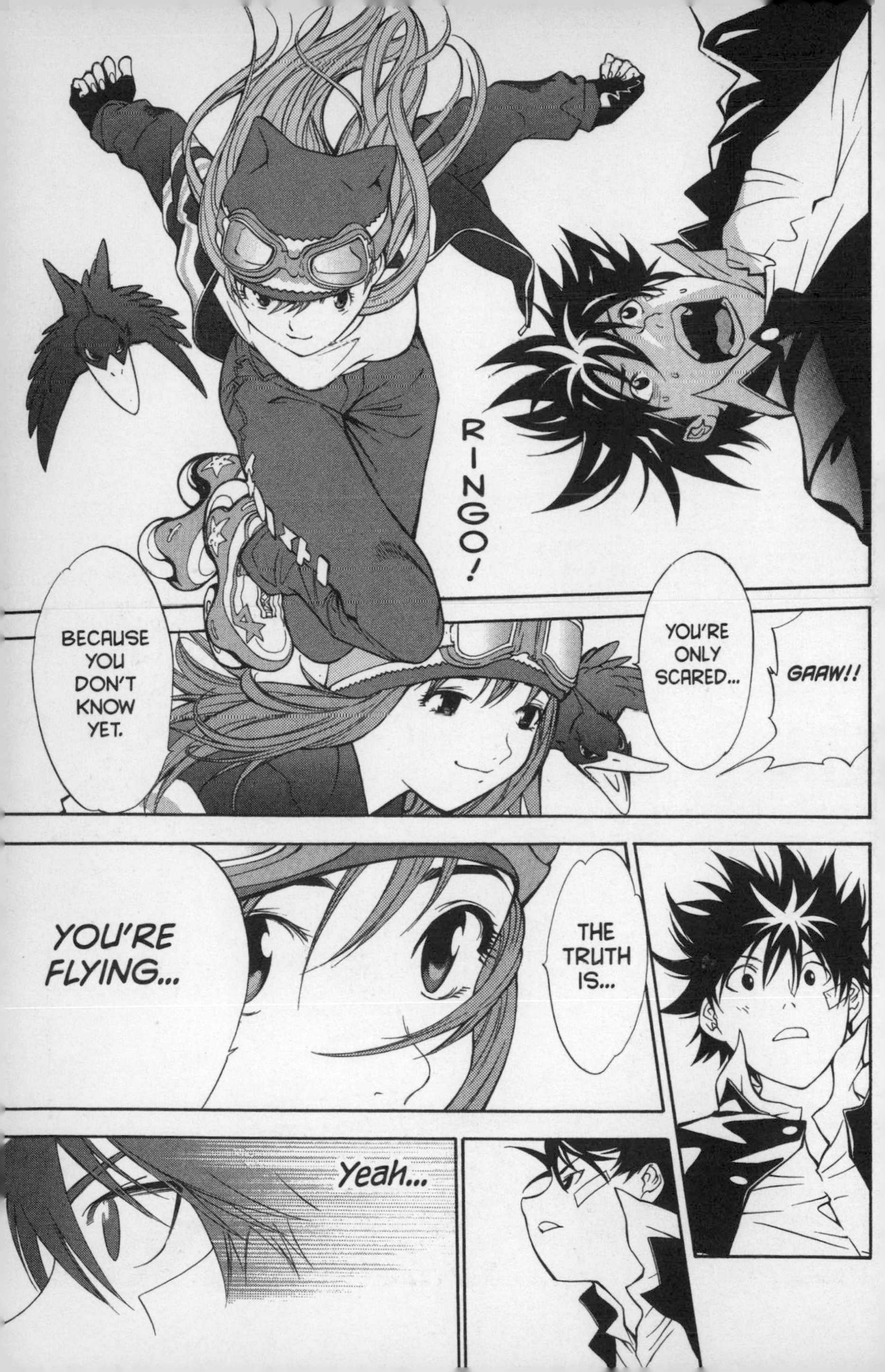

RINGO!
GAAW!!
YOU'RE ONLY SCARED...
BECAUSE YOU DON'T KNOW YET.
THE TRUTH IS...
YOU'RE FLYING...
Yeah...

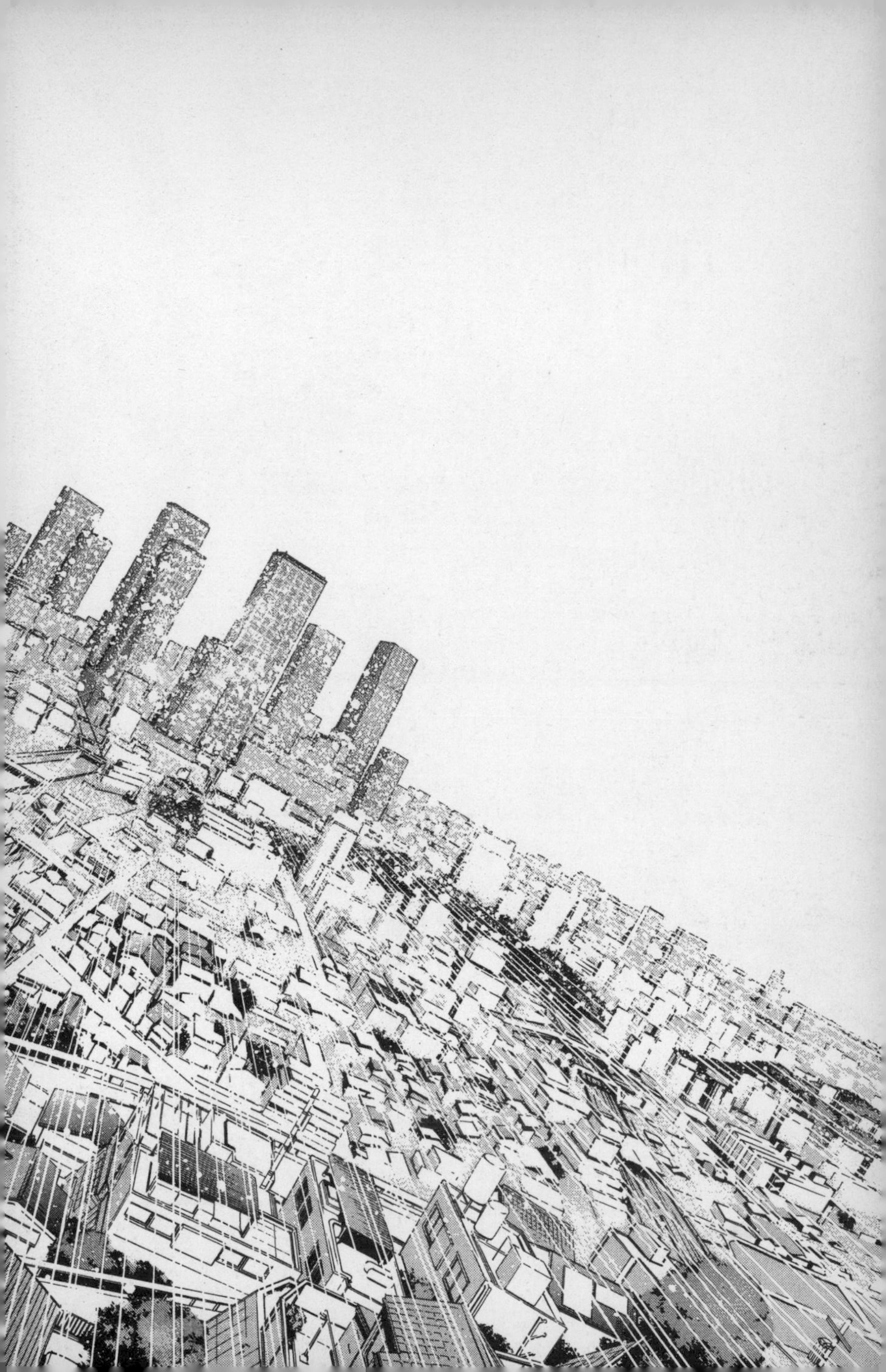

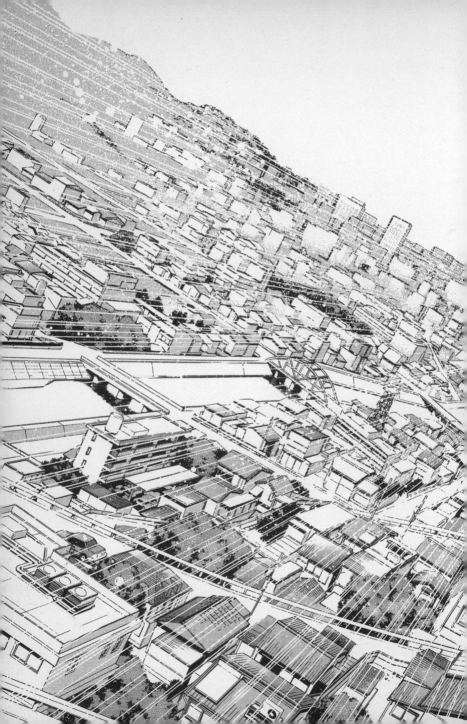

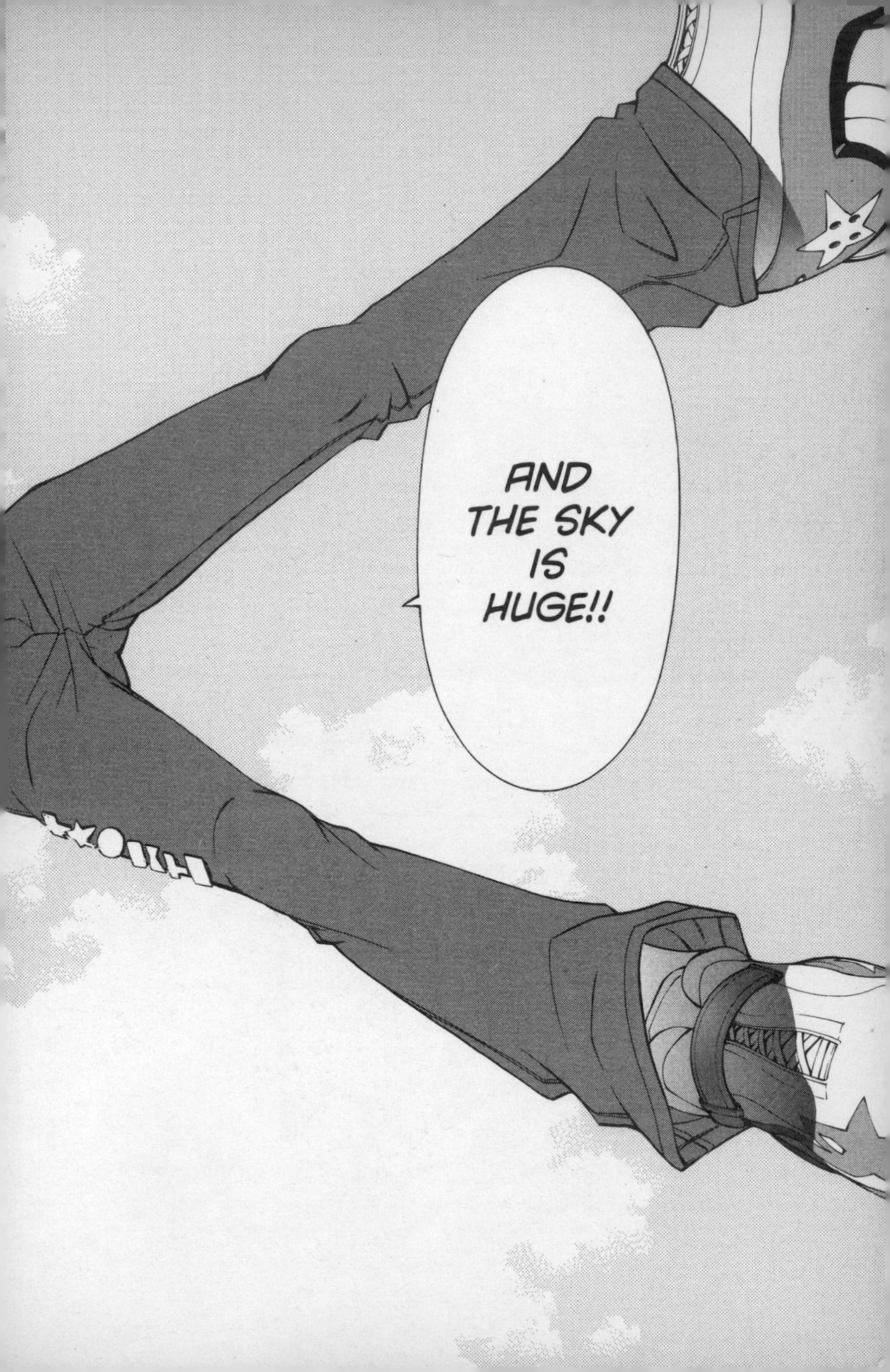
AND THE SKY IS HUGE!!

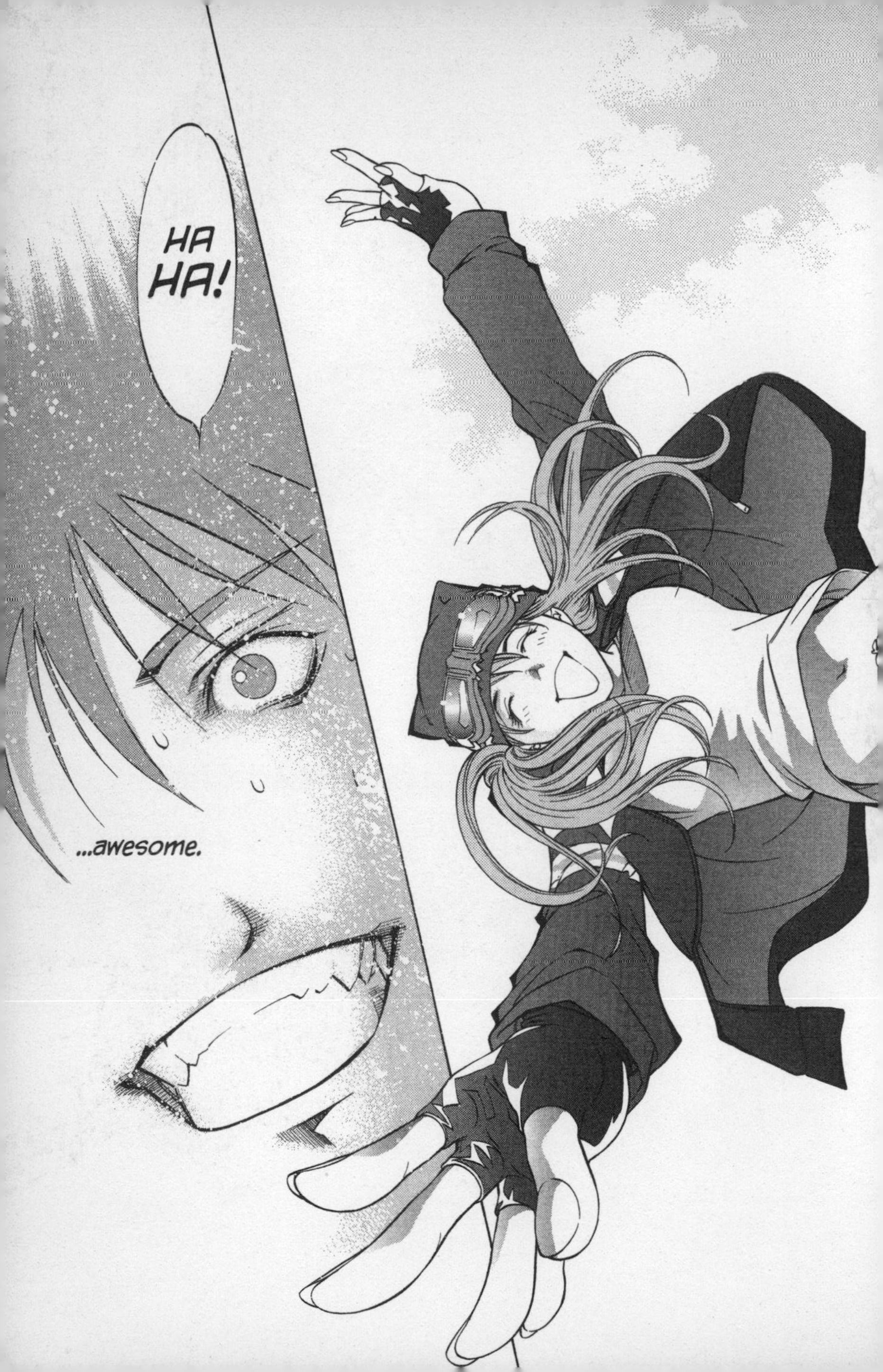
HA HA!
...awesome.

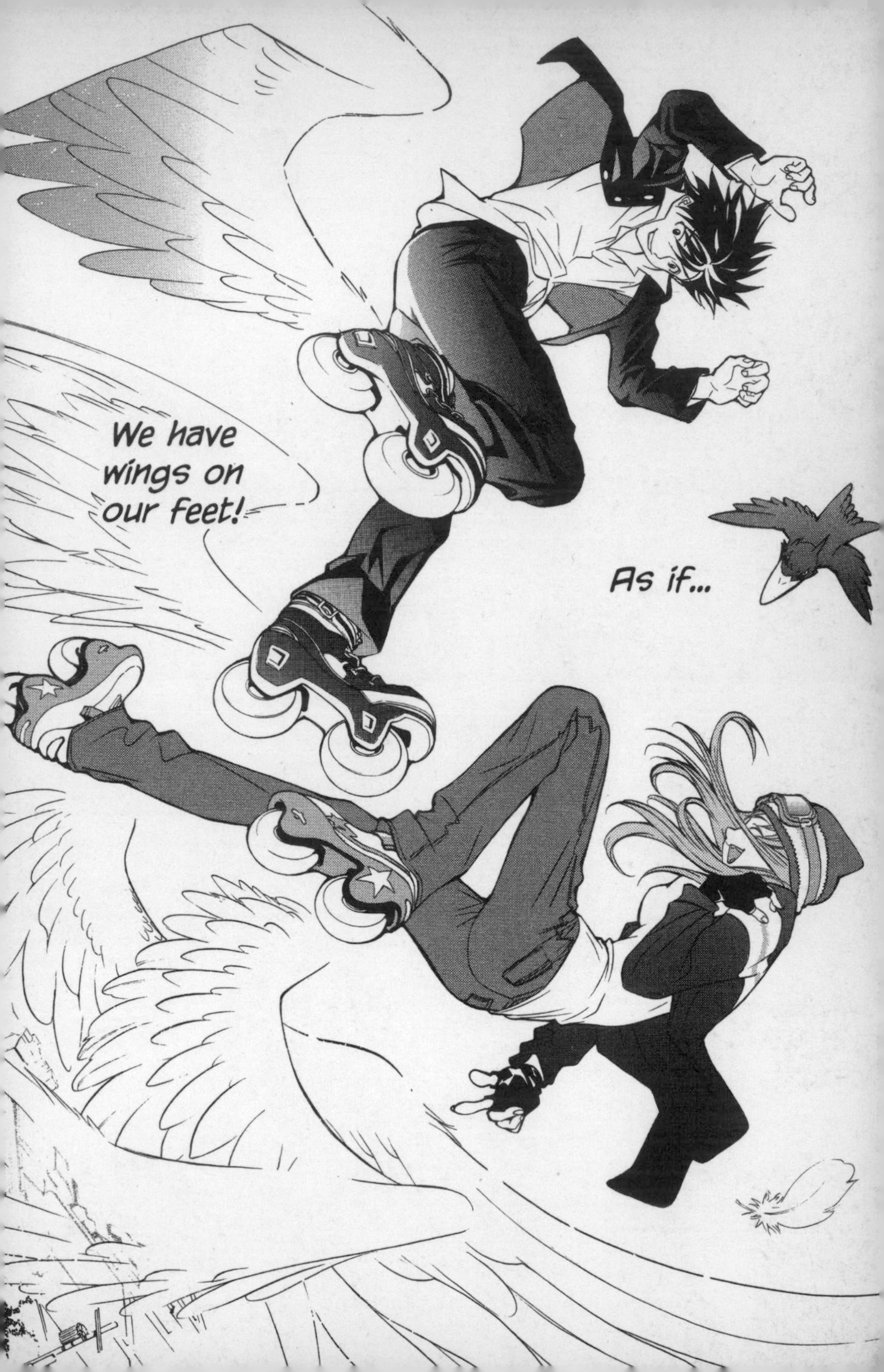
As if...
We have wings on our feet!

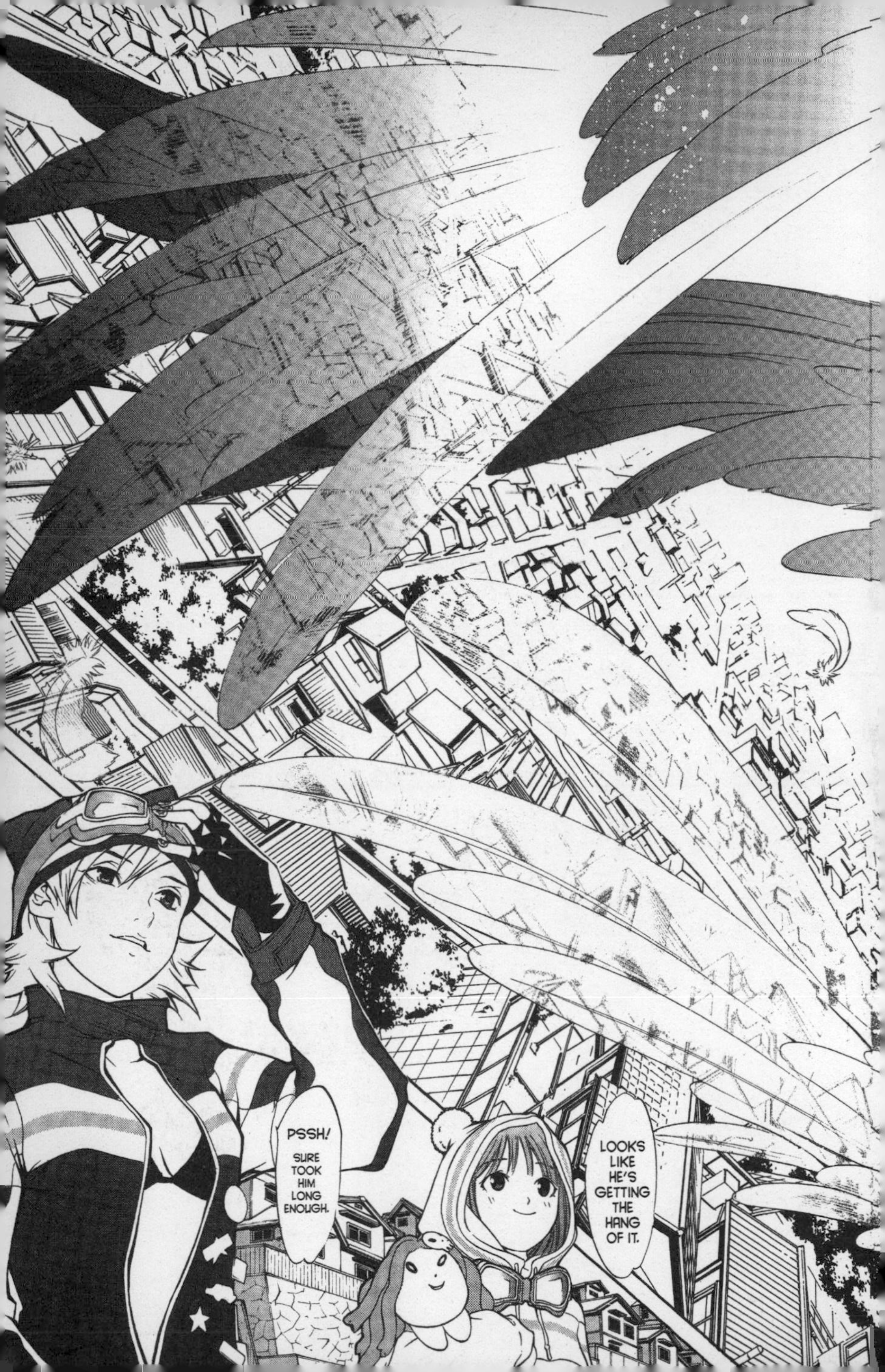
LOOKS LIKE HE'S GETTING THE HANG OF IT.
PSSH!
SURE TOOK HIM LONG ENOUGH.

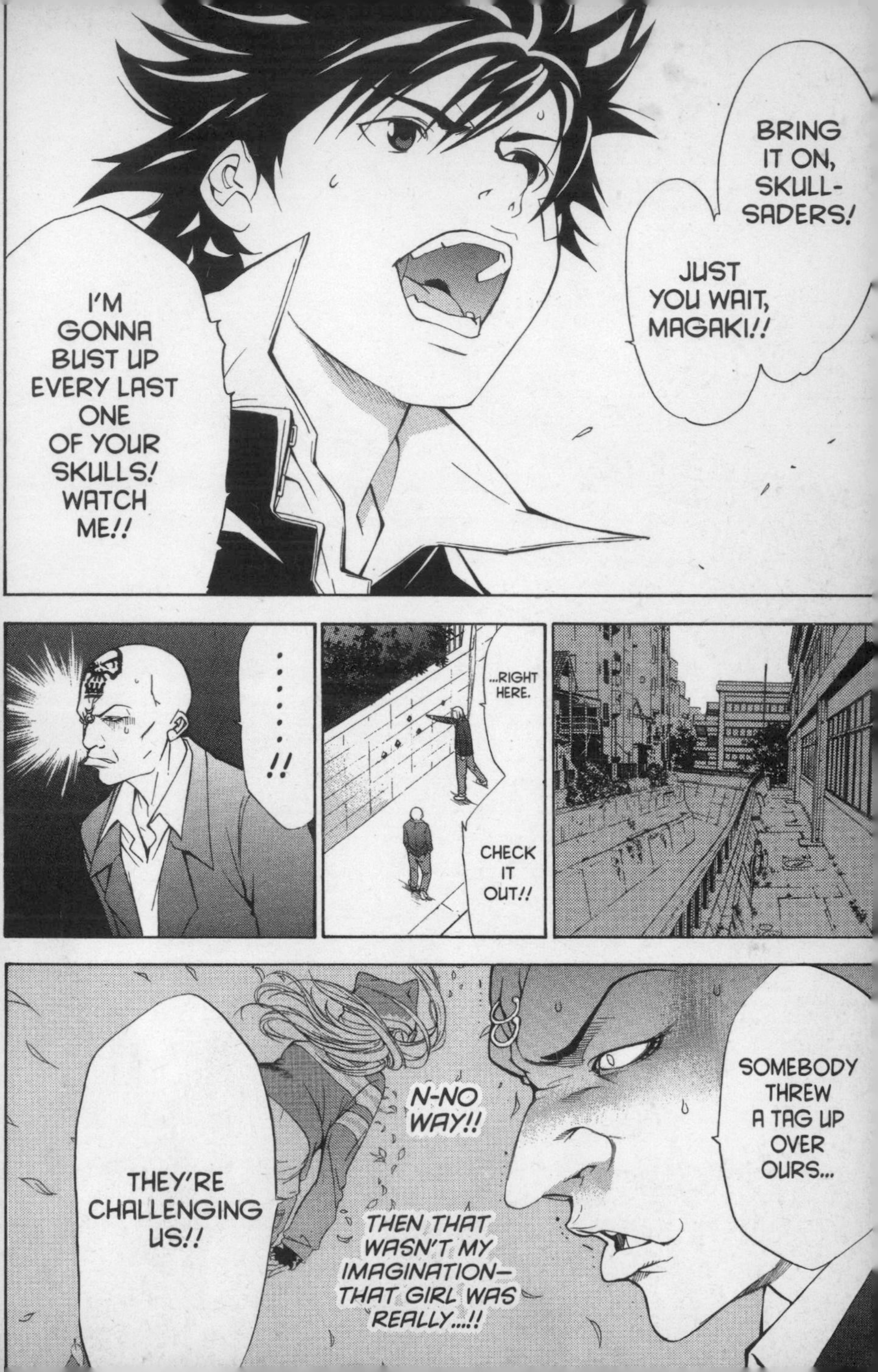
BRING IT ON, SKULL-SADERS!
JUST YOU WAIT, MAGAKI!!
I'M GONNA BUST UP EVERY LAST ONE OF YOUR SKULLS! WATCH ME!!
...RIGHT HERE.
CHECK IT OUT!!
......!!
SOMEBODY THREW A TAG UP OVER OURS...
N-NO WAY!!
THEY'RE CHALLENGING US!!
THEN THAT WASN'T MY IMAGINATION—THAT GIRL WAS REALLY...!!

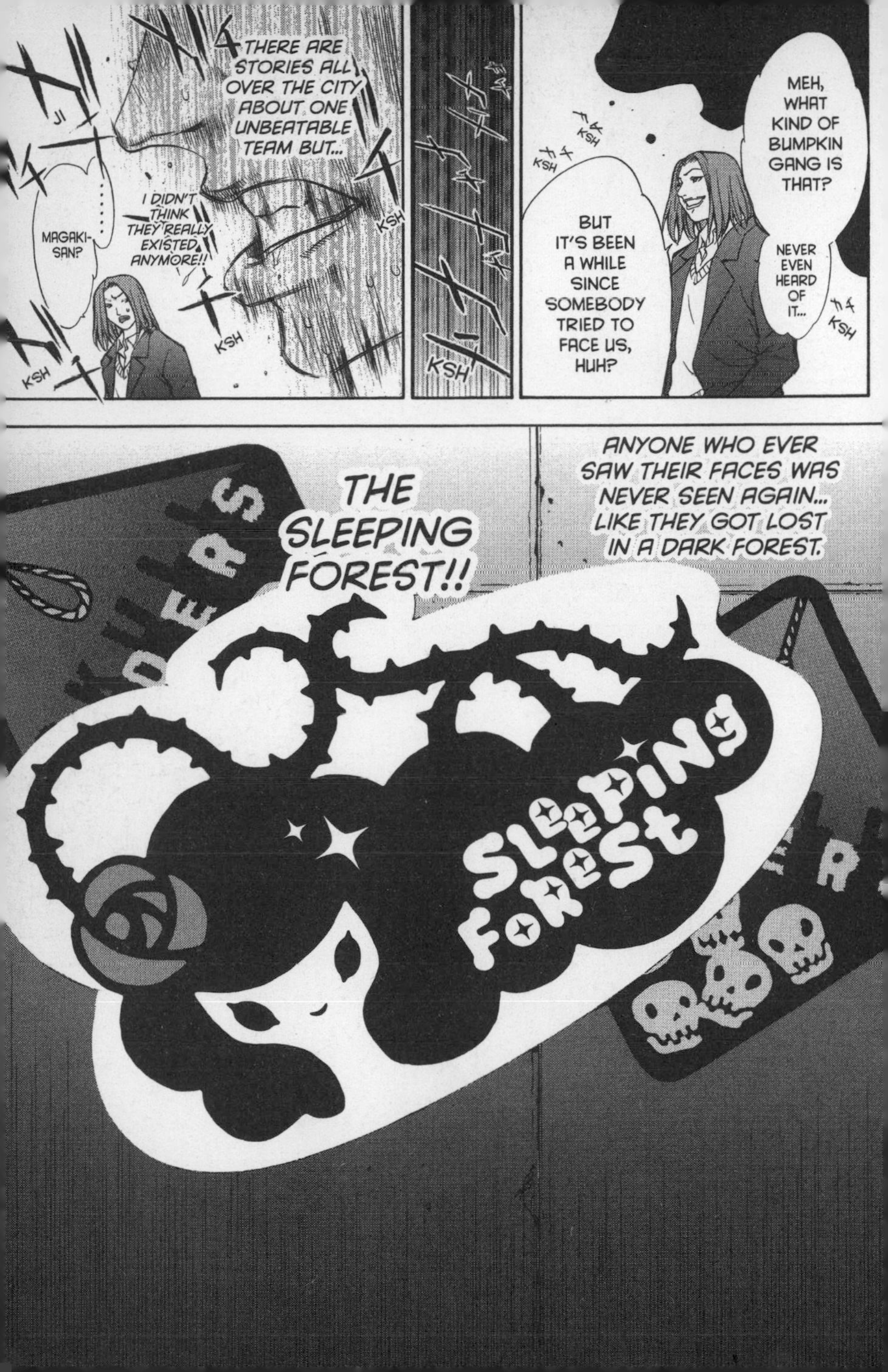
MEH, WHAT KIND OF BUMPKIN GANG IS THAT?
NEVER EVEN HEARD OF IT...
KSH
KSH
KSH
BUT IT'S BEEN A WHILE SINCE SOMEBODY TRIED TO FACE US, HUH?
KSH
THERE ARE STORIES ALL OVER THE CITY ABOUT ONE UNBEATABLE TEAM BUT...
KSH
I DIDN'T THINK THEY REALLY EXISTED ANYMORE!!
JI
KSH
MAGAKI-SAN?
KSH
ANYONE WHO EVER SAW THEIR FACES WAS NEVER SEEN AGAIN... LIKE THEY GOT LOST IN A DARK FOREST.
THE SLEEPING FOREST!!
SLEEPING FOREST

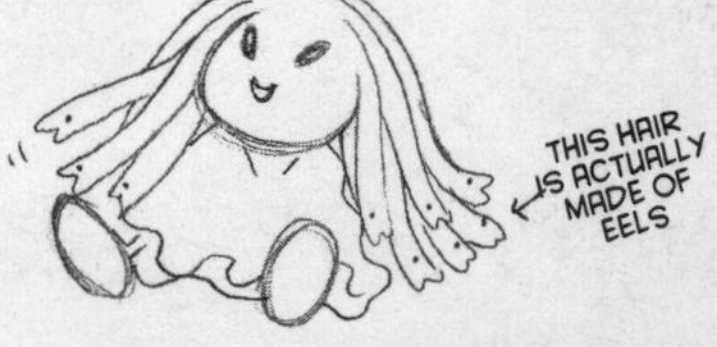
THIS HAIR IS ACTUALLY MADE OF EELS

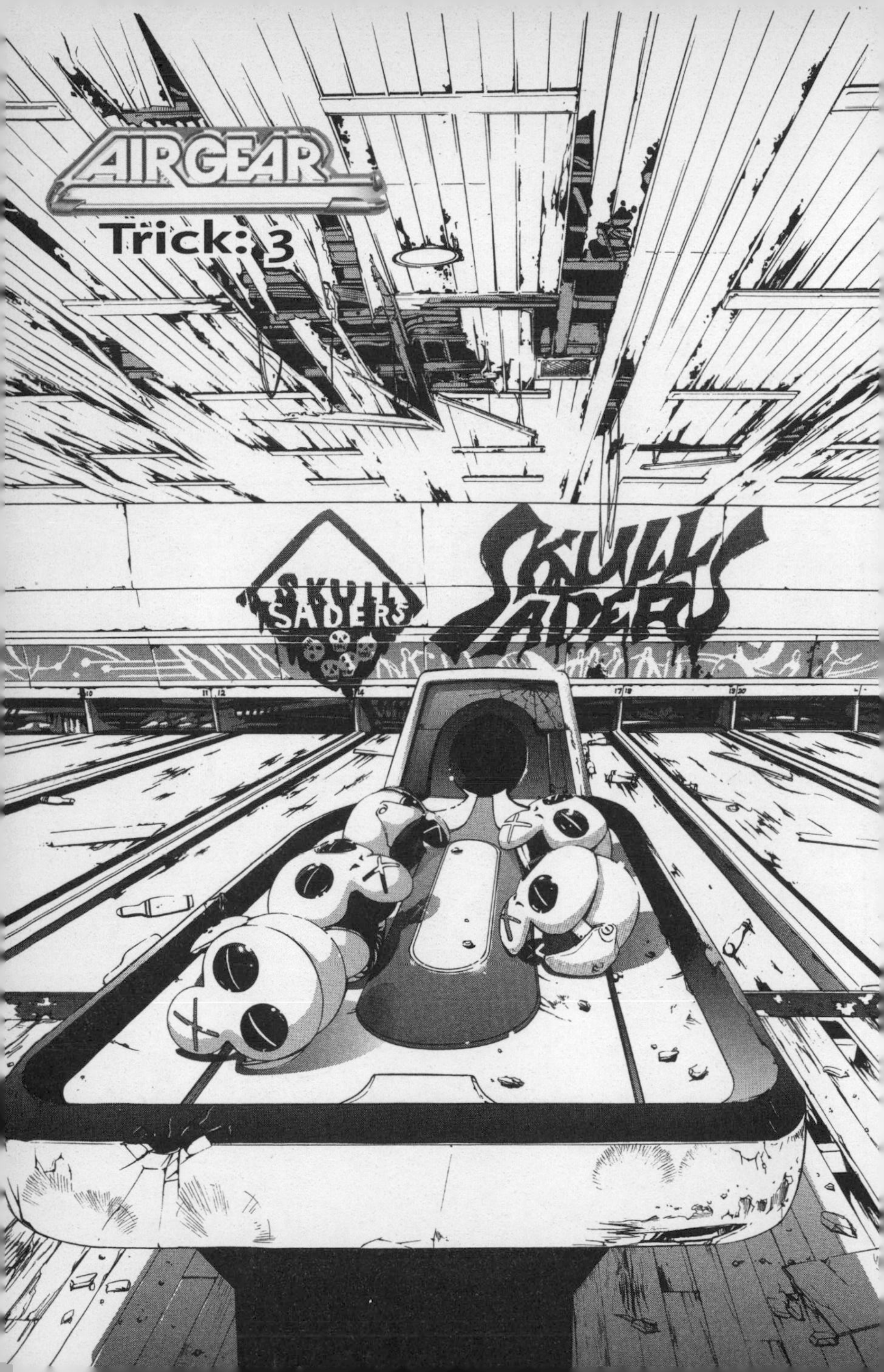
AIR GEAR
Trick: 3
SKULL SADERS

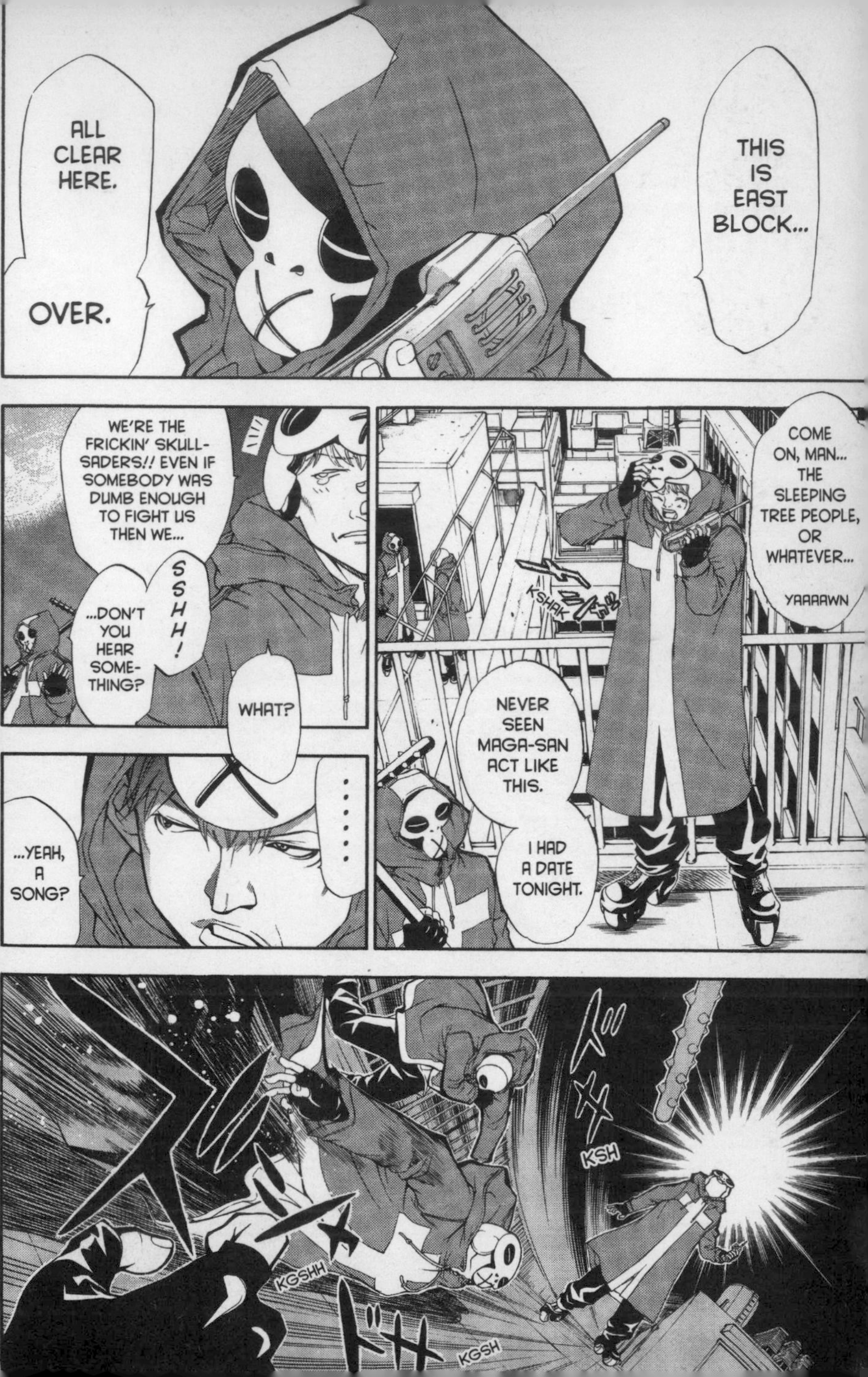
THIS IS EAST BLOCK...
ALL CLEAR HERE.
OVER.
COME ON, MAN... THE SLEEPING TREE PEOPLE, OR WHATEVER...
YAAAAWN
KSHAK
NEVER SEEN MAGA-SAN ACT LIKE THIS.
I HAD A DATE TONIGHT.
WE'RE THE FRICKIN' SKULL-SADERS!! EVEN IF SOMEBODY WAS DUMB ENOUGH TO FIGHT US THEN WE...
SSHH!
...DON'T YOU HEAR SOME-THING?
WHAT?
......
...YEAH, A SONG?
KSH
KGSHH
KGSH

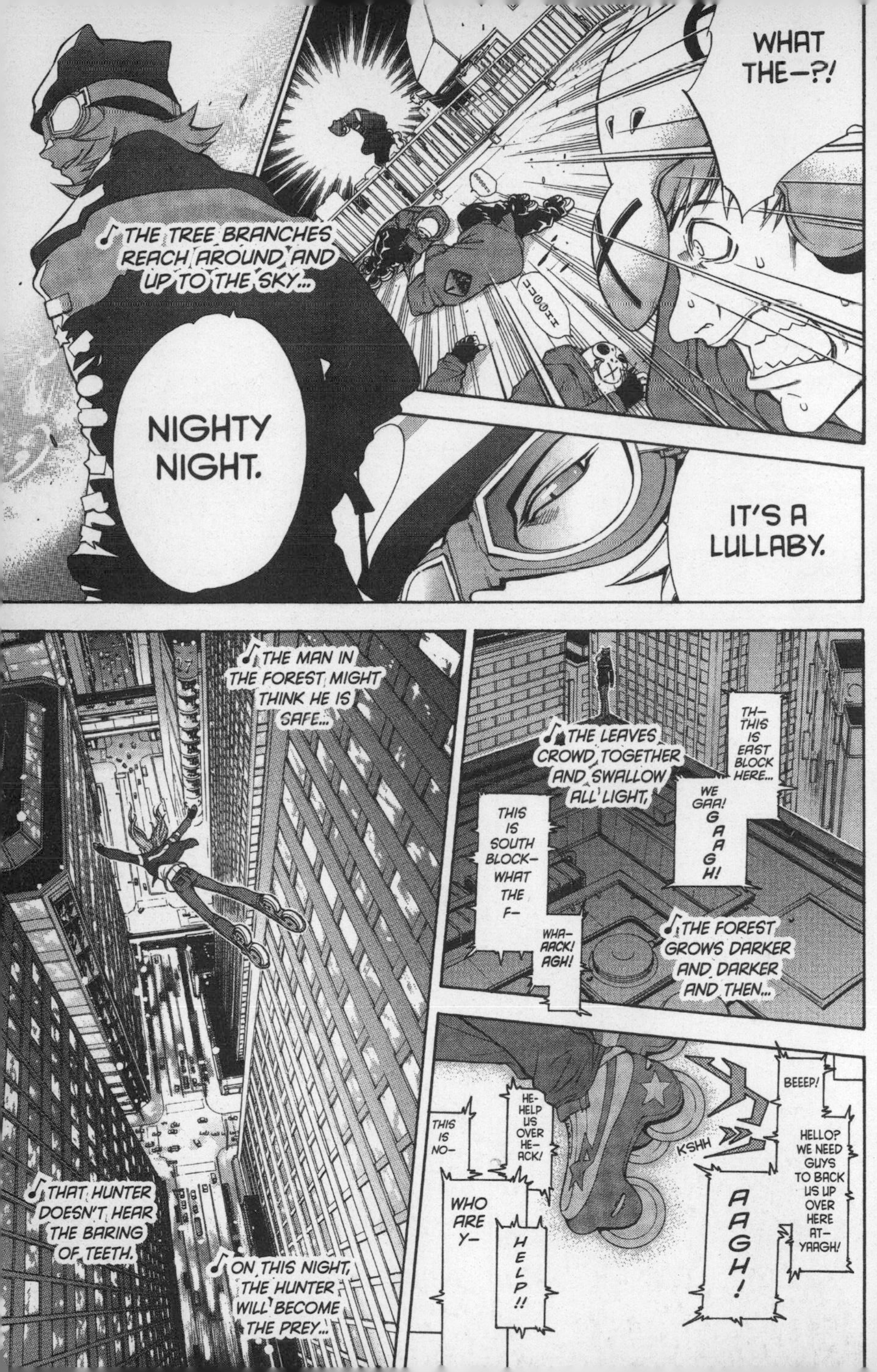
WHAT THE—?!
IT'S A LULLABY.
♪THE TREE BRANCHES REACH AROUND AND UP TO THE SKY...
NIGHTY NIGHT.
TH— THIS IS EAST BLOCK HERE...
WE GAA! GAAGH!
♪THE LEAVES CROWD TOGETHER AND SWALLOW ALL LIGHT,
THIS IS SOUTH BLOCK— WHAT THE F—
WHA— AACK! AGH!
♪THE FOREST GROWS DARKER AND DARKER AND THEN...
BEEEP!
HELLO? WE NEED GUYS TO BACK US UP OVER HERE AT— YAAGH!
KSHH
AAGH!
HE— HELP US OVER HE— ACK!
THIS IS NO—
HELP!!
WHO ARE Y—
♪THE MAN IN THE FOREST MIGHT THINK HE IS SAFE...
♪THAT HUNTER DOESN'T HEAR THE BARING OF TEETH.
♪ON THIS NIGHT, THE HUNTER WILL BECOME THE PREY...

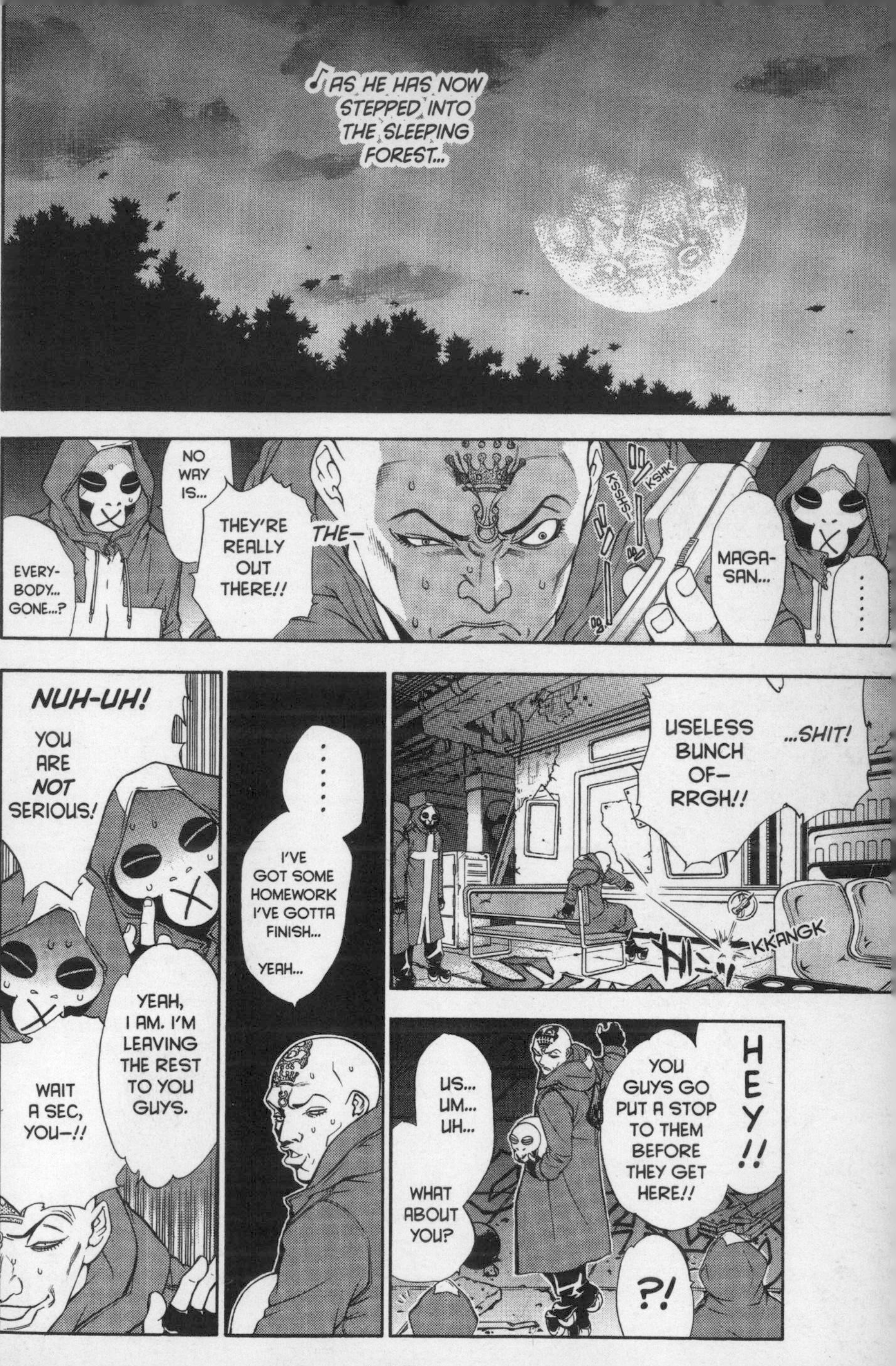
♪AS HE HAS NOW STEPPED INTO THE SLEEPING FOREST...
......
MAGA-SAN...
KSHK
KSHS
THE—
NO WAY IS...
THEY'RE REALLY OUT THERE!!
EVERY-BODY... GONE...?
...SHIT!
USELESS BUNCH OF— RRGH!!
KKANGK
HEY!!
YOU GUYS GO PUT A STOP TO THEM BEFORE THEY GET HERE!!
US... UM... UH...
WHAT ABOUT YOU?
?!
......
I'VE GOT SOME HOMEWORK I'VE GOTTA FINISH...
YEAH...
NUH-UH!
YOU ARE NOT SERIOUS!
YEAH, I AM. I'M LEAVING THE REST TO YOU GUYS.
WAIT A SEC, YOU—!!

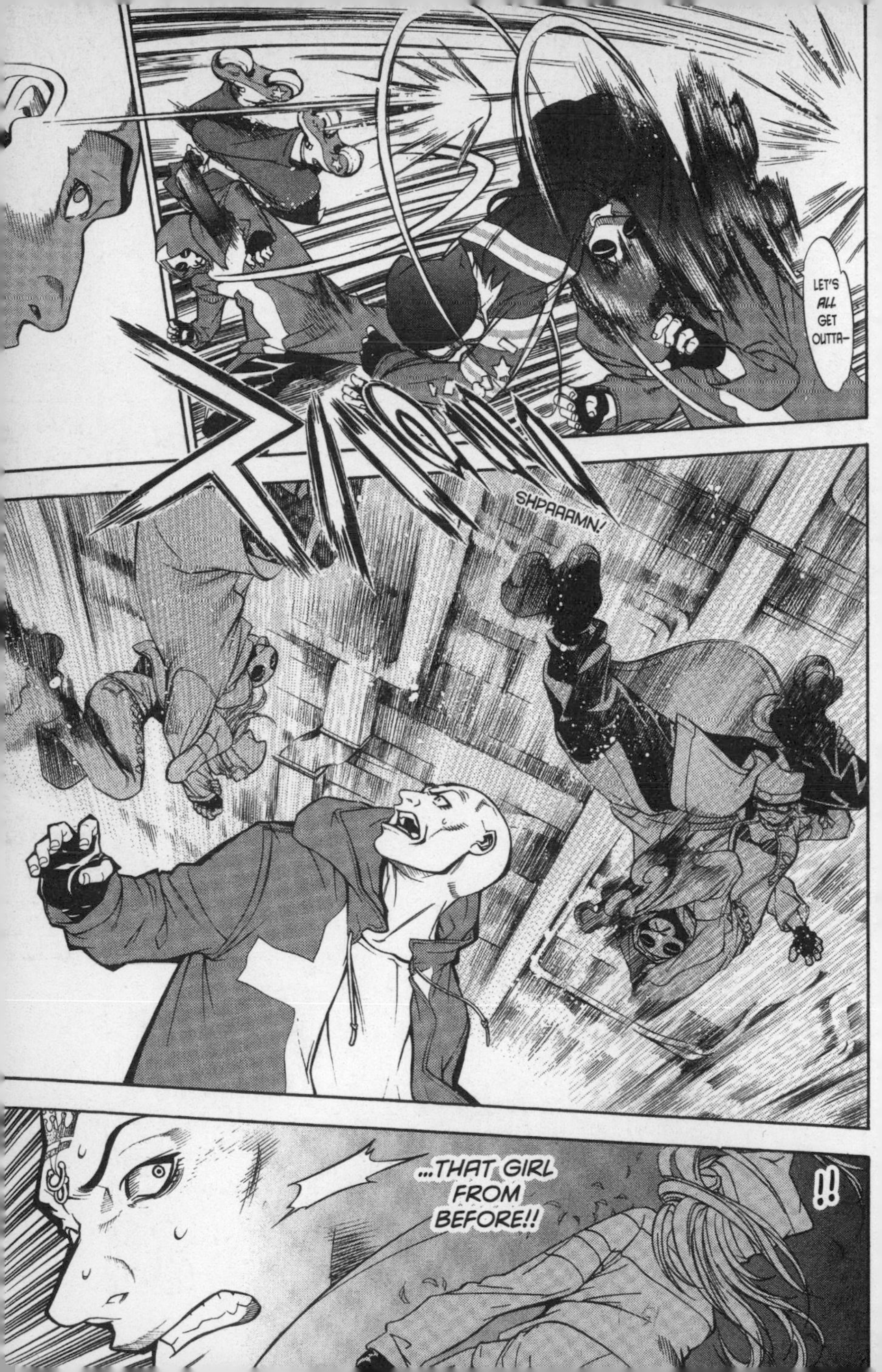
LET'S ALL GET OUTTA—
SHPAAAMN!
!!
...THAT GIRL FROM BEFORE!!

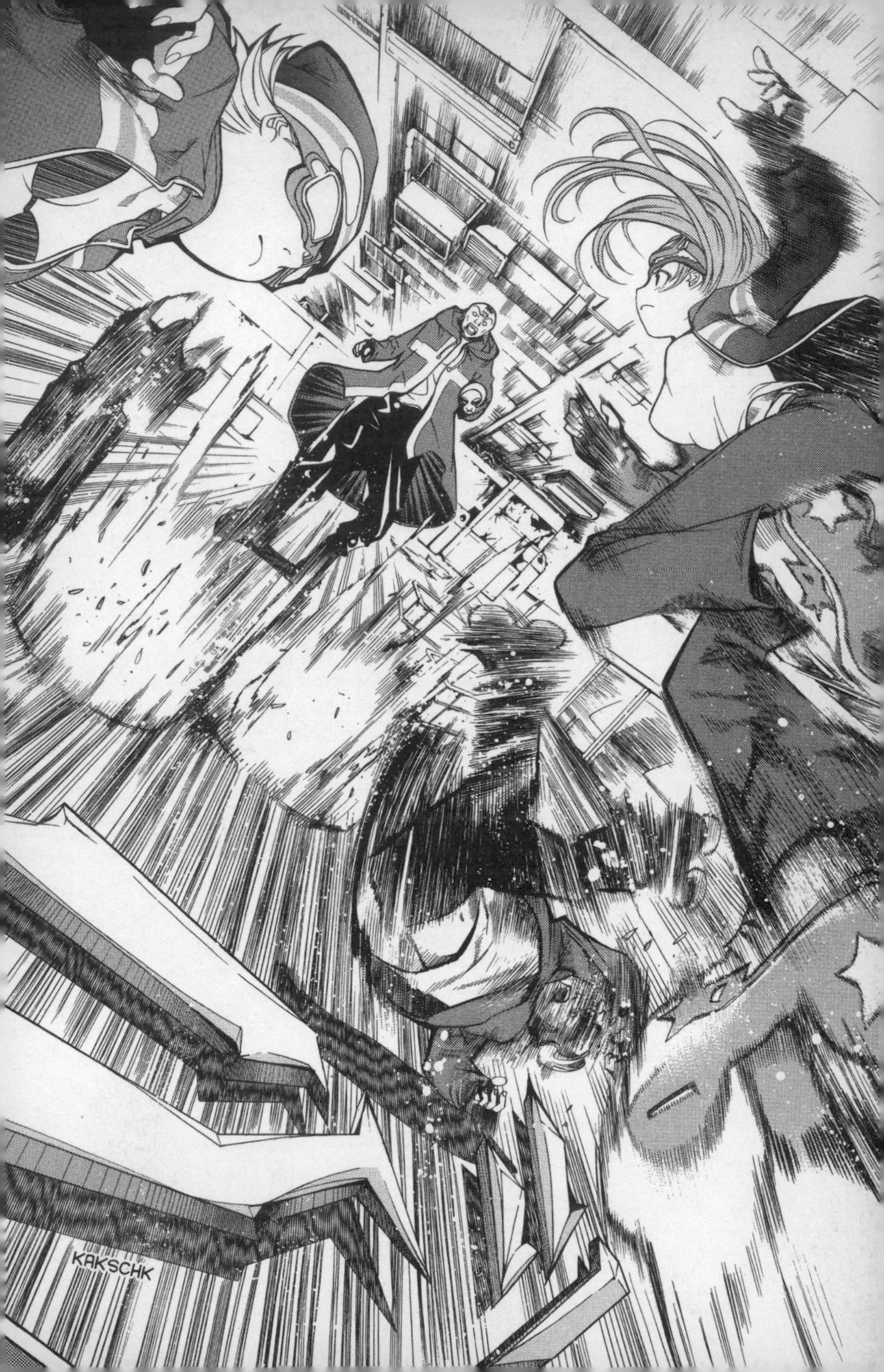
KAKSCHK

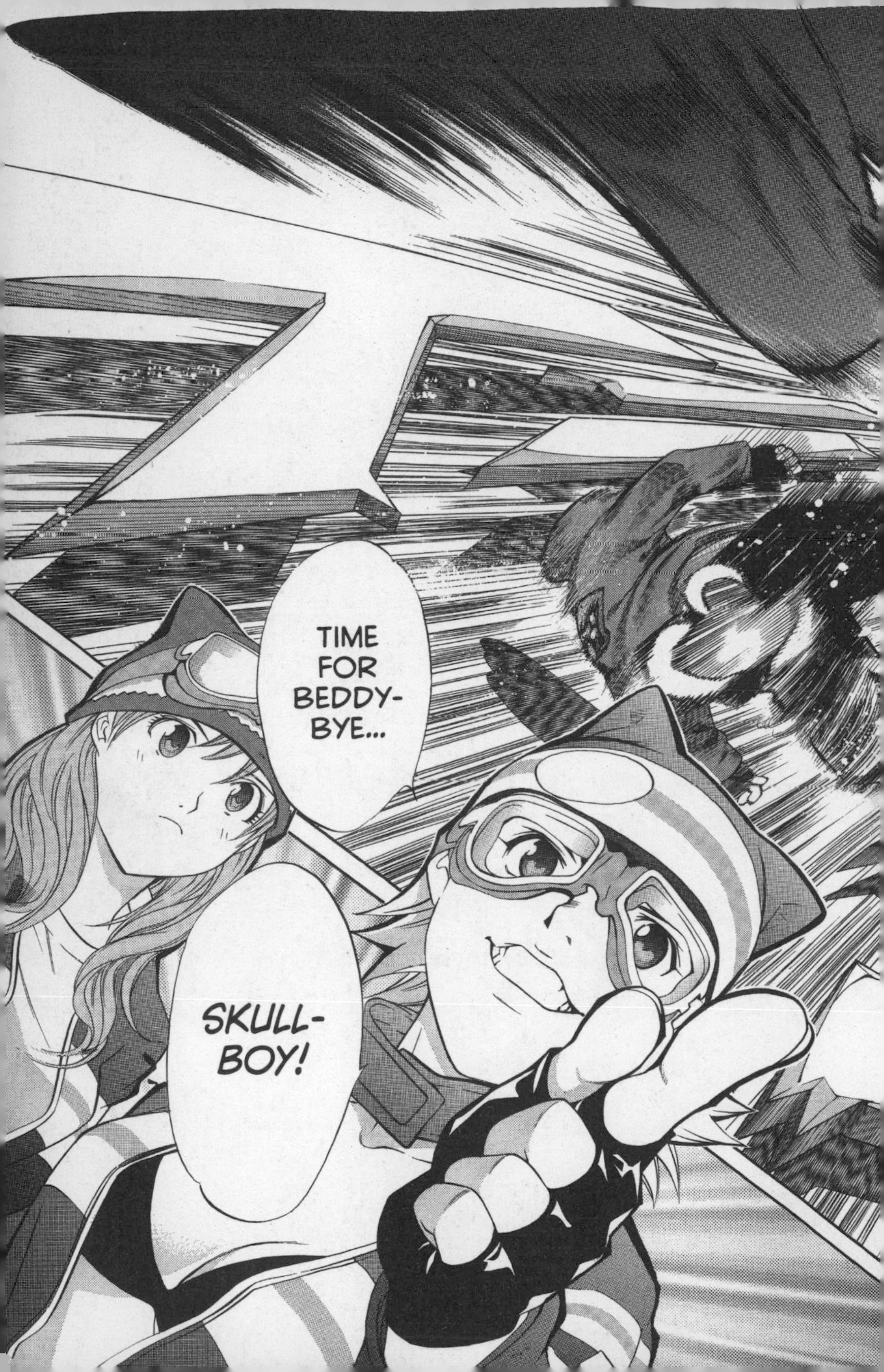
TIME FOR BEDDY-BYE...
SKULL-BOY!

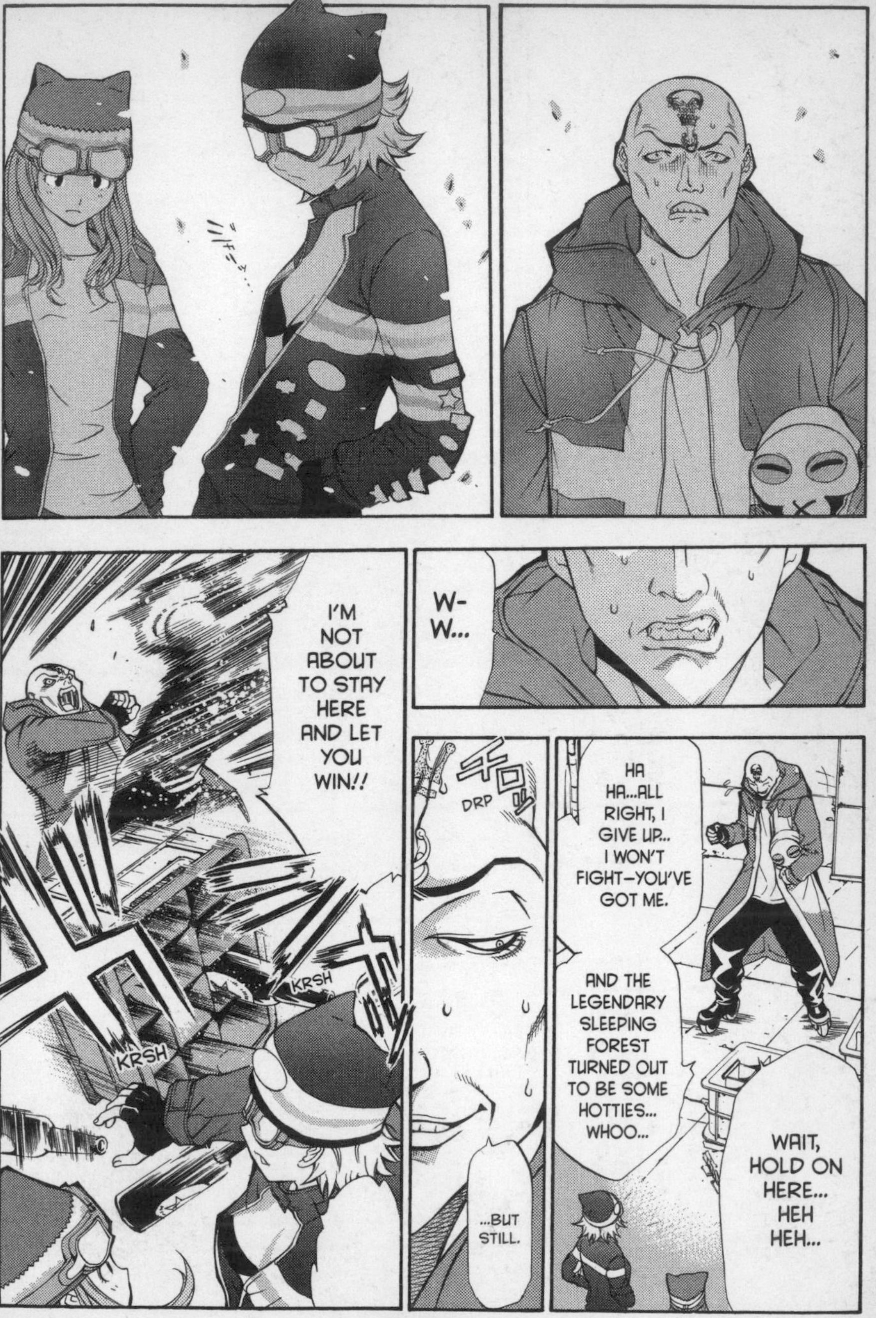
W-
W...
HA HA...ALL RIGHT, I GIVE UP... I WON'T FIGHT—YOU'VE GOT ME.
AND THE LEGENDARY SLEEPING FOREST TURNED OUT TO BE SOME HOTTIES... WHOO...
WAIT, HOLD ON HERE... HEH HEH...
DRP
...BUT STILL.
I'M NOT ABOUT TO STAY HERE AND LET YOU WIN!!
KRSH
KRSH

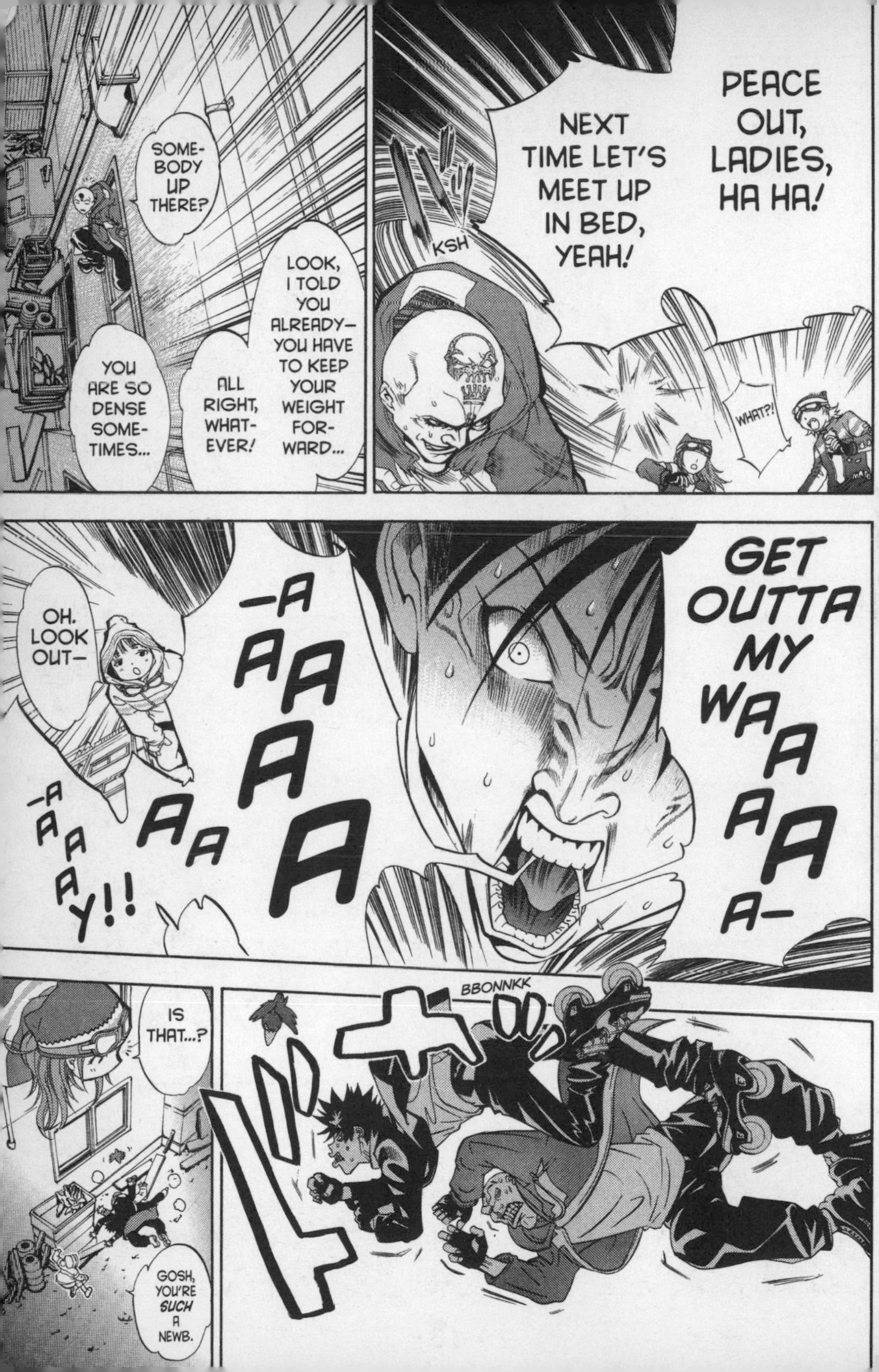

PEACE OUT, LADIES, HA HA!
NEXT TIME LET'S MEET UP IN BED, YEAH!
KSH
WHAT?!
SOME-BODY UP THERE?
LOOK, I TOLD YOU ALREADY— YOU HAVE TO KEEP YOUR WEIGHT FOR-WARD...
ALL RIGHT, WHAT-EVER!
YOU ARE SO DENSE SOME-TIMES...
GET OUTTA MY WAAAAAA—
—AAAAAAAA
OH. LOOK OUT—
—AAAAY!!
BBONNKK
IS THAT...?
GOSH, YOU'RE *SUCH* A NEWB.

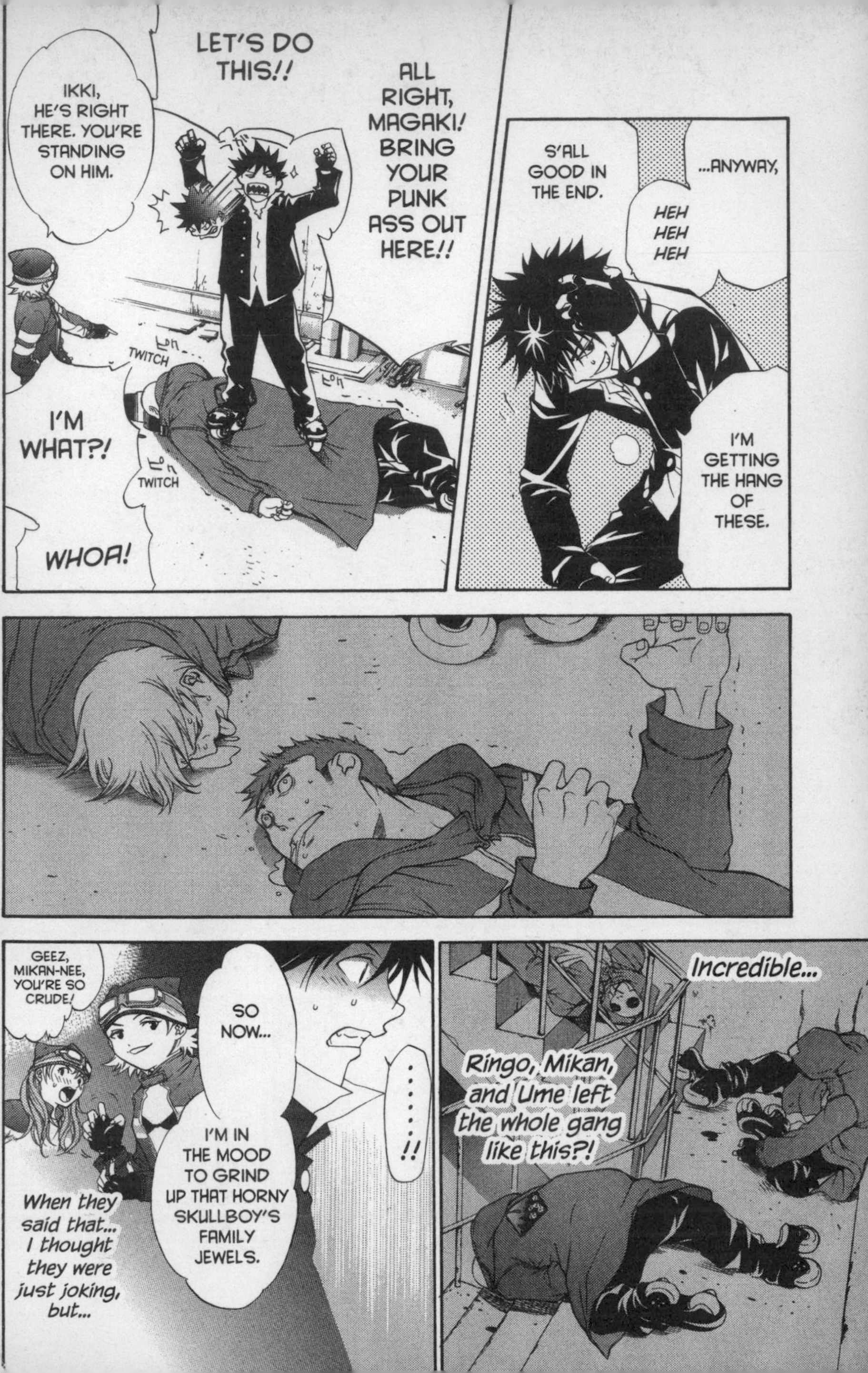
...ANYWAY,
S'ALL GOOD IN THE END.
HEH HEH HEH
I'M GETTING THE HANG OF THESE.
ALL RIGHT, MAGAKI! BRING YOUR PUNK ASS OUT HERE!!
LET'S DO THIS!!
IKKI, HE'S RIGHT THERE. YOU'RE STANDING ON HIM.
TWITCH
I'M WHAT?!
TWITCH
WHOA!
Incredible...
Ringo, Mikan, and Ume left the whole gang like this?!
......!!
SO NOW...
I'M IN THE MOOD TO GRIND UP THAT HORNY SKULLBOY'S FAMILY JEWELS.
GEEZ, MIKAN-NEE, YOU'RE SO CRUDE!
When they said that... I thought they were just joking, but...

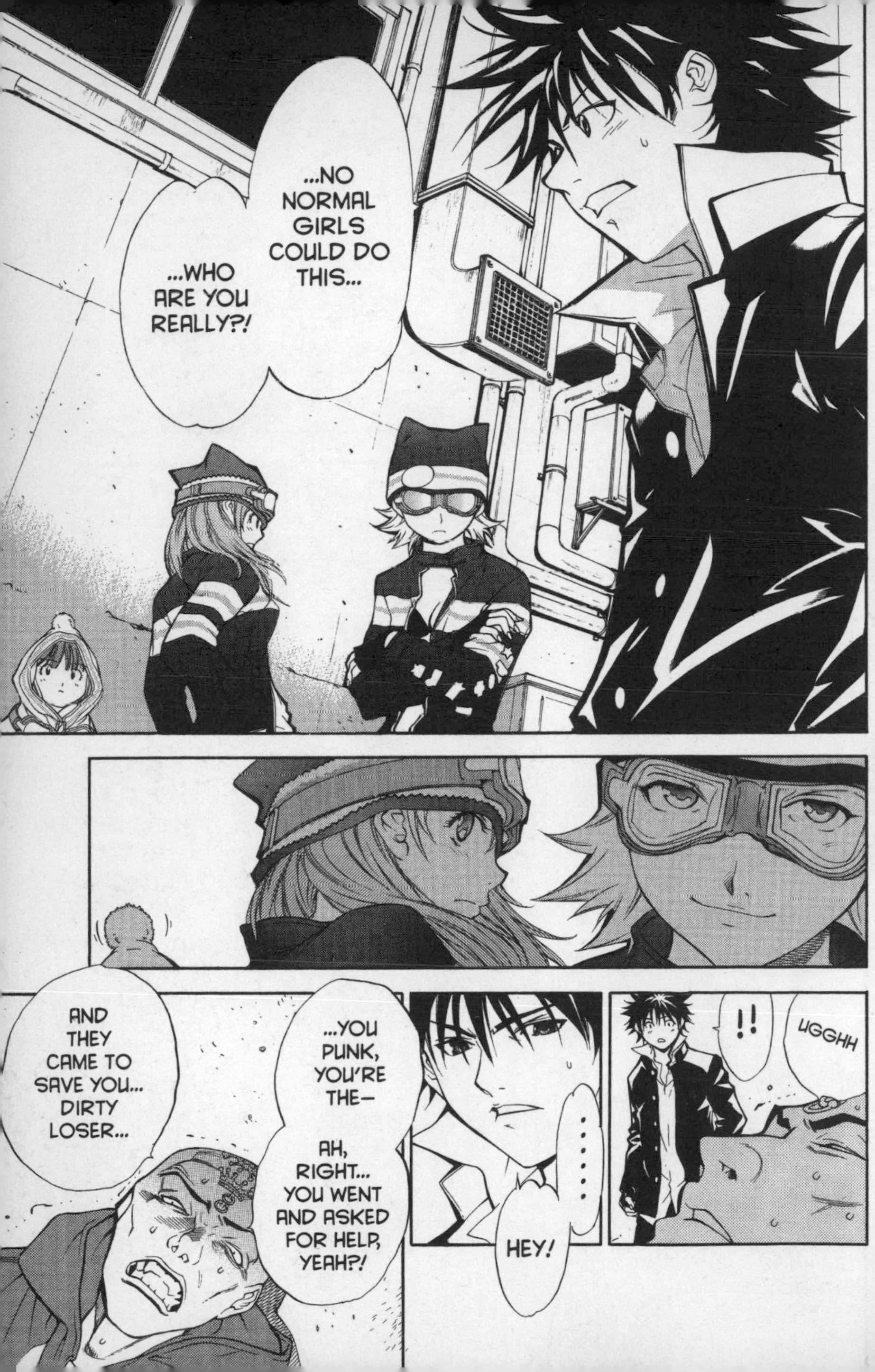
...NO NORMAL GIRLS COULD DO THIS...
...WHO ARE YOU REALLY?!
UGGHH
!!
......
HEY!
...YOU PUNK, YOU'RE THE—
AH, RIGHT... YOU WENT AND ASKED FOR HELP, YEAH?!
AND THEY CAME TO SAVE YOU... DIRTY LOSER...

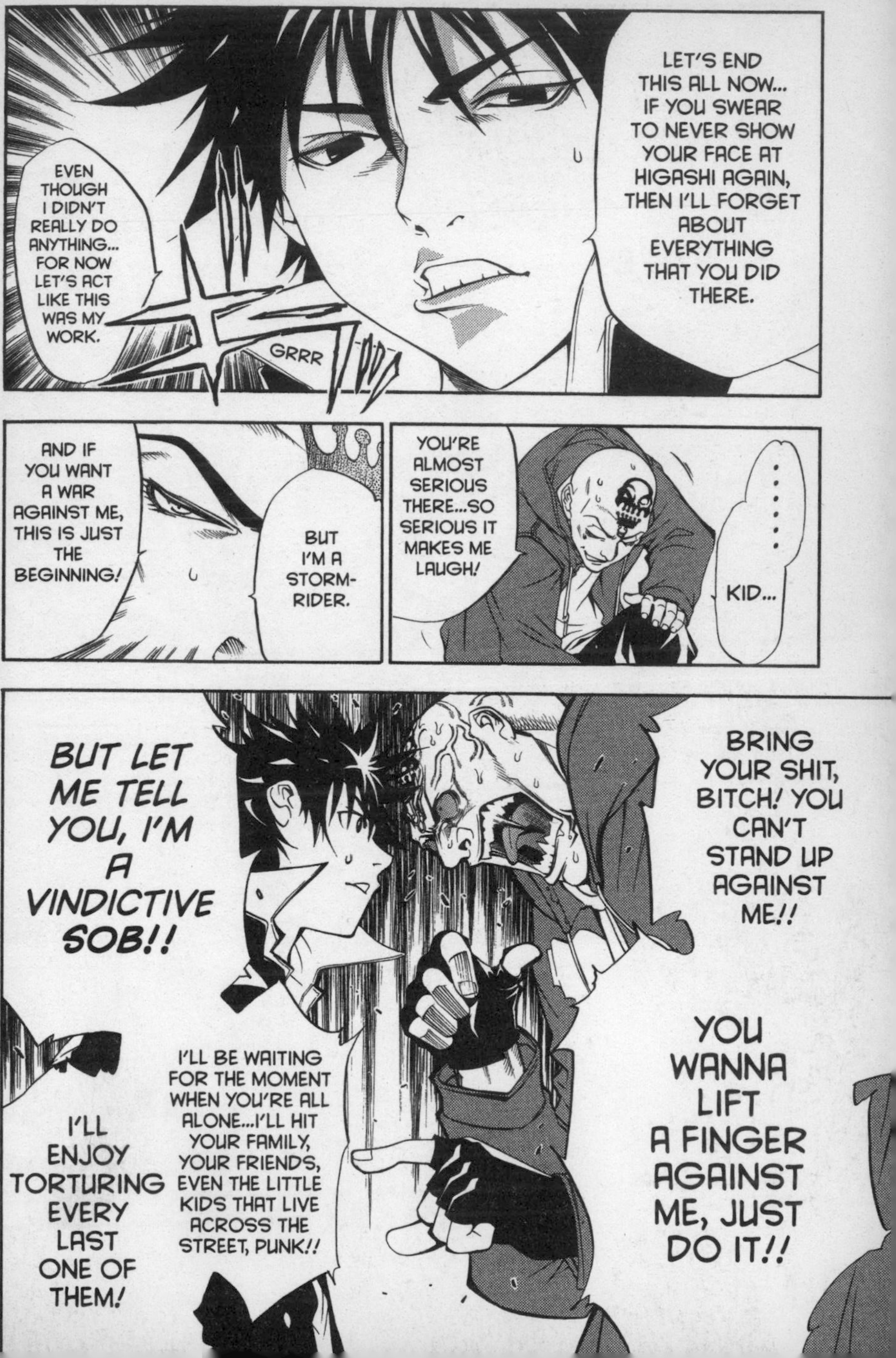
LET'S END THIS ALL NOW... IF YOU SWEAR TO NEVER SHOW YOUR FACE AT HIGASHI AGAIN, THEN I'LL FORGET ABOUT EVERYTHING THAT YOU DID THERE.
EVEN THOUGH I DIDN'T REALLY DO ANYTHING... FOR NOW LET'S ACT LIKE THIS WAS MY WORK.
GRRR
...... KID...
YOU'RE ALMOST SERIOUS THERE...SO SERIOUS IT MAKES ME LAUGH!
BUT I'M A STORM-RIDER.
AND IF YOU WANT A WAR AGAINST ME, THIS IS JUST THE BEGINNING!
BRING YOUR SHIT, BITCH! YOU CAN'T STAND UP AGAINST ME!!
BUT LET ME TELL YOU, I'M A VINDICTIVE SOB!!
YOU WANNA LIFT A FINGER AGAINST ME, JUST DO IT!!
I'LL BE WAITING FOR THE MOMENT WHEN YOU'RE ALL ALONE...I'LL HIT YOUR FAMILY, YOUR FRIENDS, EVEN THE LITTLE KIDS THAT LIVE ACROSS THE STREET, PUNK!!
I'LL ENJOY TORTURING EVERY LAST ONE OF THEM!

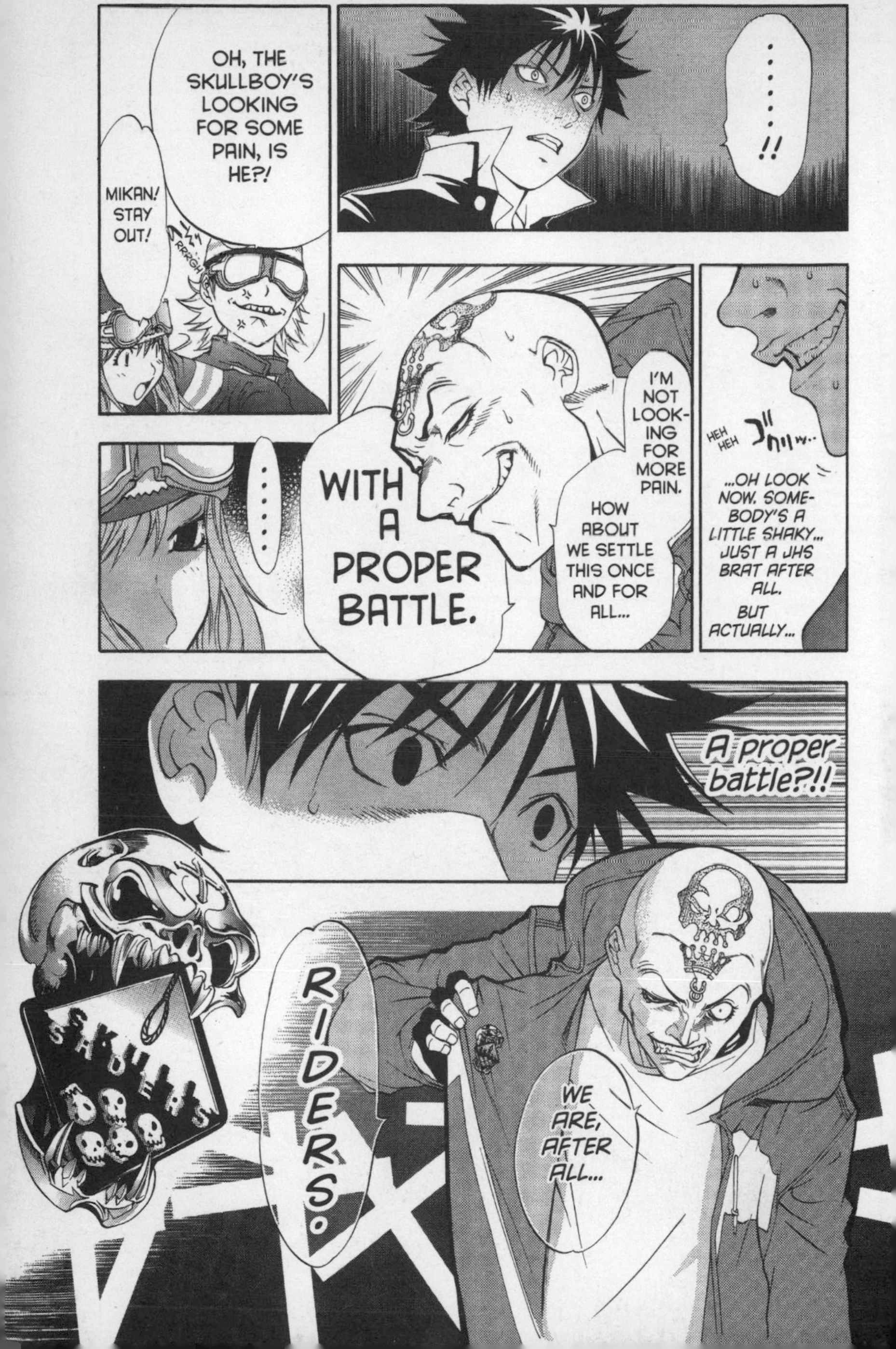
......!!
OH, THE SKULLBOY'S LOOKING FOR SOME PAIN, IS HE?!
MIKAN! STAY OUT!
RRRGH
HEH HEH
...OH LOOK NOW. SOME-BODY'S A LITTLE SHAKY... JUST A JHS BRAT AFTER ALL.
BUT ACTUALLY...
I'M NOT LOOK-ING FOR MORE PAIN.
HOW ABOUT WE SETTLE THIS ONCE AND FOR ALL...
WITH A PROPER BATTLE.
......
A proper battle?!!
WE ARE, AFTER ALL...
RIDERS.
SKULLERS

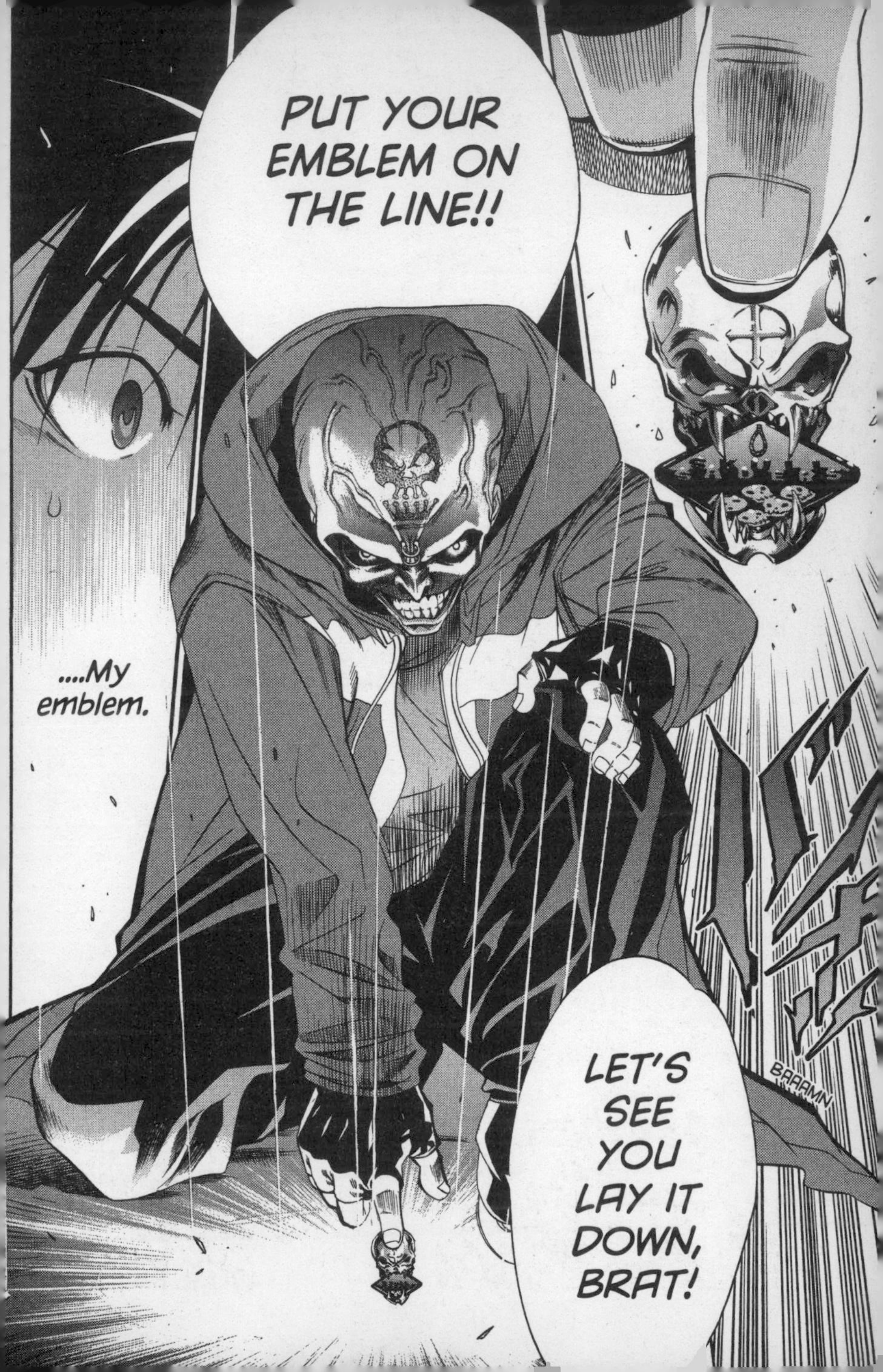
PUT YOUR EMBLEM ON THE LINE!!
LET'S SEE YOU LAY IT DOWN, BRAT!
BAAAMN
....My emblem.

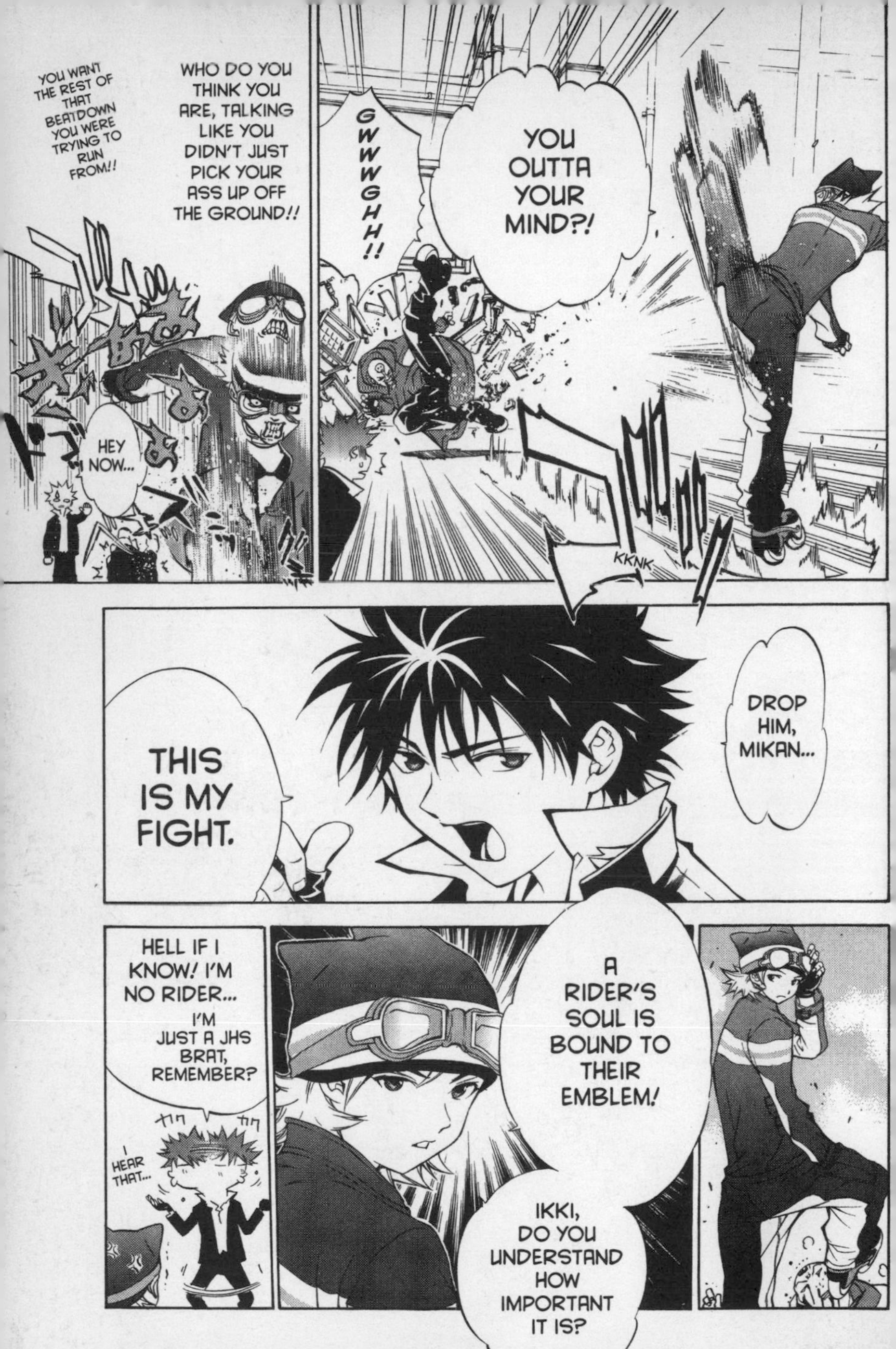
YOU OUTTA YOUR MIND?!
GWWWGHH!!
KKNK
WHO DO YOU THINK YOU ARE, TALKING LIKE YOU DIDN'T JUST PICK YOUR ASS UP OFF THE GROUND!!
YOU WANT THE REST OF THAT BEATDOWN YOU WERE TRYING TO RUN FROM!!
HEY NOW...
DROP HIM, MIKAN...
THIS IS MY FIGHT.
A RIDER'S SOUL IS BOUND TO THEIR EMBLEM!
IKKI, DO YOU UNDERSTAND HOW IMPORTANT IT IS?
HELL IF I KNOW! I'M NO RIDER...
I'M JUST A JHS BRAT, REMEMBER?
I HEAR THAT...

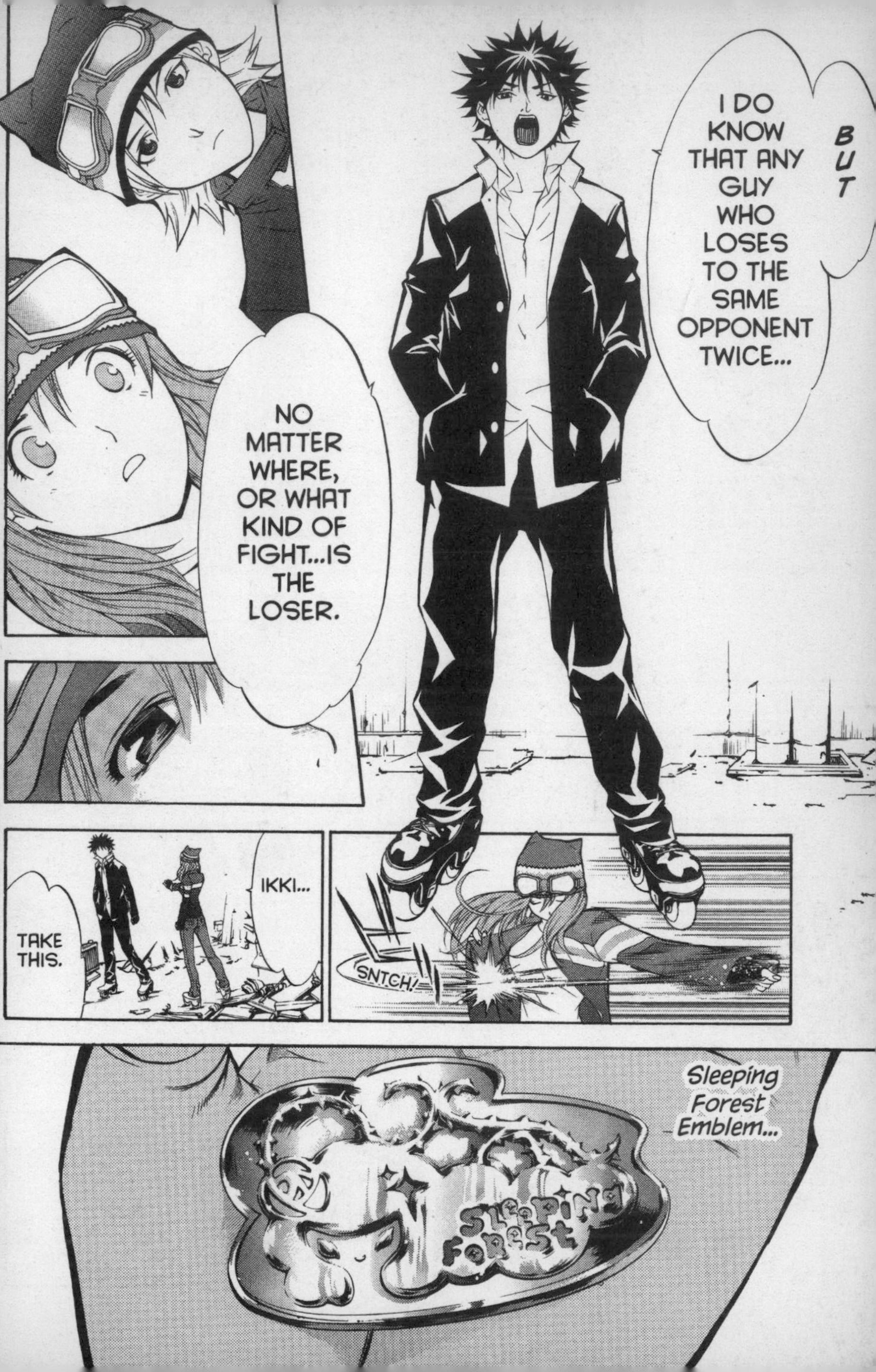
BUT
I DO KNOW THAT ANY GUY WHO LOSES TO THE SAME OPPONENT TWICE...
NO MATTER WHERE, OR WHAT KIND OF FIGHT...IS THE LOSER.
SNTCH!
IKKI...
TAKE THIS.
Sleeping Forest Emblem...
SLEEPING FOREST

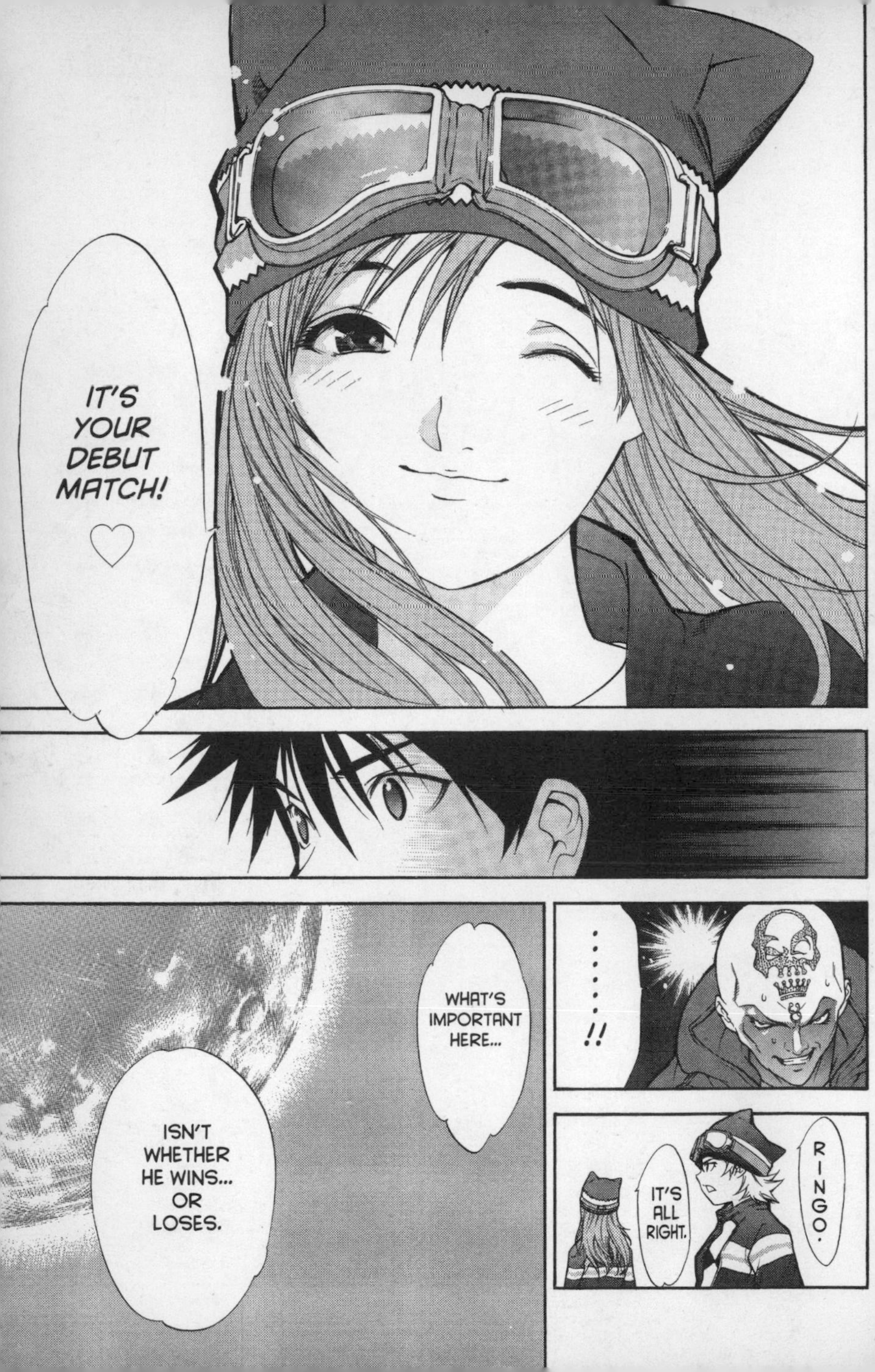
IT'S YOUR DEBUT MATCH! ♡
......!!
RINGO.
IT'S ALL RIGHT.
WHAT'S IMPORTANT HERE...
ISN'T WHETHER HE WINS... OR LOSES.

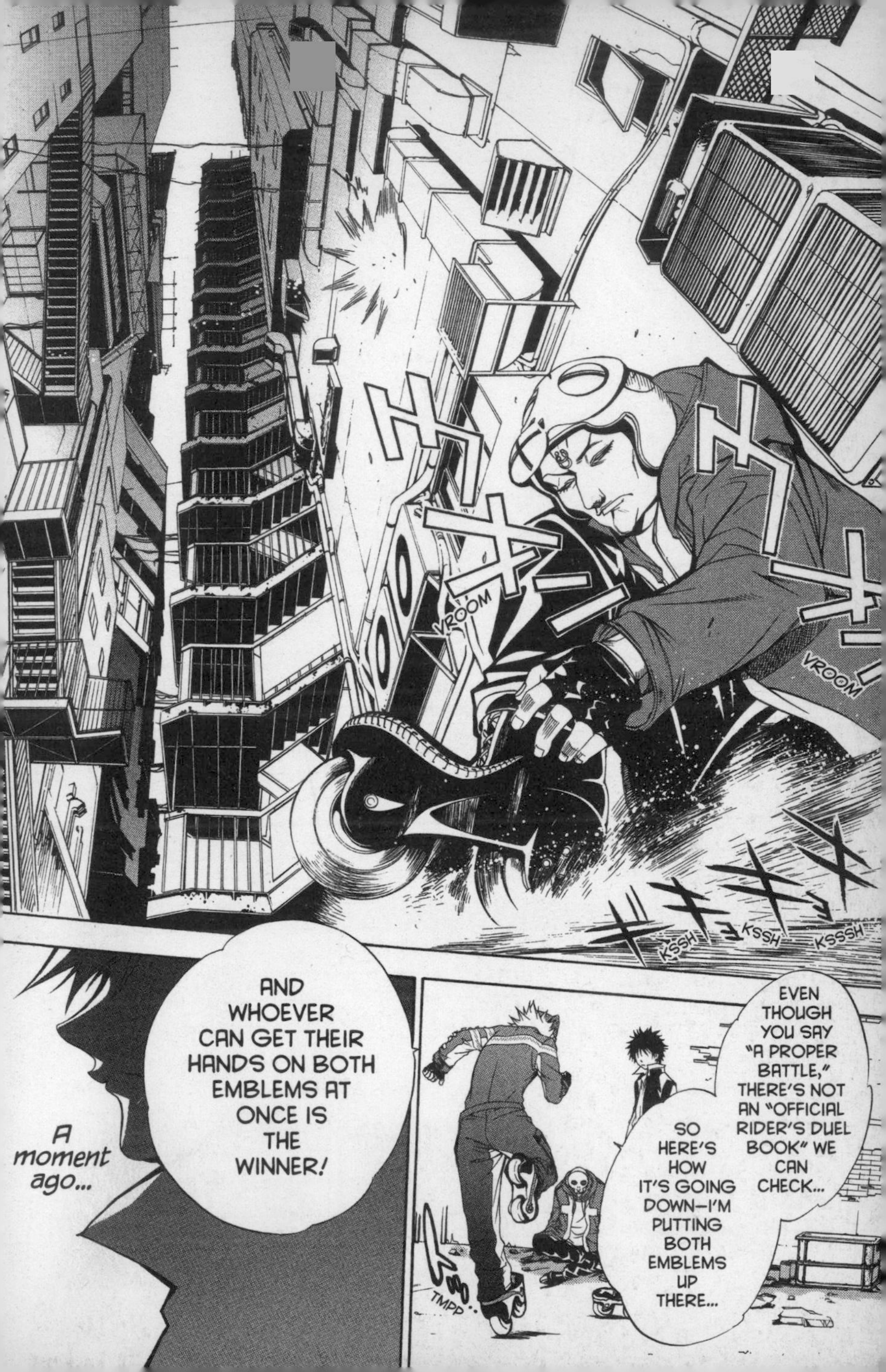
VROOM
VROOM
KSSSH
KSSH
KSSH
EVEN THOUGH YOU SAY "A PROPER BATTLE," THERE'S NOT AN "OFFICIAL RIDER'S DUEL BOOK" WE CAN CHECK...
SO HERE'S HOW IT'S GOING DOWN—I'M PUTTING BOTH EMBLEMS UP THERE...
TMPP
AND WHOEVER CAN GET THEIR HANDS ON BOTH EMBLEMS AT ONCE IS THE WINNER!
A moment ago...

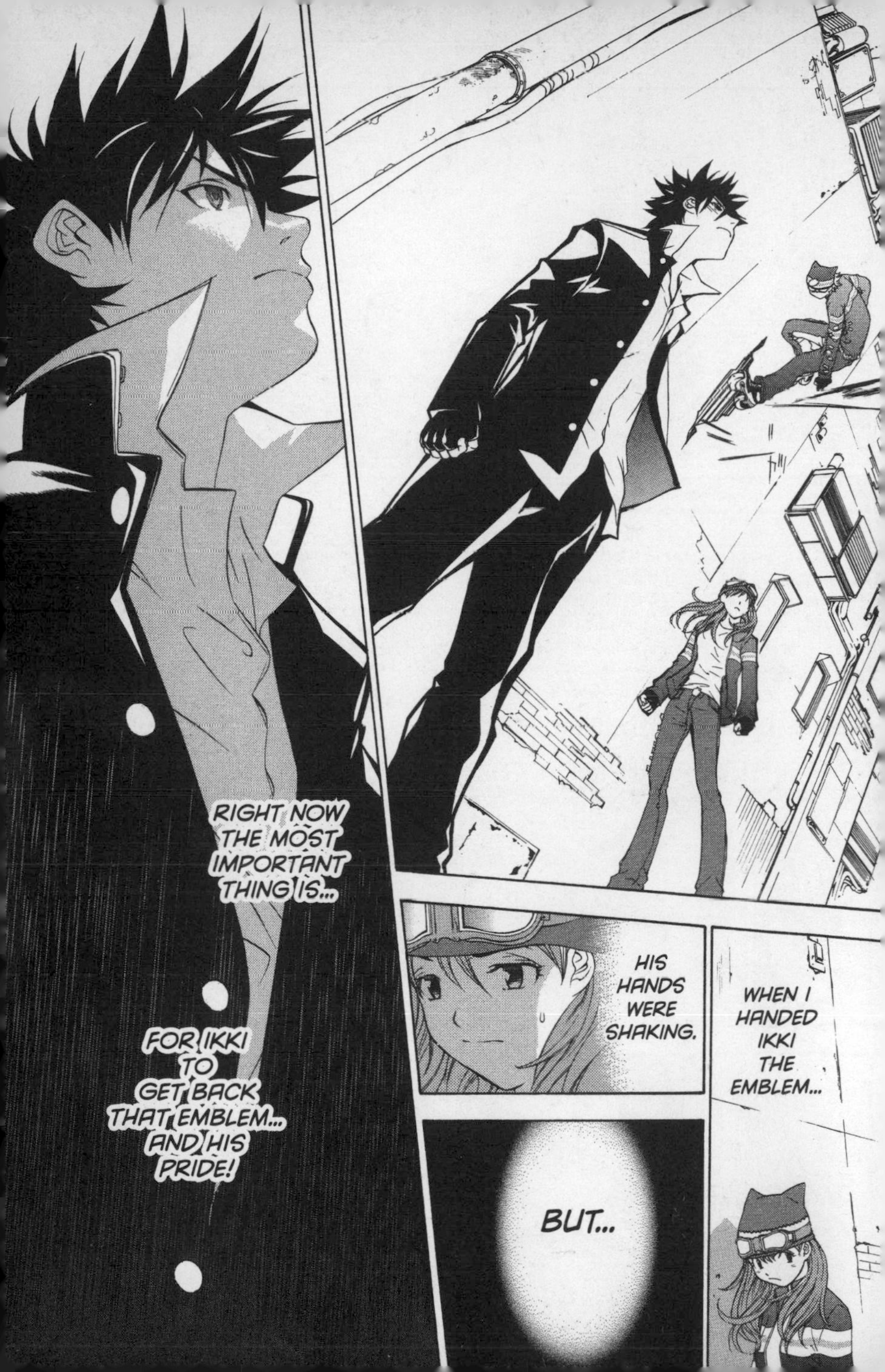
WHEN I HANDED IKKI THE EMBLEM...
HIS HANDS WERE SHAKING.
BUT...
RIGHT NOW THE MOST IMPORTANT THING IS...
FOR IKKI TO GET BACK THAT EMBLEM... AND HIS PRIDE!

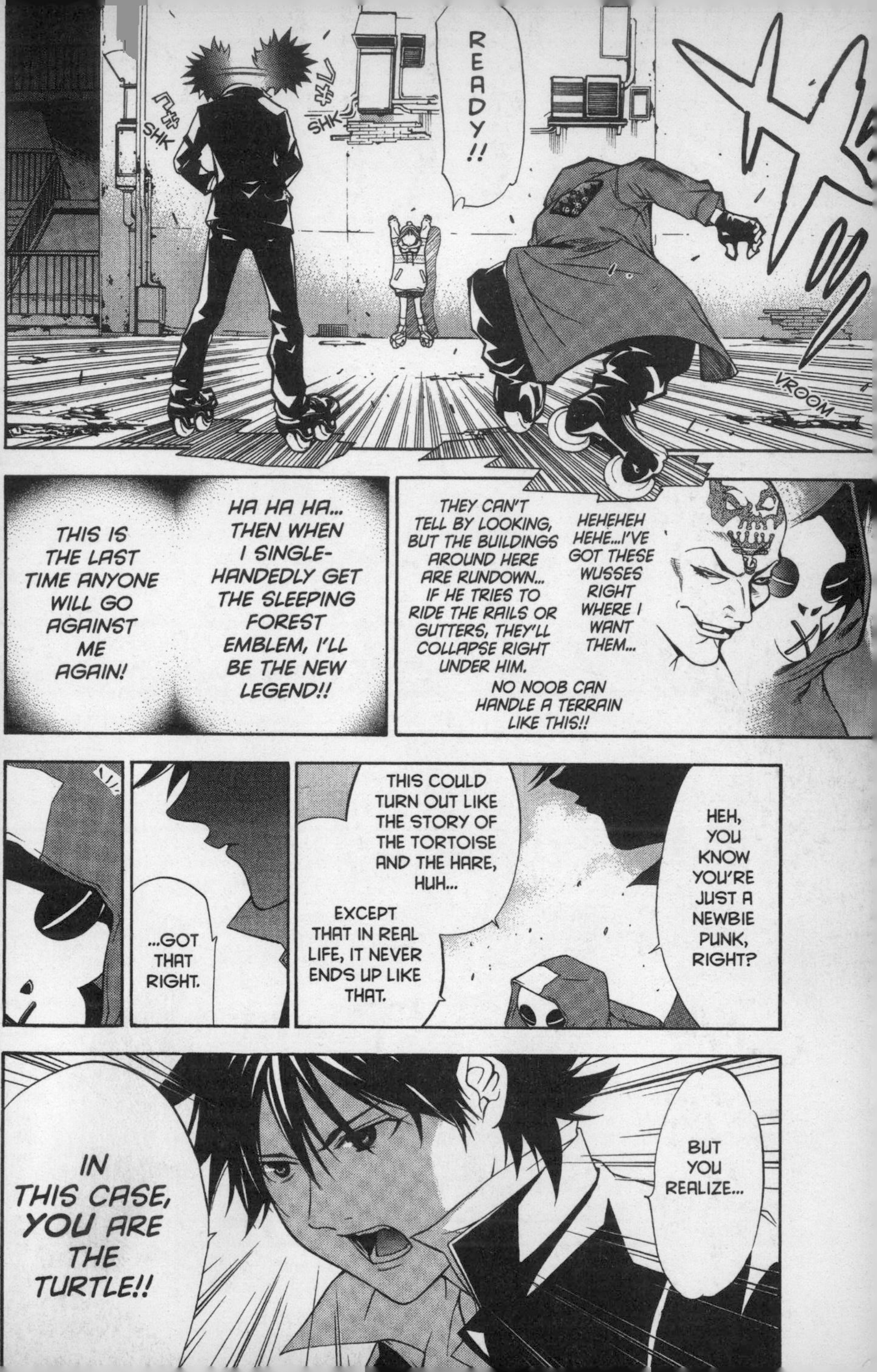
SHK
SHK
READY!!
VROOM
HEHEHEH HEHE...I'VE GOT THESE WUSSES RIGHT WHERE I WANT THEM...
THEY CAN'T TELL BY LOOKING, BUT THE BUILDINGS AROUND HERE ARE RUNDOWN... IF HE TRIES TO RIDE THE RAILS OR GUTTERS, THEY'LL COLLAPSE RIGHT UNDER HIM.
NO NOOB CAN HANDLE A TERRAIN LIKE THIS!!
HA HA HA... THEN WHEN I SINGLE-HANDEDLY GET THE SLEEPING FOREST EMBLEM, I'LL BE THE NEW LEGEND!!
THIS IS THE LAST TIME ANYONE WILL GO AGAINST ME AGAIN!
HEH, YOU KNOW YOU'RE JUST A NEWBIE PUNK, RIGHT?
THIS COULD TURN OUT LIKE THE STORY OF THE TORTOISE AND THE HARE, HUH...
EXCEPT THAT IN REAL LIFE, IT NEVER ENDS UP LIKE THAT.
...GOT THAT RIGHT.
BUT YOU REALIZE...
IN THIS CASE, YOU ARE THE TURTLE!!

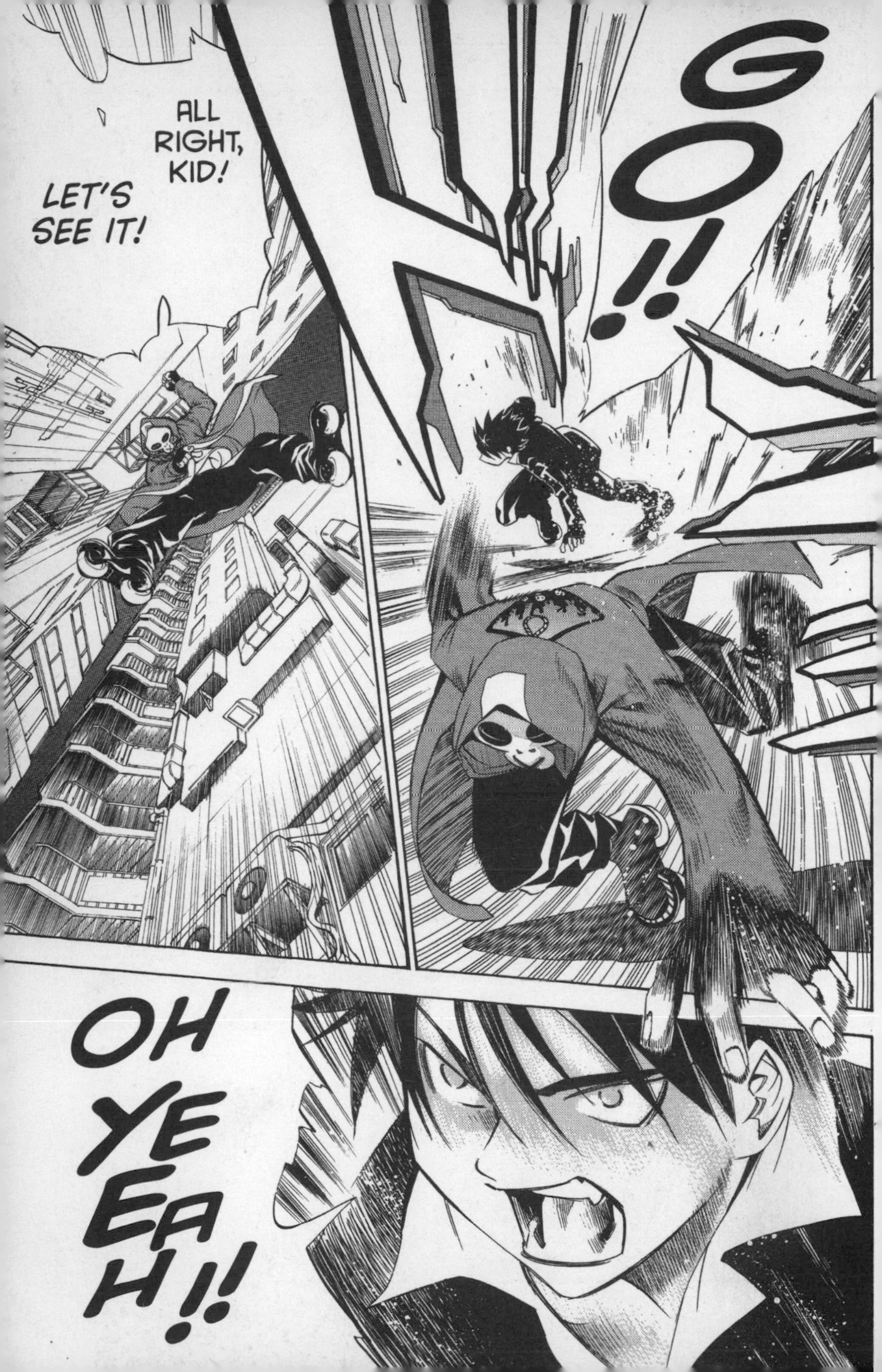
GO!!
ALL RIGHT, KID!
LET'S SEE IT!
OH YEEAH!!

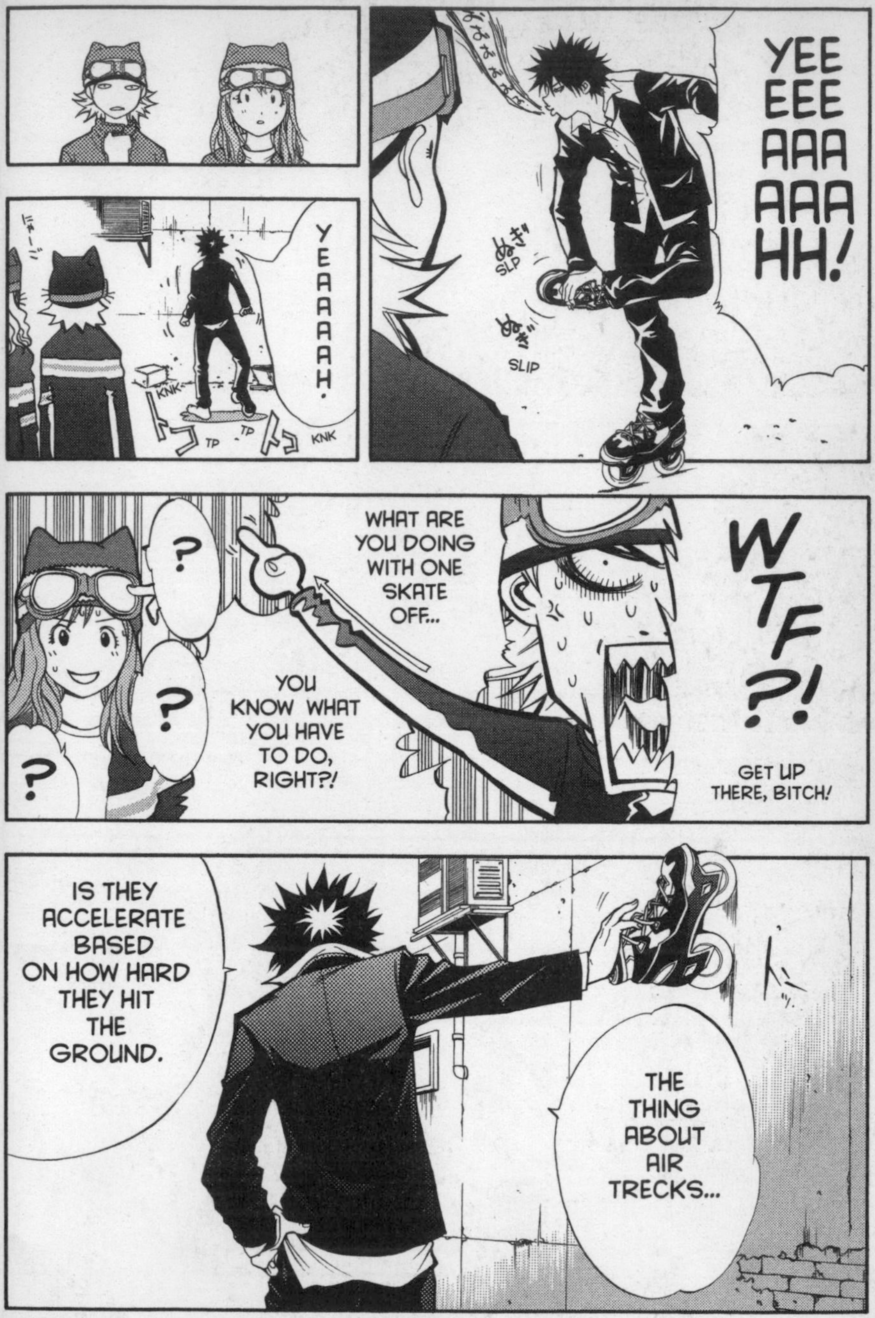
YEEEEEAAAAAAHH!
ぬぎ
SLIP
ぬぎ
SLIP
にゃーご
YEAAAAAAH.
KNK
トコ
TP
TP
トコ
KNK
WTF?!
GET UP THERE, BITCH!
WHAT ARE YOU DOING WITH ONE SKATE OFF...
YOU KNOW WHAT YOU HAVE TO DO, RIGHT?!
?
?
?
THE THING ABOUT AIR TRECKS...
IS THEY ACCELERATE BASED ON HOW HARD THEY HIT THE GROUND.

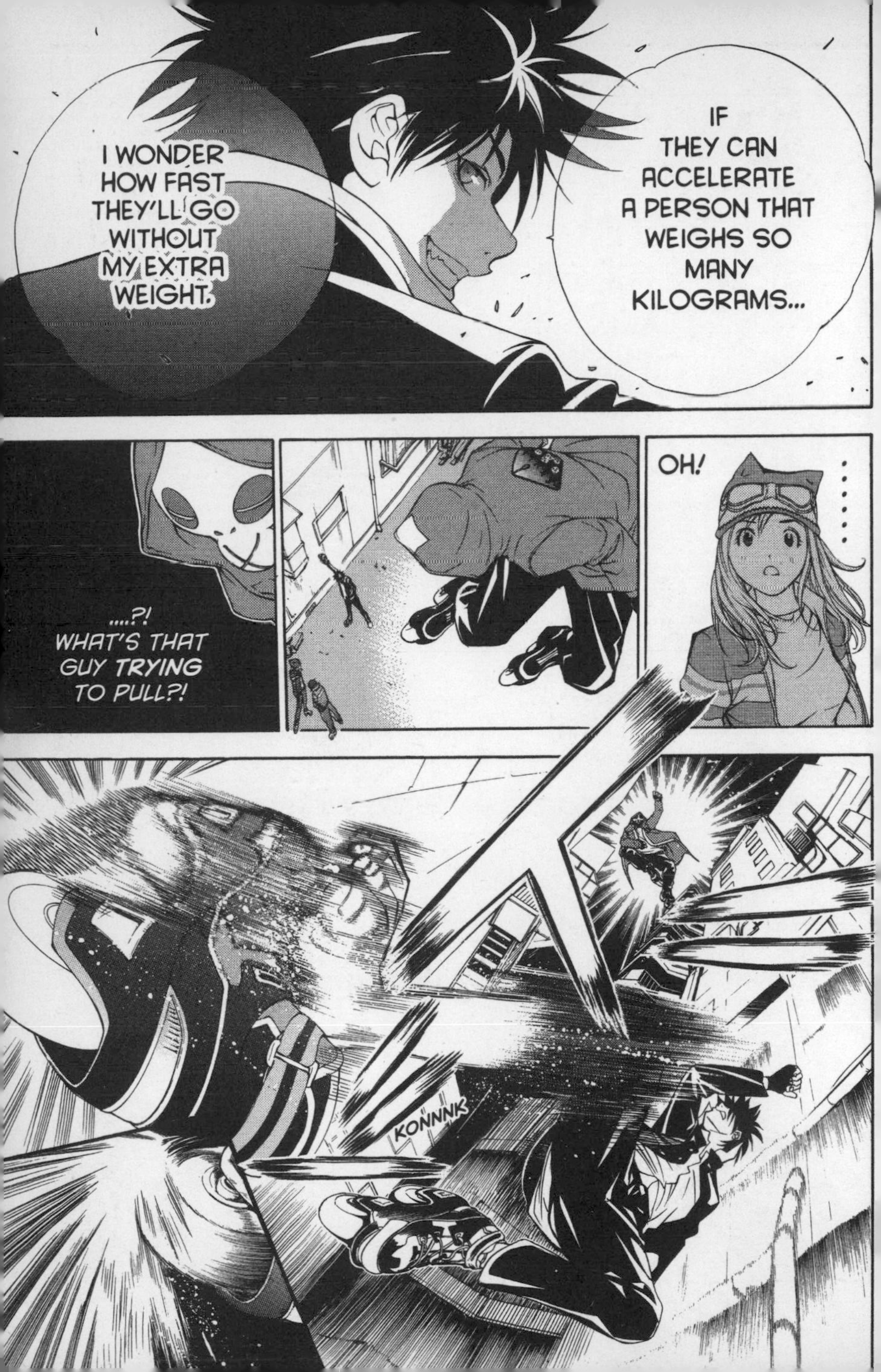
IF THEY CAN ACCELERATE A PERSON THAT WEIGHS SO MANY KILOGRAMS...
I WONDER HOW FAST THEY'LL GO WITHOUT MY EXTRA WEIGHT.
OH!
......
....?! WHAT'S THAT GUY *TRYING* TO PULL?!
KONNNK

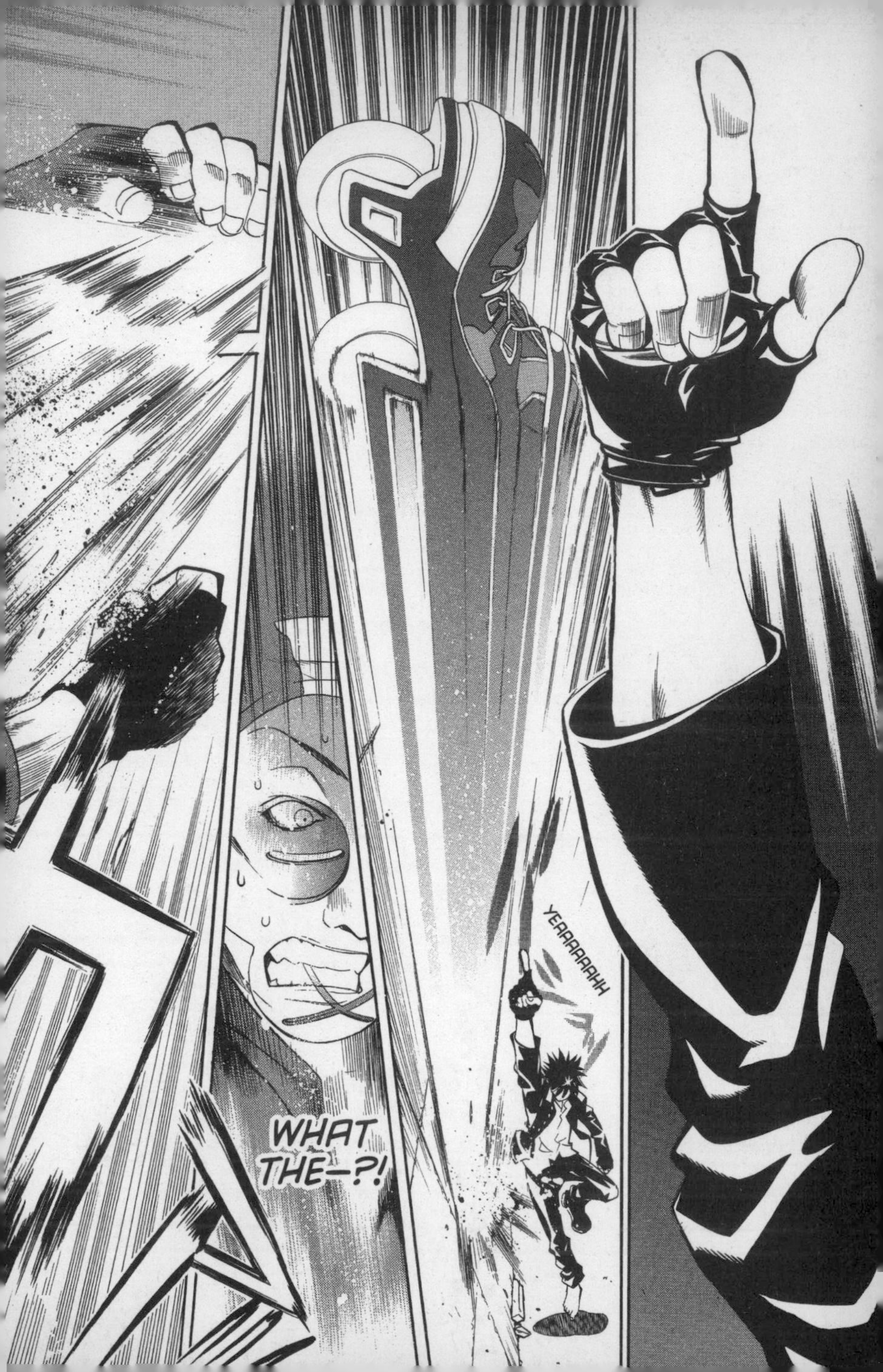
YEAAAAAAHH
WHAT THE–?!

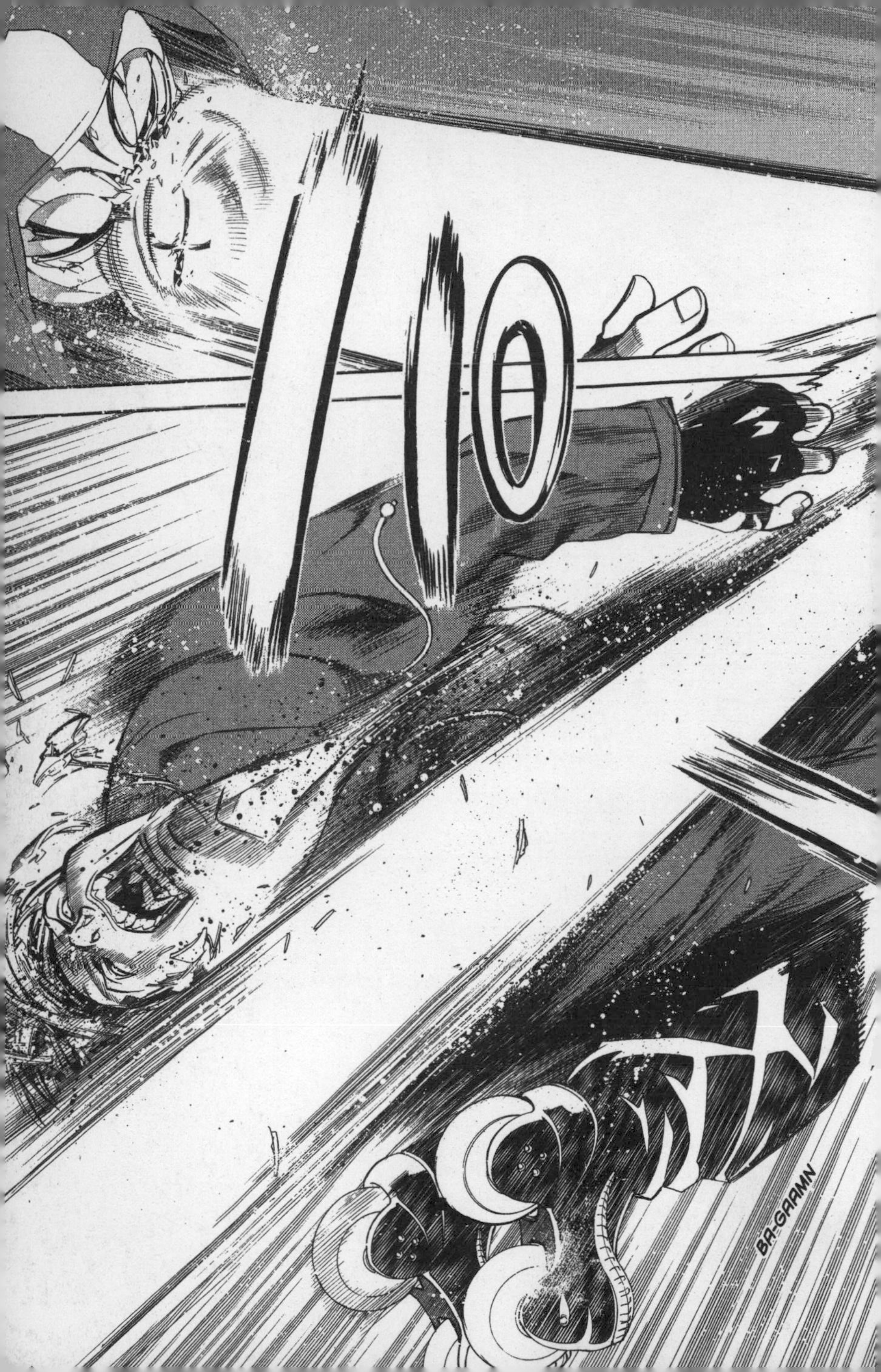
BA-GARMN

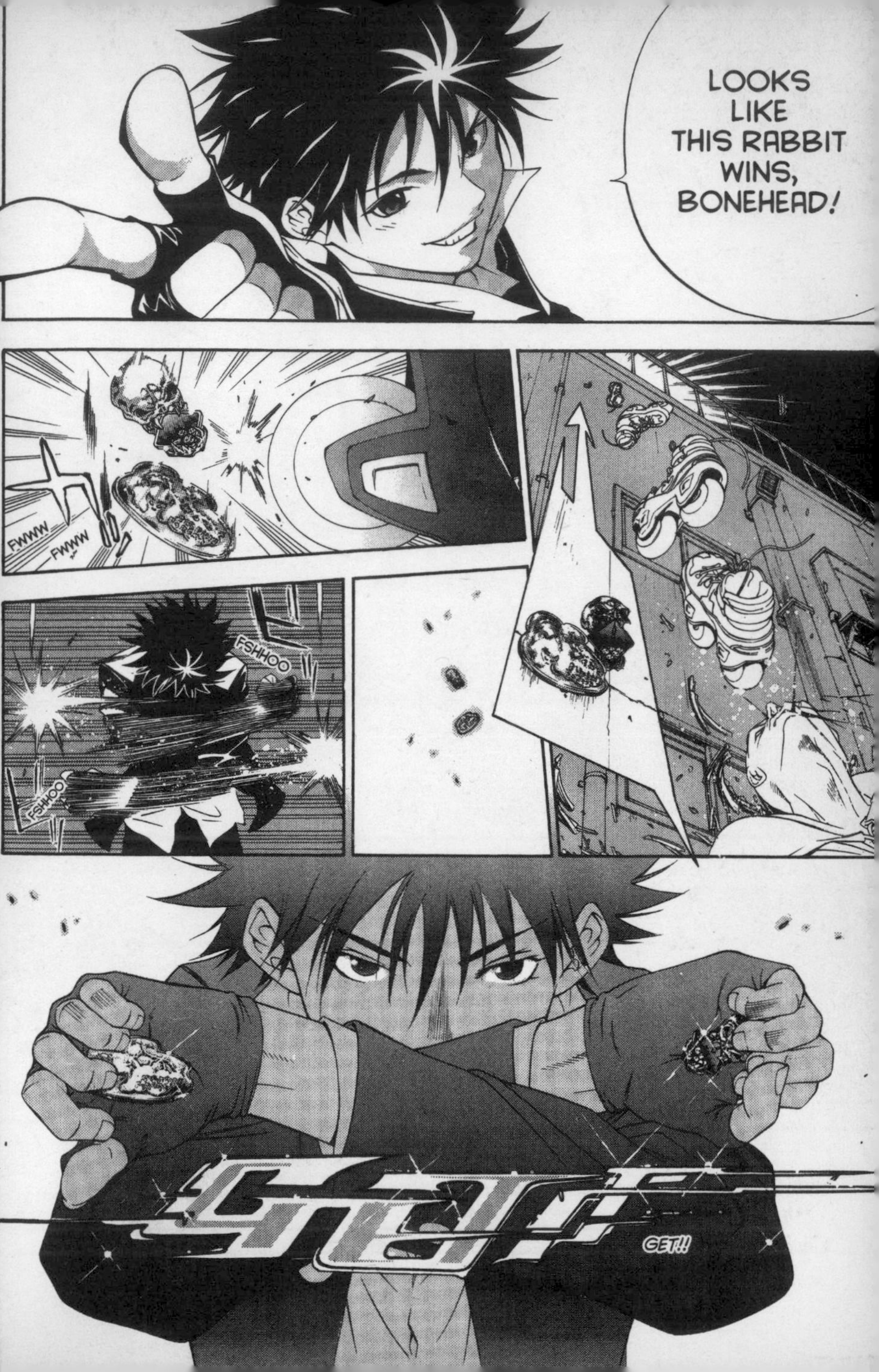
LOOKS LIKE THIS RABBIT WINS, BONEHEAD!
FWWW
FWWW
FSHHOO
FSHHOO
GET!!

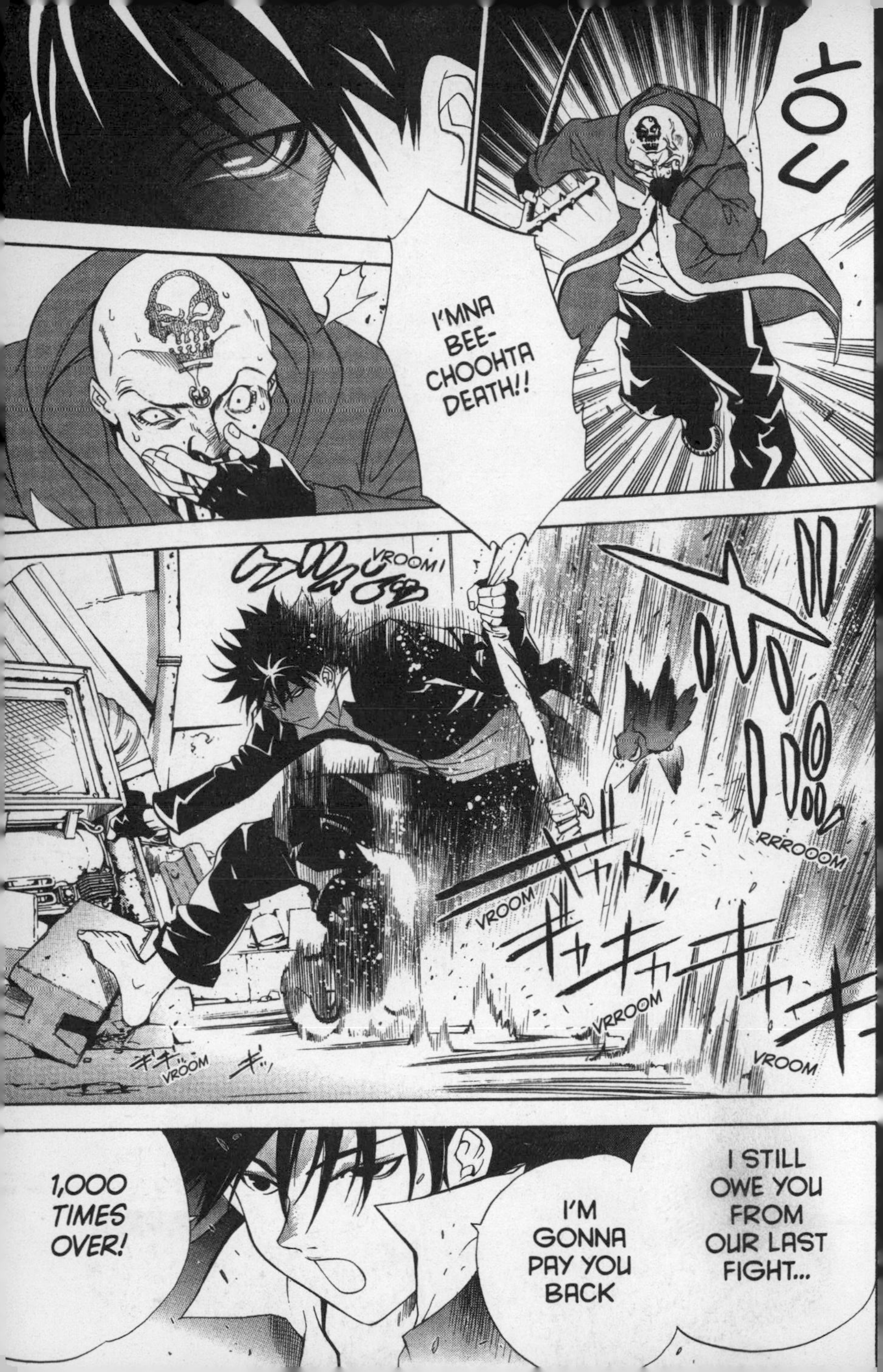
I'MNA BEE-CHOOHTA DEATH!!
VROOM!
RRROOOM
VROOM
VRROOM
VROOM
VROOM
I STILL OWE YOU FROM OUR LAST FIGHT...
I'M GONNA PAY YOU BACK
1,000 TIMES OVER!

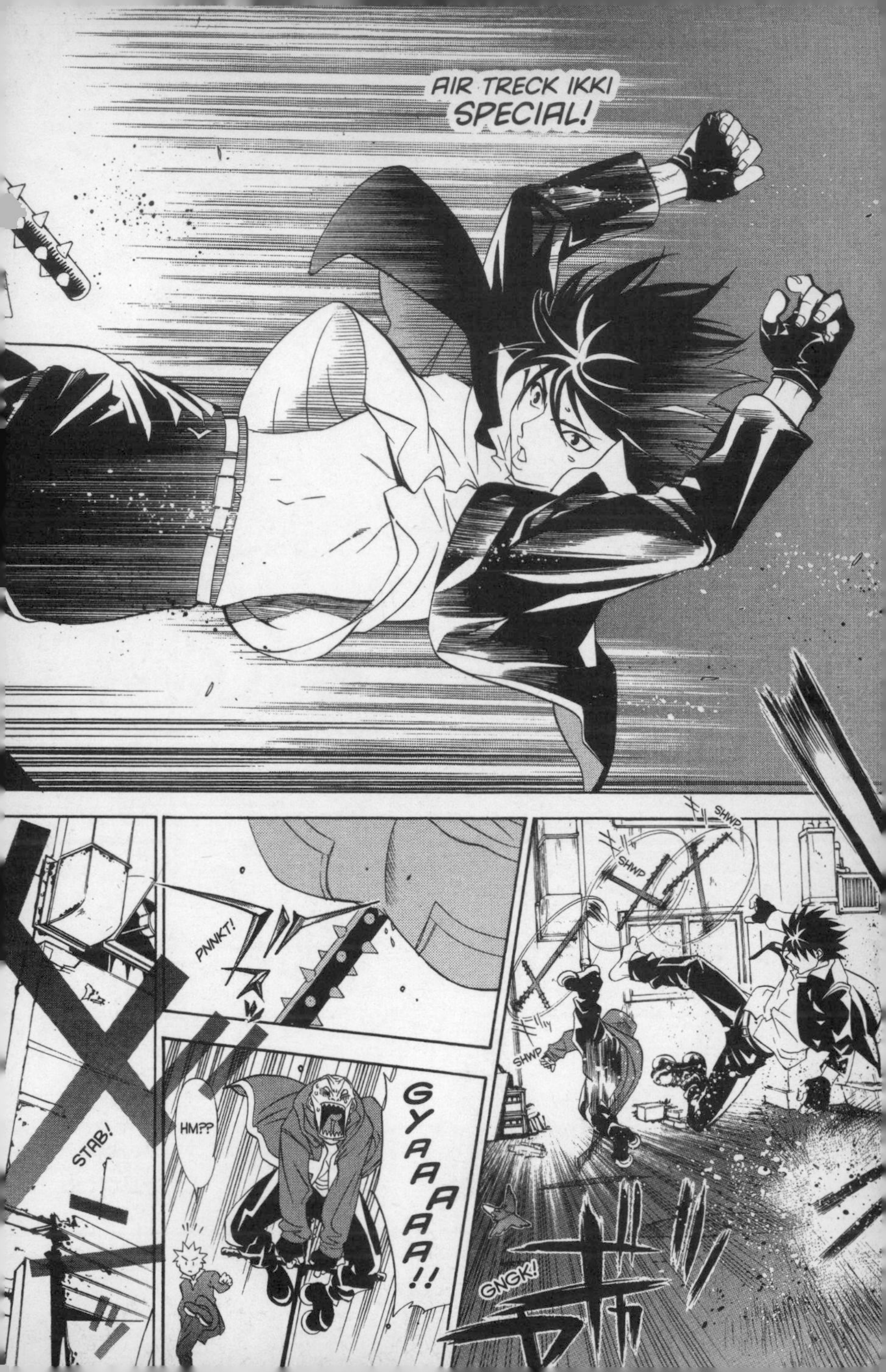
AIR TRECK IKKI SPECIAL!
SHWP
SHWP
SHWP
GNGK!
PNNKT!
GYAAAAAA!!
HM??
STAB!

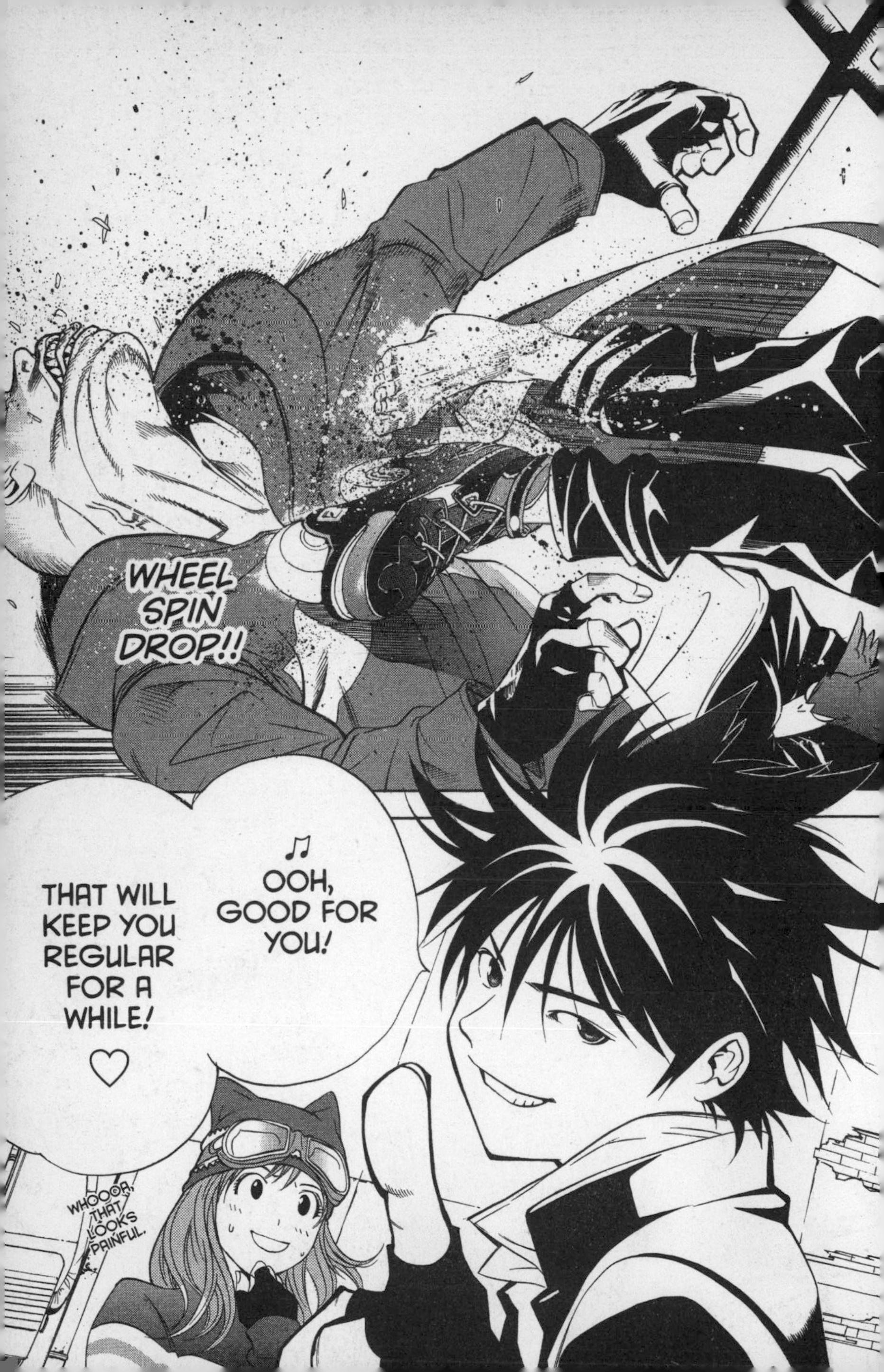
WHEEL SPIN DROP!!
♫ OOH, GOOD FOR YOU!
THAT WILL KEEP YOU REGULAR FOR A WHILE! ♡
WHOOOA, THAT LOOKS PAINFUL.

A FLOWER TO REPRESENT MAGAKI'S EVENING...

A FLOWER THAT HAS ALREADY BLOOMED

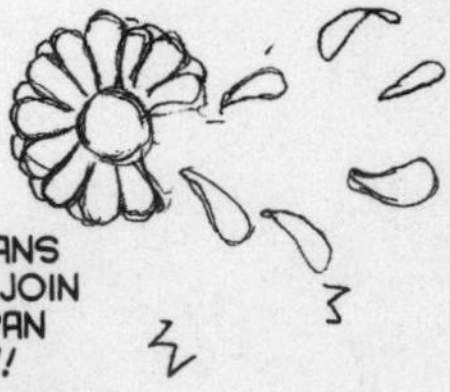

THIS MEANS HE CAN'T JOIN THE JAPAN NAVY!!

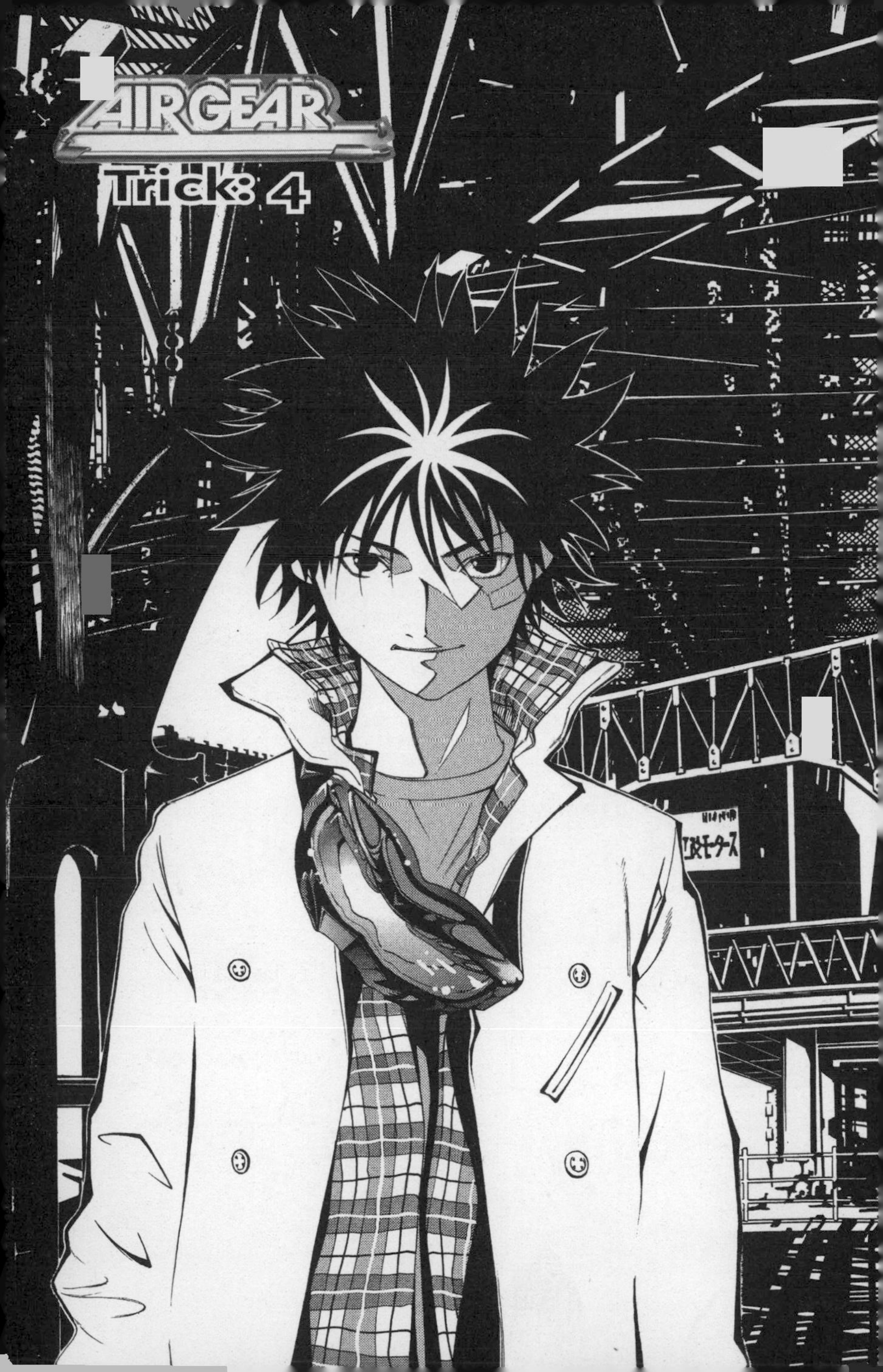
AIRGEAR
Trick: 4

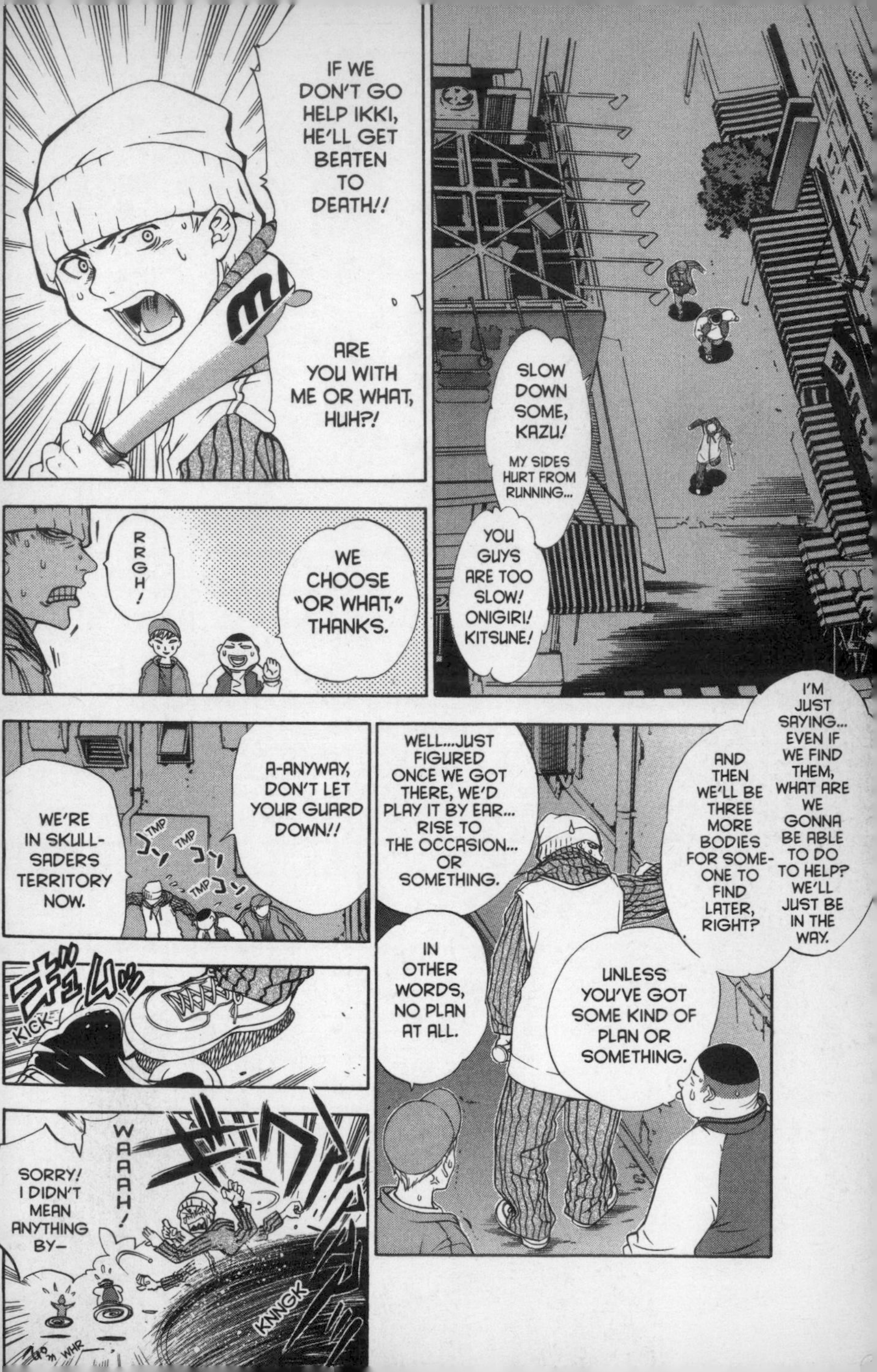
SLOW DOWN SOME, KAZU!
MY SIDES HURT FROM RUNNING...
YOU GUYS ARE TOO SLOW! ONIGIRI! KITSUNE!
IF WE DON'T GO HELP IKKI, HE'LL GET BEATEN TO DEATH!!
ARE YOU WITH ME OR WHAT, HUH?!
WE CHOOSE "OR WHAT," THANKS.
RRGH!
I'M JUST SAYING... EVEN IF WE FIND THEM, WHAT ARE WE GONNA BE ABLE TO DO TO HELP? WE'LL JUST BE IN THE WAY.
AND THEN WE'LL BE THREE MORE BODIES FOR SOME-ONE TO FIND LATER, RIGHT?
UNLESS YOU'VE GOT SOME KIND OF PLAN OR SOMETHING.
WELL...JUST FIGURED ONCE WE GOT THERE, WE'D PLAY IT BY EAR... RISE TO THE OCCASION... OR SOMETHING.
IN OTHER WORDS, NO PLAN AT ALL.
A-ANYWAY, DON'T LET YOUR GUARD DOWN!!
WE'RE IN SKULL-SADERS TERRITORY NOW.
TMP TMP TMP
KICK
WAAAH!
SORRY! I DIDN'T MEAN ANYTHING BY—
KNNGK
WHR

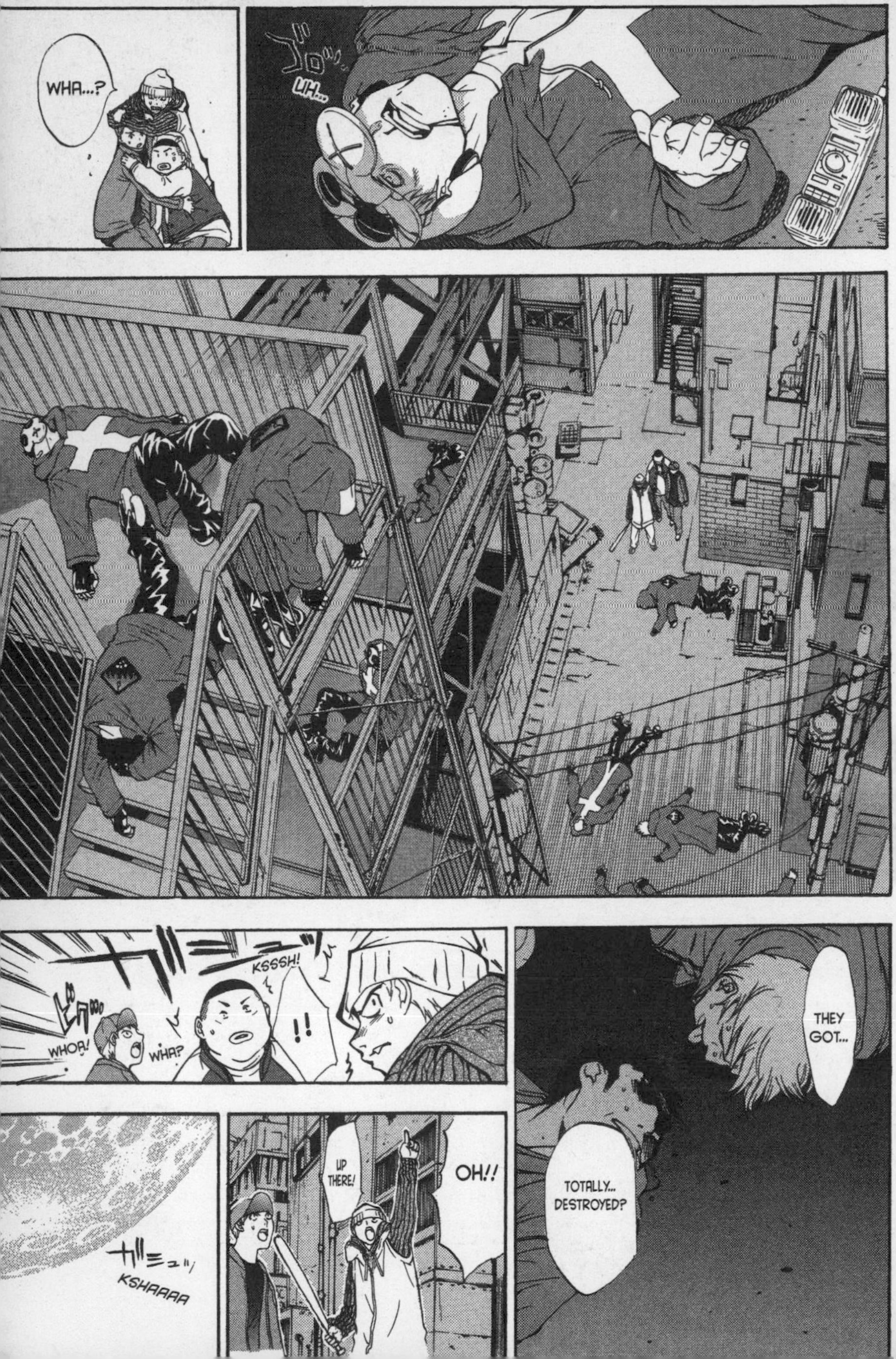
UH...
WHA...?
THEY GOT...
TOTALLY... DESTROYED?
KSSSH!
!!
WHA?
WHOA!
OH!!
UP THERE!
KSHAAAA

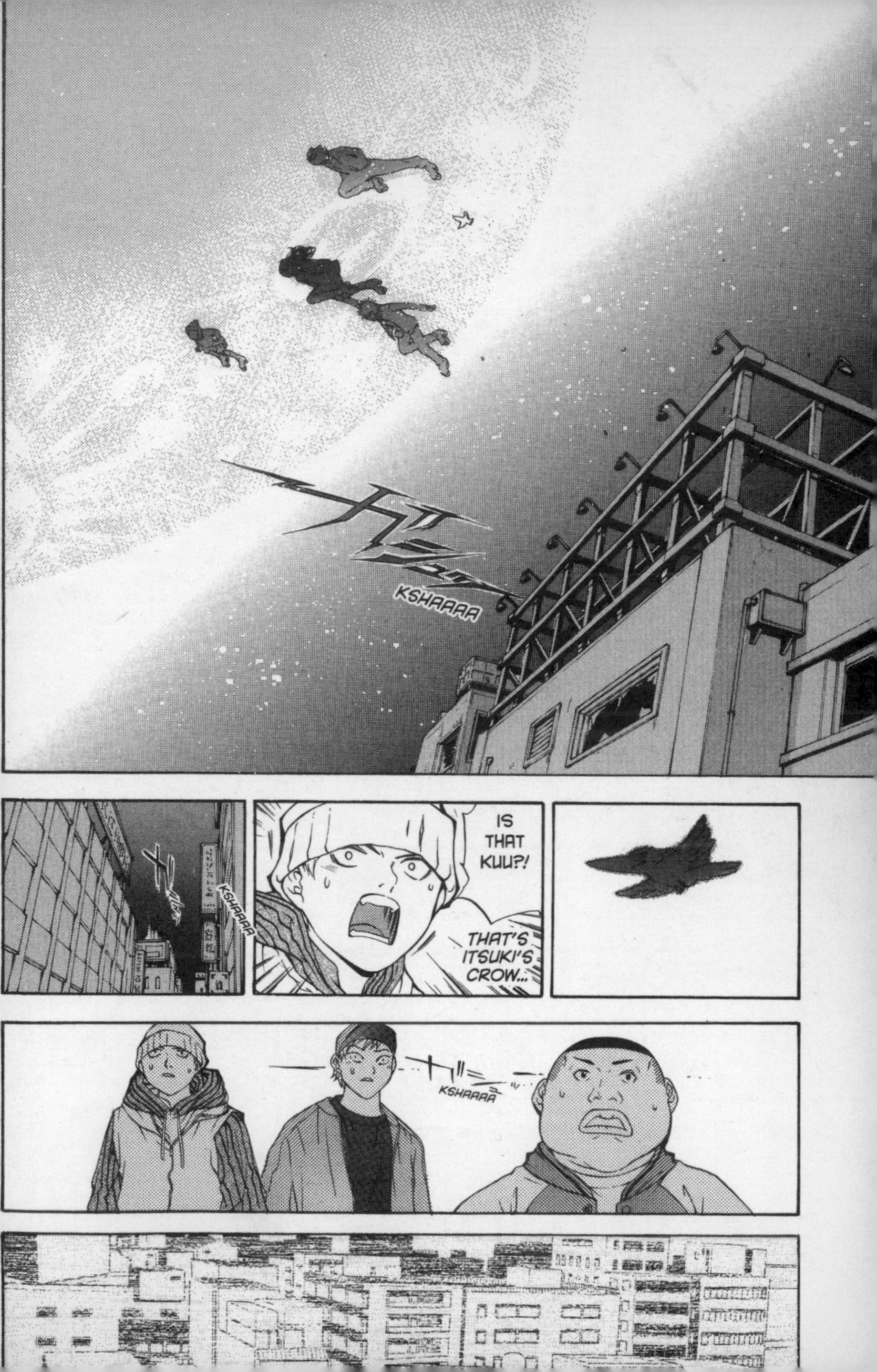
KSHAAAA
IS THAT KUU?!
THAT'S ITSUKI'S CROW...
KSHAAAA
KSHAAAA

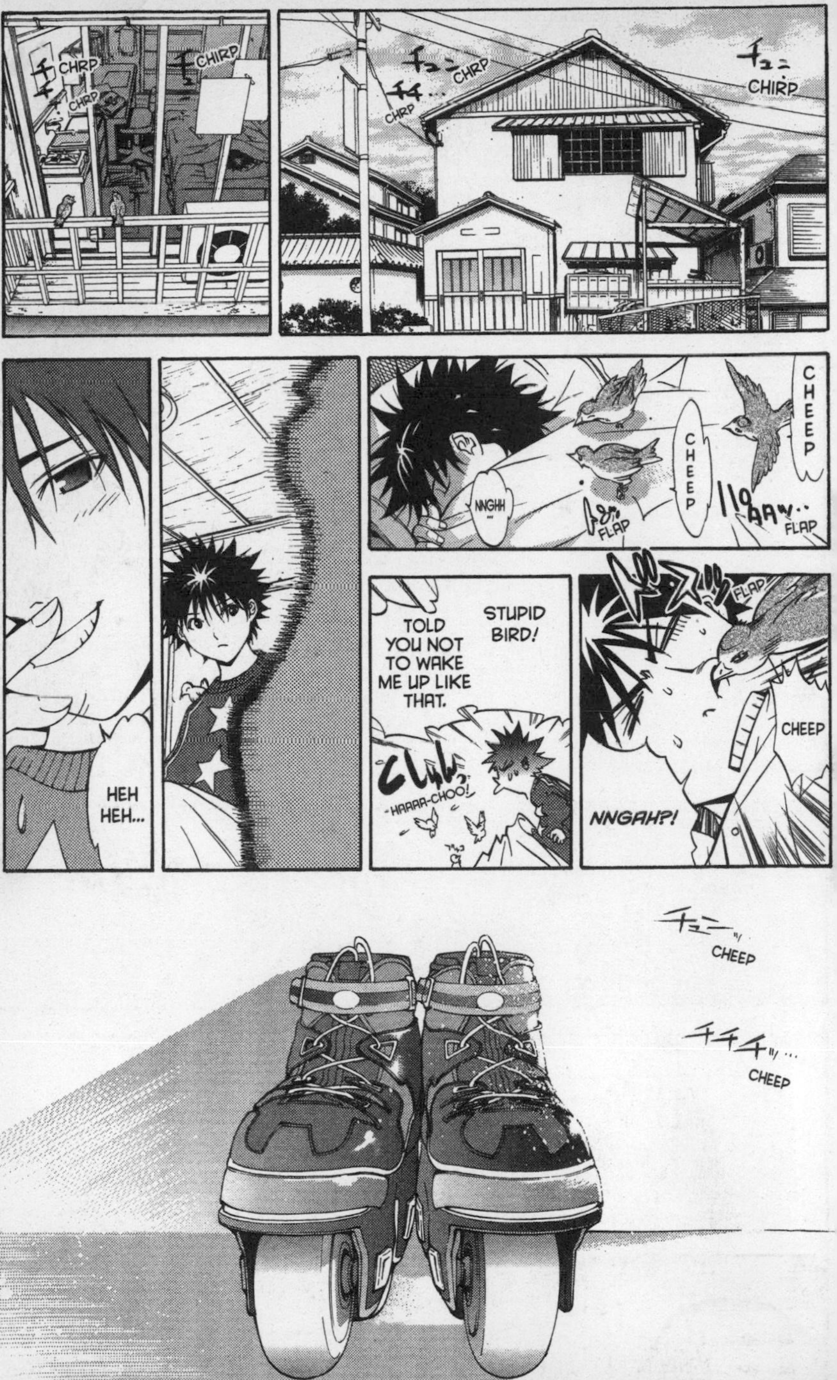
チュン
CHIRP
CHRP
CHRP
CHIRP
CHRP
CHRP
CHEEP
CHEEP
NNGH...
FLAP
FLAP
FLAP
CHEEP
NNGAH?!
STUPID BIRD!
TOLD YOU NOT TO WAKE ME UP LIKE THAT.
HAAAA-CHOO!
HEH HEH...
CHEEP
CHEEP

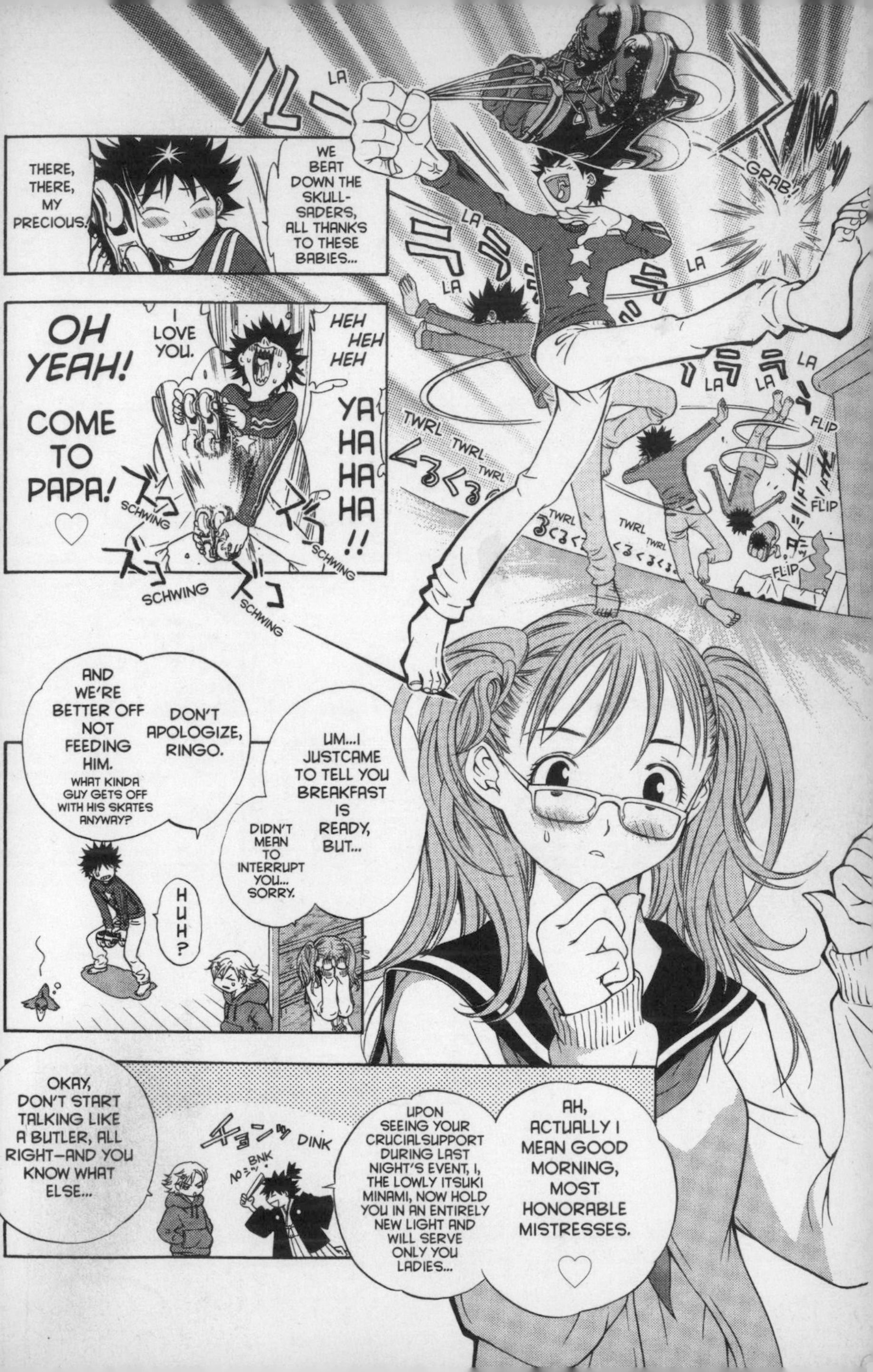
LA
GRAB!
LA
LA
LA
LA
LA
TWRL
TWRL
TWRL
TWRL
TWRL
FLIP
FLIP
FLIP
WE BEAT DOWN THE SKULL-SADERS, ALL THANKS TO THESE BABIES...
THERE, THERE, MY PRECIOUS.
HEH HEH HEH
I LOVE YOU.
OH YEAH!
COME TO PAPA! ♡
YA HA HA HA!!
SCHWING
SCHWING
SCHWING
SCHWING
UM...I JUSTCAME TO TELL YOU BREAKFAST IS READY, BUT...
DIDN'T MEAN TO INTERRUPT YOU... SORRY.
DON'T APOLOGIZE, RINGO.
AND WE'RE BETTER OFF NOT FEEDING HIM.
WHAT KINDA GUY GETS OFF WITH HIS SKATES ANYWAY?
HUH?
AH, ACTUALLY I MEAN GOOD MORNING, MOST HONORABLE MISTRESSES. ♡
UPON SEEING YOUR CRUCIALSUPPORT DURING LAST NIGHT'S EVENT, I, THE LOWLY ITSUKI MINAMI, NOW HOLD YOU IN AN ENTIRELY NEW LIGHT AND WILL SERVE ONLY YOU LADIES...
DINK
BNK
OKAY, DON'T START TALKING LIKE A BUTLER, ALL RIGHT—AND YOU KNOW WHAT ELSE...

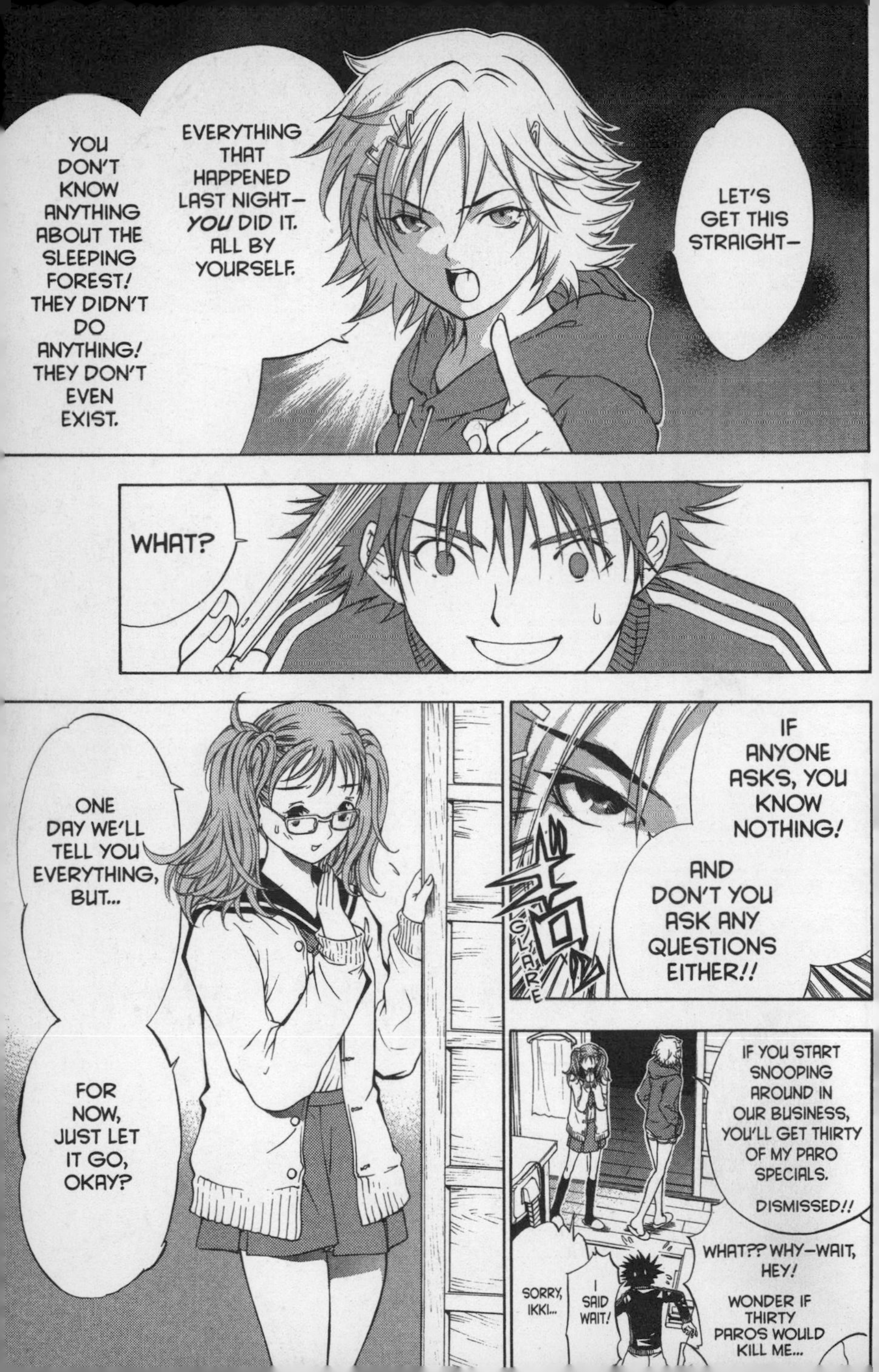
LET'S GET THIS STRAIGHT—
EVERYTHING THAT HAPPENED LAST NIGHT—*YOU* DID IT. ALL BY YOURSELF.
YOU DON'T KNOW ANYTHING ABOUT THE SLEEPING FOREST! THEY DIDN'T DO ANYTHING! THEY DON'T EVEN EXIST.
WHAT?
IF ANYONE ASKS, YOU KNOW NOTHING!
AND DON'T YOU ASK ANY QUESTIONS EITHER!!
GLARE
IF YOU START SNOOPING AROUND IN OUR BUSINESS, YOU'LL GET THIRTY OF MY PARO SPECIALS.
DISMISSED!!
WHAT?? WHY—WAIT, HEY!
I SAID WAIT!
SORRY, IKKI...
WONDER IF THIRTY PAROS WOULD KILL ME...
ONE DAY WE'LL TELL YOU EVERYTHING, BUT...
FOR NOW, JUST LET IT GO, OKAY?

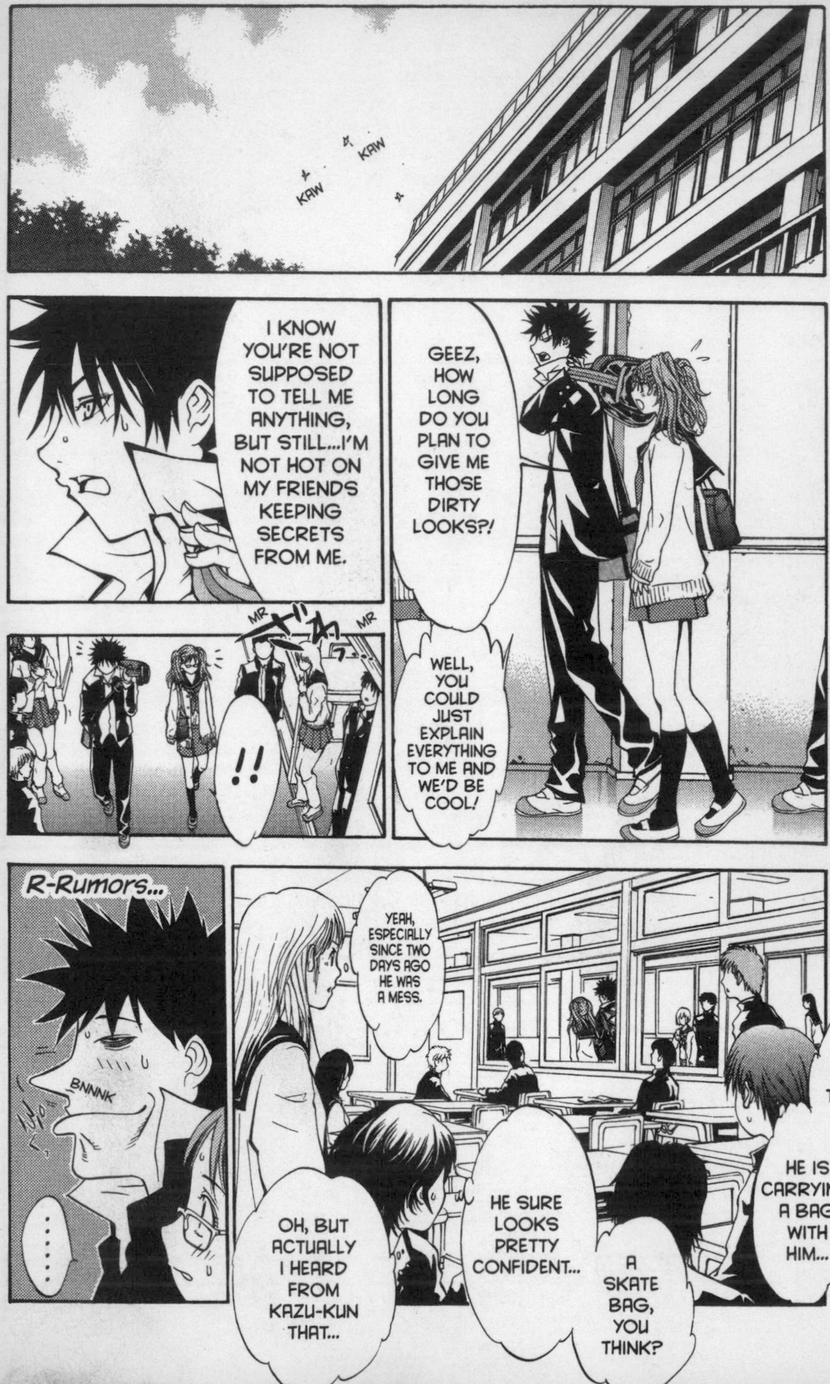
KAW
KAW
GEEZ, HOW LONG DO YOU PLAN TO GIVE ME THOSE DIRTY LOOKS?!
WELL, YOU COULD JUST EXPLAIN EVERYTHING TO ME AND WE'D BE COOL!
I KNOW YOU'RE NOT SUPPOSED TO TELL ME ANYTHING, BUT STILL...I'M NOT HOT ON MY FRIENDS KEEPING SECRETS FROM ME.
MR
MR
!!
HEY, THERE'S IKKI-KUN...
HE IS CARRYING A BAG WITH HIM...
A SKATE BAG, YOU THINK?
HE SURE LOOKS PRETTY CONFIDENT...
YEAH, ESPECIALLY SINCE TWO DAYS AGO HE WAS A MESS.
OH, BUT ACTUALLY I HEARD FROM KAZU-KUN THAT...
R-Rumors...
BNNNK
......

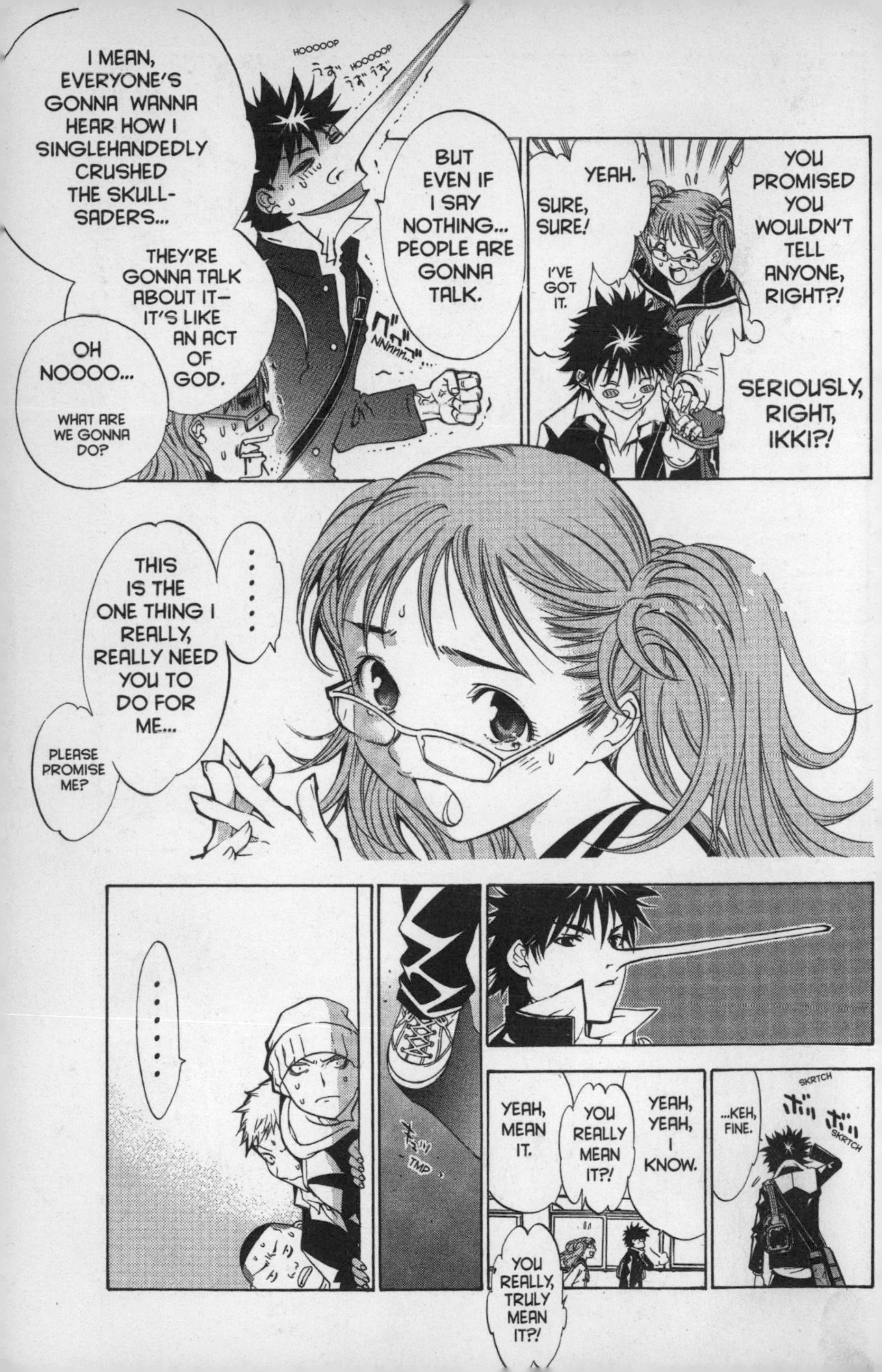
YOU PROMISED YOU WOULDN'T TELL ANYONE, RIGHT?!
YEAH.
SURE, SURE!
I'VE GOT IT.
SERIOUSLY, RIGHT, IKKI?!
BUT EVEN IF I SAY NOTHING... PEOPLE ARE GONNA TALK.
HOOOOOP
HOOOOOP
I MEAN, EVERYONE'S GONNA WANNA HEAR HOW I SINGLEHANDEDLY CRUSHED THE SKULL-SADERS...
THEY'RE GONNA TALK ABOUT IT— IT'S LIKE AN ACT OF GOD.
OH NOOOO...
WHAT ARE WE GONNA DO?
......
THIS IS THE ONE THING I REALLY, REALLY NEED YOU TO DO FOR ME...
PLEASE PROMISE ME?
SKRTCH
SKRTCH
...KEH, FINE.
YEAH, YEAH, I KNOW.
YOU REALLY MEAN IT?!
YEAH, MEAN IT.
YOU REALLY, TRULY MEAN IT?!
TMP
......

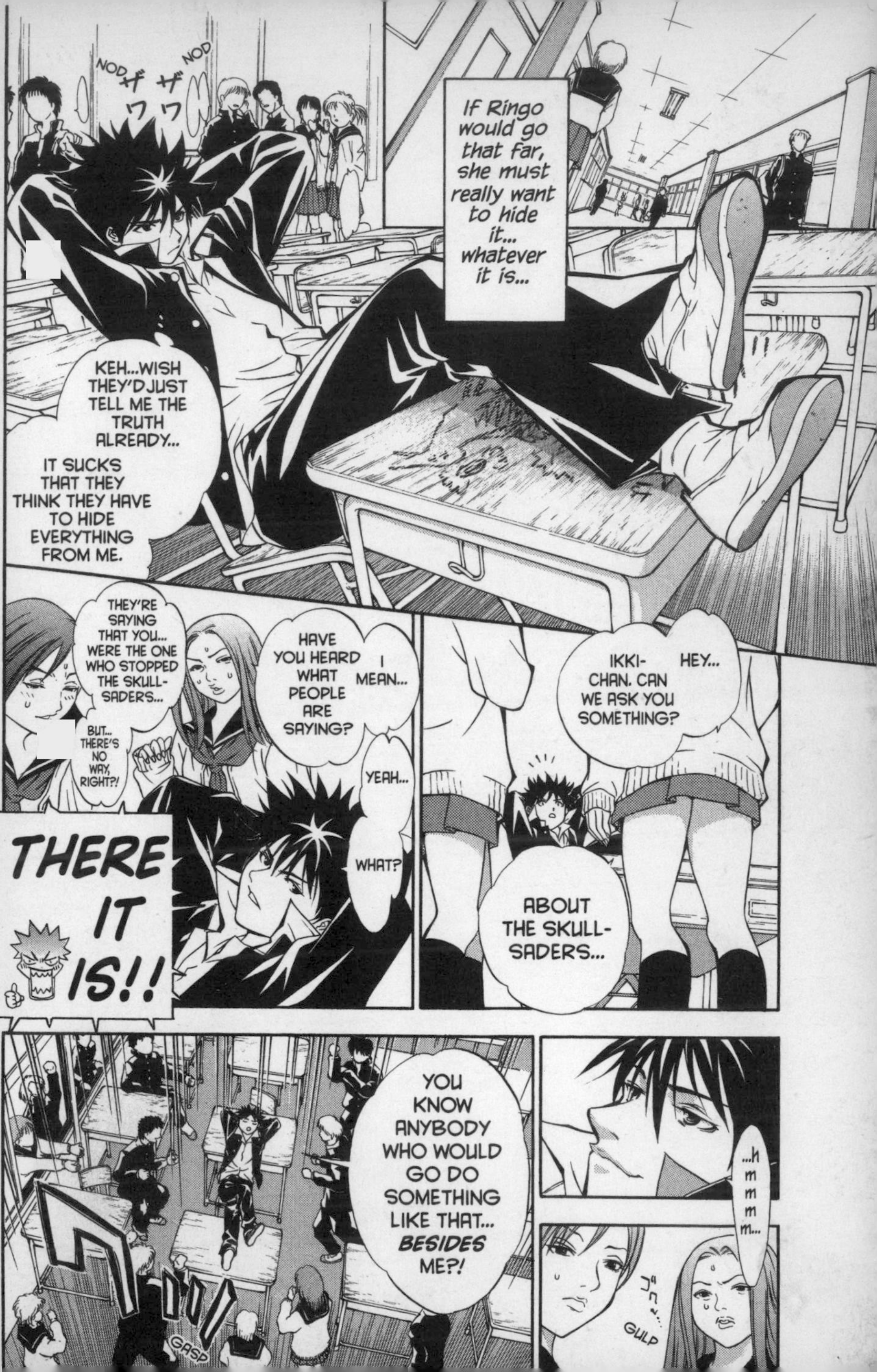

If Ringo would go that far, she must really want to hide it... whatever it is...
NOD NOD
ザワザワ
KEH...WISH THEY'D JUST TELL ME THE TRUTH ALREADY...
IT SUCKS THAT THEY THINK THEY HAVE TO HIDE EVERYTHING FROM ME.
HEY...
IKKI-CHAN. CAN WE ASK YOU SOMETHING?
ABOUT THE SKULL-SADERS...
I MEAN...
HAVE YOU HEARD WHAT PEOPLE ARE SAYING?
THEY'RE SAYING THAT YOU... WERE THE ONE WHO STOPPED THE SKULL-SADERS...
BUT... THERE'S NO WAY, RIGHT?!
YEAH...
WHAT?
THERE IT IS!!
...hmmmm...
GULP
YOU KNOW ANYBODY WHO WOULD GO DO SOMETHING LIKE THAT... *BESIDES* ME?!
GASP

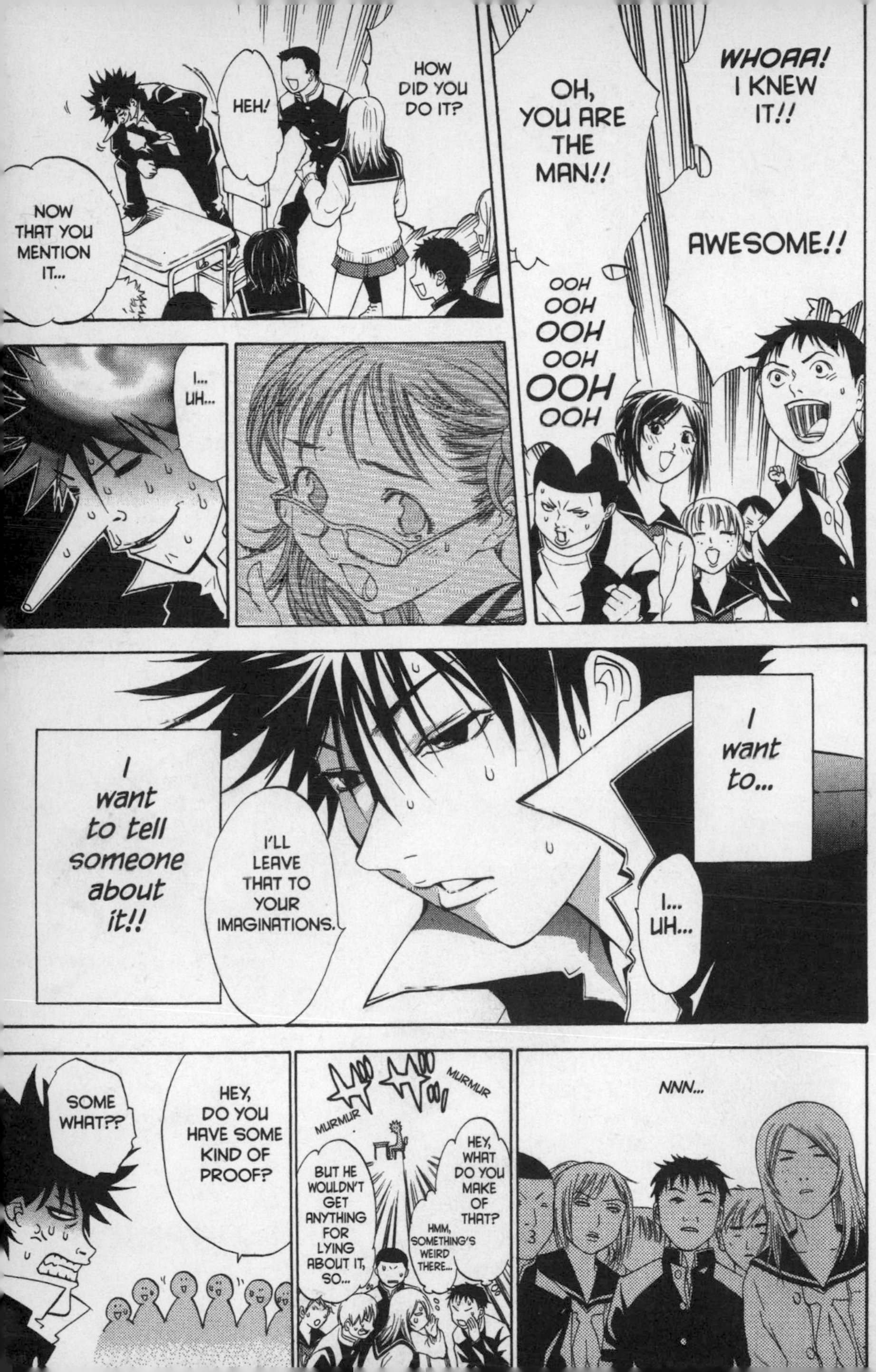
WHOAA! I KNEW IT!!
OH, YOU ARE THE MAN!!
AWESOME!!
OOH OOH OOH OOH OOH OOH
HOW DID YOU DO IT?
HEH!
NOW THAT YOU MENTION IT...
I... UH...
I want to...
I... UH...
I'LL LEAVE THAT TO YOUR IMAGINATIONS.
I want to tell someone about it!!
NNN...
MURMUR
HEY, WHAT DO YOU MAKE OF THAT?
HMM, SOMETHING'S WEIRD THERE...
MURMUR
BUT HE WOULDN'T GET ANYTHING FOR LYING ABOUT IT, SO...
HEY, DO YOU HAVE SOME KIND OF PROOF?
SOME WHAT??

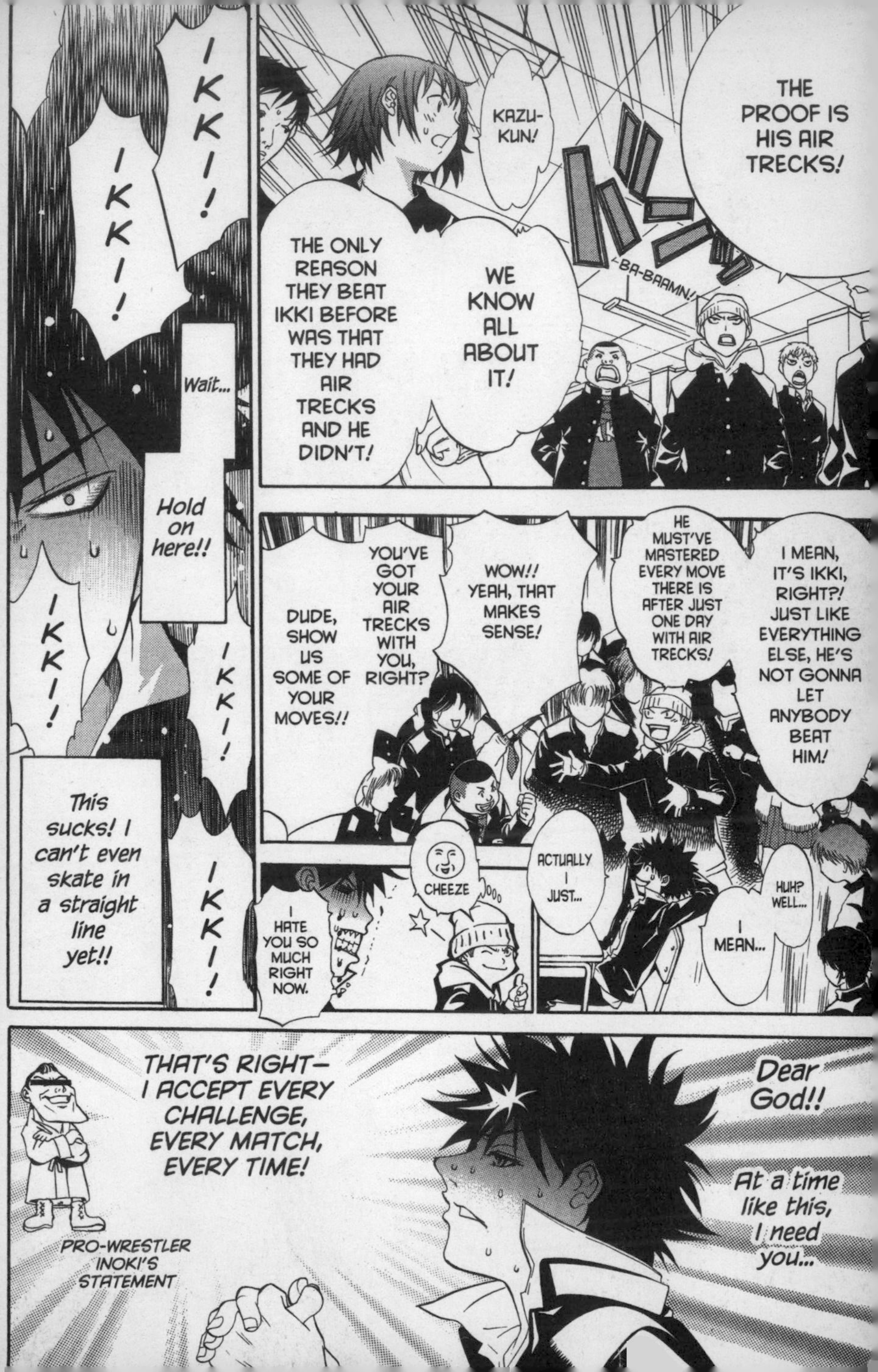
THE PROOF IS HIS AIR TRECKS!
BA-BAAMN!
KAZU-KUN!
WE KNOW ALL ABOUT IT!
THE ONLY REASON THEY BEAT IKKI BEFORE WAS THAT THEY HAD AIR TRECKS AND HE DIDN'T!
I MEAN, IT'S IKKI, RIGHT?! JUST LIKE EVERYTHING ELSE, HE'S NOT GONNA LET ANYBODY BEAT HIM!
HE MUST'VE MASTERED EVERY MOVE THERE IS AFTER JUST ONE DAY WITH AIR TRECKS!
WOW!! YEAH, THAT MAKES SENSE!
YOU'VE GOT YOUR AIR TRECKS WITH YOU, RIGHT?
DUDE, SHOW US SOME OF YOUR MOVES!!
HUH? WELL...
I MEAN...
ACTUALLY I JUST...
CHEEZE
I HATE YOU SO MUCH RIGHT NOW.
IKKI!
IKKI!
Wait...
Hold on here!!
IKKI!
IKKI!
This sucks! I can't even skate in a straight line yet!!
IKKI!
Dear God!!
At a time like this, I need you...
THAT'S RIGHT— I ACCEPT EVERY CHALLENGE, EVERY MATCH, EVERY TIME!
PRO-WRESTLER INOKI'S STATEMENT

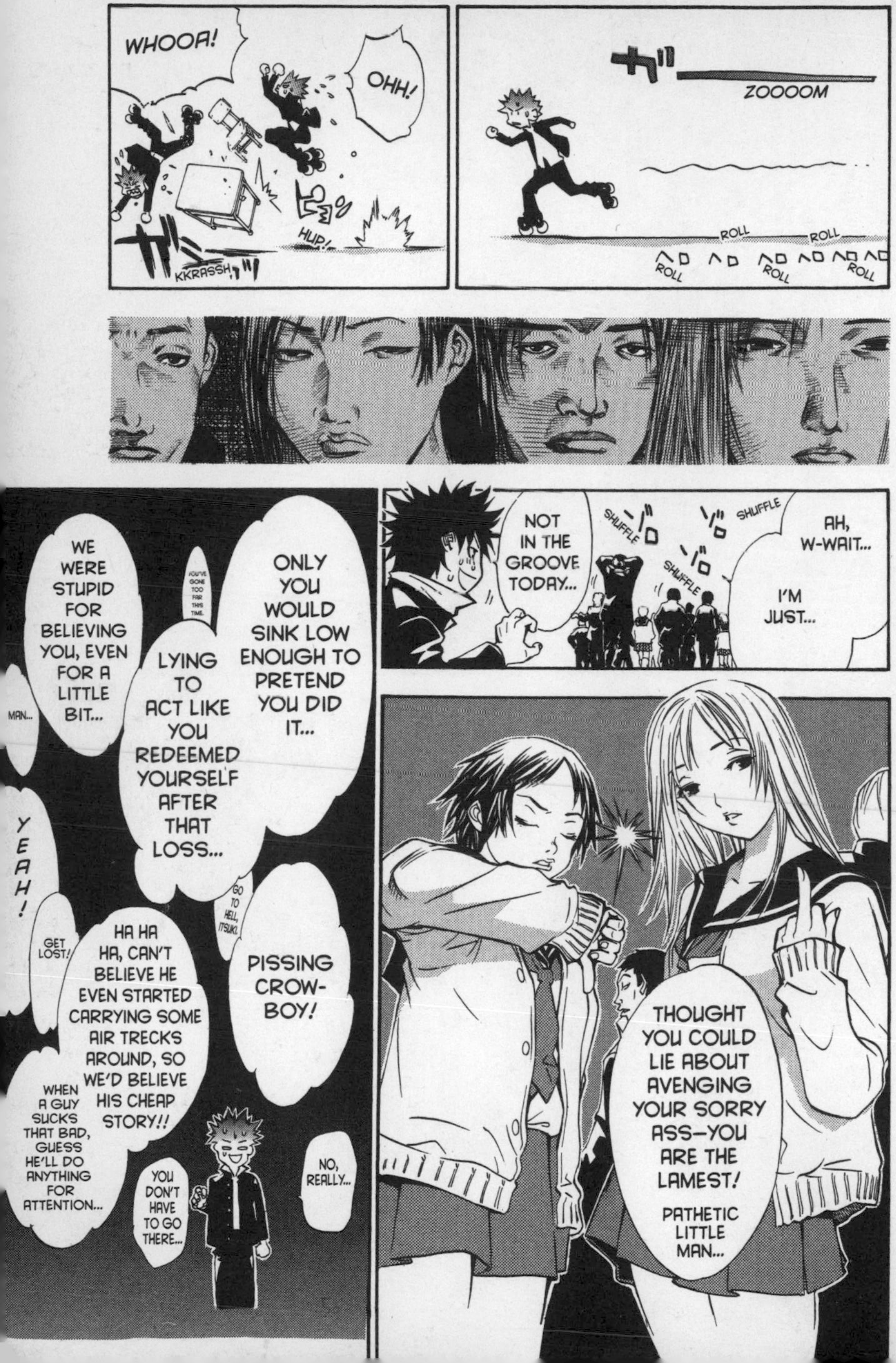
ZOOOOM
ROLL
ROLL
ROLL
ROLL
ROLL
WHOOA!
OHH!
HUP!
KKRASSH
AH, W-WAIT...
I'M JUST...
SHUFFLE
SHUFFLE
SHUFFLE
NOT IN THE GROOVE TODAY...
THOUGHT YOU COULD LIE ABOUT AVENGING YOUR SORRY ASS—YOU ARE THE LAMEST!
PATHETIC LITTLE MAN...
ONLY YOU WOULD SINK LOW ENOUGH TO PRETEND YOU DID IT...
YOU'VE GONE TOO FAR THIS TIME.
WE WERE STUPID FOR BELIEVING YOU, EVEN FOR A LITTLE BIT...
LYING TO ACT LIKE YOU REDEEMED YOURSELF AFTER THAT LOSS...
MAN...
YEAH!
GO TO HELL, ITSUKI.
PISSING CROW-BOY!
HA HA HA, CAN'T BELIEVE HE EVEN STARTED CARRYING SOME AIR TRECKS AROUND, SO WE'D BELIEVE HIS CHEAP STORY!!
GET LOST!
WHEN A GUY SUCKS THAT BAD, GUESS HE'LL DO ANYTHING FOR ATTENTION...
NO, REALLY...
YOU DON'T HAVE TO GO THERE...

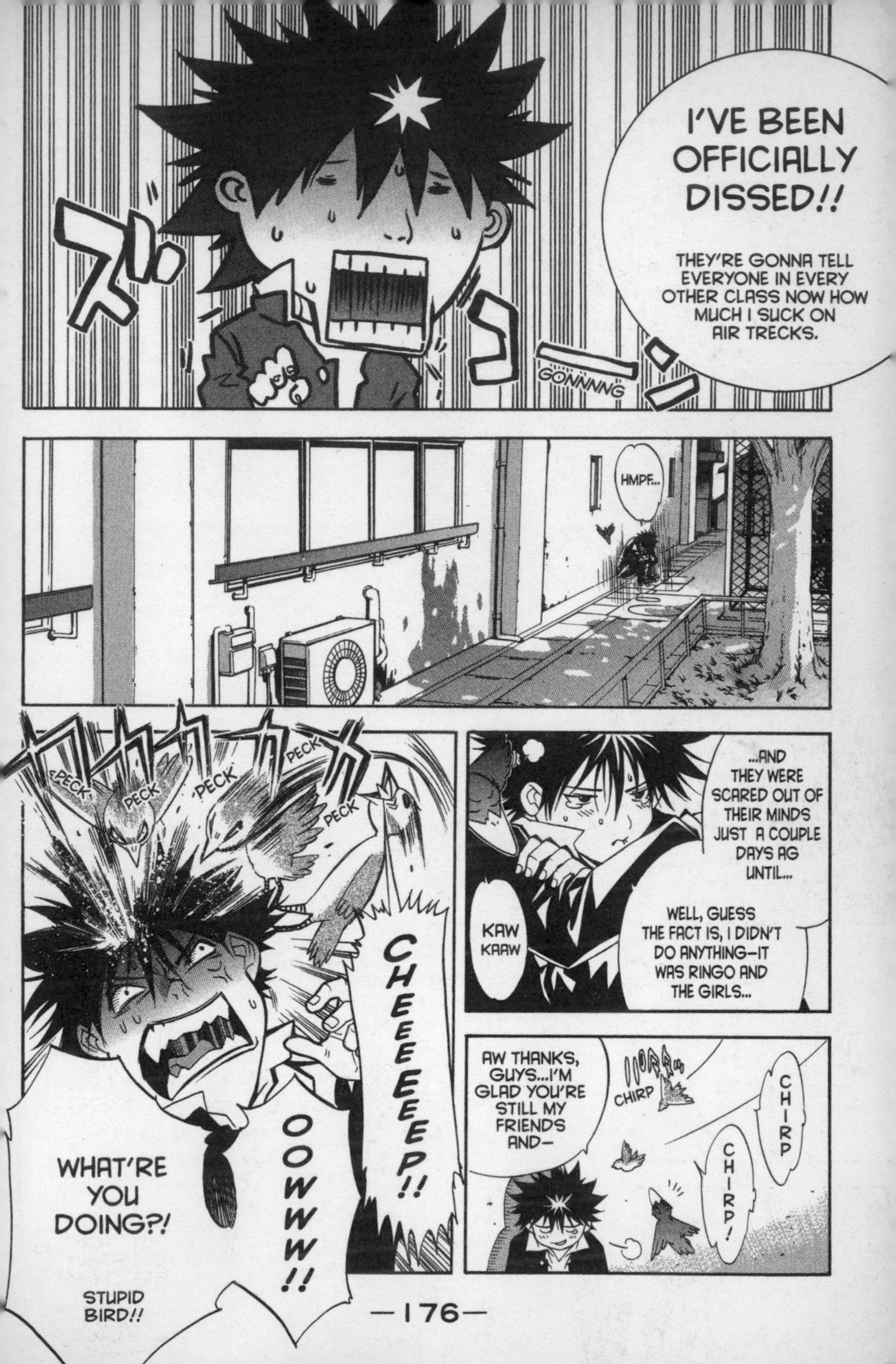
I'VE BEEN OFFICIALLY DISSED!!
THEY'RE GONNA TELL EVERYONE IN EVERY OTHER CLASS NOW HOW MUCH I SUCK ON AIR TRECKS.
GONNNNG
HMPF...
...AND THEY WERE SCARED OUT OF THEIR MINDS JUST A COUPLE DAYS AG UNTIL...
WELL, GUESS THE FACT IS, I DIDN'T DO ANYTHING—IT WAS RINGO AND THE GIRLS...
KAW KAAW
CHIRP
CHIRP!
CHIRP
AW THANKS, GUYS...I'M GLAD YOU'RE STILL MY FRIENDS AND—
PECK
PECK
PECK
PECK
PECK
CHEEEEEEP!!
OOWWWW!!
WHAT'RE YOU DOING?!
STUPID BIRD!!

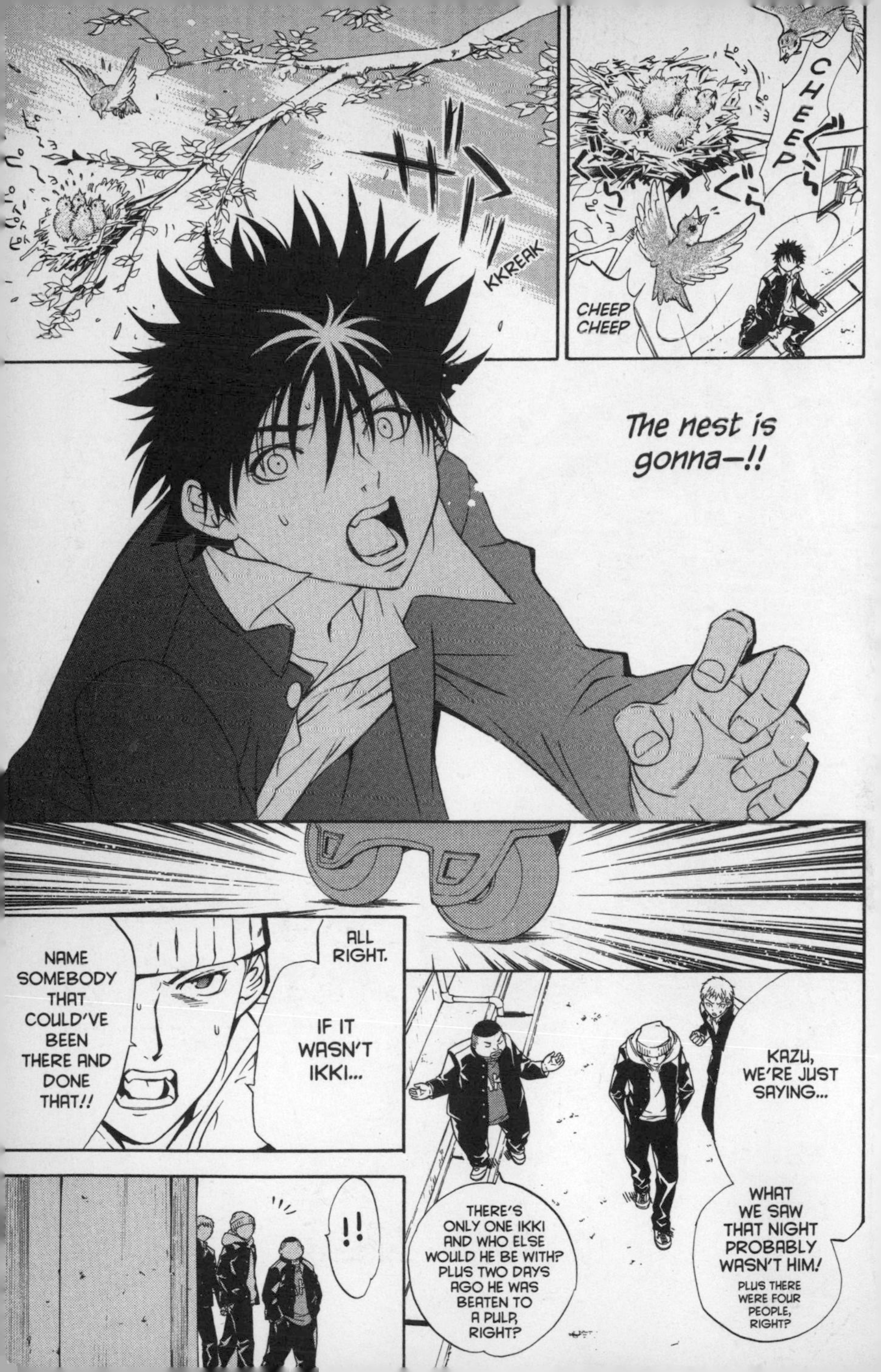
CHEEP
CHEEP CHEEP
KKREAK
The nest is gonna–!!
KAZU, WE'RE JUST SAYING...
WHAT WE SAW THAT NIGHT PROBABLY WASN'T HIM!
PLUS THERE WERE FOUR PEOPLE, RIGHT?
THERE'S ONLY ONE IKKI AND WHO ELSE WOULD HE BE WITH? PLUS TWO DAYS AGO HE WAS BEATEN TO A PULP, RIGHT?
ALL RIGHT.
IF IT WASN'T IKKI...
NAME SOMEBODY THAT COULD'VE BEEN THERE AND DONE THAT!!
!!

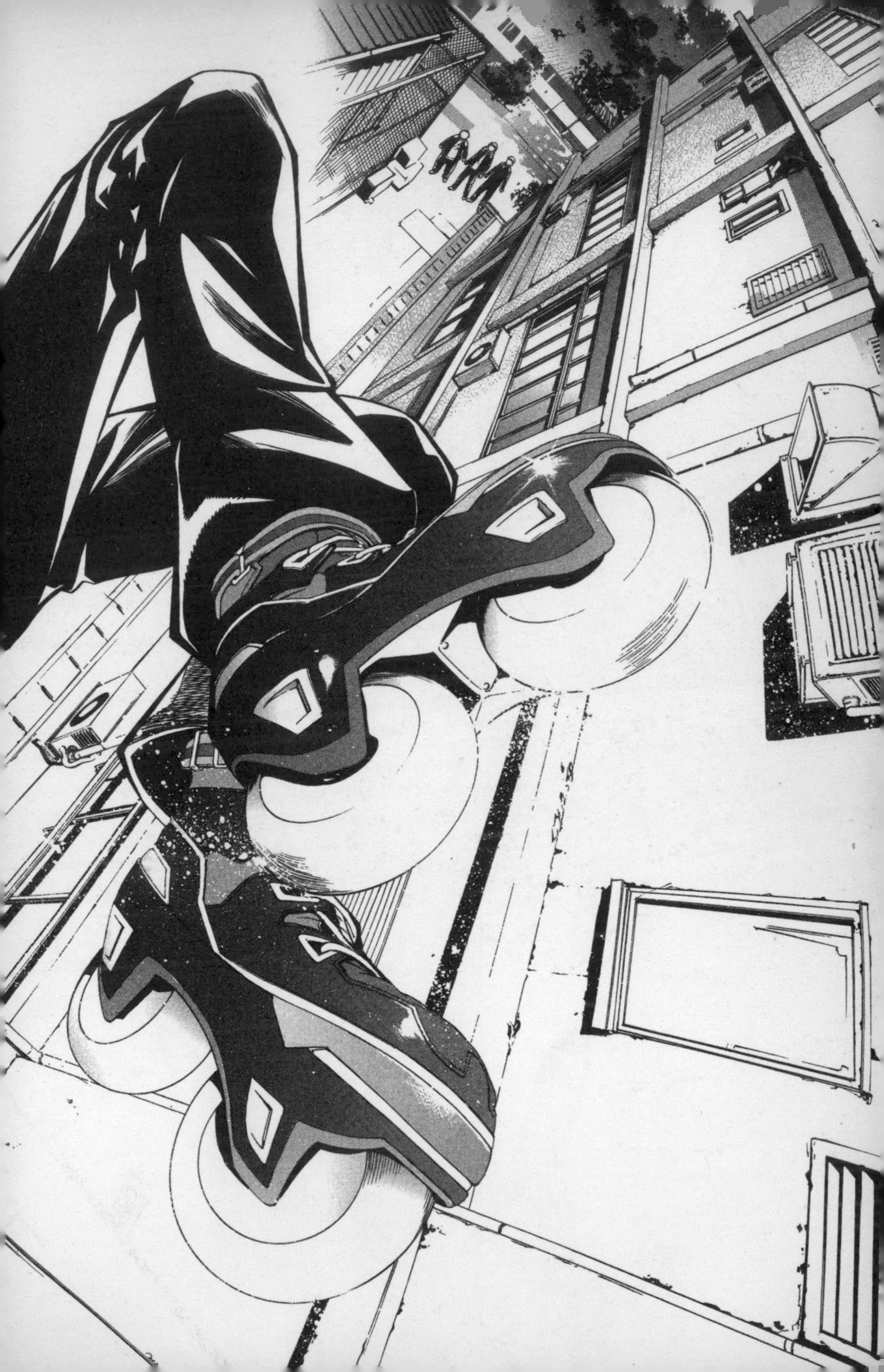

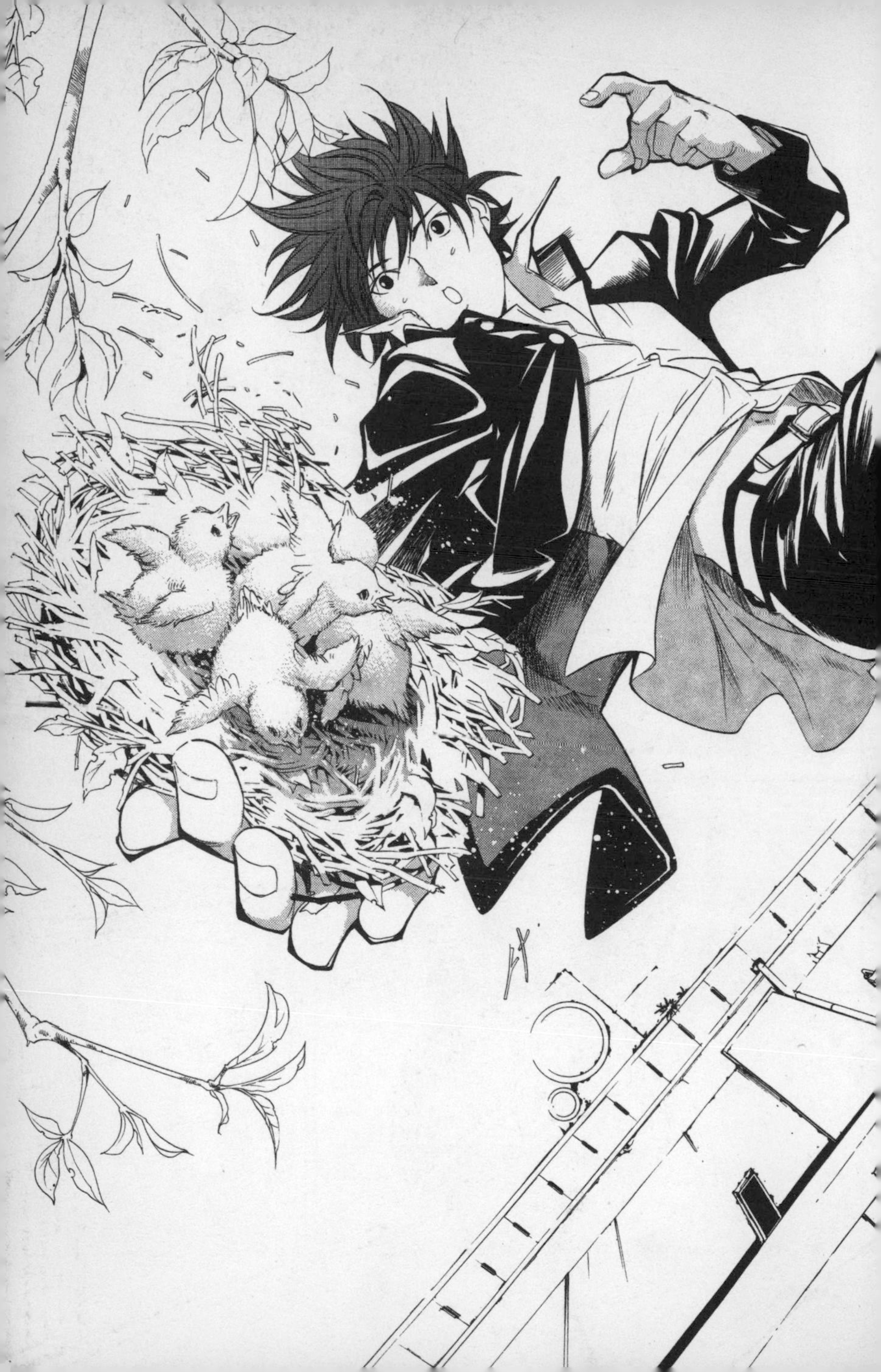

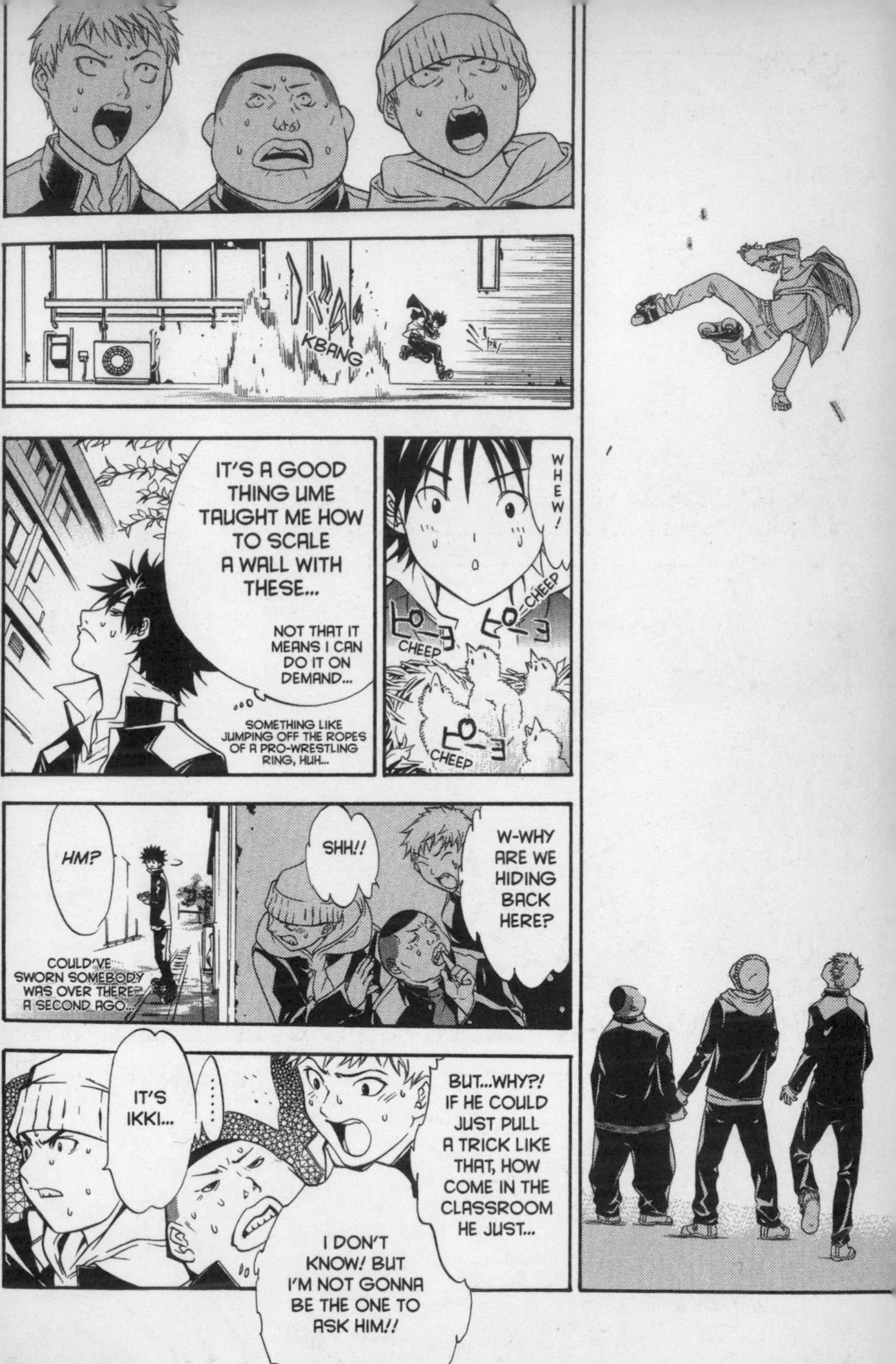
KBANG
WHEW!
CHEEP
CHEEP
CHEEP
IT'S A GOOD THING UME TAUGHT ME HOW TO SCALE A WALL WITH THESE...
NOT THAT IT MEANS I CAN DO IT ON DEMAND...
SOMETHING LIKE JUMPING OFF THE ROPES OF A PRO-WRESTLING RING, HUH...
W-WHY ARE WE HIDING BACK HERE?
SHH!!
HM?
COULD'VE SWORN SOMEBODY WAS OVER THERE A SECOND AGO...
BUT...WHY?! IF HE COULD JUST PULL A TRICK LIKE THAT, HOW COME IN THE CLASSROOM HE JUST...
...
IT'S IKKI...
I DON'T KNOW! BUT I'M NOT GONNA BE THE ONE TO ASK HIM!!

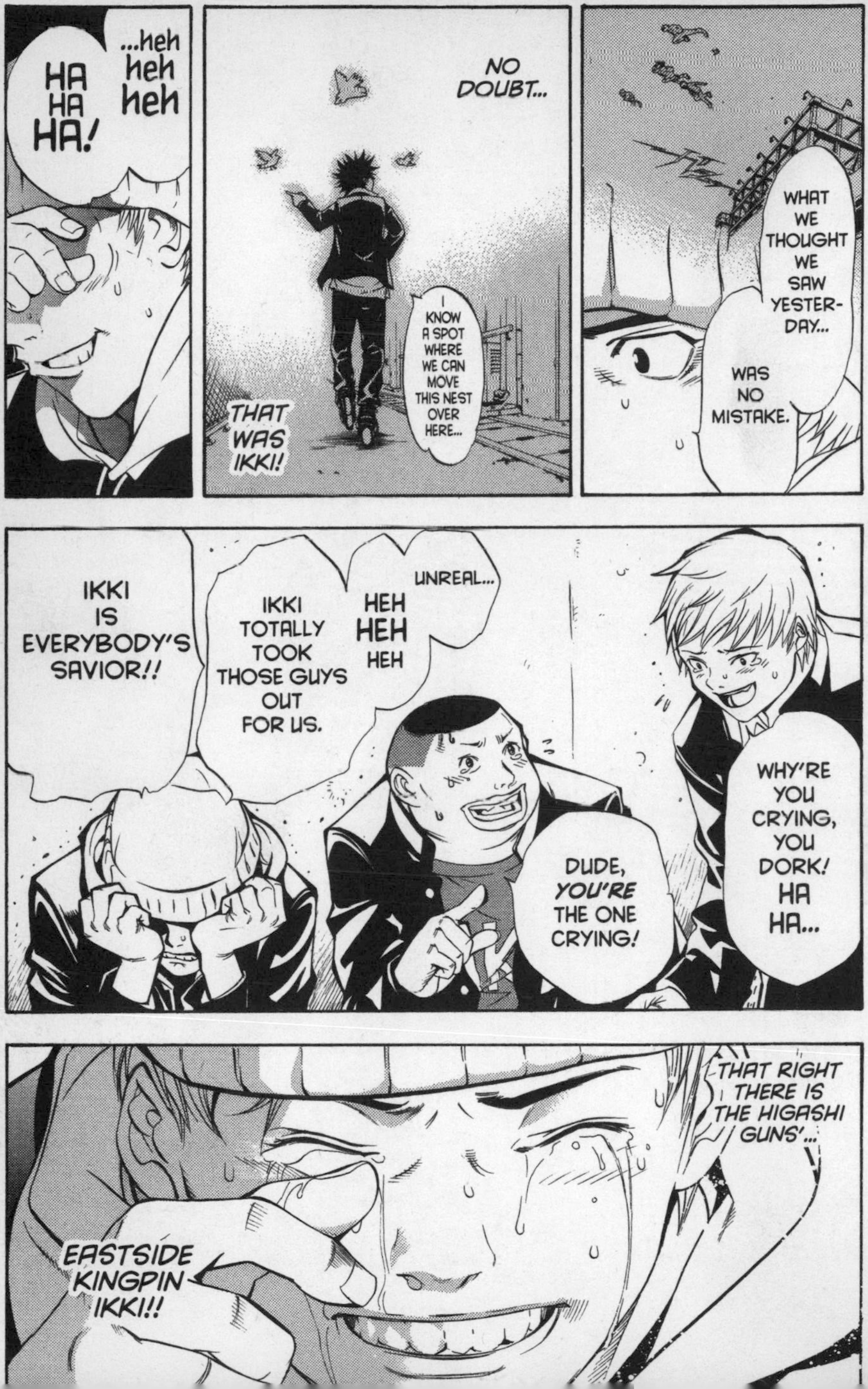
WHAT WE THOUGHT WE SAW YESTERDAY...
WAS NO MISTAKE.
NO DOUBT...
I KNOW A SPOT WHERE WE CAN MOVE THIS NEST OVER HERE...
THAT WAS IKKI!
...heh heh heh
HA HA HA!
WHY'RE YOU CRYING, YOU DORK! HA HA...
DUDE, *YOU'RE* THE ONE CRYING!
UNREAL...
HEH HEH HEH
IKKI TOTALLY TOOK THOSE GUYS OUT FOR US.
IKKI IS EVERYBODY'S SAVIOR!!
THAT RIGHT THERE IS THE HIGASHI GUNS'...
EASTSIDE KINGPIN IKKI!!

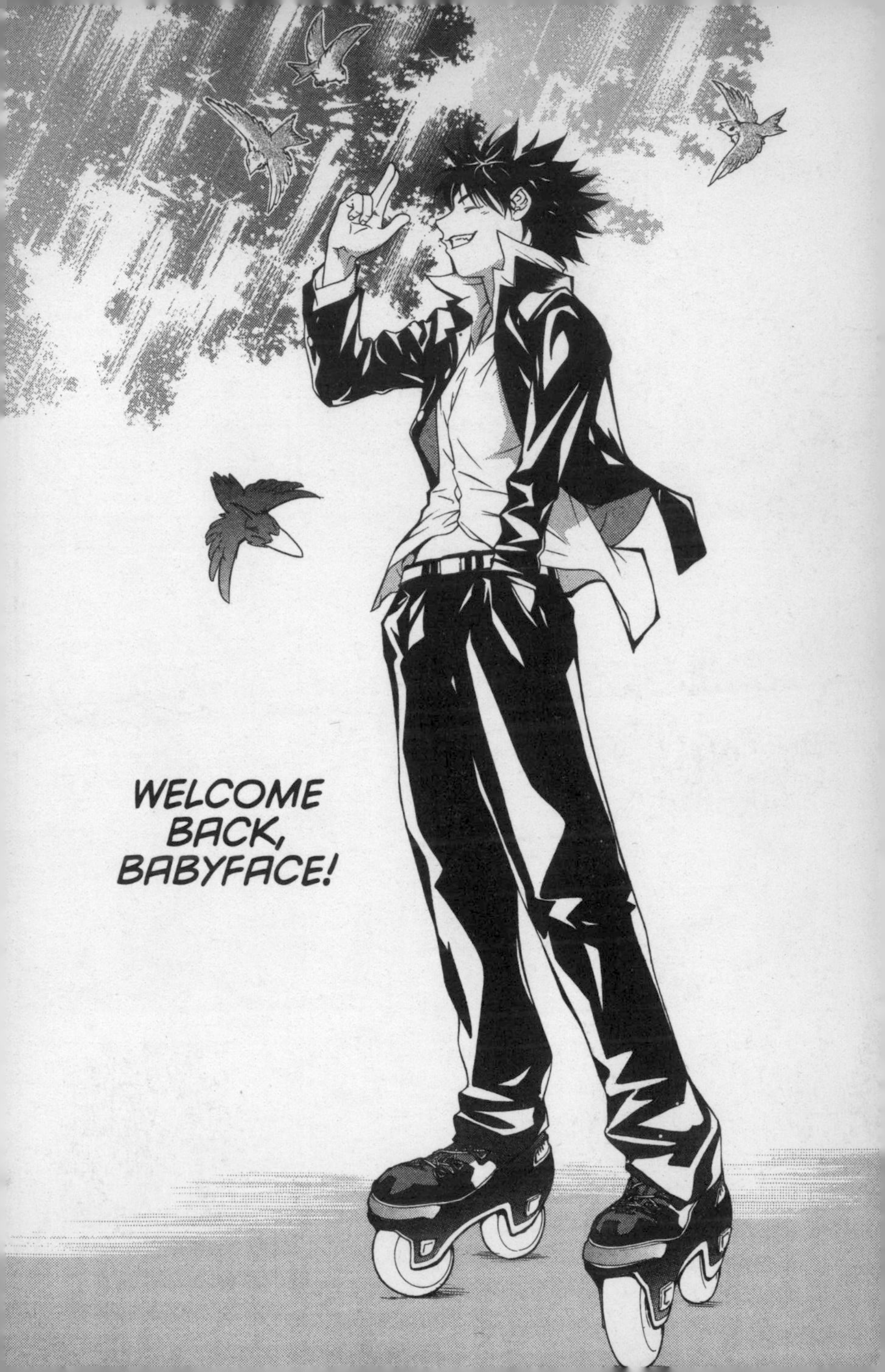
WELCOME BACK, BABYFACE!

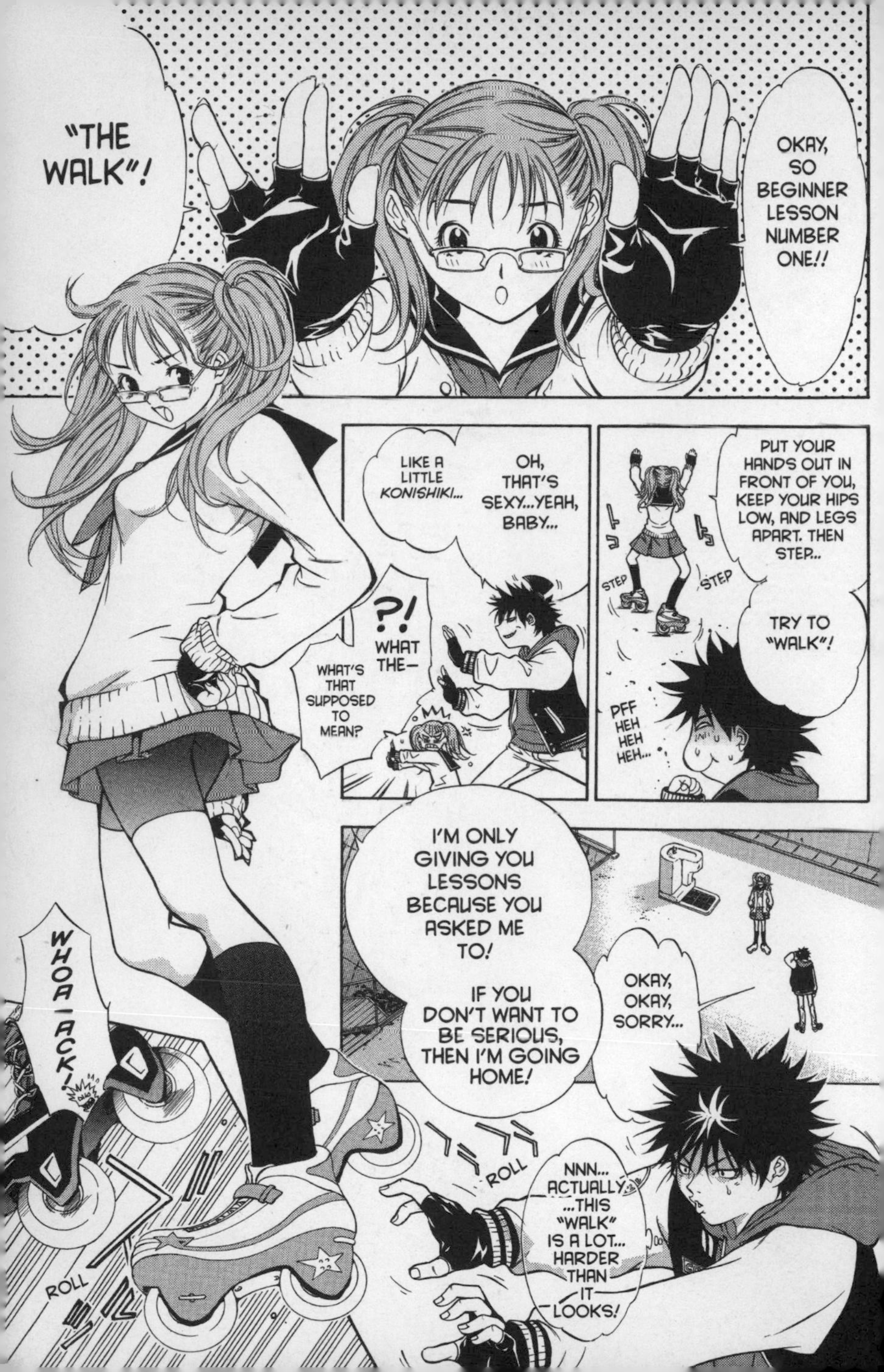
OKAY, SO BEGINNER LESSON NUMBER ONE!!
"THE WALK"!
PUT YOUR HANDS OUT IN FRONT OF YOU, KEEP YOUR HIPS LOW, AND LEGS APART. THEN STEP...
STEP
STEP
TRY TO "WALK"!
PFF HEH HEH HEH...
OH, THAT'S SEXY...YEAH, BABY...
LIKE A LITTLE *KONISHIKI*...
?!
WHAT THE—
WHAT'S THAT SUPPOSED TO MEAN?
I'M ONLY GIVING YOU LESSONS BECAUSE YOU ASKED ME TO!
IF YOU DON'T WANT TO BE SERIOUS, THEN I'M GOING HOME!
OKAY, OKAY, SORRY...
ROLL
NNN... ACTUALLY ...THIS "WALK" IS A LOT... HARDER THAN IT LOOKS!
WHOA—ACK!
ROLL

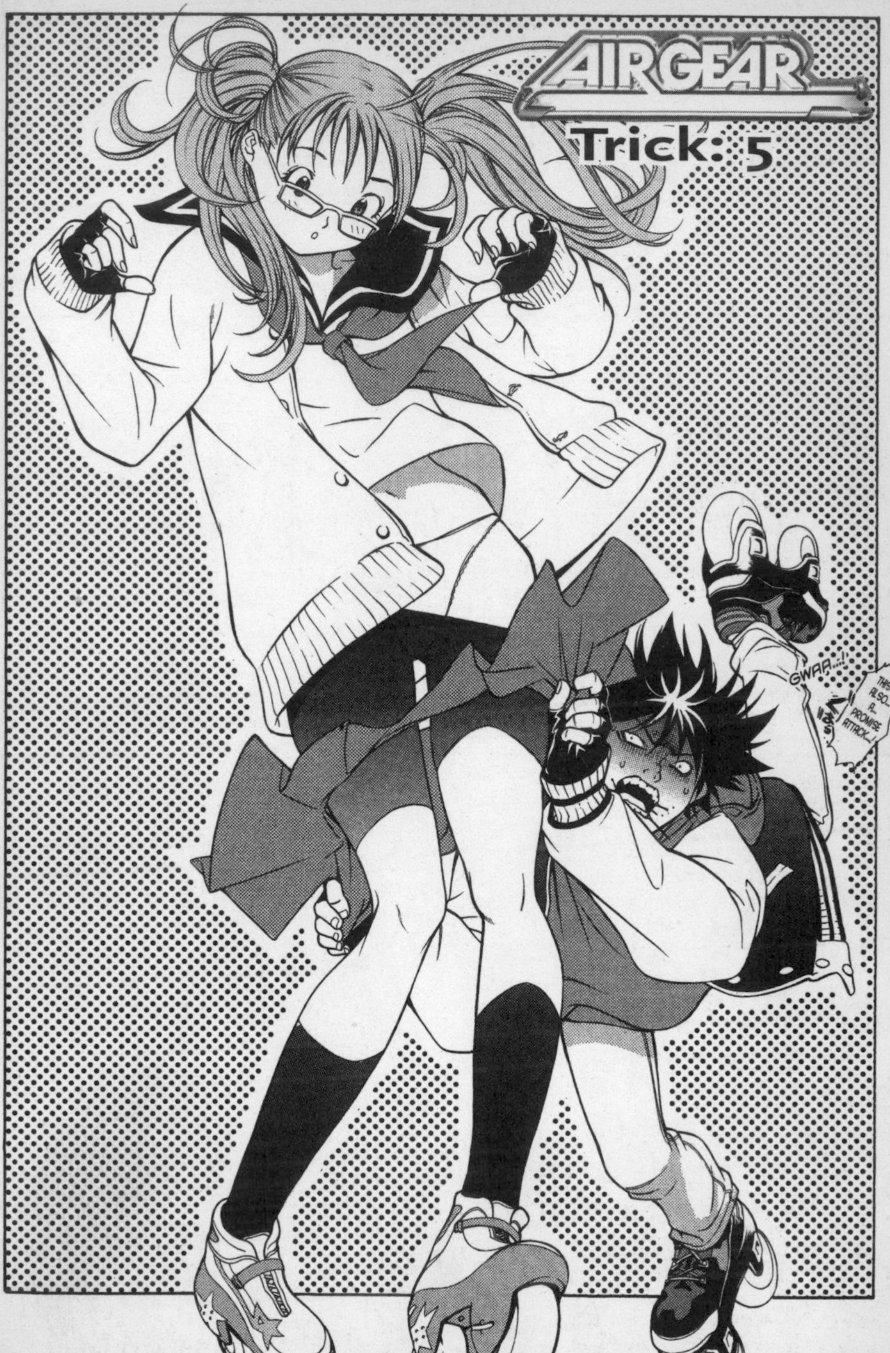
AIR GEAR
Trick: 5
GWAA...!
THIS IS ALSO... A... PROMISE ATTACK...!

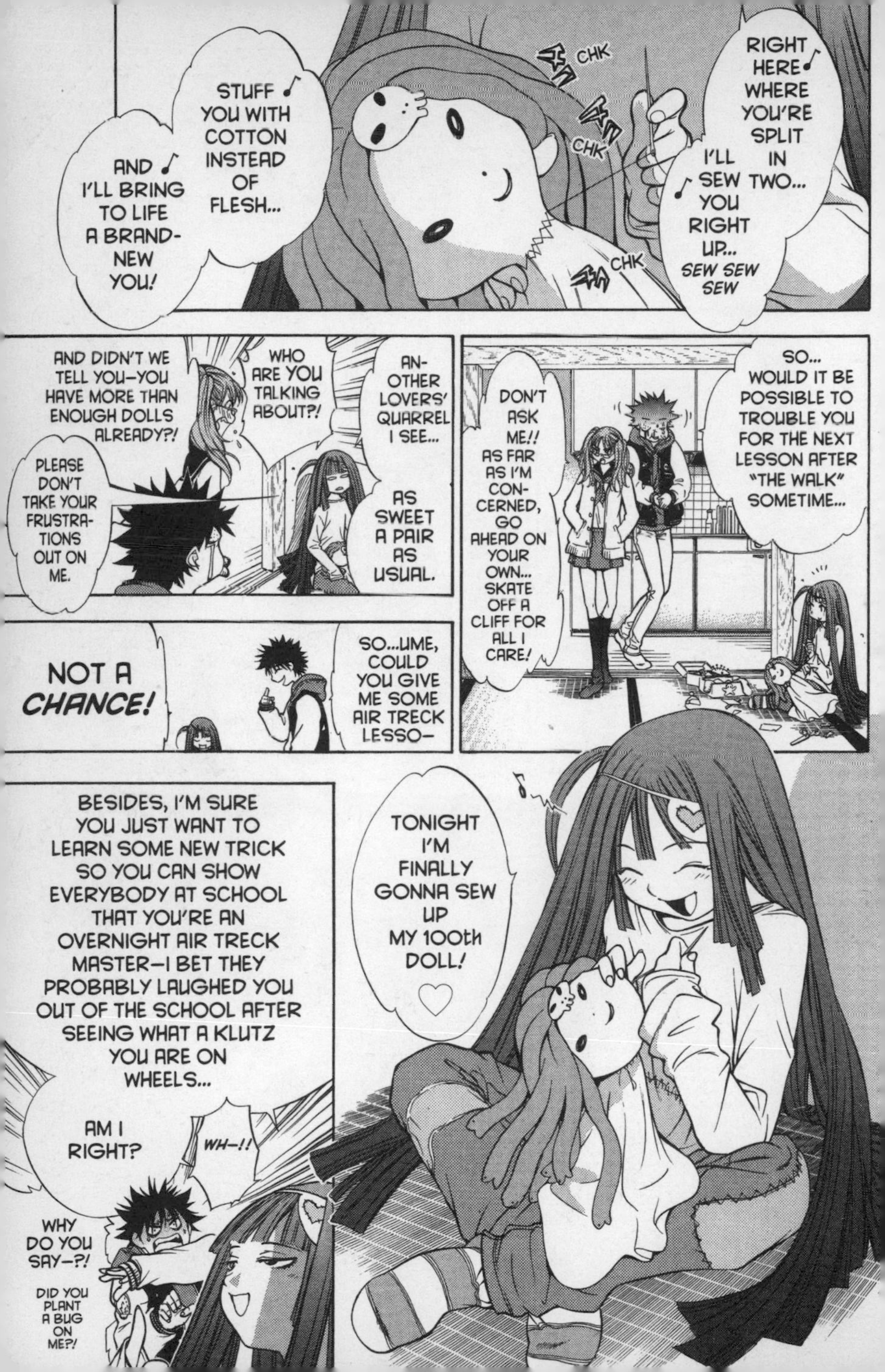
RIGHT HERE♪ WHERE YOU'RE SPLIT IN TWO...
♪ I'LL SEW YOU RIGHT UP... SEW SEW SEW
CHK
CHK
CHK
STUFF♪ YOU WITH COTTON INSTEAD OF FLESH...
AND♪ I'LL BRING TO LIFE A BRAND-NEW YOU!
SO... WOULD IT BE POSSIBLE TO TROUBLE YOU FOR THE NEXT LESSON AFTER "THE WALK" SOMETIME...
DON'T ASK ME!! AS FAR AS I'M CONCERNED, GO AHEAD ON YOUR OWN... SKATE OFF A CLIFF FOR ALL I CARE!
AN-OTHER LOVERS' QUARREL I SEE...
AS SWEET A PAIR AS USUAL.
WHO ARE YOU TALKING ABOUT?!
AND DIDN'T WE TELL YOU—YOU HAVE MORE THAN ENOUGH DOLLS ALREADY?!
PLEASE DON'T TAKE YOUR FRUSTRATIONS OUT ON ME.
SO...UME, COULD YOU GIVE ME SOME AIR TRECK LESSO—
NOT A *CHANCE!*
TONIGHT I'M FINALLY GONNA SEW UP MY 100th DOLL! ♡
BESIDES, I'M SURE YOU JUST WANT TO LEARN SOME NEW TRICK SO YOU CAN SHOW EVERYBODY AT SCHOOL THAT YOU'RE AN OVERNIGHT AIR TRECK MASTER—I BET THEY PROBABLY LAUGHED YOU OUT OF THE SCHOOL AFTER SEEING WHAT A KLUTZ YOU ARE ON WHEELS...
AM I RIGHT?
WH—!!
WHY DO YOU SAY—?!
DID YOU PLANT A BUG ON ME?!

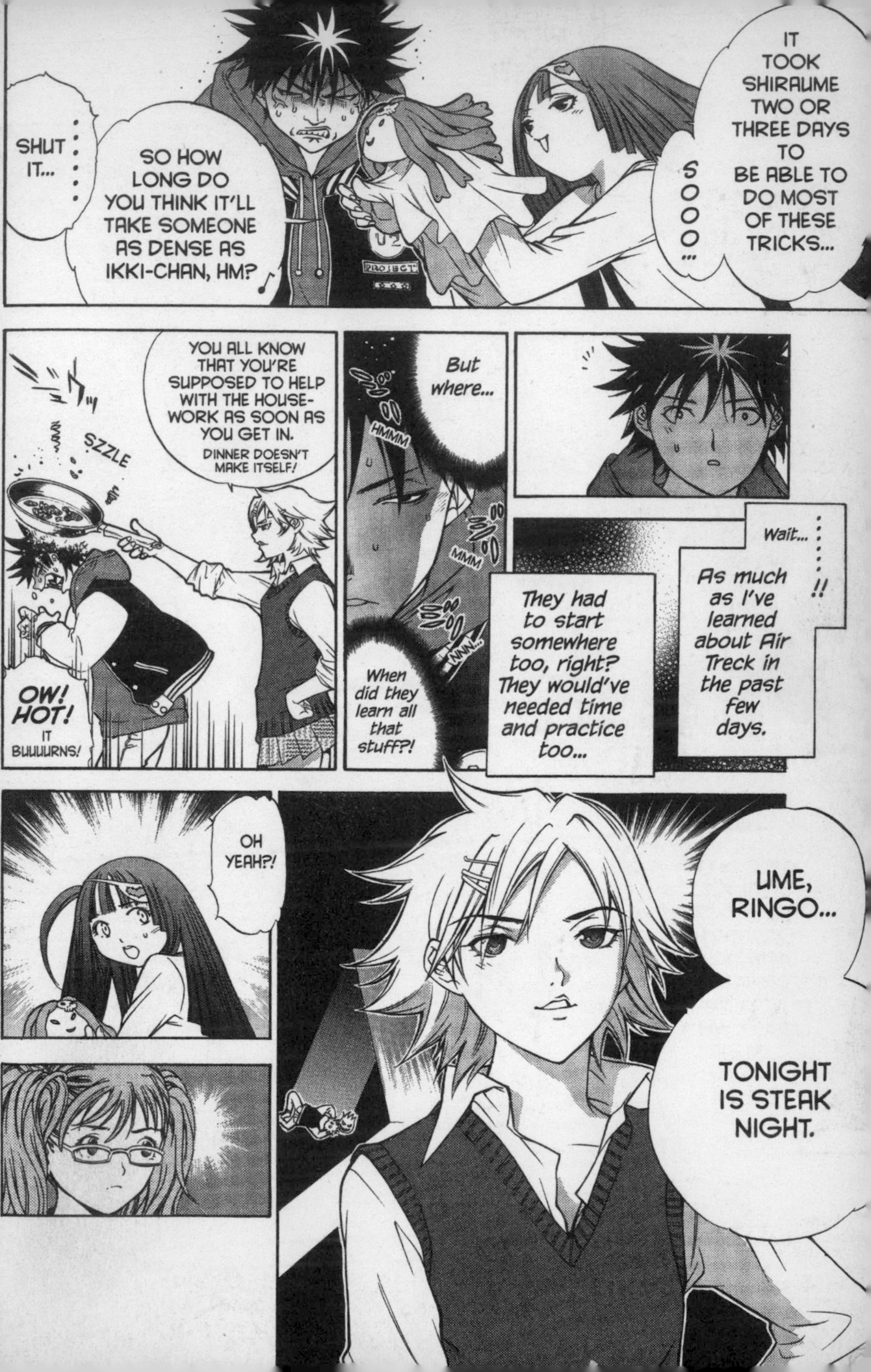
IT TOOK SHIRAUME TWO OR THREE DAYS TO BE ABLE TO DO MOST OF THESE TRICKS...
SOOOO...
SO HOW LONG DO YOU THINK IT'LL TAKE SOMEONE AS DENSE AS IKKI-CHAN, HM?
SHUT IT......
!
Wait......!!
As much as I've learned about Air Treck in the past few days.
They had to start somewhere too, right? They would've needed time and practice too...
But where...
HMMM
MMM
NNN...
When did they learn all that stuff?!
YOU ALL KNOW THAT YOU'RE SUPPOSED TO HELP WITH THE HOUSE-WORK AS SOON AS YOU GET IN.
DINNER DOESN'T MAKE ITSELF!
SZZLE
OW! HOT!
IT BUUUURNS!
UME, RINGO...
TONIGHT IS STEAK NIGHT.
OH YEAH?!

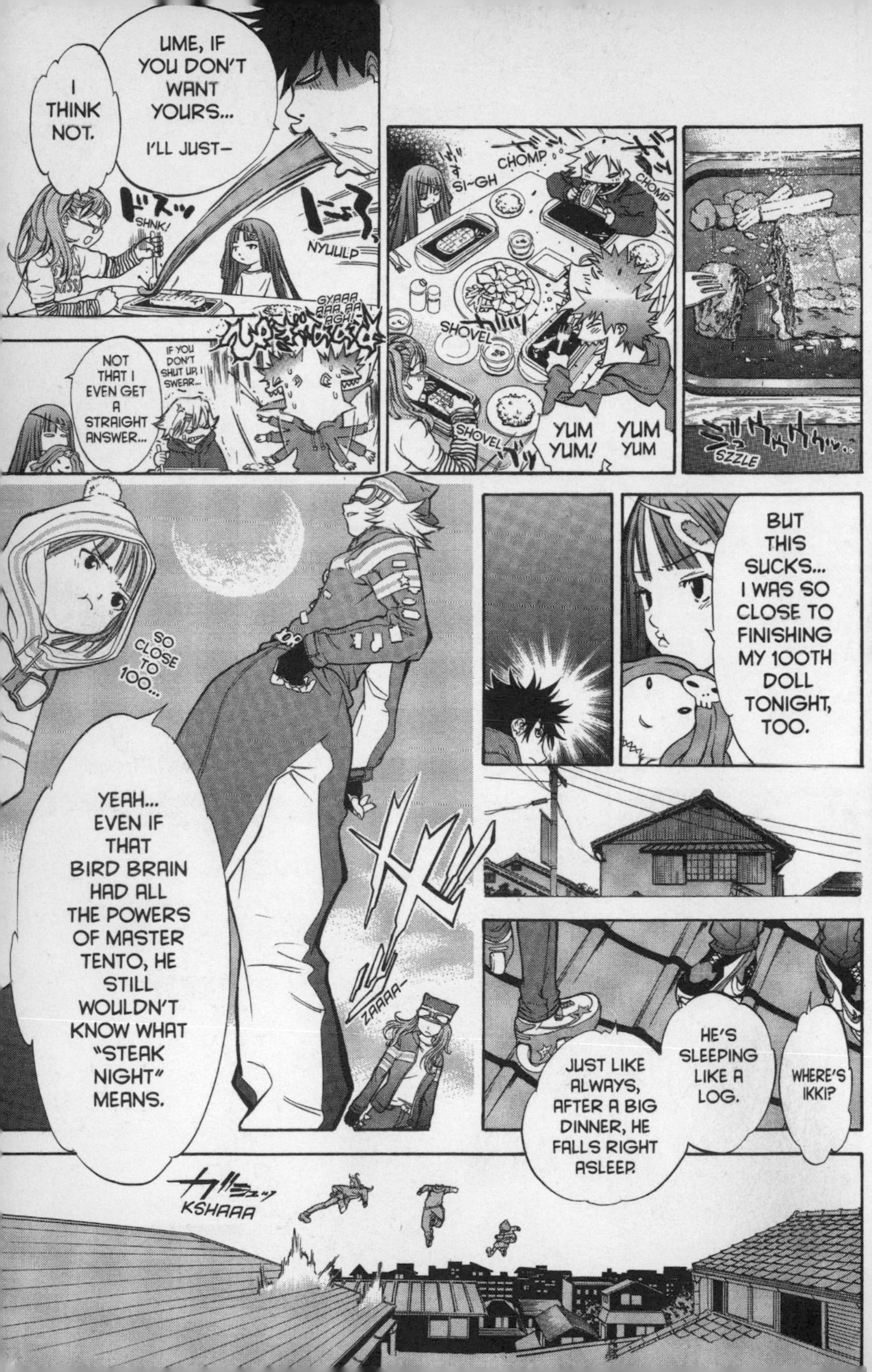
SZZLE
SI~GH
CHOMP
CHOMP
SHOVEL
SHOVEL
YUM YUM!
YUM YUM
UME, IF YOU DON'T WANT YOURS... I'LL JUST–
I THINK NOT.
SHNK!
NYUULP
GYAAA AAA AA AGH!
IF YOU DON'T SHUT UP, I SWEAR...
NOT THAT I EVEN GET A STRAIGHT ANSWER...
BUT THIS SUCKS... I WAS SO CLOSE TO FINISHING MY 100TH DOLL TONIGHT, TOO.
WHERE'S IKKI?
HE'S SLEEPING LIKE A LOG.
JUST LIKE ALWAYS, AFTER A BIG DINNER, HE FALLS RIGHT ASLEEP.
SO CLOSE TO 100...
YEAH... EVEN IF THAT BIRD BRAIN HAD ALL THE POWERS OF MASTER TENTO, HE STILL WOULDN'T KNOW WHAT "STEAK NIGHT" MEANS.
ZAAAA–
KSHAAA

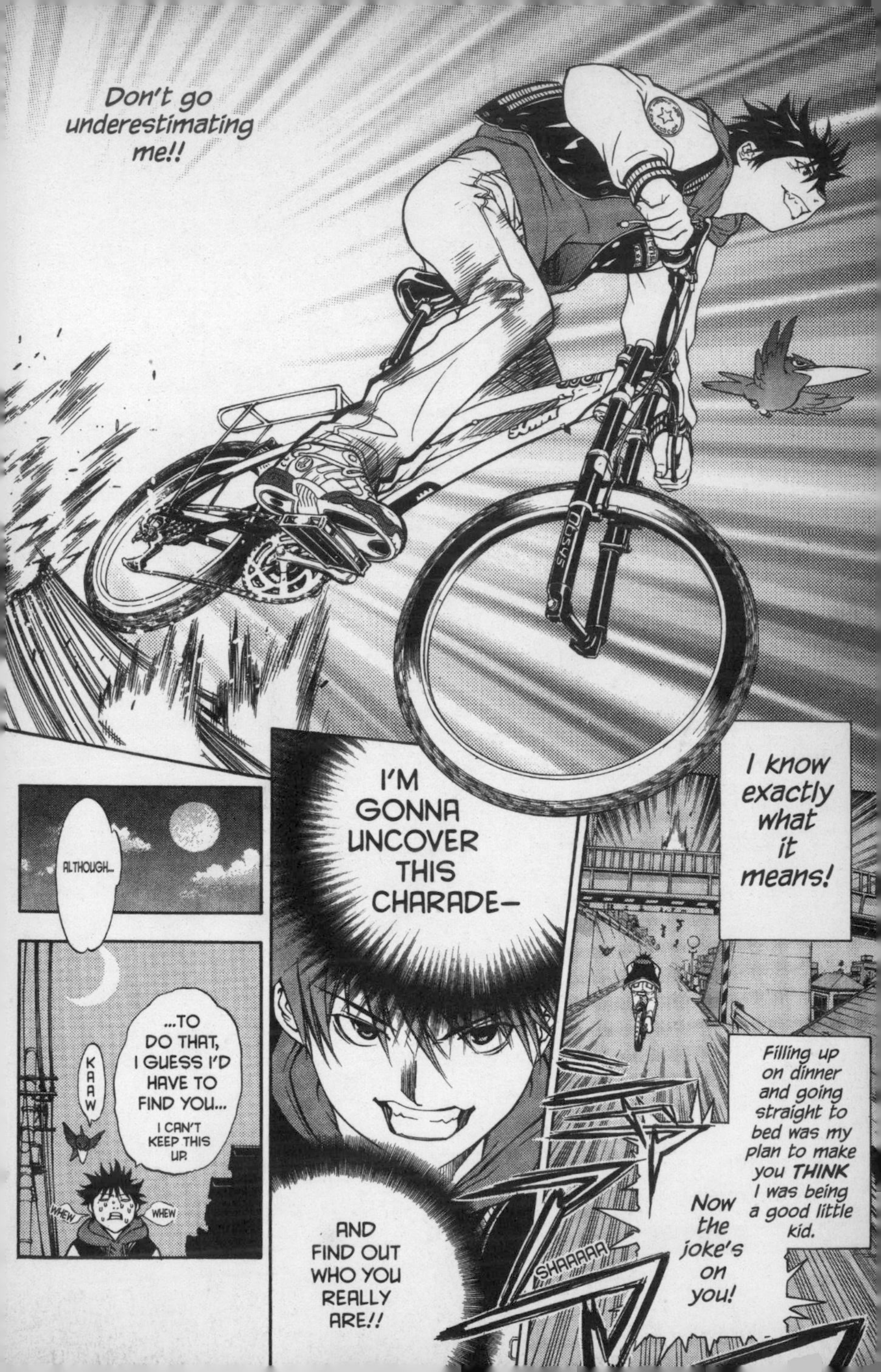
Don't go underestimating me!!
I know exactly what it means!
Filling up on dinner and going straight to bed was my plan to make you THINK I was being a good little kid.
Now the joke's on you!
SHAAAAA
I'M GONNA UNCOVER THIS CHARADE—
AND FIND OUT WHO YOU REALLY ARE!!
ALTHOUGH...
...TO DO THAT, I GUESS I'D HAVE TO FIND YOU...
I CAN'T KEEP THIS UP.
KAAAW
WHEW
WHEW

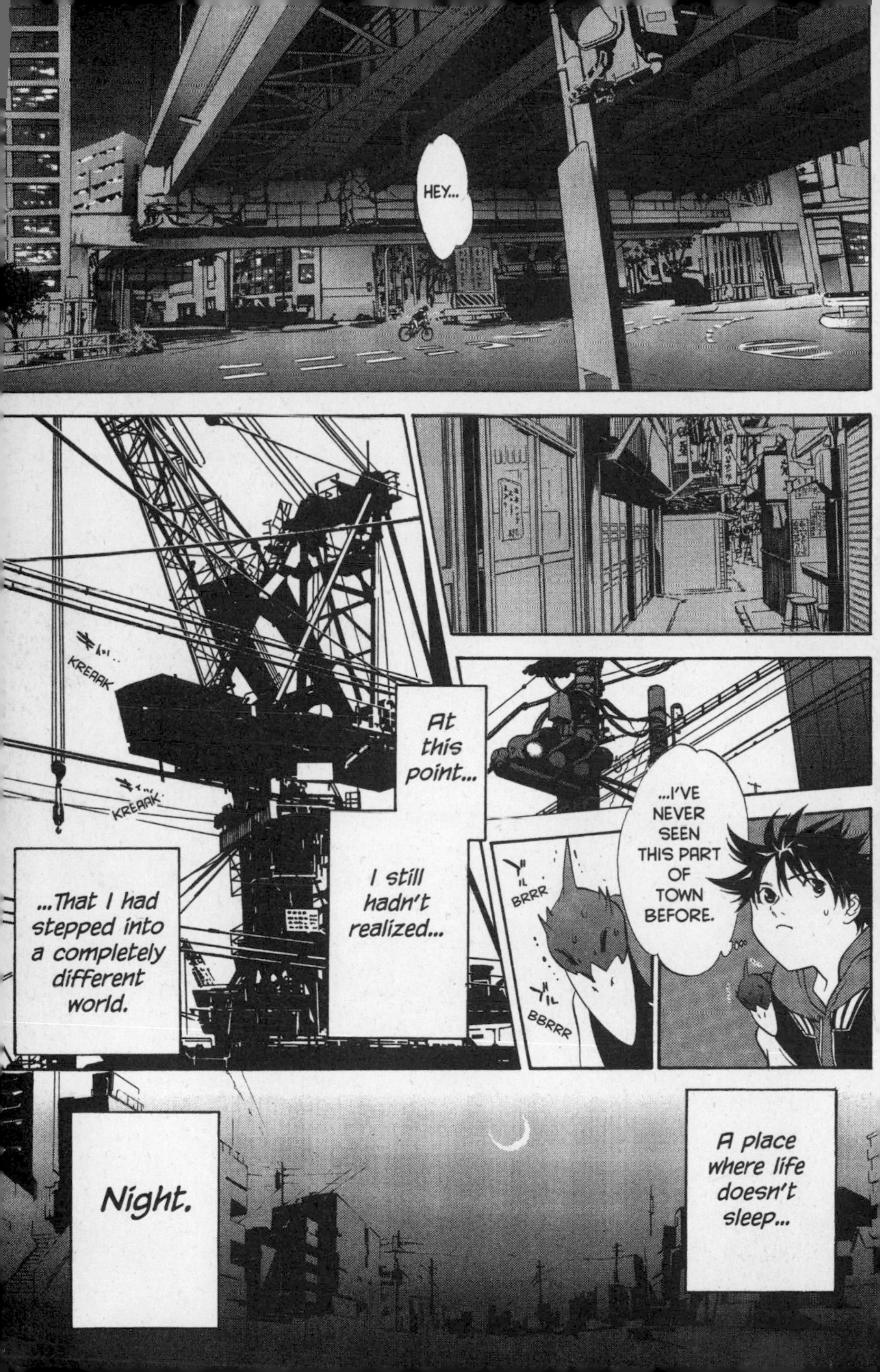
HEY...
...I'VE NEVER SEEN THIS PART OF TOWN BEFORE.
BRRR
BRRRR
KREAAK
KREAAK
At this point...
I still hadn't realized...
...That I had stepped into a completely different world.
A place where life doesn't sleep...
Night.

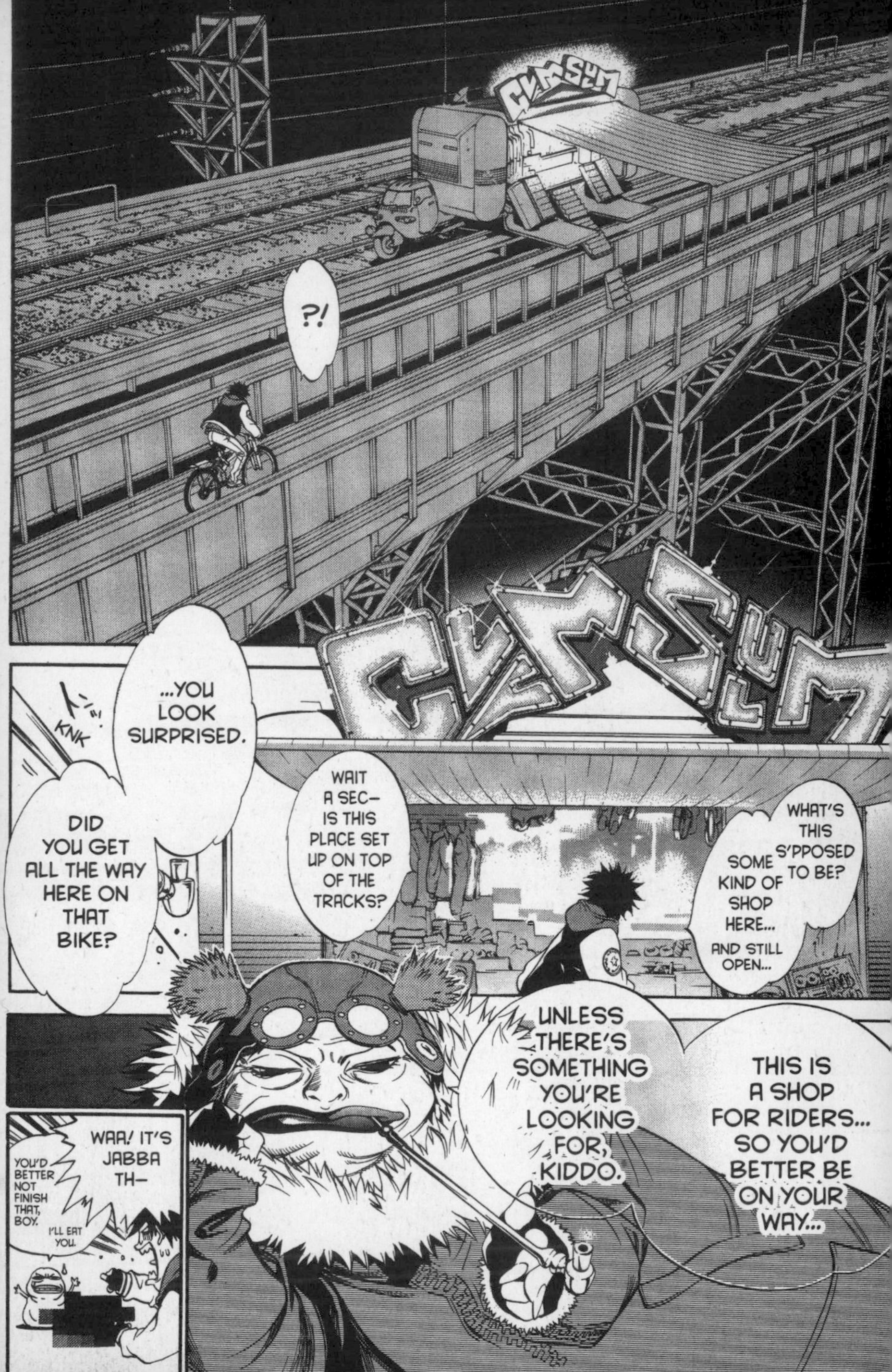

CYMSUM
?!
CYMSUM
WHAT'S THIS S'PPOSED TO BE?
SOME KIND OF SHOP HERE...
AND STILL OPEN...
WAIT A SEC— IS THIS PLACE SET UP ON TOP OF THE TRACKS?
...YOU LOOK SURPRISED.
KNK
DID YOU GET ALL THE WAY HERE ON THAT BIKE?
THIS IS A SHOP FOR RIDERS... SO YOU'D BETTER BE ON YOUR WAY...
UNLESS THERE'S SOMETHING YOU'RE LOOKING FOR, KIDDO.
WAA! IT'S JABBA TH—
YOU'D BETTER NOT FINISH THAT, BOY.
I'LL EAT YOU.

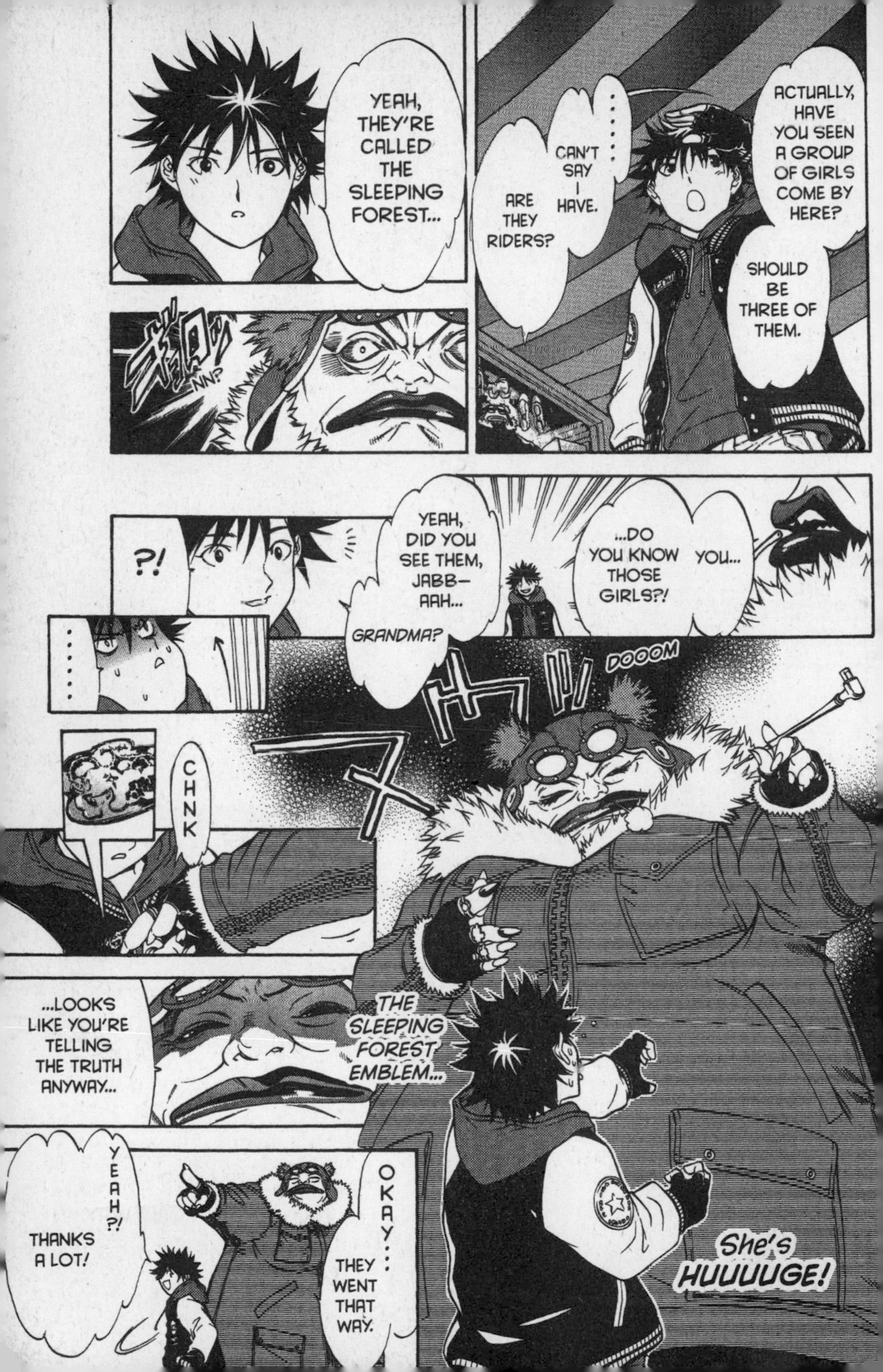
ACTUALLY, HAVE YOU SEEN A GROUP OF GIRLS COME BY HERE?
SHOULD BE THREE OF THEM.
......
CAN'T SAY I HAVE.
ARE THEY RIDERS?
YEAH, THEY'RE CALLED THE SLEEPING FOREST...
NN?
YOU...
...DO YOU KNOW THOSE GIRLS?!
YEAH, DID YOU SEE THEM, JABB—AAH...
GRANDMA?
?!
......
DOOOM
CHNK
THE SLEEPING FOREST EMBLEM...
She's HUUUUGE!
...LOOKS LIKE YOU'RE TELLING THE TRUTH ANYWAY...
OKAY...
THEY WENT THAT WAY.
YEAH?!
THANKS A LOT!

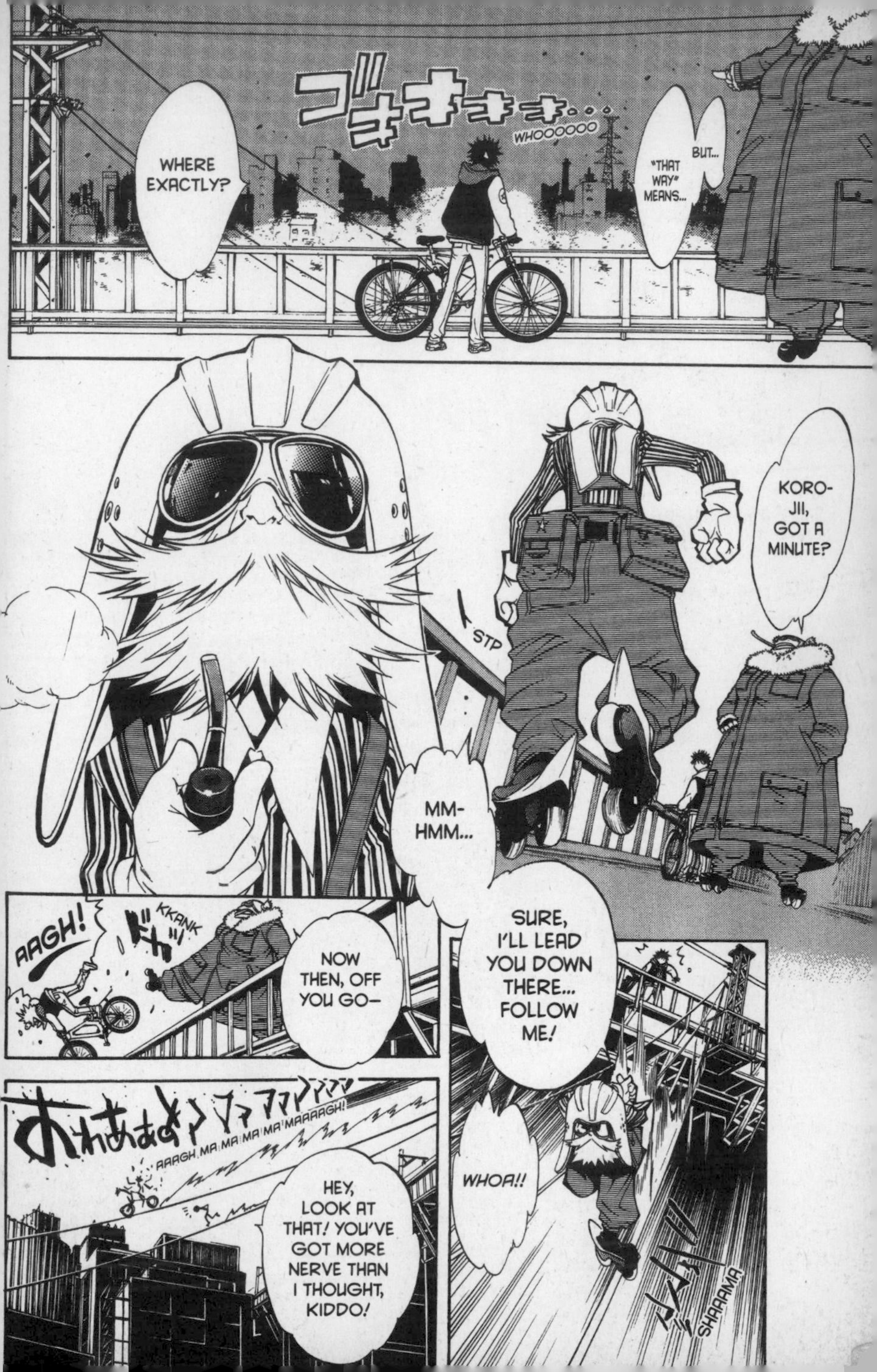

BUT...
"THAT WAY" MEANS...
ゴォォォォ...
WHOOOOOO
WHERE EXACTLY?
KORO-JII, GOT A MINUTE?
STP
MM-HMM...
SURE, I'LL LEAD YOU DOWN THERE... FOLLOW ME!
WHOA!!
SHAAAMA
NOW THEN, OFF YOU GO—
KKANK
AAGH!
AARGH MA MA MA MA MAAAAGH!
HEY, LOOK AT THAT! YOU'VE GOT MORE NERVE THAN I THOUGHT, KIDDO!

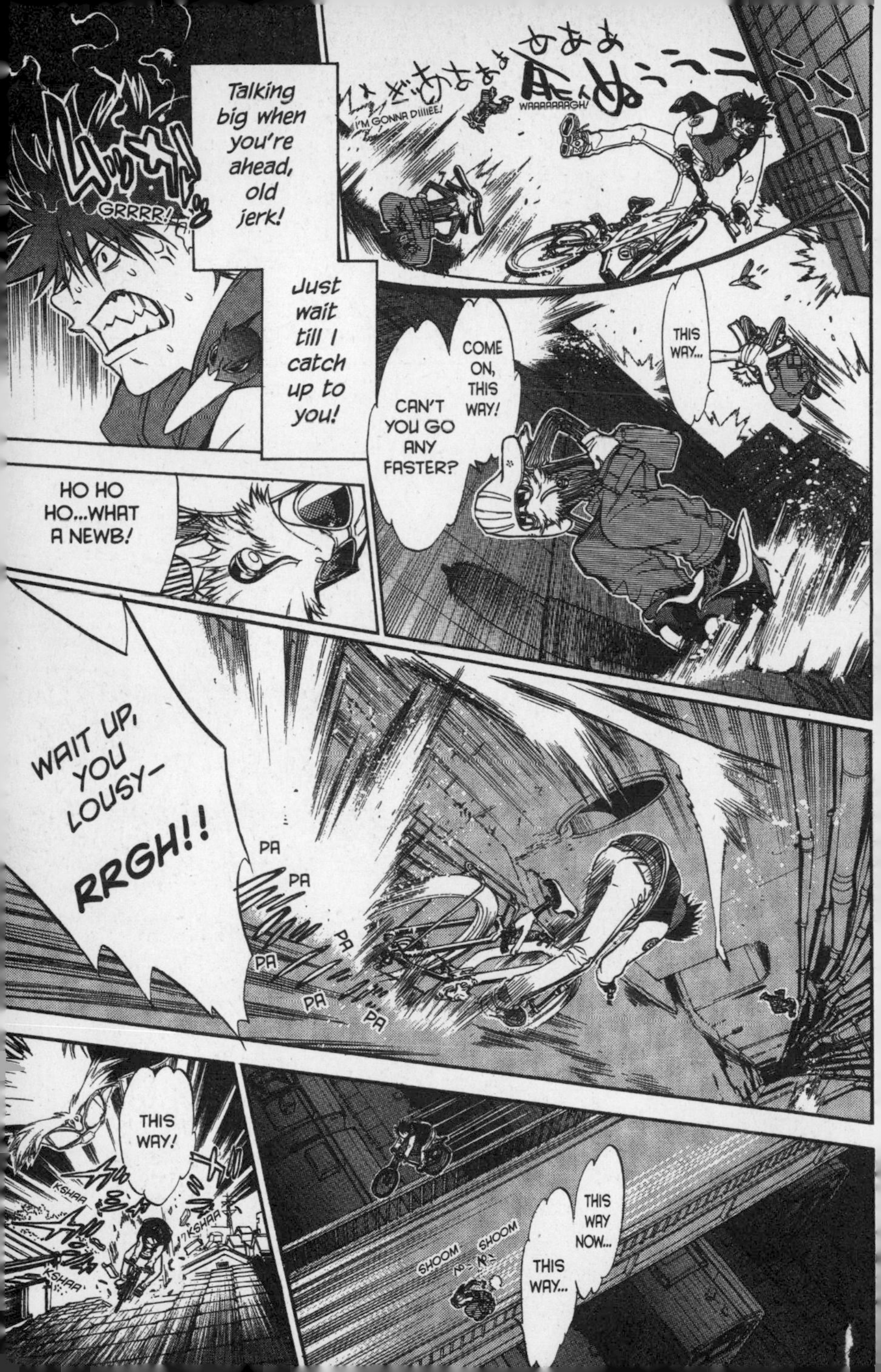
I'M GONNA DIIIIEE!
WAAAAAAAGH!
GRRRR!
Talking big when you're ahead, old jerk!
Just wait till I catch up to you!
THIS WAY...
COME ON, THIS WAY!
CAN'T YOU GO ANY FASTER?
HO HO HO...WHAT A NEWB!
WAIT UP, YOU LOUSY-
RRGH!!
PA
PA
PA
PA
PA
PA
THIS WAY NOW...
THIS WAY...
SHOOM
SHOOM
THIS WAY!
KSHAA
KSHAA
KSHAA

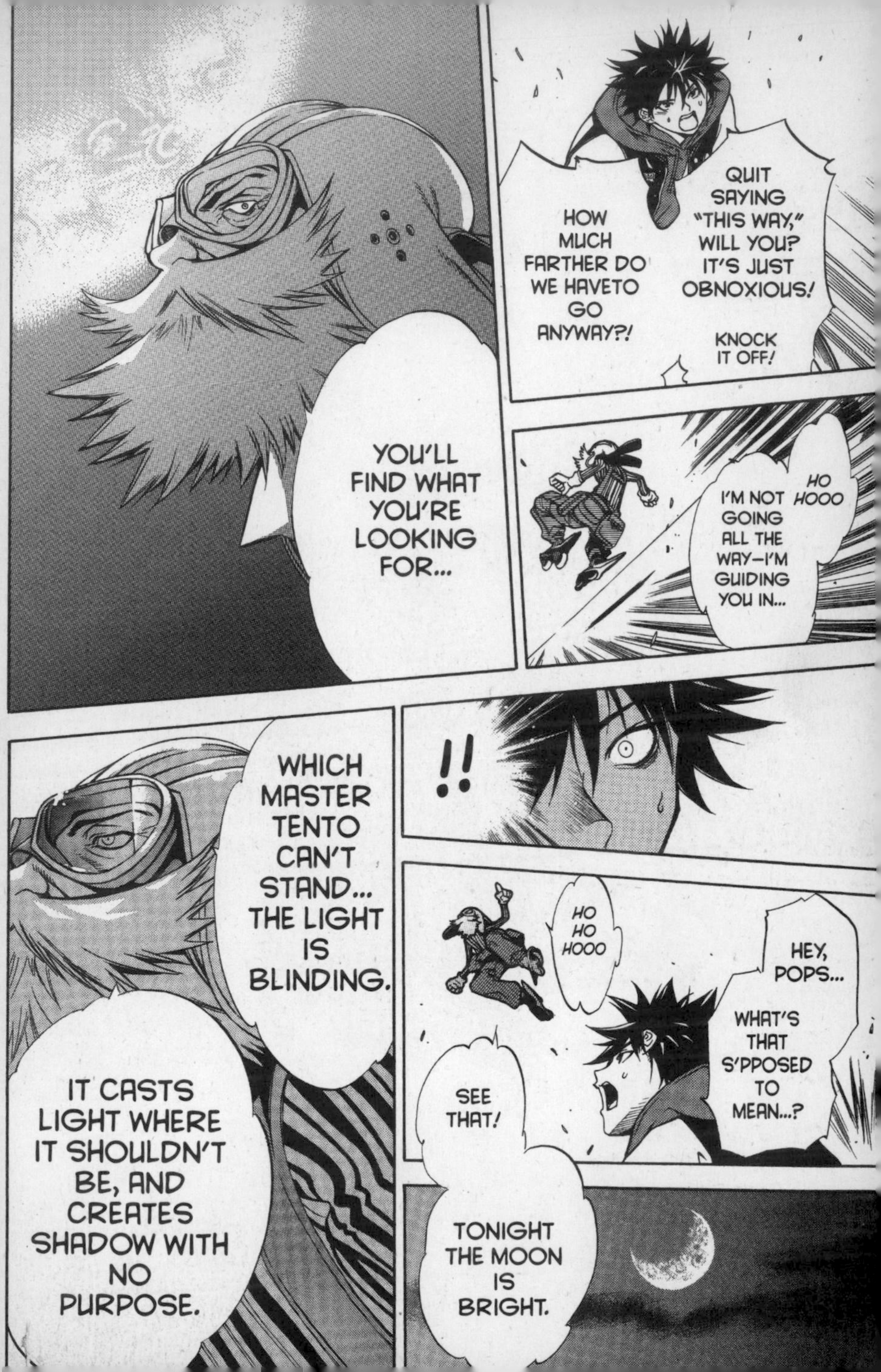
QUIT SAYING "THIS WAY," WILL YOU? IT'S JUST OBNOXIOUS!
HOW MUCH FARTHER DO WE HAVETO GO ANYWAY?!
KNOCK IT OFF!
HO HOOO
I'M NOT GOING ALL THE WAY—I'M GUIDING YOU IN...
YOU'LL FIND WHAT YOU'RE LOOKING FOR...
!!
HEY, POPS...
WHAT'S THAT S'PPOSED TO MEAN...?
HO HO HOOO
SEE THAT!
TONIGHT THE MOON IS BRIGHT.
WHICH MASTER TENTO CAN'T STAND... THE LIGHT IS BLINDING.
IT CASTS LIGHT WHERE IT SHOULDN'T BE, AND CREATES SHADOW WITH NO PURPOSE.

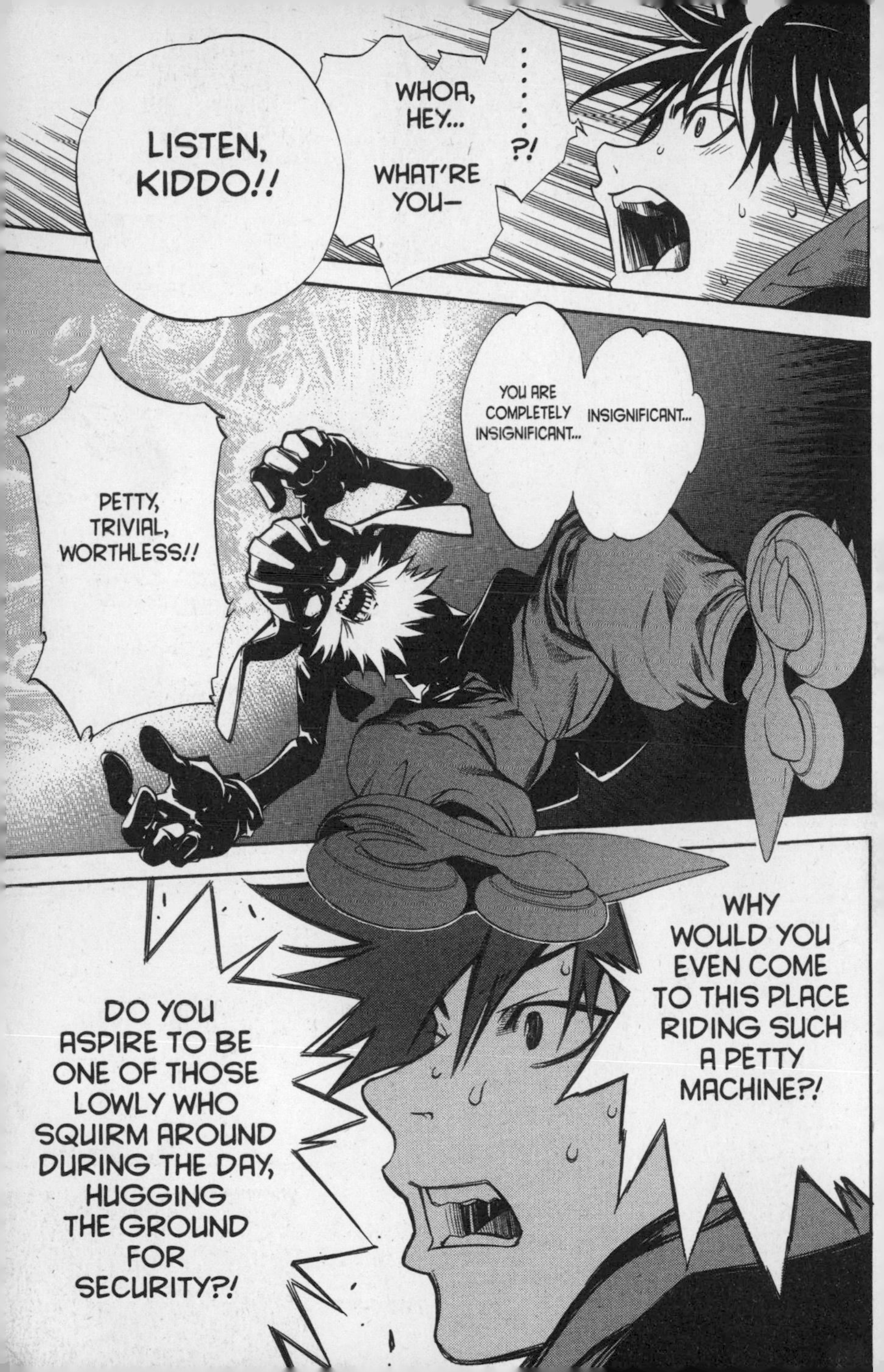
......?!
WHOA, HEY... WHAT'RE YOU—
LISTEN, KIDDO!!
YOU ARE COMPLETELY INSIGNIFICANT... INSIGNIFICANT...
PETTY, TRIVIAL, WORTHLESS!!
WHY WOULD YOU EVEN COME TO THIS PLACE RIDING SUCH A PETTY MACHINE?!
DO YOU ASPIRE TO BE ONE OF THOSE LOWLY WHO SQUIRM AROUND DURING THE DAY, HUGGING THE GROUND FOR SECURITY?!

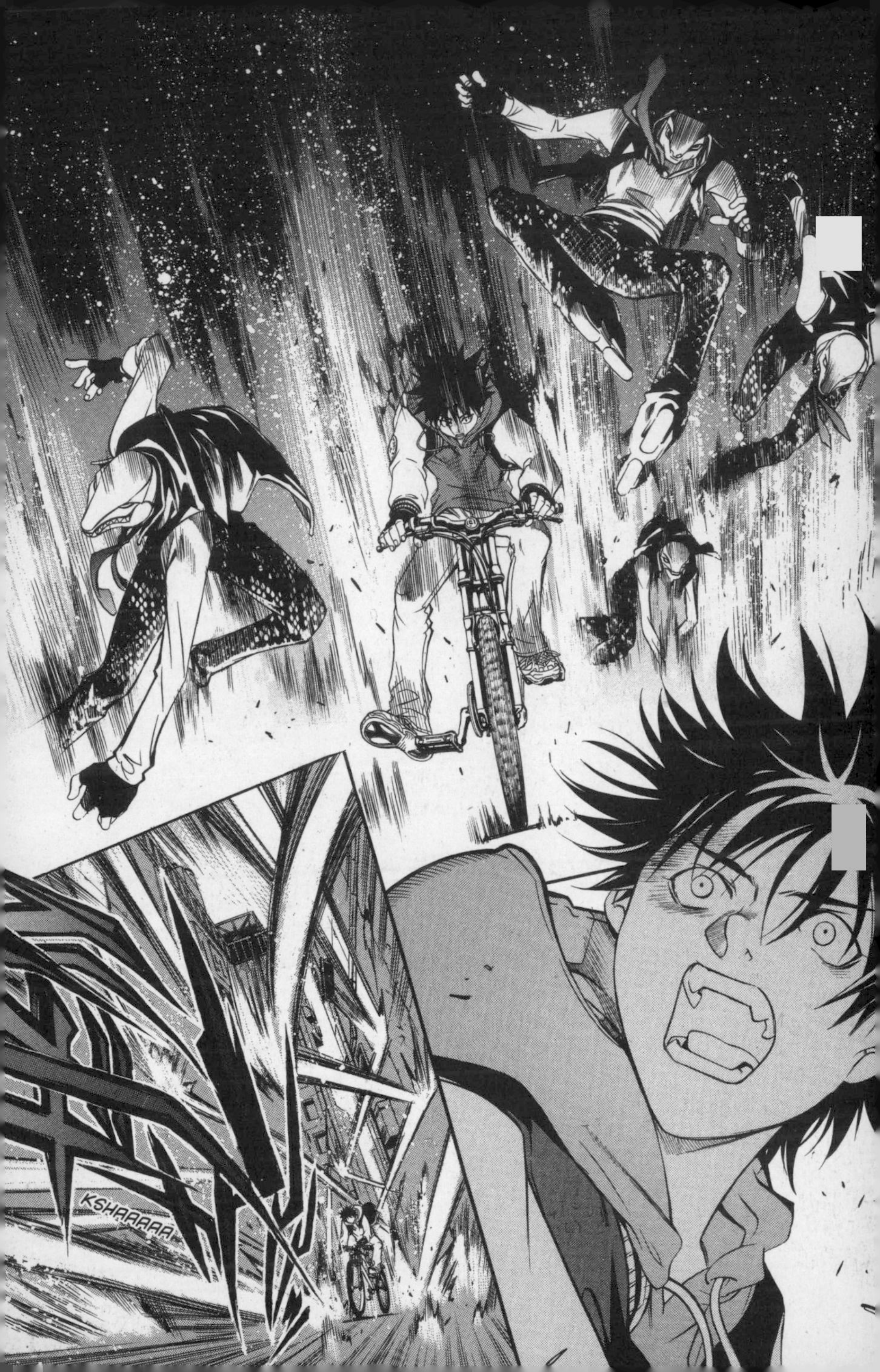
KSHAAAAA

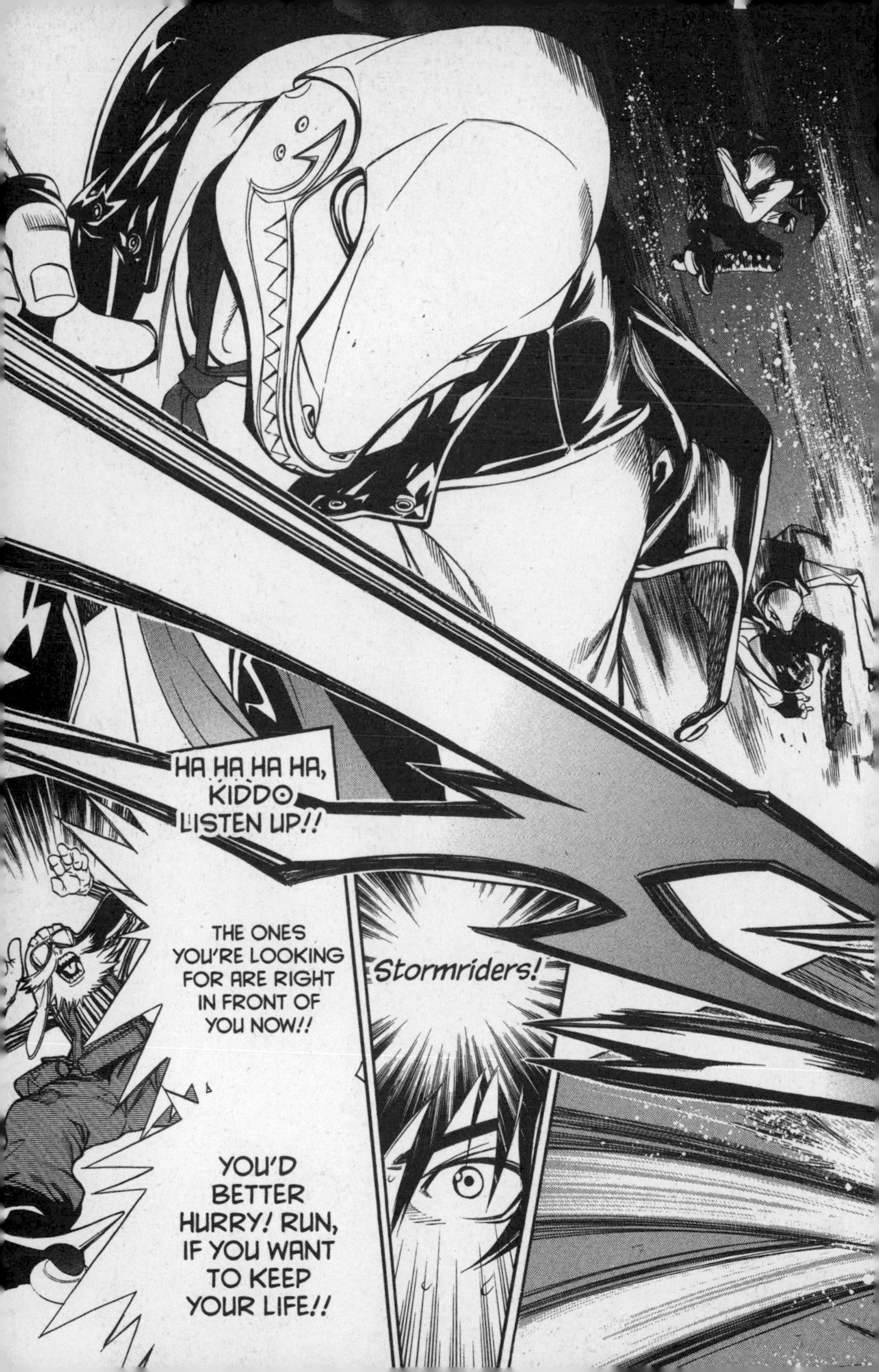
HA HA HA HA, KIDDO LISTEN UP!!
Stormriders!
THE ONES YOU'RE LOOKING FOR ARE RIGHT IN FRONT OF YOU NOW!!
YOU'D BETTER HURRY! RUN, IF YOU WANT TO KEEP YOUR LIFE!!

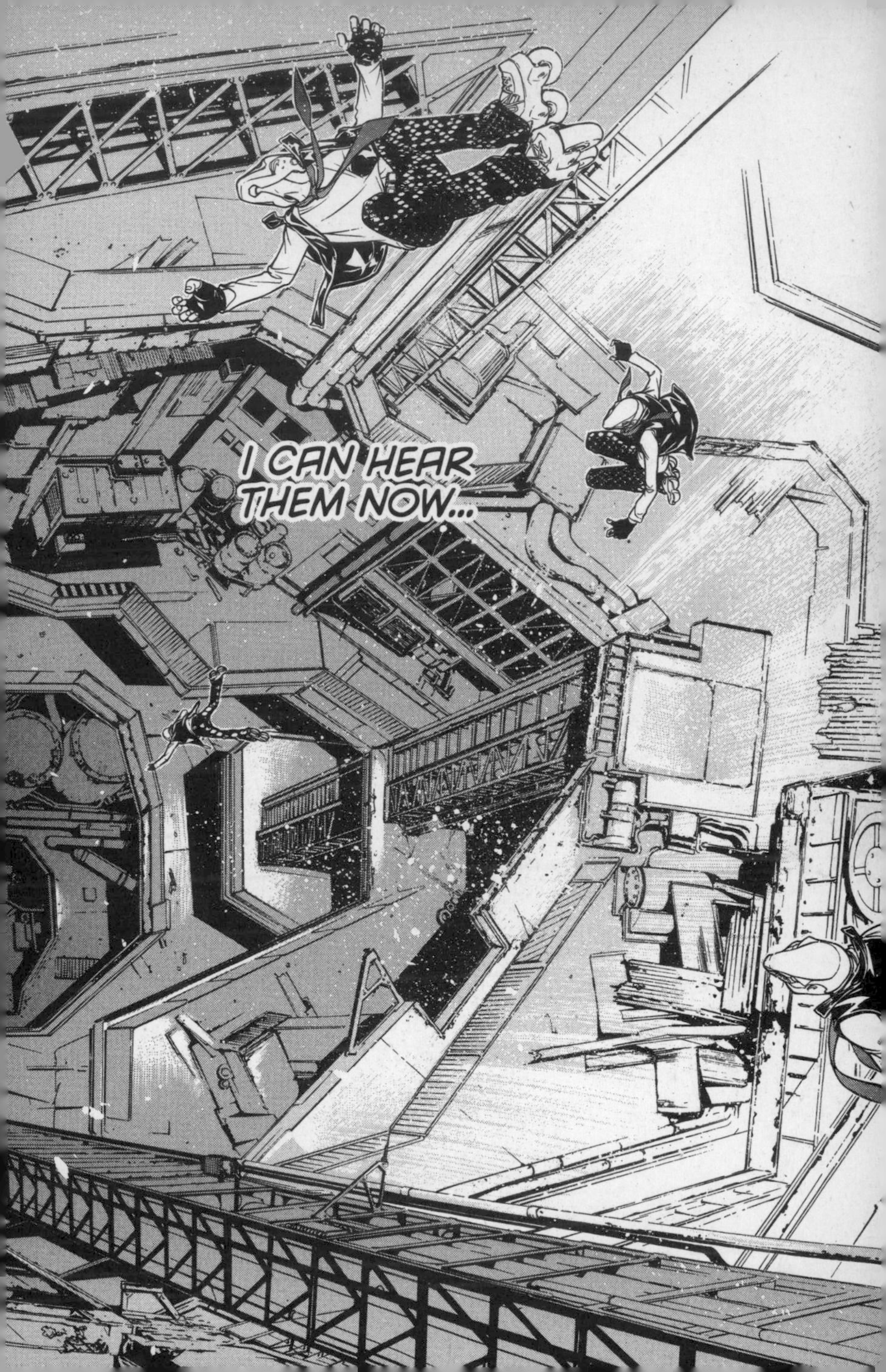
I CAN HEAR THEM NOW...

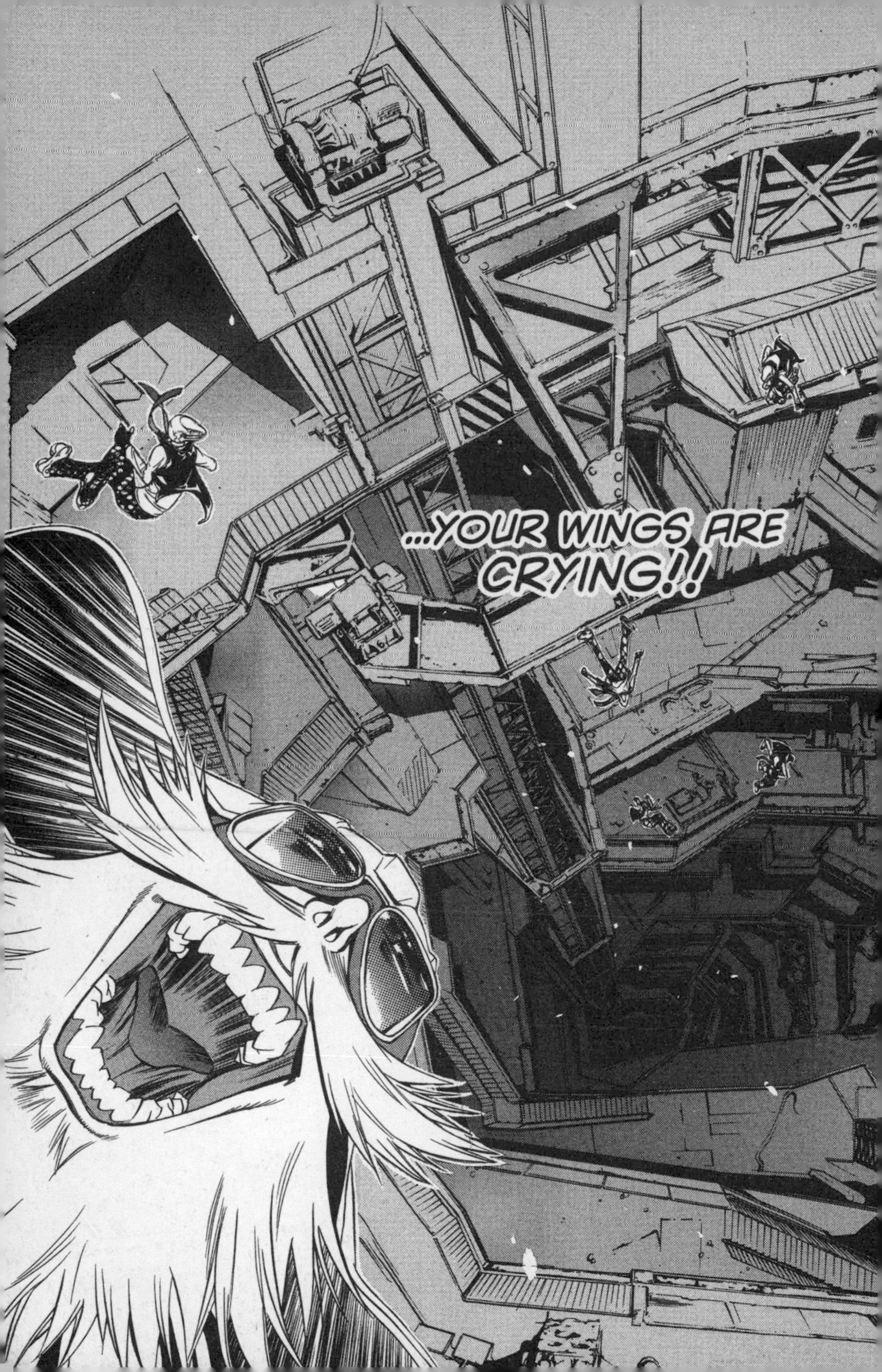
...YOUR WINGS ARE CRYING!!

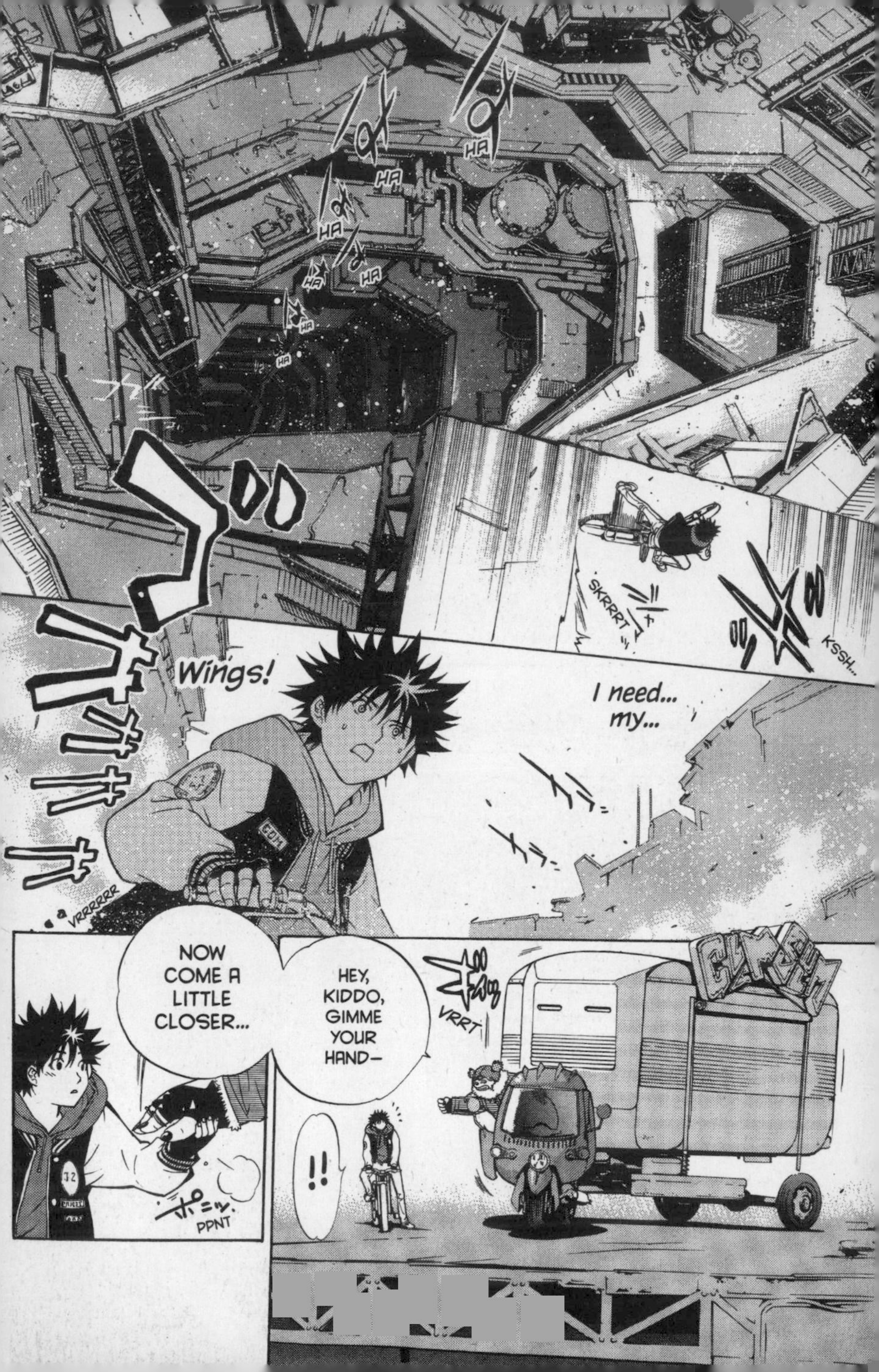
HA
HA
HA
HA
HA
HA
HA
SKRRRT
KSSH...
I need... my...
Wings!
VRRRRRR
HEY, KIDDO, GIMME YOUR HAND—
VRRT
!!
NOW COME A LITTLE CLOSER...
PPNT

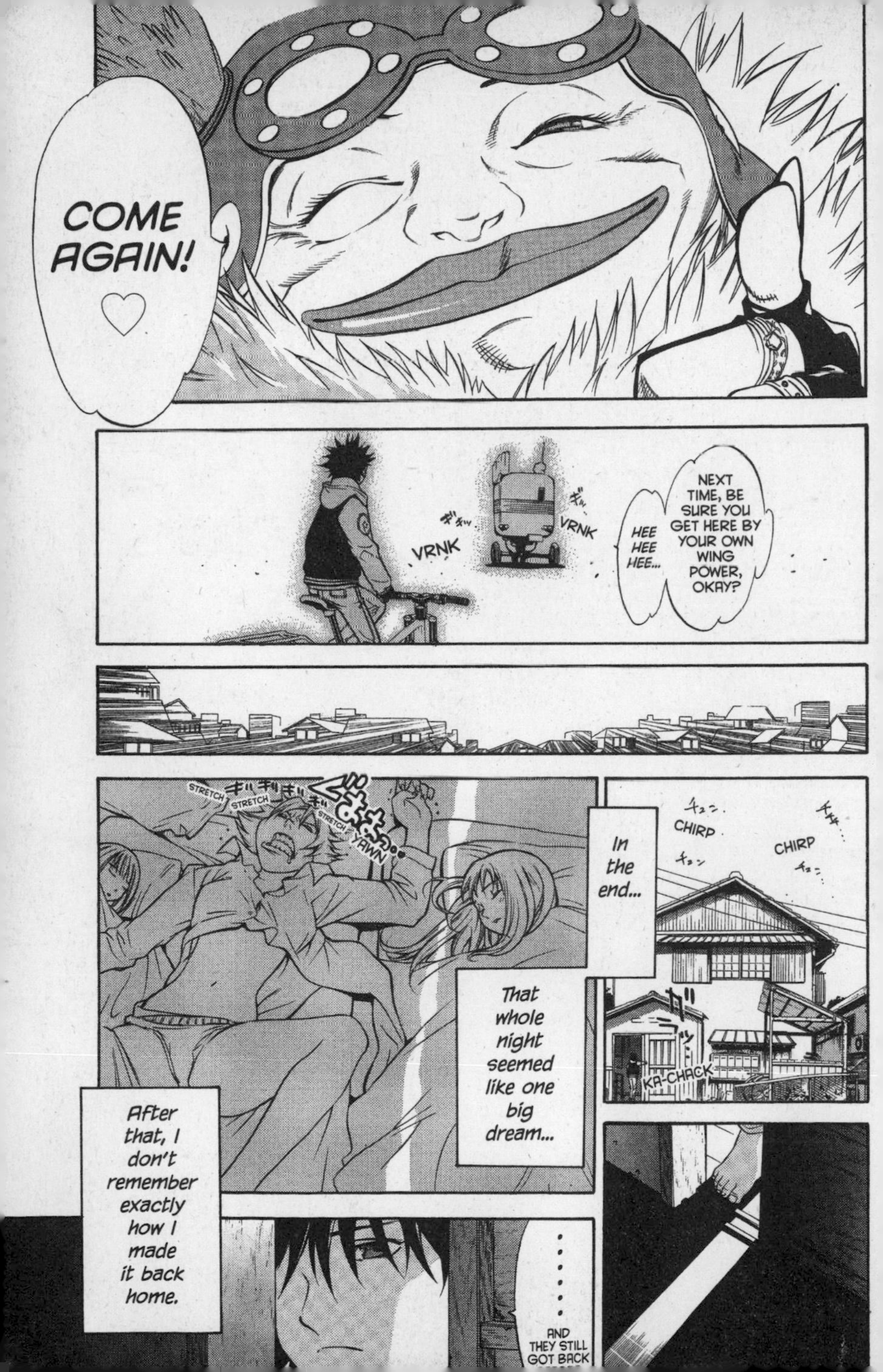
COME AGAIN! ♡
NEXT TIME, BE SURE YOU GET HERE BY YOUR OWN WING POWER, OKAY?
HEE HEE HEE...
VRNK
VRNK
CHIRP
CHIRP
KA-CHACK
In the end...
That whole night seemed like one big dream...
STRETCH
STRETCH
STRETCH
YAWN
After that, I don't remember exactly how I made it back home.
......
AND THEY STILL GOT BACK

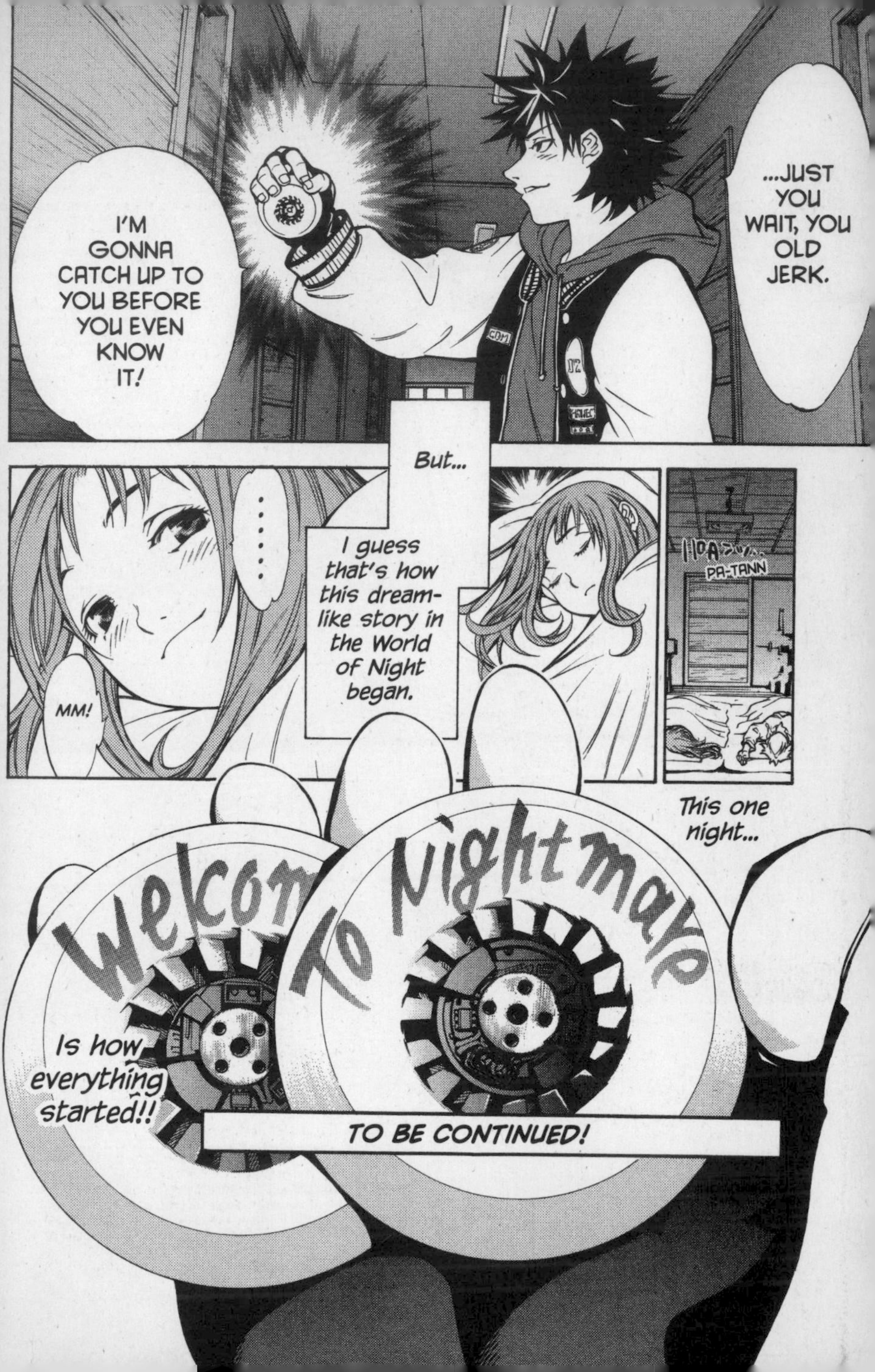
...JUST YOU WAIT, YOU OLD JERK.
I'M GONNA CATCH UP TO YOU BEFORE YOU EVEN KNOW IT!
PA-TANN
But...
I guess that's how this dream-like story in the World of Night began.
......
MM!
This one night...
Welcome to Nightmare
Is how everything started!!
TO BE CONTINUED!

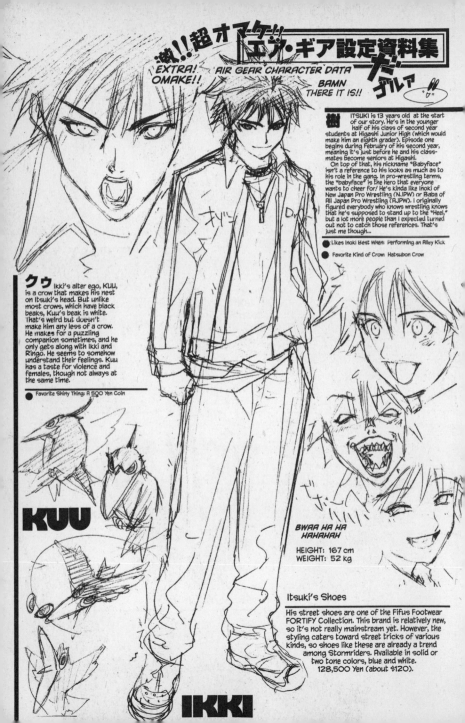

激!!超オマケ!! エア・ギア設定資料集だゴルァ

EXTRA! OMAKE!!

AIR GEAR CHARACTER DATA

BAMN THERE IT IS!!

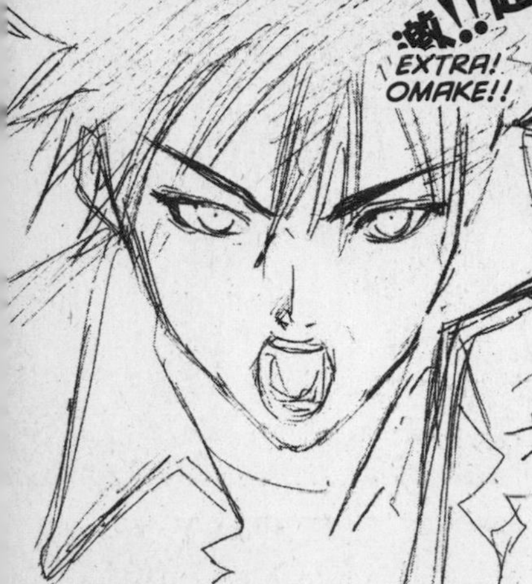

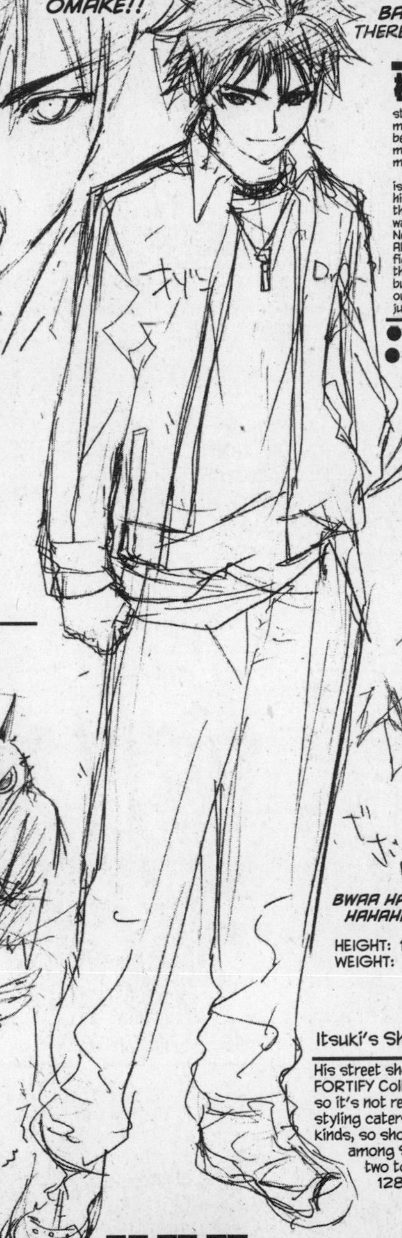

樹 ITSUKI is 13 years old at the start of our story. He's in the younger half of his class of second year students at Higashi Junior High (which would make him an eighth grader). Episode one begins during February of his second year, meaning it's just before he and his classmates become seniors at Higashi.

On top of that, his nickname "Babyface" isn't a reference to his looks as much as to his role in the gang. In pro-wrestling terms, the "babyface" is the hero that everyone wants to cheer for! He's kinda like Inoki of New Japan Pro Wrestling (NJPW) or Baba of All Japan Pro Wrestling (AJPW). I originally figured everybody who knows wrestling knows that he's supposed to stand up to the "Heel," but a lot more people than I expected turned out not to catch those references. That's just me though...

- Likes Inoki Best When: Performing an Alley Kick
- Favorite Kind of Crow: Hatsubon Crow

クゥ Ikki's alter ego, KUU, is a crow that makes his nest on Itsuki's head. But unlike most crows, which have black beaks, Kuu's beak is white. That's weird but doesn't make him any less of a crow. He makes for a puzzling companion sometimes, and he only gets along with Ikki and Ringo. He seems to somehow understand their feelings. Kuu has a taste for violence and females, though not always at the same time.

- Favorite Shiny Thing: A 500 Yen Coin

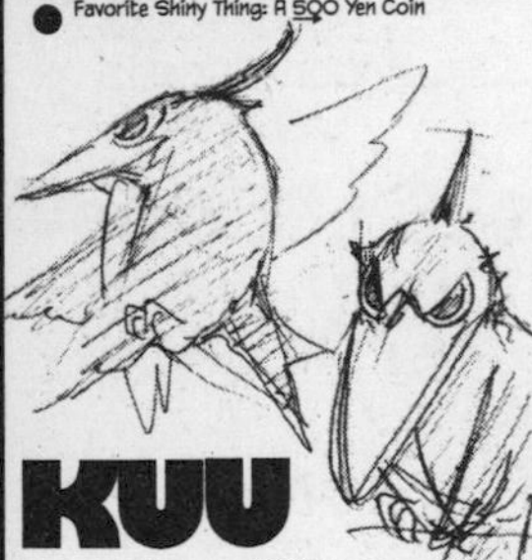

KUU

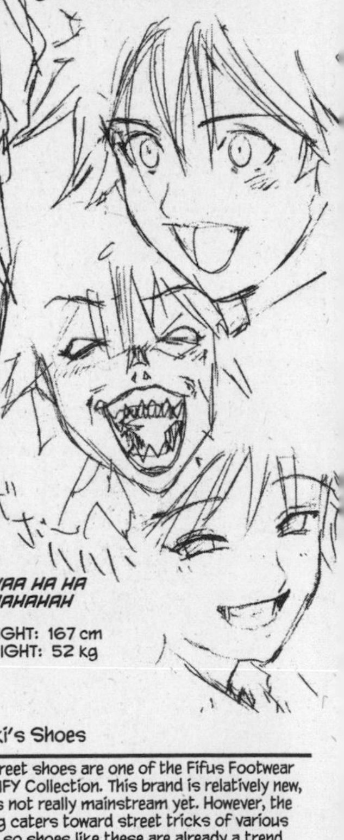

BWAA HA HA HAHAHAH

HEIGHT: 167 cm
WEIGHT: 52 kg

Itsuki's Shoes

His street shoes are one of the Fifus Footwear FORTIFY Collection. This brand is relatively new, so it's not really mainstream yet. However, the styling caters toward street tricks of various kinds, so shoes like these are already a trend among Stormriders. Available in solid or two tone colors, blue and white. 128,500 Yen (about $120).

IKKI

林檎

RINGO

The third-born daughter in the Noyamano family; also a second-year student, along with Ikki, at Higashi Junior High School. Fourteen years old; Height: 157 cm, Bust: 84 cm, Waist: 57 cm, Hip: 81 cm.

Ringo and Ikki have grown up together like brother and sister, but he's the only one who hasn't noticed her feelings might be a little different. Everyone else around them can see her affections for him. She's always in glasses which makes her irresistible to those fanboys who like the geeky schoolgirl type, but she also has a rough side, which she rarely shows—but when she does get violent, it might remind you of Mikan. Most of the time however, she ends up as Ikki and Mikan's babysitter.

- Likes Inoki Best When: Actually, she prefers Baba over Inoki.

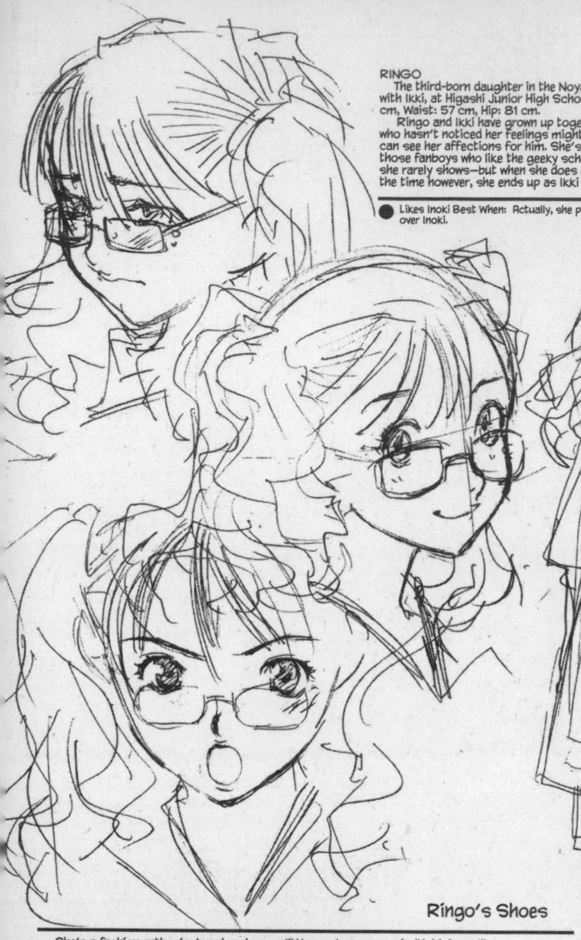

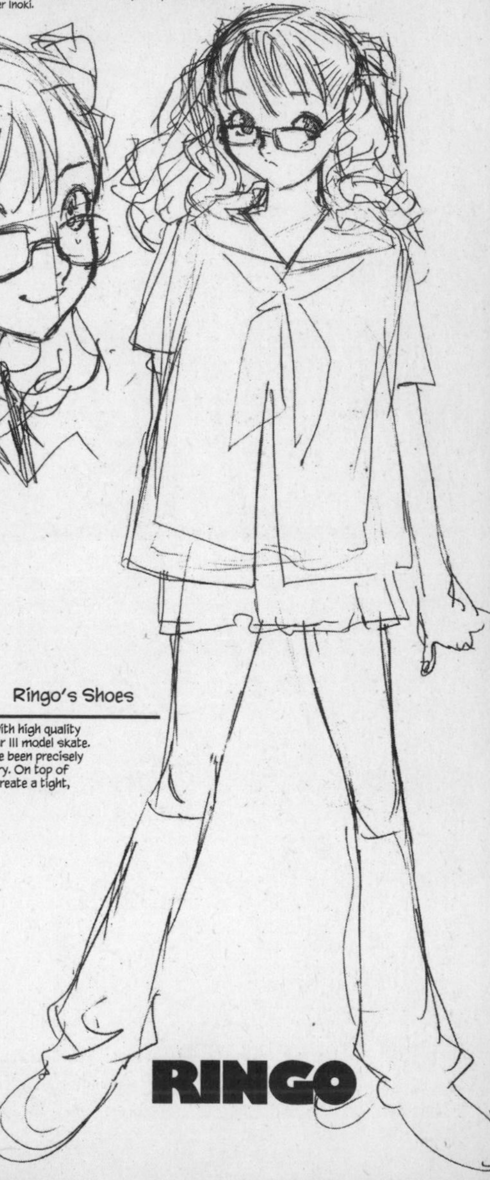

Ringo's Shoes

She's a fashion enthusiast and perhaps a little overly concerned with high quality clothing and accessories. She wears a Basing Bape brand Bapestar III model skate. They're the high-mobility model, but the wheels and suspension have been precisely adjusted, making her skates even faster and smoother than ordinary. On top of that, they're equipped with extra shocks and power, combining to create a tight, solid, super-technical pair of Air Trecks.

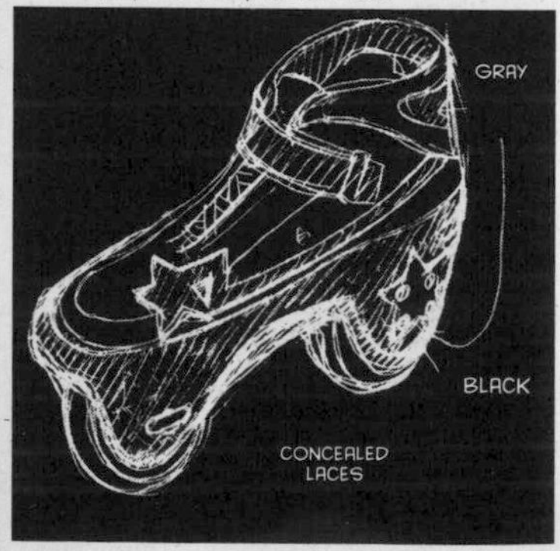
GRAY
BLACK
CONCEALED LACES

RINGO

蜜柑

MIKAN

Second-born daughter in the family, a 17-year-old high school junior. Height: 164 cm, Bust: 79 cm, Waist: 60 cm, Hip: 79 cm. She's a candid, explosive and formidable fighter who likes torture and ramen. Mikan's not too busty and might seem a little pear-shaped, but her fans say "We like it like that"... so there she is.

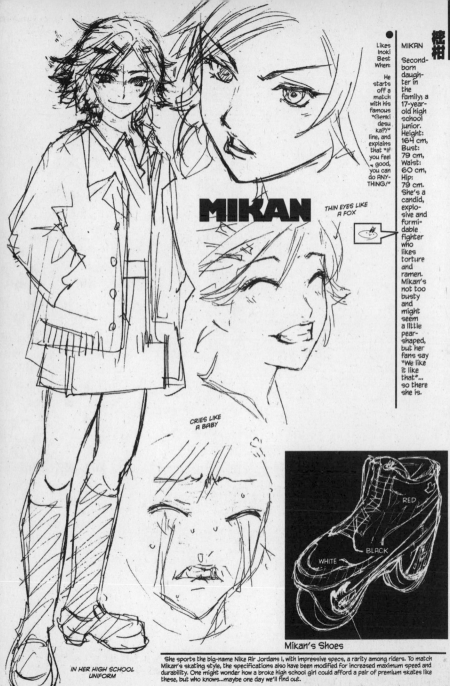

Likes Inoki Best When:

He starts off a match with his famous "Genki desu ka?!" line, and explains that "If you feel good, you can do ANYTHING!"

MIKAN

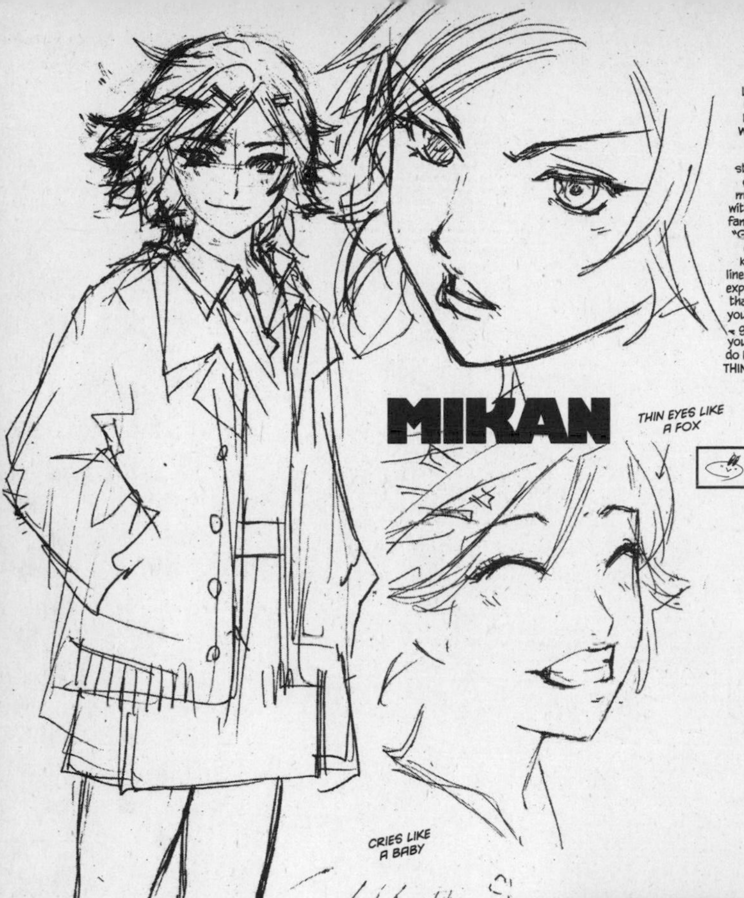
THIN EYES LIKE A FOX
CRIES LIKE A BABY

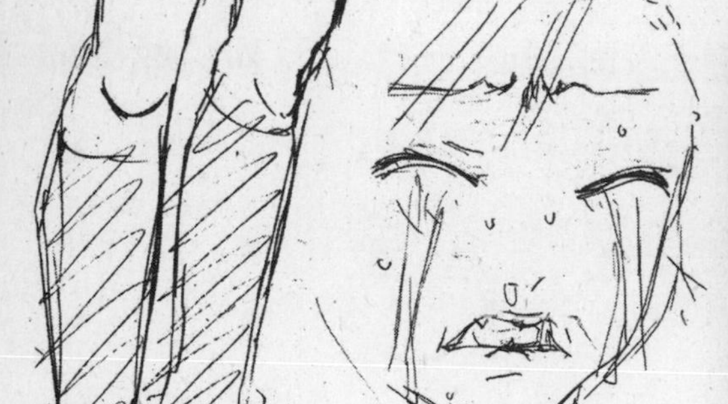
IN HER HIGH SCHOOL UNIFORM

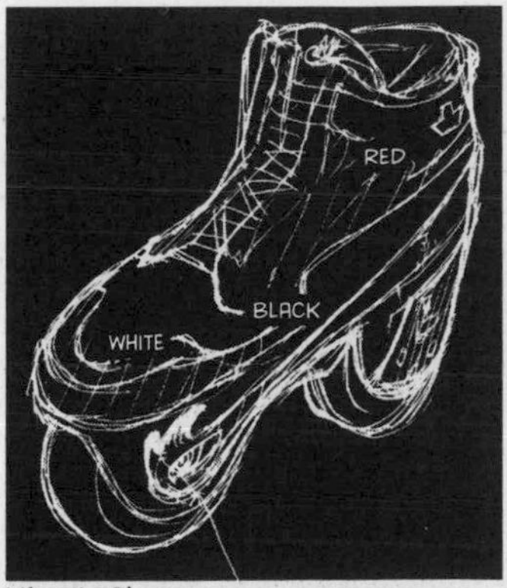
RED
BLACK
WHITE

Mikan's Shoes

She sports the big-name Nike Air Jordans I, with impressive specs, a rarity among riders. To match Mikan's skating style, the specifications also have been modified for increased maximum speed and durability. One might wonder how a broke high school girl could afford a pair of premium skates like these, but who knows...maybe one day we'll find out.

白梅

SHIRAUME
Fourth daughter in the Noyamano family, she's an elementary school fourth grader, at age 10. It seems the four sisters had to start taking care of themselves just after she was born. Perhaps that's why she's a little spoiled and can be quite selfish sometimes. Could also explain why everything around her has a slightly creepy feel to it. She admires Kei Machida's design work, and handiwork like crafts and sewing are her specialty. She's always carrying a raggedy doll with her and believe it or not, she has 98 others exactly like it! Making them has become her life's work (at least so far). Her usual response to things she doesn't like is to growl...

● Likes Bob Sapp When: She can see the lines on the back of his neck...

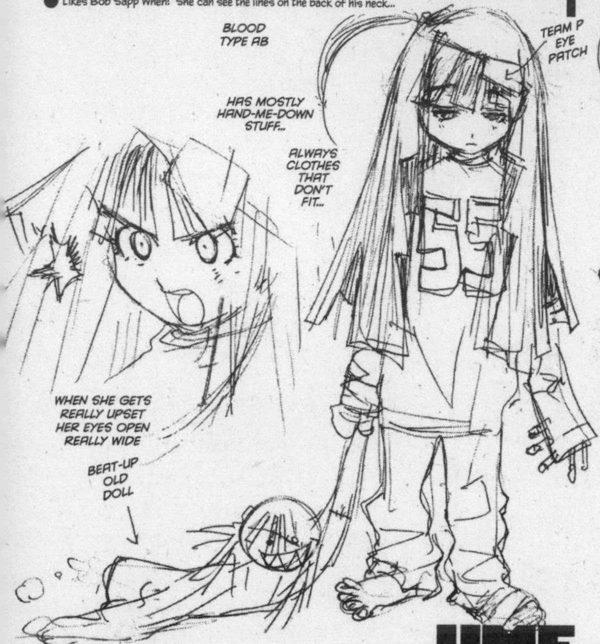
TEAM P EYE PATCH
BLOOD TYPE AB
HAS MOSTLY HAND-ME-DOWN STUFF...
ALWAYS CLOTHES THAT DON'T FIT...
WHEN SHE GETS REALLY UPSET HER EYES OPEN REALLY WIDE
BEAT-UP OLD DOLL

UME

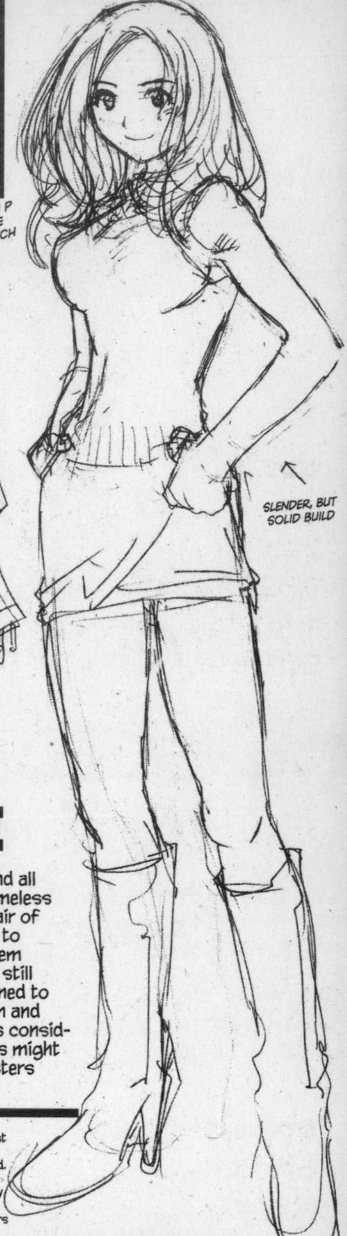
SLENDER, BUT SOLID BUILD

Ume's Shoes

If there were one supreme shoe maker... a "shoe maker to end all shoemakers" if you will... it would be Conberse. Each pair a timeless classic, with endless variations, and Ume specifically has a pair of customized Oll-Stars. She's so lightweight that extra mods to improve agility and speed aren't needed. Her skates might seem pretty normal, but they're still extremely high-end and tuned to help her keep up with Mikan and Ringo on the go. All things considered, their awesome skates might be the only thing these sisters really have in common.

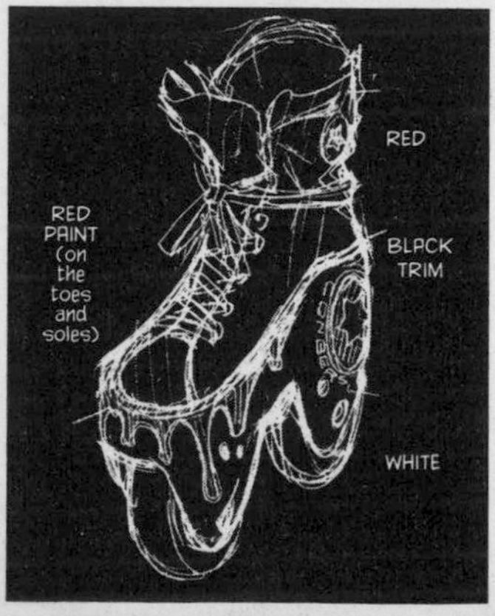
RED
RED PAINT (on the toes and soles)
BLACK TRIM
WHITE

梨花

RIKA
The eldest daughter of the Noyamano family, at 22 years old. Height: 172 cm, Bust: 92 cm, Waist: 61 cm, Hip: 88 cm. She has whole-heartedly accepted the job of taking care of this "super party" ever since she was 12 years old. She's taken care of her three other sisters, the honorary brother and his pet since then, and now she's grown into a very responsible and efficient young woman. She wants everyone in the Noyamano family to be successful, especially Mikan. Because she didn't get the chance to finish school herself, Rika lives vicariously through Mikan. When Rika loses her temper, it's truly terrifying.

RIKA

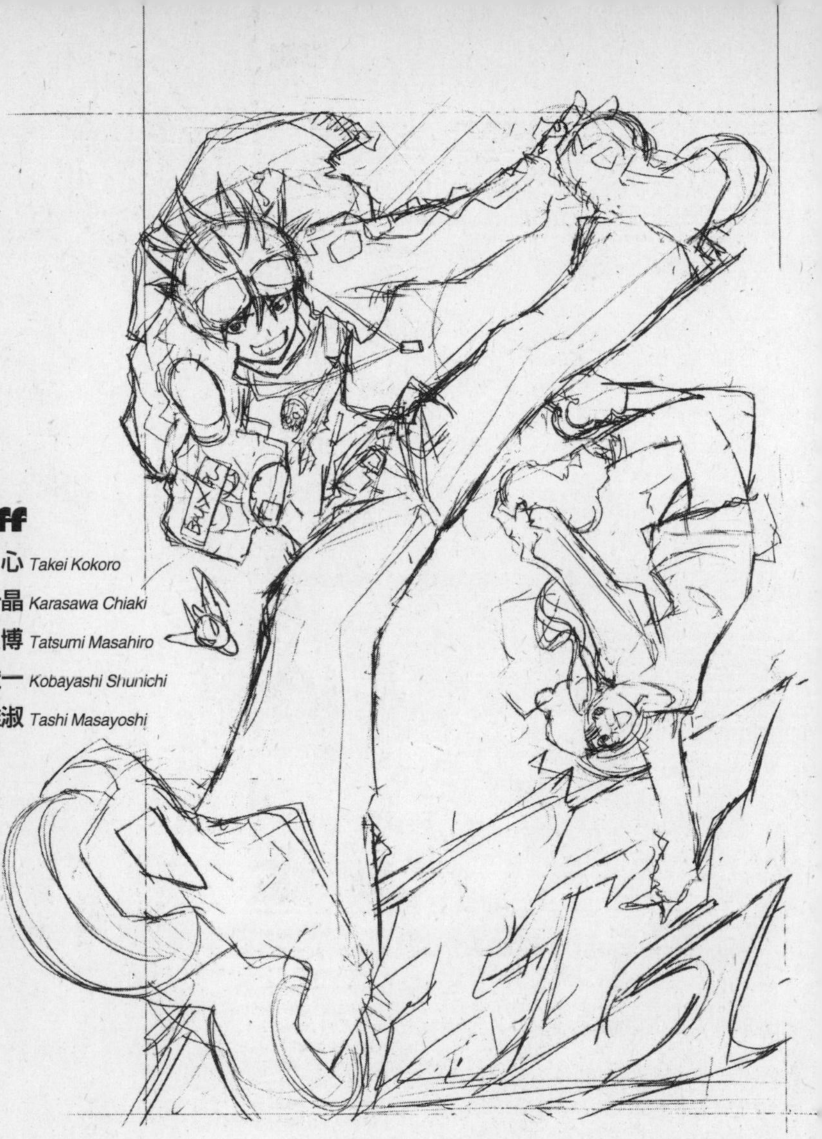

staff

竹井　心 *Takei Kokoro*

唐沢千晶 *Karasawa Chiaki*

辰己正博 *Tatsumi Masahiro*

小林俊一 *Kobayashi Shunichi*

田仕雅淑 *Tashi Masayoshi*

special thanks

石神由紀子 *Ishigami Yukiko*

pacific

屋代川隆史 *Yashirogawa Takashi*

青木　優 *Aoki Yu*

Translation Notes

Japanese is a tricky language for most Westerners, and translation is often more art than science. For your edification and reading pleasure, here are notes on some of the places where we could have gone in a different direction in our translation of the work, or where a Japanese cultural reference is used.

Hon ja maka, page 16

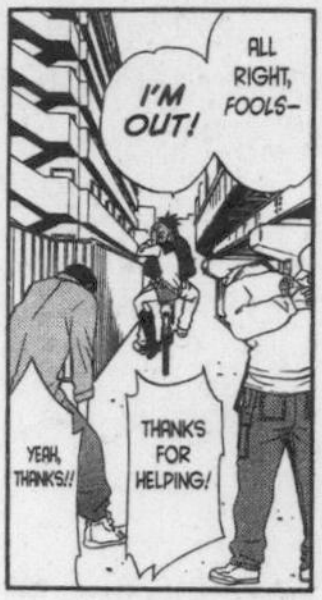
ALL RIGHT, FOOLS–
I'M OUT!
THANKS FOR HELPING!
YEAH, THANKS!!

As he leaves, Itsuki says to a couple of guys, "Hon ja maka," which is also the name of a comedy duo in Japan. It's a play on words for "*Sore ja, mata,*" which is a casual way to say, "Catch you later."

Yakuza, page 19

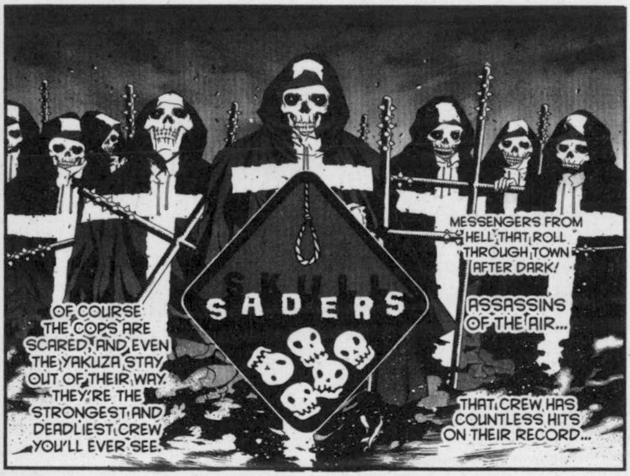
MESSENGERS FROM HELL THAT ROLL THROUGH TOWN AFTER DARK!
ASSASSINS OF THE AIR...
SKULL SADERS
THAT CREW HAS COUNTLESS HITS ON THEIR RECORD...
OF COURSE THE COPS ARE SCARED, AND EVEN THE YAKUZA STAY OUT OF THEIR WAY. THEY'RE THE STRONGEST AND DEADLIEST CREW YOU'LL EVER SEE.

The Yakuza are crime rings in Japan, dealing in money, loans, and gambling. Similar to the Italian Mafia.

Yakinku, page 29

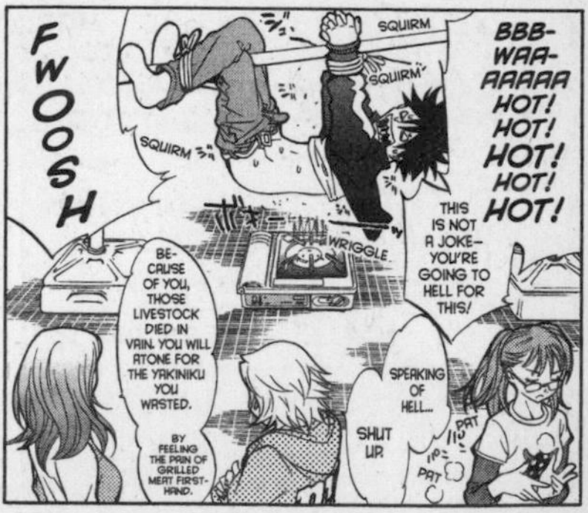
BBB-WAA-AAAAA HOT! HOT! HOT! HOT! HOT!
SQUIRM
SQUIRM
SQUIRM
FWOOSH
WRIGGLE
THIS IS NOT A JOKE– YOU'RE GOING TO HELL FOR THIS!
BE-CAUSE OF YOU, THOSE LIVESTOCK DIED IN VAIN. YOU WILL ATONE FOR THE YAKINIKU YOU WASTED.
BY FEELING THE PAIN OF GRILLED MEAT FIRST-HAND.
SPEAKING OF HELL...
SHUT UP.
PAT
PAT

Yakiniku is grilled meat, often served with special sauces. It's usually pork, beef, tripe, and various other meats all served together—which is why knocking over a table of *yakiniku* means a number of animals died in vain!

Tsubame, page 36

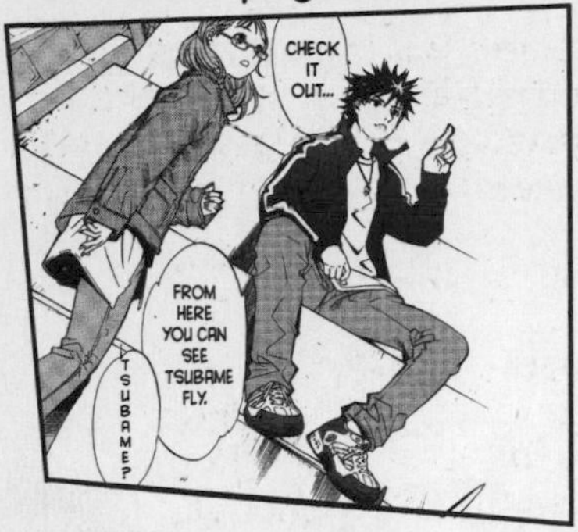
CHECK IT OUT...
FROM HERE YOU CAN SEE TSUBAME FLY.
TSUBAME?

Itsuki calls the mysterious girl with the skates "Tsubame," which is Japanese for swallow. These petite birds aren't rare—they're commonly found in Japan, even in the city—but they stll grab attention by swooping low and zooming in and out of obstacles.

Suplex, page 104

A German Suplex is a wrestling move—it involves grabbing your opponent from behind, locking his arm, and squeezing him at the waist. Itsuki can't imagine how that would help if he got hit in the face, but...

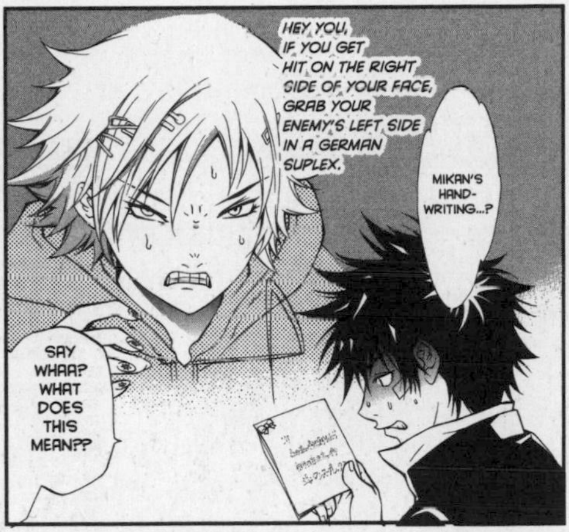
HEY, YOU, IF YOU GET HIT ON THE RIGHT SIDE OF YOUR FACE, GRAB YOUR ENEMY'S LEFT SIDE IN A GERMAN SUPLEX.
MIKAN'S HAND-WRITING...?
SAY WHAA? WHAT DOES THIS MEAN??

Paro, page 169

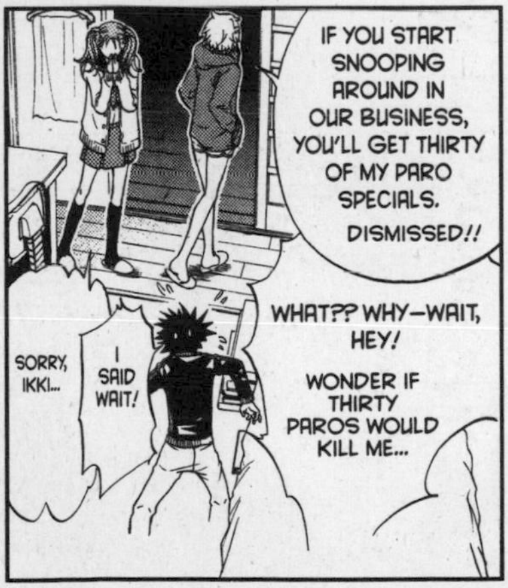
IF YOU START SNOOPING AROUND IN OUR BUSINESS, YOU'LL GET THIRTY OF MY PARO SPECIALS.
DISMISSED!!
WHAT?? WHY—WAIT, HEY!
WONDER IF THIRTY PAROS WOULD KILL ME...
I SAID WAIT!
SORRY, IKKI...

Paro Special is a pro-wrestling move in which you wrap your legs around the opponent's waist and pull his arms above his head, thus hyper-extending his torso with all your weight on his back.

Inoki, page 174

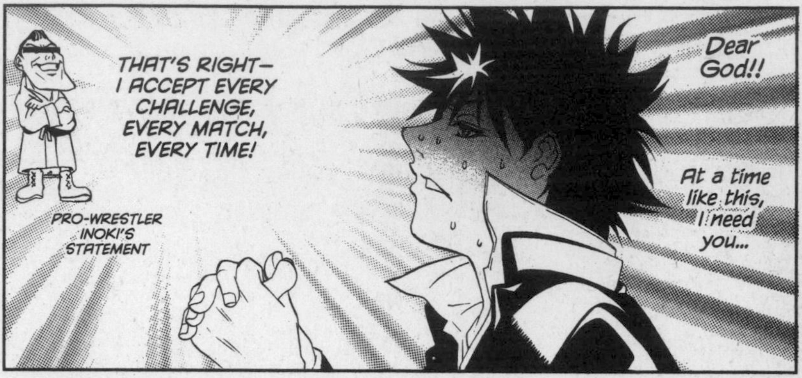
Dear God!!
At a time like this, I need you...
THAT'S RIGHT— I ACCEPT EVERY CHALLENGE, EVERY MATCH, EVERY TIME!
PRO-WRESTLER INOKI'S STATEMENT

Anotonio Inoki is a very famous and well-respected pro wrestler in Japan. He started New Japan Pro Wrestling (NJPW) and is credited with having raised the status of the sport by publicizing its strength, sportsmanship, and great mottos. In this case, Itsuki is being inspired to show off his skills by remembering one of Inoki's mottos.

Konishiki, page 183

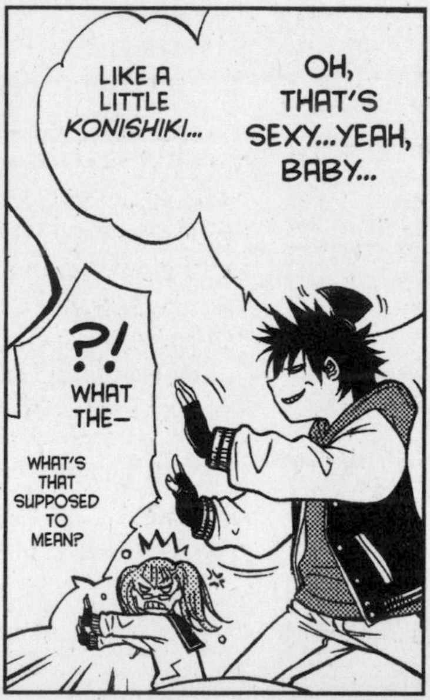
OH, THAT'S SEXY...YEAH, BABY...
LIKE A LITTLE KONISHIKI...
?! WHAT THE—
WHAT'S THAT SUPPOSED TO MEAN?

Konishiki is a famous Sumo wrestler in Japan . . . Itsuki likens Ringo to the Sumo master because of how she "walks" in her skates.

Grand Slum, page 190

She's taken graphic liberties with the sign, so it might be hard to read, but the name of the shop is "Glam Slum"—which in katakana is pronounced the same as "Grand Slam."

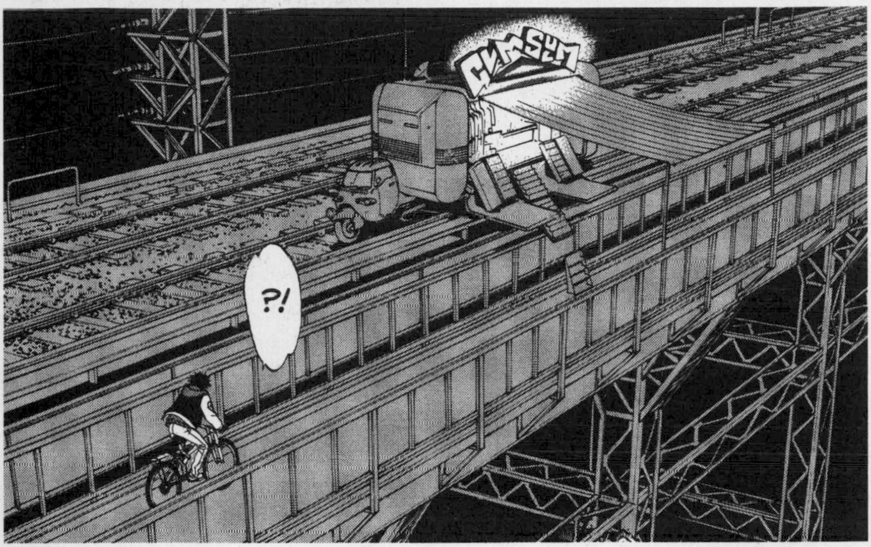
?!

Kocchi kocchi, page 194

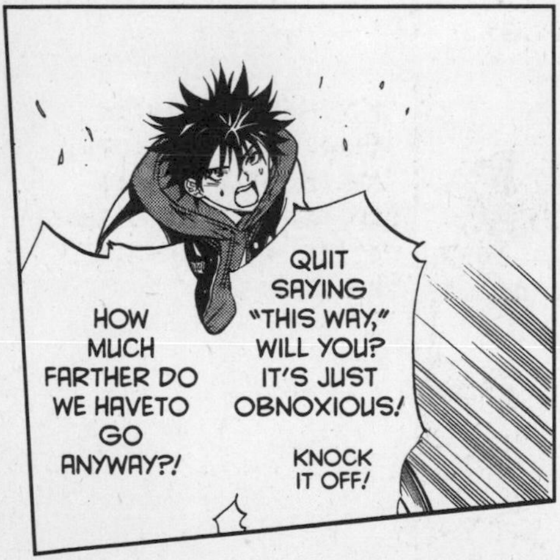
QUIT SAYING "THIS WAY," WILL YOU? IT'S JUST OBNOXIOUS!
KNOCK IT OFF!
HOW MUCH FARTHER DO WE HAVETO GO ANYWAY?!

In Japanese, the old man, Kojor-jii, keeps saying "Kocchi, kocchi, kocchi," which sounds something like a clock ticking. Itsuki's actual response to it is, "Stop saying that, you sound like an old clock." However in English, saying "This way, this way" doesn't bring to mind any household machines . . . except perhaps a broken record player.

**Air Gear volume 2
is available now.
Here is a preview
from volume 2
in Japanese.**

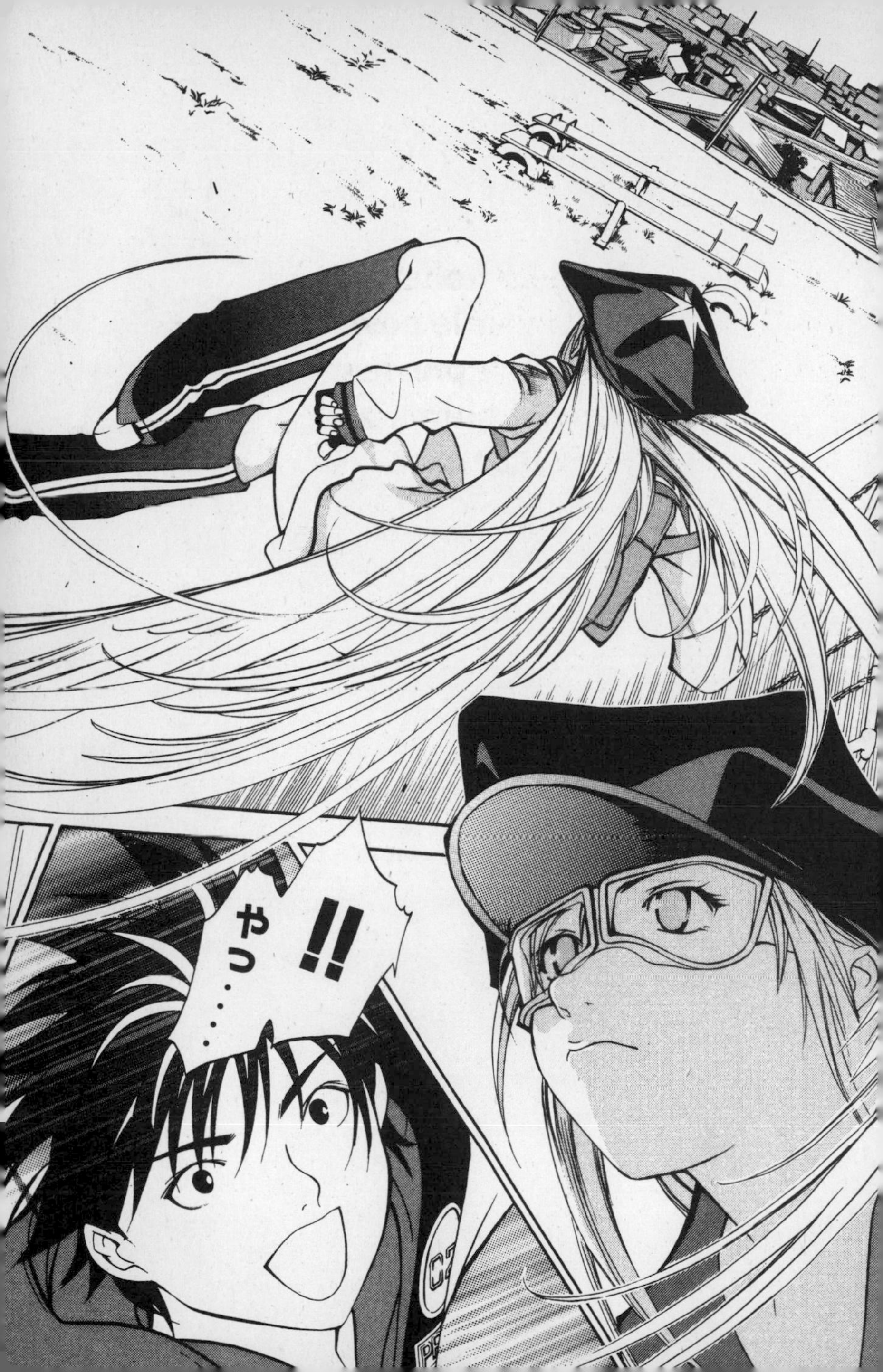
やっ‥‥!!

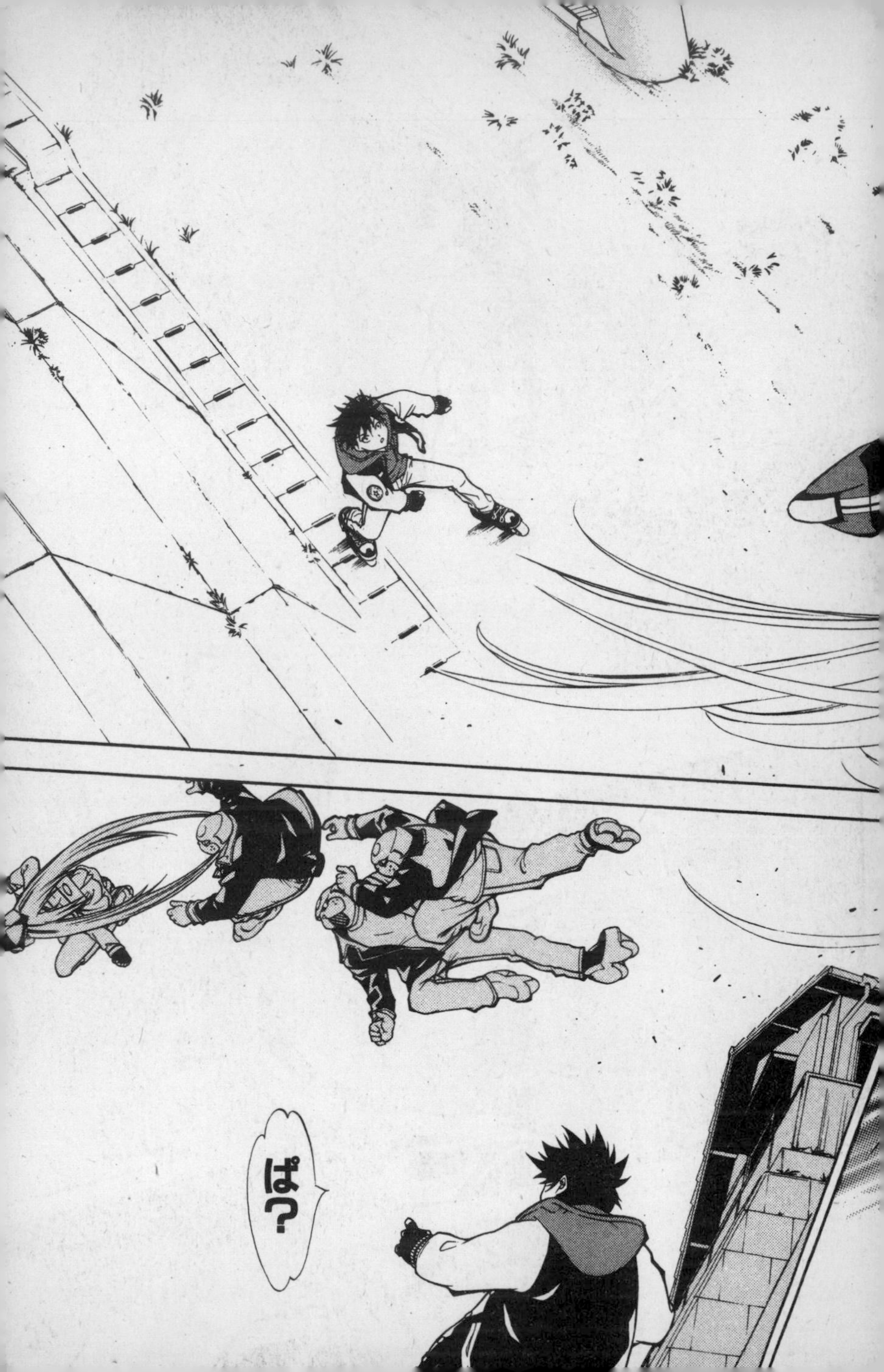
ぱっ?

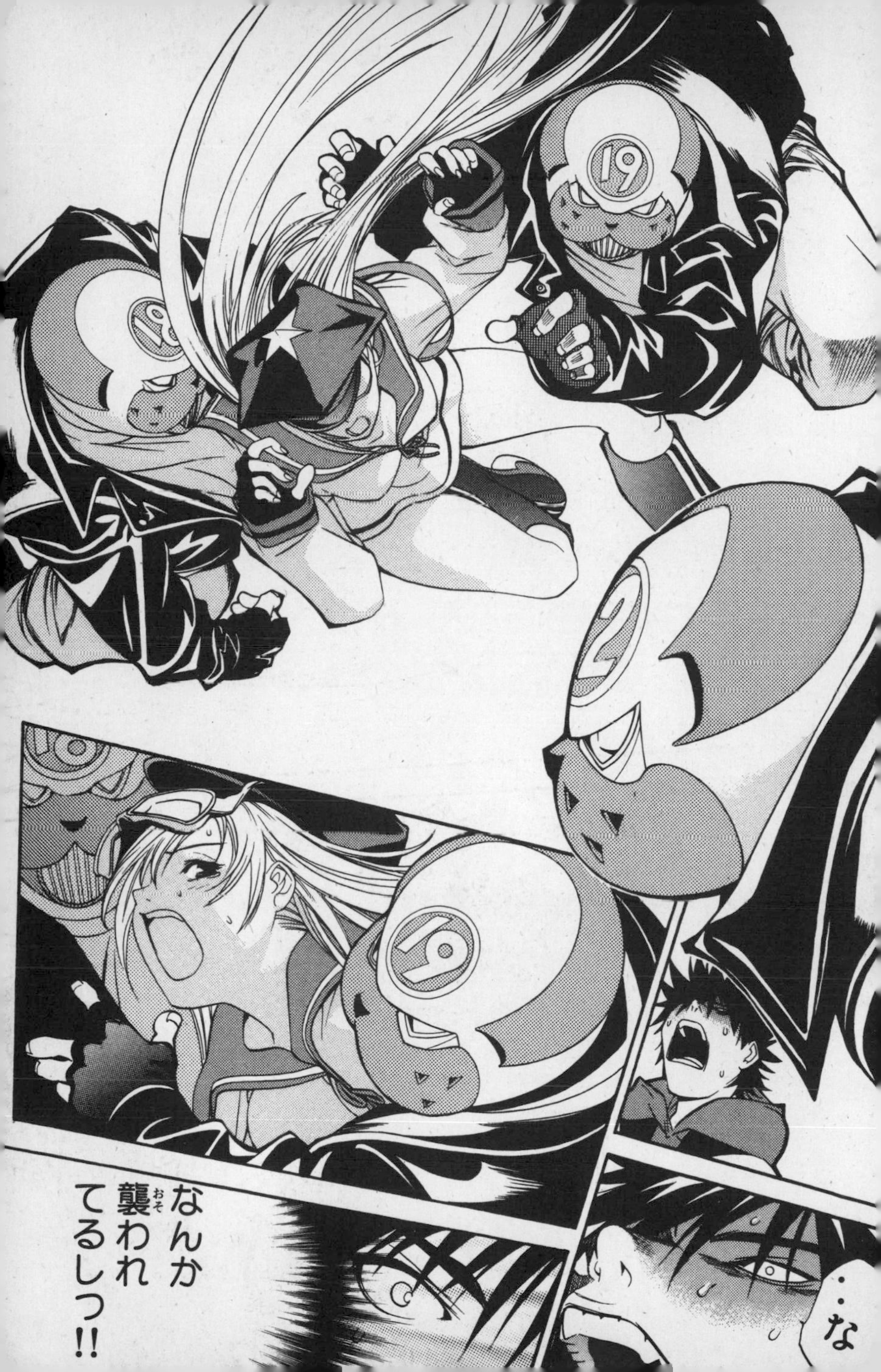
・・な
なんか襲われてるしっ!!

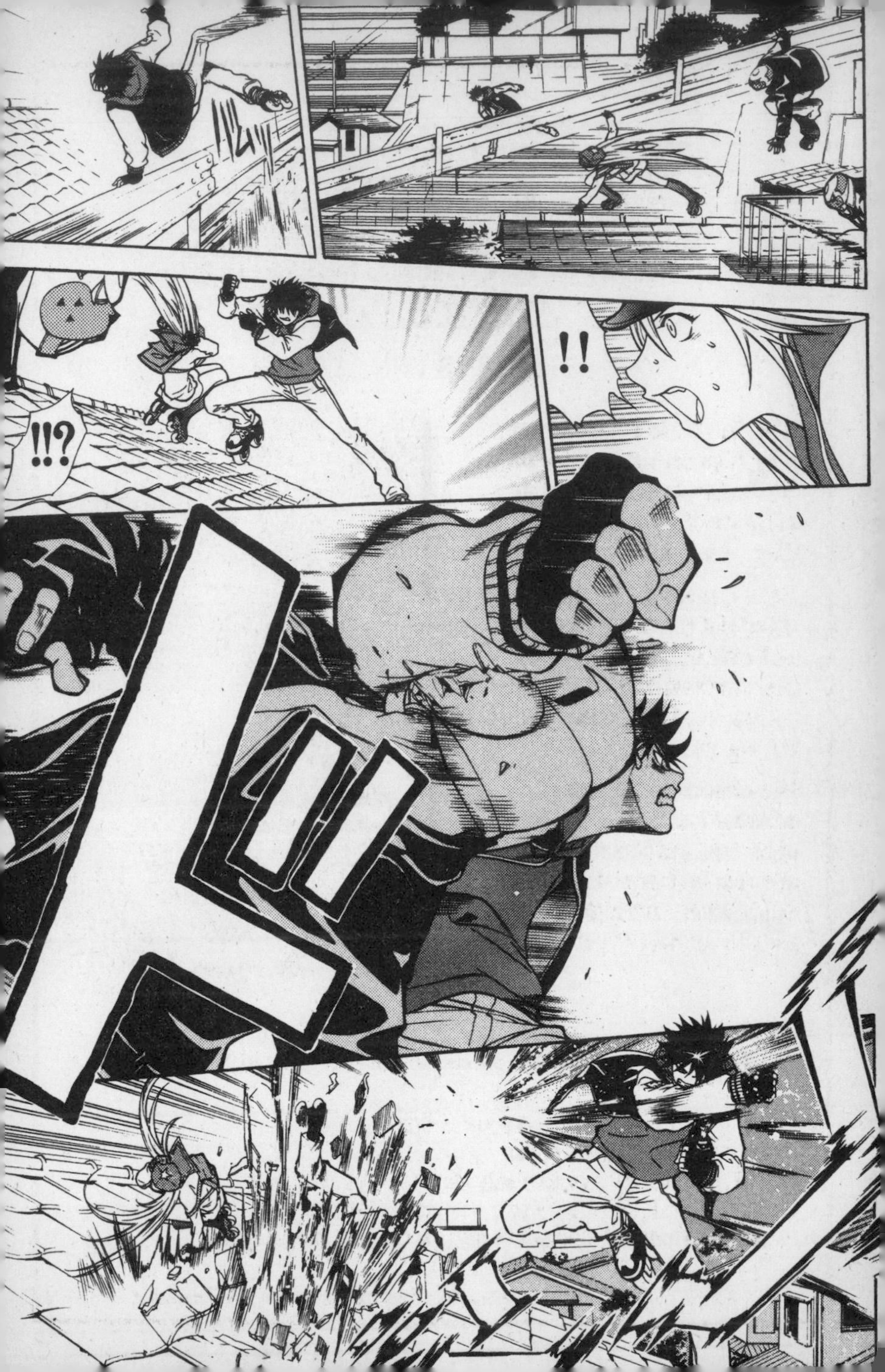
!!
!!?

BY JIN KOBAYASHI

SUBTLETY IS FOR WIMPS!

She . . . is a second-year high school student with a single all-consuming question: Will the boy she likes ever really notice her?

He . . . is the school's most notorious juvenile delinquent, and he's suddenly come to a shocking realization: He's got a huge crush, and now he must tell her how he feels.

Life-changing obsessions, colossal foul-ups, grand schemes, deep-seated anxieties, and raging hormones—School Rumble portrays high school as it really is: over-the-top comedy!

Ages: 16+

Special extras in each volume! Read them all!

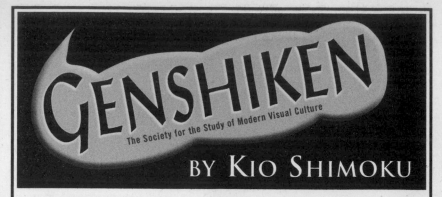
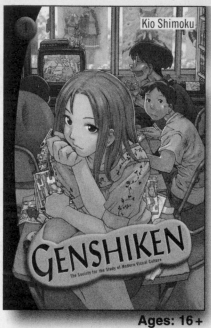

BY UEDA HAJIME

A HILARIOUS STORY OF AN ALIEN GIRL SENT TO INVADE PLANET EARTH

In the near-future on planet Earth, a world gone mad where never-ending war is a fact of life, Kirio is the coolest kid at school. Up in the sky, a giant robot is fighting a fleet of gunships, but the brilliant and distant Kirio is far from fazed—until the battling 'bot makes an unexpected landing in Kirio's front yard and rings the bell. But the worst threat for Kirio could be what stands on the other side of the door: an alien invader robot with the face of an adorable girl!

Ages: 13+

Special extras in each volume! Read them all!

TOMARE!
[STOP!]

You are going the wrong way!

Manga is a completely different
type of reading experience.

To start at the *beginning*, go to the *end*!

That's right! Authentic manga is read the traditional Japanese
way—from right to left. Exactly the *opposite* of how American
books are read. It's easy to follow: Just go to the other end of
the book, and read each page—and each panel—from right side
to left side, starting at the top right. Now you're experiencing
manga as it was meant to be.